Sacred Pathways

Sacred Pathways

The Brain's Role In Religious and Mystic Experiences

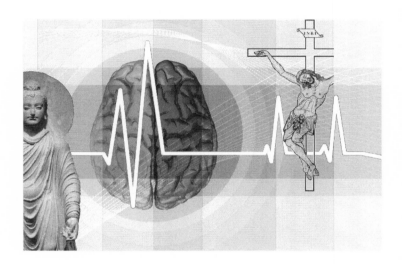

Todd Murphy

Forward by His Holiness, the Dalai Lama of Tibet

Forward by Dr. Michael Persinger

Forward by His Grace,
(Eastern Catholic) Bishop +Nazarin

Cover art public domain, from 1) Wiki Commons. 2) Paid Graphic service.

Library of Congress Cataloging-in-Publication Data

Murphy, Todd Raymond

"Sacred Pathways: The Brain's Role in Religious and Mystic Experiences" / Todd R. Murphy—1ˢᵗ Print Edition.

Includes Bibliographic references.

1. Neuroscience 2. mysticism 3. Near-Death Experiences.

ISBN: 978-0-6158-9048-7 (sc)
ISBN: 978-1-4834-0210-9 (e)

Lulu Publishing Services rev. date: 11/25/2013

Table of Contents

Dedication

This book is dedicated to my teachers, scientific
and spiritual; past and present.

Dr. Michael Persinger, Stan Koren, Edgar "Karmu" Warner, George
Olebar, Carey C. Briggs, "Bigfoot", "Lightening Bear", E. Theo
Hedding, Paul Lowe, Osho, Dorothy "Ma" Deome, Dr. Bernard Yeh,
Dr. Nan Chao, Ven. U Silananda, and many others.

Acknowledgements

I would also like to acknowledge the many people who helped me
complete this work and encouraged me to bring it to publication. M.
Chelnenza, D. Arbeeney, Pailin Murphy, Omega Patterson-Fox, Cheri
Kruger, "Mi-Chan", His Grace, Fr. Robert Hartman, J. Dvivedi, Shri
Shailendra Sharma, Noel Murphy, Drago Plecko, Anne Prehn, and a
host of others. My thanks to all.

5th of November, 2013

NOTE:

See us online at:

www.sacred-pathways.org

Foreword

By His Holiness, The Dalai Lama

THE DALAI LAMA

Over the last thirty years, despite my lack of formal scientific training I have held many personal meetings and discussions with scientists. I believe that spirituality and science are different but complimentary exploratory approaches with the same greater goal, that of understanding the nature of reality by means of critical investigation. There is much each may learn from the other, and together they may contribute to expanding human knowledge and fulfilling the well-being of humanity.

In relation to science, we should always adopt the view that accords with the facts. If, upon investigation, we find that there are reasons and proofs for a conclusion, then we should accept it. However, a clear distinction should be made between what is not found by science, and what is found to be non-existent by science. What science finds to be non-existent, we should accept as non-existent but what science merely does not find is a completely different matter.

An example is consciousness itself. Although sentient beings, including human beings have experienced consciousness for centuries, we still do not know what consciousness actually is, how it functions or what is its complete nature. Things that have no form, no shape, and no color are in a category of phenomena that cannot be understood in the way that external phenomena are investigated. Therefore, a study of consciousness involving both scientists and experienced meditator has significant potential to extend our understanding.

In this book, Professor Todd Murphy recounts what he has discovered about the brain's role in religious and mystic experience; findings that interested readers will no doubt find illuminating.

October 5th, 2013

Foreword

By Dr. Michael A. Persinger

In this book, Todd Murphy develops the concept of neurotheology from a unique and fresh perspective that finely balances the common sense of subjective experience with the general principles of neuroscience. Professor Murphy describes the essential human microanatomy and function, allowing the reader to appreciate, understand and explore neurotheology and its implications with an optimal level of detail. There is a chapter containing primary principles of neural function, which allows the reader to explain and predict behaviors. These principles are then applied with ease and pedagogical clarity to the phenomena of near-death-experiences, the sensed presence of a Sentient Being, and the attributions of God. Professor Murphy systematically develops these concepts and offers examples and parallel phenomena from eastern and western cultures.

Spirituality offers a dilemma comparable to the particle-wave duality of the photon that we can see reflected in the continuity of scientific thought since the emergence of metaphysics, where contemporary scientific thought began. In addition to the perennial question of what spirituality actually is, the primary wonder has been the inference of a default totality that includes all of space and time. If we accept that all our experiences are generated from brain activity (or at least strongly correlated with it), then we must also accept that the concept of God and feeling of oneness with "Him" should be related to brain structure and function. The billions of human brains all share the same essential genetic sequence, so the occurrence of a universal commonality, made unique for each person through modulation of the factors that affect its expression, is only to be expected. Neurotheology is the contemporary manifestation of this examination. As in any science, the rate at which exploration occurs depends on experiments and technology that allows the manipulation of key parameters to verify or refute explanations. The powers of social institutions are also diminished by the return of control over spirituality to the individual, though the development of adequate technology, and the understanding of its principles.

With a perspicacity and courage rarely found in the writing by contemporary academics, Professor Murphy explores the beliefs of reincarnation and the implications for its validity in context of modern neuroscience and quantum biology.

Supported by experimental data, Professor Murphy develops the explanation, theory, and parallel experiences from other cultures, that the sense of self is a "left hemispheric" phenomenon coupled to language processes. However, during periods of enhanced interhemispheric coherence, the right hemispheric equivalent of this left hemispheric sense of self, as well as the sensed presence, can occur concomitantly with changes that herald enlightenment and altered perceptions with respect to the self and the universe in which it exists. Because the brain influences all of the organs and tissues of the body, which are in turn represented in the brain, the consequences of the neural processes associated with enlightenment can affect the adaptability of the person. Many neuroscientists have considered the sense of self to be the final problem; one whose solution will be as significant to our civilization as the heliocentric universe was in Copernicus' time or evolutionary reasoning was to the 19th century Victorians.

The mechanisms and processes by which the entire species might access these experiences as collectives or as transient phenomena are related to an informative description of the earth's magnetic field within which we all exist. In all levels of discourse in science, the phenomena associated with the locality of how units interact are determined by the medium in which they are immersed together. Human brains are immersed within the magnetic and gravitational fields of this planet. From this perspective many of the "non-local" phenomena that have eluded science (but have co-existed within spiritual traditions) become expected, if not necessary.

Sacred Pathways is the *Principia* of the scientific investigation of spiritual experiences. Individuals who appoint themselves protectors of "true knowledge" may find this book disquieting. After all, scientists, philosophers, and theologians are human beings who display the expected aggression towards the concepts and the person whose writings frustrate their beliefs. So when you read this book remember the writer's courage and imagine infinite possibilities.

Dr. Michael A. Persinger
Full Professor
Behavioral Neuroscience, Biomolecular Sciences and
Human Studies Programs
Departments of Psychology and Biology
Laurentian University
Sudbury, Ontario, Canada P3E 2C6
mpersinger@laurentian.ca
14 April, 2012

Foreword

By His Grace,
(Eastern Catholic) Bishop +Nazarin

St. Ephriam's House
Rev. Fr. +Nazarin, Director
574 Valley St.
San Francisco, CA 94131

The church has an obligation to explore new avenues of knowledge, and it should not turn its back to the kind of science in this book. Although it's not written from a believer's perspective, it offers new reason to pray and to engage God's presence.

Science and religion are not in conflict with each other, and this volume brings them together.

The theology behind *Sacred Pathways* is based on science, but it shows a deep respect for religion, and tells us that its one of the things that makes us human. As a clergyman, I agree completely. It does not attempt to strip us of our free will and force us to choose between atheism and faith in God. It only says that our brains are the foundation for all our experiences, including God.

The author, Professor Todd Murphy, is right when he says that feeling God's presence is a part of the deepest prayer. He is also right when he implies that we are accountable for our actions when we die.

His work, though based in science, asks us to grapple with the fact that we all know what is moral and right, and that's a good thing, whether it comes from the Teachings of our Lord or reasoning from anthropology. This book asks us to pray, and that can only bring us closer to God, whether it comes from the pulpit or the ideas at work in today's neuroscience.

This is not a work of Christian theology; it's an illuminating work that's well worth reading because it affirms the value of faith, prayer, morality, compassion and above all, coming closer to God.

+ Nazarin

Bishop +Nazarin (Eastern Catholic)
October, 2013

CHAPTER 1

Introduction

If reincarnation is a human behavior (however hard to observe), and Darwin was right, then reincarnation is an evolutionary adaptation that contributed to the survival of our species at some point in our evolutionary history.

There is a saying that no book is completed as much as it's abandoned. Eventually, the writer must decide that it's time to stop, even though there are still things they would like to change and improve. That's the case here. I have no doubt that some scientists will see things that could be stated more accurately, or that could take better account of their own theories. This book has a rather wide scope. Primarily, it draws from neuroscience, but there is also some discussion that relates to anthropology, physics, psychology, and sociology. I have tried to work with concepts that most scientists can agree on, even if only for the sake of argument. This means, among other things, that our starting point is the view of human beings that begins with Darwinian evolution.

This is a book in neurotheology, and we will use the idea that spirituality, like everything else in the mind, depends on brain activity. Modern science accepts that all subjective experiences depend on the brain, but this idea becomes controversial when it's applied in the context of religion and spirituality.

Spiritual Experiences

When I say spiritual experience, I'm referring to altered states of consciousness that appear with positive emotions. Nearly any altered state that feels good can be labeled as spiritual. Romantic love, unless it's unrequited, is often spoken of as though it were a mystic experience. The connection between lovers can seem spiritual, and their relationship can seem to have a higher purpose, or perhaps even be predestined. The experience of romantic love is within both the normal range of human states of consciousness, and our definition for spirituality. Whether or not love is a spiritual state depends on who you're talking to, whether or not they're in love, and whether their religious beliefs include a connection between love and spirituality. Other ordinary states of consciousness, like creativity, the urge to help others, and the thrills that accompany things like skydiving, mountain climbing and bungee jumping, may stand on the line between spiritual and normal states of consciousness.

Religion, and more especially mysticism, can be seen as a way of trying to achieve positive altered states of consciousness, and sometimes trying to avoid negative ones.

Materialism

The approach we're taking in this book is materialistic, but that doesn't mean that either the author or its readers are materialists. I don't claim that everything can be reduced to matter, energy or physical forces, or that all features of consciousness are nothing but the brain at work. I do claim that the only way to find out if it's true is to take it for granted, and then see how well that assumption works as we try to use it to understand consciousness and the mind. If consciousness is ultimately a thing of spirit, then science will one day encounter it as it studies the mind, and the materialist position will break down. That breakdown point, whatever it is, will offer neuroscience a challenge. The only way the world will ever learn if the mind is more than the brain is to *encourage* materialism. If the foundation of the mind is in the *spirit*, then no amount of challenge will ever change it. The best way to prove that there is more to the mind than the brain is to assume that it's nothing but the brain, and then see where that belief fails. This could take a long time, if it happens at all.

Theories are only replaced after they have been *correctly* challenged and then fail to survive. Science will only abandon materialism after it's been challenged, fails to survive the challenge, and is then replaced. It will take a revolution in science, or it won't happen at all. No matter how compelling the non-materialist view is, scientific materialism will dominate the sciences unless evidence that shatters it appears, *and* that evidence is put into a theoretical frame work – a paradigm. This is why the skeptical viewpoint fails to put nonsensical scientific ideas to rest. The enduring pseudosciences address things that science can't explain. Astrology explains the vicissitudes of ordinary life. Science doesn't have any explanation for why your luck might be bad, but astrology does, so astrology survives, no matter what science has to say about it. The truth or falsehood of astrology has nothing to do with it. Old ideas stay with us until better ones appear.

One of the guiding rules of science is called *falsificationism*. It says that you can't prove that an idea or theory is true. New theories and ideas can only be tested by doing experiments to try and prove them wrong. If a new theory survives enough such tests, it is eventually treated as scientific truth. Theories must be challenged and survive or they are eventually replaced. If something is true, no amount of challenge will ever change it. In the end, failing theories invite their own replacements.

The same is true for the belief that mind is nothing but the brain. Such neuroscientific explanations for the phenomena of mind need to be developed before they can be challenged. At one time, materialism was a philosophical position; something philosophers debated. Today, it guides several active areas of study within neuroscience, physics and other fields of science. Many of these studies are not yet complete. A host of questions remain open and no one knows which unanswered question might eventually cause either the downfall or the validation of materialism. The only way to challenge the idea that mind is nothing but brain is by continuing to gather evidence; continuing to make observations; and continuing to amend the theories when conflicting evidence appears.

Let me offer a metaphor. I once had an automotive dynamometer, a device to test engine parts. I literally found it in the street in a city not far from Detroit, the car manufacturing center of the United States. There are many kinds of dynamometers, and this one was intended to test one particular kind of carburetor. It was a box with a carburetor connected to a motor. The motor moved the carburetor's parts, allowing the engineers to test it in action. The carburetor would work, mixing air and gasoline, in a lab, not in an actual car. It was then turned on and left to run for hours, days, weeks or even months. Later, it was taken apart. Engineers would then examine it to see which parts were worn down, and find the weak points in the whole assembly. Then, they put the carburetor back on the dynamometer, and run it some more. You run it until it breaks. The place where it breaks shows which part needs to be re-designed.

Another metaphor is in *breakdown voyages* for naval ships. There are special crews whose only job is to test new ships. They take them out and run them at high speed and in bad weather. They even run them into rocks. All of this is to find out which of the ship's parts need to be strengthened before it's ready for battle. They fire every gun, test every tool and, if necessary, make some adjustments. The idea is that flaws and problems should appear in testing, not during an ocean battle.

That's what I want neurotheology to do with the idea that *mind is brain*. I want to run it until it breaks. If it never breaks, then neurotheology, with its distinct materialist bias, will become a part of science. If it does break, then the breaking point will have been found, and pinpoint where to look to find a nonphysical basis for consciousness, the existence of an actual God, a supreme mind or a higher intelligence. It might even tell us what *non-physical* really means. I don't think the idea that mind is brain is going to fail, but I recognize that many others hold the opposite opinion. Putting this concept through a breakdown voyage is the only position that both atheists and the religious faithful will be able to agree on.

Others, with less materialist views, have only two choices. The first is to reject materialism and declare that mind is much more than just the brain. However, such declarations won't mean much without proof the scientific community can accept. The second option is to have faith in one's spiritual beliefs and *encourage* work based on the idea that mind is brain. At the same time, religious believers can and will have faith that the breaking point will appear and one day reveal God, or show that science will never be able to understand Him. Like good lawyers, we should try to understand the value of opinions we may not agree with. Science won't ever be convinced by arguments for the existence of God that come from religion; it will only be convinced by its own failure to explain the world and the mind without positing His existence. Those who believe in God will say that such a failure is inevitable. Those who don't will say that it could never happen. Opinions on both sides are often held with real passion, so it may take a long time for the question to be answered.

We have to invoke a few principles to help us understand the brain's role in spirituality. The first is that we must only look within the brain for our explanations, because this will help us to make more discoveries than assuming that there is a higher intelligence at work. We can't study this higher intelligence, but we *can* study the brain. Because we can observe the brain and how it operates, perhaps we'll find something there that's beyond analysis, both now and in the future. Until then, as much as we can we should do science according to its rules, because otherwise we won't be doing it at all. One of the rules is that assumptions are allowed, so long as it's made clear that they *are* assumptions. We'll need to make a few of them in this book, and those who cry 'foul!' when we do so only show an ignorance of scientific methods. We should also remember that there is no Pope of science; no final authority on what is science and what isn't, or what methods it should or shouldn't use.

As a work uniting spirituality with science, religious scholars may like to see some changes. Some of them will be offended, but in the same ways that they are already offended by the scientific view of the world.

There have been attempts to merge religion and science in the past, and most of these have not worked out very well. Some religious thinkers have worked out vast bodies of theory that attempt to reconcile the two, but their standards for what constitutes a legitimate merger of science and spirituality came from religion. I take the position that any meaningful synthesis of science and religion must follow the rules of science, and be based on science that most scientists can agree with. Instead of looking for scientific verification of religious beliefs, we begin with scientific evidence about religion itself; from simple faith to the profound experiences that shape the minds of mystics.

A great deal of brain research is motivated by clinical concerns. That's how it should be. Understanding the brain in order to heal its disorders is neuroscience's most important job. In discussing the brain's role in spirituality, we'll emphasize the brain functions that play a role in spirituality. Understanding how the brain works during prayer, for example, means making inferences from scientific evidence, some of which is taken from clinical studies and there will always be scientists who draw different conclusions from the same evidence.

Ultimately, it's the public who pays for all scientific research. Even when research is funded by private companies, they do so out of profits that comes from money spent by large numbers of people. The scientific questions of the uneducated public are worth considering, and their concerns are important. Most people want to know what will happen when they die. Most people want to know what God is. Answering these questions is a worthwhile pursuit for science. Even if the answers are not completely certain, the questions are still valid. There are scientists who feel that the only worthwhile questions for science to answer are those that come from scientists. Naturally, I do not agree. Scientific answers for questions that come from people who are interested in spirituality are worth pursuing, if only because they are intrinsically interesting to the ordinary people who pay for it all. However, because such questions flow from human concerns, and not from previous research, they may receive less rigorous answers than the science that sends rockets to the moon.

In some cases, we will take spiritual beliefs, hone them down to their simplest elements, turning them into postulates (*explicit* assumptions), and try to develop hypotheses that have the power to explain a wide range of facts based on them. This method yields real science, but a kind that's sometimes speculative, but we must remember

6

that scientific speculations are still science. There are also ideas in this book that cannot be proven or disproven yet, and that usually attracts criticism from scientists. However, I don't believe there's anything wrong with hypotheses that cannot be verified so long as they're presented as hypotheses, and not theories, and their authors don't *claim* to have a way to prove them. The rules of science allow a great deal of freedom, so long as the shortcomings of new hypotheses are stated openly. There is often an interval between a hypothesis being proposed, and the development of an experiment that proves or disproves it. Some skeptics will point to a hypothesis and say that there is no evidence to support it, but this, by itself, doesn't mean that it's wrong. It only means that scientists should be careful about how they use it. Hypotheses built on unproven ones are less stable. Building speculations on other speculations may be allowed, but the resulting 'thought experiments' may yield answers that soon fall down.

Instead of trying to prove that anyone's religious beliefs are right, we will try and reshape certain spiritual ideas, so that they fit into the scientific perspective. In some cases, this will mean all but abandoning the original religious beliefs. For example, my view of reincarnation has very little in common with the beliefs of ordinary Hindus and Buddhists. It has more points of agreement with advanced Buddhist psychology than it does with ordinary believers, but advanced Buddhist psychology (Abhidharma philosophy) is almost unknown - both to ordinary Buddhist believers and to scientists. Religious and scientific paradigms are so different that almost nothing you can say in the language of religion makes any sense in the language of science; and vice-versa. The challenge is not to prove that reincarnation actually happens. It's to express a hypothesis concerning reincarnation that makes sense in the language of science. That's very different from trying to prove that it's true. When someone says "it has no proof" you can answer them, asking if they mean to say that aspirin didn't help with headaches until after the first experiments proved it.

This book offers explanations for near-death experiences, and those who are skeptical are faced with two challenges. The first is to devise experiments that disprove these explanations, and the second is to come up with better explanations for the same phenomenon.

There is a saying that repetition is the first law of learning. Another is that if you want to explain something new to someone, first tell them what you're going to tell them, and then tell them. After that, tell them what you've told them. This is the first time many readers will be thinking about some of the brain concepts and neural hardware we'll be talking about, so a lot is repeated. Just like an introductory course in school, this book reviews its material each time we need to be sure we understand something. Many ideas in this book are based on the work of Dr. M.A. Persinger and we'll read about his work several times. I'm happy to acknowledge my intellectual debt to him, but the reader should understand that I am solely responsible for this book.

Skepticism

This book, and the hypotheses it offers, are temporary. Even if every idea I offer is accepted by the scientific community, they will inevitably be replaced by ideas that do better a better job of explaining the relevant facts, or are a better fit with prevailing scientific ideas. The challenge before this book is not to find the "truth". It's to address the perennial religious questions in ways that mean something in scientific language. To do this, we have to build new concepts; ones that replace some older spiritual ideas. In the course of this book, we'll engage new ways of seeing things like virtue, karma, enlightenment, sin, psychic perceptions, and prayer. Their old meanings have to be put aside, and replaced with concepts expressed in scientific vocabulary.

Science is an ongoing process. The solid theories that guided it in the past are often left behind today. The hypotheses in this book are no exception to this rule. Even if they look valid today, they will be put aside tomorrow.

Ordinary people, who understand the methods of police investigation but not those used in the laboratory, consider courtroom evidence as valid as scientific evidence. In a courtroom, several people testifying to the same thing is enough to establish it as true. In the law, reports are accepted as true, unless there is reason to regard them with suspicion. In the sciences, especially in the eyes of skeptics who examine paranormal

in the history of science were supported by evidence when they were first proposed. It took centuries to prove Copernicus was right. Aspirin worked long before it was proven effective. Ideas, hypotheses, and theories make predictions which are then used to prove the theory is false. If it survives the falsification process, the idea is taken as true. Proponents of a theory decide if an experiment is a valid test, and skeptics oversee it. Testing a scientific hypothesis is a cooperative effort that involves both skeptics and believers. Today's skeptics have forgotten that they cannot help science advance without the very people they denounce most.

The reader should know that this is a first edition. Readers are invited to send in their questions, comments, and criticisms, though I can't promise that they will receive a response.

Note About References

Most readers will need to learn about the brain parts and principles we'll be discussing, and it will help them if they are reminded when these things come up in the discussions. For some readers, who have already learned about brain science, the material will seem a bit repetitive at times. This can't be helped. If it's written to be easy for people who are already at home with concepts of neuroscience, it will be very difficult for everyone else. If it is written for people who are encountering these ideas for the first time, it will be difficult for some neuroscientists.

This book is intended to be as readable as possible. A couple of editors have added convoluted language, hoping to make it 'sound scientific', and the final edits have focused on replacing the academic style with more ordinary writing. However, because of the subject matter, academic references have been added to support as many statements as possible. This makes it something of a hybrid of academic and popular science writing. Some of the earlier chapters are more heavily referenced than later ones, because there isn't much point in providing the same references for our points each time we mention them, and some of them are mentioned several times.

This book has been proofread several times, but it seems no matter how many people go over it, a few errors always remain. All the proofreaders were so engaged by its material that they forgot to look for typos and errors, and focused on what it had to say instead. If you, gentle reader, notice any mistakes, please let the author know.

If you are reading this book wondering if I believe in God or not, you may be disappointed. I make no attempt to answer that question. In fact, I may seem to contradict myself. I allow my faith (my religious feelings) to run separately from my beliefs. If something *feels* good to me, I will often *act* as though it were true. If I *conclude* that an idea has a high probability of being valid, I will *think* as though it is - But go on acting just the same.

"Men turned to stone when they ceased to believe in the beauty of the impossible." – *Arabian Nights*.

CHAPTER 2

Reincarnation in Human Evolution

Although this book is about Spirituality and the Brain, there won't be a lot of brain science in this chapter. Here the discussion will include some anthropology, a few brain functions and a touch of physics. The ideas will be based on "The Structure and Function of NDEs: An Algorithmic Reincarnation Hypothesis"[1] (by the author of this book), which was published in the (peer-reviewed) Journal for Death Studies. This concept of reincarnation was reviewed by a group of scientists, who collectively agreed that it was worth publishing. Because of this publication, reincarnation has become a matter of science. It can now be discussed without using any religious authority or traditions for its basis.

This view of reincarnation begins with Near-Death Experiences (NDEs). It rests on the explicit assumption that NDE reports are not just 'near death' experiences; they reflect the death-process as it occurs in human beings. In other words, if you die and *don't* come back, you end up with the same experiences as those who died and *did* come back. This allows us to use the experiences of those who've died and come back to life as evidence in building a hypothesis.

Belief in reincarnation seems to have several points of origin in history. Many early Greek philosophers believed in it. Some Gnostic

Christians seemed to accept it. It has a long history, but it seems to have begun in India, well before the time of the Buddha.

In the older Hindu traditions, the experiences people had when they were deep in meditation had experiences which they thought somehow 'opened death's door', and allow them to 'look into the other side'. They felt that the profound states of consciousness that appeared in meditation, yoga and other spiritual practices showed them what was going on in the "realms beyond death". Later, we will look at the idea that religious and mystic experiences are based on the neural pathways that function at death, but working while we're still alive, so that there may be some truth to this.

During NDEs, Visions of God usually only come after the realization that one has died. When the same experience happens during yoga or intense prayer, it can seem like a very different thing; perhaps 'grace' or the fruits of spiritual practice. The fundamental hypothesis of this book is that both the death-process and mystic experiences both rely on the same states of consciousness, as well as their sources within the brain.

Here, the starting point is in Biological Evolution. Human behaviors, emotions and ways of thinking come from the result of adaptations that appeared during our evolutionary history, as we passed through the filters of natural selection.

If reincarnation is a human behavior (however hard to observe), and Darwin was right, then reincarnation is an evolutionary adaptation that contributed to the survival of our species at some point in our evolutionary history.

If there is such a thing as reincarnation, and the features of our species come from our evolution, then reincarnation must come from the same kind of processes that gave us upright posture, binocular vision and of course, language. Everything about us comes from our evolution[2]. This behavior - 'taking rebirth' - can't be observed. We can't prove that it happens. We must instead make an assumption or *postulate*[3] and explore the hypothesis that comes from it. We will work with the idea that:

Reincarnation is a human trait, in which information derived from a human mind at death, confers advantages to individuals and is recruited by another during gestation or infancy.

To begin, we need to think about the evolutionary advantage (or survival value) reincarnation would have given us. Then we should look at the mechanisms involved in the process, and how it might take place. We'll explore our idea's *explanatory power,* and see how much it can explain. We'll also try to see which traditional Hindu and Buddhist teachings can be included in the view of reincarnation we'll develop here.

Primarily, it will explain aspects of NDEs, which we explicitly assume reflect the death-process in humans. To satisfy religious believers who accept reincarnation, we have to provide a better description than the older religions offer, as well as answering questions that the traditional teachings can't address.

Until very recently, much of the world believed that experiences after death were dominated by the effects of our sins and our virtues. Some religions believe that people go to heaven or hell after death, after being judged for the sins they committed during their lives. One might reincarnate as a king, a beggar or even an insect, depending on one's morality. Believers are told that they will reincarnate as a fly if they swatted too many flies during their lives. Obviously, these are not scientific ideas, and there are lots of questions they can't answer. One is 'How does the population rise?' If each person is someone else reincarnated, then the number of people should be constant, but it's not. Another is '*Why* do people reincarnate?' 'Why does it happen at all?'

Traditional teachings on reincarnation appear designed to guide people into moral behavior. If a person believes they will be tortured after their death for being violent during their lives, there is more reason for them to avoid violence. If they believe their hands will be cut off in their next life if they steal in this one, they are less likely to steal things. Enforcing the social rules is easier if they come from a divine source.

The mechanisms involved in reincarnation, being a matter of birth and death, are probably very different from those involved in keeping human behavior moral or, as we see it, adaptive. One mechanism will involve biological processes. Another will involve social ones. The link between the two, traditionally upheld by Eastern religions, might really exist.

Because NDEs offer a wealth of observations about the death-process, any theory about reincarnation should be able to explain aspects of NDEs. They offer a kind of evidence that neither classical reincarnation theory nor beliefs about heaven, hell, judgment and God can interpret.

There is a fundamental anomaly[4] in NDE research; a question researchers haven't been able to answer. How can individuals die, each in their own way, yet also share a set of experiences with others? Once the moment of death has arrived, all opportunities for mating will have passed. So how can this trait be passed on to the next generation? We can't say those who died undergoing the human death-process survived, while those who died without it didn't. When nobody survives an experience, survival of the fittest can't explain how people come to have it. How could we develop a trait that gives us certain experiences when we die, when people those without it didn't survive any better than those who have it. This is the normal filter in biological evolution. However, everyone fails to survive death.

The classical 'method' of evolution is that some members of the species have a trait. Those who have it are able to survive better than others. The survivors survive and reproduce better then others, and eventually the trait is found throughout the population.

If we are the result of natural selection, then how is it possible that we die one way instead of another? There are no survivors from death. With today's modern medicine, people who have heart attacks are often defibrillated back into consciousness. Doctors can often revive really badly injured people. Yet, until about 30 years ago, almost everybody who died - stayed dead. How could evolution distinguish those who died one way from those who died another? If there is a snippet of DNA that makes it possible to have Near-Death Experiences, it must have been put into place by some other means than the demise of those who didn't have it.

Near-Death Experiences

We have assumed that the human death-process (made explicit in NDEs) is the result of biological evolution. We are also obliged to think that its individual episodes perform functions that contribute to the adaptive value of the whole process. In other words, each phase of the death-process has a job to do. We will look at these phases, one by one, now and at several points in this book.

1 – Out-of Body Experiences, Meeting a harbinger of Death.

Out of Body experiences (OBEs) are one of the most common first episodes in NDEs. During OBEs, people often find themselves floating below the ceiling, seeing their own body when they look down at the scene below them. Others don't see their own body, but they do see the same environment they were in before they left their body. Viewing the scene from an out of body perspective cannot help but convince people that they're dead.

We will use NDEs from Thailand for comparison with Western NDEs in much of this book. In Thailand, near-death experiences typically begin with a visitation by a *Yamatoot*, a servant who comes from the underworld to claim the souls of dying people, and bring them to Yama, their master; the Lord of the underworld.

In this illustration[5] an old man, who was tired of carrying his burden of firewood, thought out aloud how nice it would be if only his life could end – then and there. Immediately, a Yamatoot appeared and said, "If you really want to die, I can arrange it for you". The old man quickly changed his mind, and decided he'd rather go on living. When a Thai person meets a Yamatoot, they know it's someone from 'the other side', and their life is over.

The Grim Reaper probably once played the same role in Europe. Angels have long been believed to play the role of *psychopomp*, one who assists the souls of the dead on their journey to the afterlife.

There are many Western NDEs where they do just that. Their appearance can take the place of OBEs, and going to heaven with them often takes the place of going through the Tunnel or a Void[6].

> "I saw a road, and wondered where it went. I walked along the road. Suddenly, I heard two people talking very loudly. I looked and saw that they were Yamatoots. One of them spoke to me saying 'we've come to take you to hell[7]'."

Yamatoots come and take one to the underworld, a journey that begins in this world, and ends in the next, not only conveys that you're dead, but also that you've 'arrived' at the place you belong. In Thailand, it's a walk down a road accompanied by a Yamatoot, but this isn't the only form it can take. In one Thai case, the person flew while holding a "figure's" (probably a Yamatoot's) arm. In ancient Greece, we find the same motif of moving from one realm to another in the ferryboat that6 takes them to the land of the dead. OBEs, Yamatoots, the Grim Reaper, and arrival at the River Styx all effectively convince people that they're dead.

2 – Leaving the "Real" World.

OBEs are not the only way NDEs can begin, and the phase that follows also takes more than one form. One can go through *The Tunnel*, moving towards a light at its end. Eventually, you enter this Light. You don't just look into the tunnel, you move down its length. It's longer than it is wide, thus defining a space. It seems no one who has experienced it has ever stood still in the Tunnel. Its more than just a place or a vision. It's an experience[8].

Typically, the Tunnel comes after the OBE, but another experience often appears in its place during the same phase of NDEs, sometimes called *The Void,* a vast and dark empty space. In some ways it's like the Tunnel. It looks darker towards the edge of one's vision, and there is often a point of light in the center which expands into *The Light.*

In some cases, this second phase may even be completely absent. The absence of a phase in the NDE could be because the person offered no resistance to its function. Many writers, discussing NDEs, often give the impression that most NDEs are about the same. If the number of NDE phases is seven and if each of them has only three different manifestations, then there are hundreds of ways the process can be expressed. Interestingly, later phases seem to show more variety than earlier ones.

The third stage involves being 'on the other side'; in the spirit world; in the land of the dead; or in heaven. Often, one sees dead friends and relatives, which shows that one has entered the land of the dead. The place we go when we die varies according to each person's expectations. These expectations will usually, although not always, reflect the ideas about death and dying found in the local culture. The ideas about death and dying of a culture will usually, but not always, reflect those of its dominant religion.

3 & 4 – Arriving in the Next World, meeting the Being of Light.

Illustration from a Greek vase[9].

This phase of the death-process makes it clear that one is no longer in 'physical reality', and has gone to 'the other side'. It could be a walk down a road, a trip through a tunnel, flying through space with an angel or a short trip across the River Styx. Here, we see a man getting into a boat, and paying the ferryman (Charon) to take him across the river Styx into the land of the dead. Behind him is the god Mercury, (who serves as a guide to the underworld) with his Caduceus baton.

In the West, 'the other side' is almost always pictured as heavenly. Typical Christian images of heaven show it as a space full of clouds and angelic beings. The air is filled with the rapturous sound of angelic choirs. Everything is magnificent and blissful. There can be a joyous reunion with dead friends and relatives. God's presence fills the space with light.

After entering this 'new reality', it's time to move on to the next phase. Here one meets a deity that some NDE researchers call *The Being of Light*.

19th Century illustration[10].

People meeting the *Being of Light* usually feel they're in God's presence, but the *Being of Light* may also appear as an angel, a holy man or another being that's sacred for the person.

To be in the presence of the *Being of Light* means being filled with love, acceptance and the sense that everything is perfect and peaceful. It often includes a feeling of 'coming home', though this feeling can also appear in other phases. However, the *phenomena* that appear in the various phases are what separate them from each other; our emotional responses to them seem to be less important.

Several emotions can appear in the presence of the *Being of Light*. Usually, they are overwhelmingly positive, and the words used to describe them almost always have religious overtones ("rapturous' "forgiving" "comforting"). This phase, where the person finds themselves in 'the other world' can also take the form of a visit to hell, where there are negative *Beings of Darkness,* like Yama, the frightening Lord of the underworld, who inspires fear.

5 – The Life Review

The meeting with the *Being of Light* puts people in a mood that prepares them for the next phase, where they're confronted with the life they have just lived, whether it inspires pride or shame. The unconditional and comforting love that comes from the Being of Light makes it possible to review their actions during their lives without fear or guilt, so there is no need for denial. They are able to go through the *Life Review* in a spirit of self-acceptance and the feeling that God has already forgiven all their negative actions; their sins. The abject fear and dread Yama inspires makes people feel that denial is impossible. The Being of Light inspires such strong emotions that we're overwhelmed, and can't think of any other way to interpret our own behavior than the one we see in our Life Review. We accept our actions the way they're shown to us. If the Life Review shows us that an action was bad or sinful, then for us, it was. The only time I've read about anyone 'pleading their case' was in a Thai NDE, where the person was falsely accused of being a butcher.

The Life Review can take several forms. It can consist of re-experiencing one's life or seeing it flash before one's eyes. Sometimes it doesn't appear at all. Like all the other NDE phenomena, it tends to change according to a person's age, culture, religion and their ability to anticipate their death. The Life Review is more likely to appear when death comes suddenly and unexpectedly, and less likely when a person has time to anticipate their death, like when they are slowly dying of an illness[10]. Perhaps reflecting on one's life, knowing it's about to end, can supplant the functions of the Life Review.

There are at least two published cases where people saw their lives projected onto a wall covered with television screens. The scenes spanned decades, but they appeared all at once.

The *Life Review* can rely on a single perception, where a person sees their lives symbolically; all at once. Although there are exceptions, most people undergoing *the Life Review* have feelings about both the events they see and their lives as a whole. It's possible that some people have emotional responses so brief that they might not be aware of them. The Life Review isn't only just the person seeing their life; it's also how they feel about what they see.

The central figure of the afterlife (the being of light or the lord of the underworld) usually appears just before the Life Review. There are two parts of the experience of meeting him. In the first part, one comes into his presence. The second part is the Life Review, often with him standing by. In Thailand, one is brought into Yama's presence, and then there is a reading from what we'll call *The Book of Karma*. In spite of the Buddhist belief that one's past lives can go back for many centuries, only actions from the most recent life are read out.

As the lord of the underworld, Yama is a frightening, even terrifying being. His authority is absolute, and there's no way to appeal his decisions - everyone around him obeys. Yama has the power to condemn anyone who stands before him to be tortured, repeatedly killed and brought back to life or forced to endure powerful frustrations. He can also sentence one to reincarnate into a very difficult life. He can even command someone to become his servant (a Yamatoot), or send them to any one of several heavens.

> "Yama looked into a book in which the patients actions were written. Before the judgment could begin, Yama said that he was the wrong person and had to be taken back.[11]"

Yama did not make any of these rulings in any of the 11 translated accounts of NDEs from Thailand[12]. In those accounts, he invariably sent people back to life, often with instructions on how to improve their Karma. Just as the Being of Light is at the center of heaven, radiating love, joy and peace, Yama is at the center of hell, inspiring terror and despair. Yama is a character Thai in cartoons, religious books, advertising, etc., usually with people kneeling in front of him, pleading for mercy. Hell and its tortures are believed to exist to punish people. It's as though sins cannot be forgiven in the afterlife and pain is the way to 'balance' or heal one's Karma, even though Asian religions don't say that bad Karma is either an illness or a wound.

Witnessing the tortures of hell may have the same function in Asian NDES as seeing dead friends and relatives or entering heaven in Western NDEs. It serves to convince the person, not only that they have died, but they have come to the place they are *supposed* to be after death. The tortures of hell aren't to punish the person, but to convey two messages to the person – to see that they are now in the realm of the dead, and that they are most certainly no longer in the world of the living.

The easiest way to get someone to understand and accept being dead is to allow their expectations about death to shape their experiences. People believe in the tortures of hell because it's part of their religious upbringing. When they meet what they thought they'd find after death, they either give up any hope of resistance or come to feel that the easiest way to get through the hells that surround them ("abandon hope all ye who enter here") is to stop resisting, and walk the path before them willingly.

> As soon as I was under anesthesia, I saw the same Yamatoot. I remembered from the last time I had died

and been revived. As he led me to hell's gate, I walked past a torture chamber. The first thing I saw was a big copper pot full of boiling water. It was full of people who cried out from fear. A Yamatoot stood by guarding the people who were being tortured in this way. I walked away from this scene and came to a stand of barren tamarind trees. Their normal bark was replaced by thousands of sharp spikes. Yamatoots at the foot of the tree forced people to climb these trees by prodding them with spears. I didn't ask why these people were being tortured in this way. I already knew. They were being punished (for sexual wrongdoing)[13].

These tortures appear in the death mythologies of Asia, and NDEs from India, Thailand and medieval Europe. The beliefs about hell seen in Dante's work was widely accepted in medieval times. In Japan, NDEs often feature landscapes, rivers, and ponds[14], and don't show traditional Buddhist motifs. These can be explained as reflecting Shinto sensibilities, and the belief that landscapes, rivers, and ponds embody *Kami* (spirits). It encompasses Shinto Gods, the spirits of one's ancestors, as well as nature spirits that invest trees, rocks, water, and mountains with a sacred essence. The 'realm of the dead' is a sacred place in every religion, and in Shintoism, the land itself is sacred.

Image from Thai Religious Poster[15].

A less frightening Yama appears in this illustration from a Thai religious poster showing Yama's scales of virtue and sin. Interestingly,

Yama doesn't read the Book of Karma himself. He keeps his attention on the person he's judging.

From The Greenfield Papyrus, C. 1025 B.C.

The image of the scales of virtue also appears in other cultures. The Egyptian god Anubis would weight the souls of the dead. If the balance shows that the person wasn't virtuous and their soul was heavy with sin, Anubis gives it to the beast *Ammit*, who eats it, destroying it forever. If the scale showed that the person was without sin, their soul could go on to eternal life. The divine pair of scales used to weigh a person's virtue is an ancient theme, and may survive today in the lawyer's scales of justice.

Illustration from Wiki Commons

The image of multiple hells, with specific punishments for specific sins, appears in every country influenced by Hinduism or Buddhism. Here, we see a Hindu religious poster showing Yama, or *Yamaraj* (Lord Yama) at the center of hell (Sanskrit - *Naraka*), with horned Yamdoods (messengers of Yama) attending him. People before him plead for mercy, as his attendant reads from the book of Karma. The word Yama literally means "Death", so his Sanskrit name means The Lord of

Death. He is also a form of The God *Dharma*, the god of truth and righteousness.

Unlike the eternal Christian hell, the Hells of Hinduism and Buddhism are temporary stopping places in the cycles of death and rebirth.

From Wiki Commons

When Buddhism was brought to China, Yama's name changed to *Yanluowang*. He is as much the master of the underworld in China as anywhere else. In front of him is a scroll from which the person's sins and merits are being read. In the forefront, naked people are being tortured with whips and spears. When people in Asian hell are naked, it's usually a sign of sexual sins. There are also people being subjected to various tortures elsewhere in the picture.

The myth of an afterlife featuring the lord of the underworld, judgments and various hells for people with different sins, is found all over the old world.

Islamic women suspended by their hair while burning in hell, a punishment for immodesty. Image from Wiki Commons.

The Quran says: "…and whosoever disobeys God and His Messenger, then surely, for him is the fire of Hell, he shall dwell therein forever." (Quran 72:23).

A similar belief, in which all sinners receive the same punishment, appears in Christianity, based on at least three verses in the Bible. The first is: "And whosoever was not found written in the book of life was cast into the lake of fire." (Revelation 20:15). The second is also from the Book of (Revelation 20:12) …

another book was opened, which is the book of life: and the dead were judged out of those things which were written in the books, according to their works." The third (Matthew 25:41) is seen in the final panel below.

A common conception of the Christian Judgment day as described in the Book of Revelation, with a shining God, the Book of Life, and a soul being condemned to burn in hell.[16]

We can speculate that this widespread myth may have originated in our earliest civilizations, possibly as far back as Babylon around 1500 B.C., when the codes of law included different punishments for different crimes.

"The devils went into Uruk, they seized Innana, the holy one. ... (who carried a boy) "... down into the great dark city ... down into hell, ... stricken with terror she gave (him) into the power of the devils. They said 'this boy, put fetters on his feet, truss him up, pinion his neck in stocks'. They flew at his face with hooks and bits and bodkins, they slashed at his body with a heavy axe, they made him stand and they made him squat; they pinioned that boy by the arms and covered his face with a mask of agony...[17]"

The concepts of law from that time and place seem to strive for balance between wrongdoings and their corresponding punishments. "An eye for an eye, and a tooth for a tooth". There are many examples of this in the code of Hammurabi[18]. It seems natural to symbolize the sense of justice and absolute even-handedness with a scale. It allows the user to find perfect balance, an ideal that no judge, ancient or modern, has been able to achieve. The idea that the punishment should fit the crime may have begun in civil law, and later brought into religion.

Many Life Reviews accomplish their function using symbolism instead of literal reviews of the events in a person's life. In these NDEs, only one or two incidents from the person's life are read out to them. It's as though they aren't being judged for sinful actions, but rather a behavior *pattern*. In the Catholic sacrament of confession, one confesses a specific sin to a priest and receives forgiveness. That sin is removed from one's debts to God. If someone does wrong and fails to confess it, that particular sin is left on the person's soul, and still has to be accounted for before God. Catholics can't generalize their sins. Thailand is a Buddhist country, and in Buddhism, sin is as much matter of the mind as of action. Sin and wrongdoing are motivated by three mental habits, called *kilesa* (defilements). These are ignorance, attachment, and aversion. To put it simply, our sins are the outward manifestations of these three mental habits. In Catholicism and Western culture, specific sins matter more than the moods that inspired them. A Life Review that allows you to see the mental habits that motivated your sinful or especially virtuous actions can accomplish the same thing as a review that looks at your actions one by one. Of course, Western Life Reviews don't always focus on sin, but witnessing one's own acts can still trigger a person's sense of right and wrong.

The most common NDE Life Reviews found in Western countries today are much harder to imagine. One of its more common forms is when your life passes rapidly before your eyes. It might seem like an extremely high-speed movie, but you take in every single incident. You still have emotional responses to what you see. When you see yourself doing something you feel is wrong, you feel bad about it. I would suggest that the emotion appears, even if it's only for milliseconds[19], or even if it's completely subconscious.

In another common manifestation, the person goes through their whole life in an instant. In some cases, people don't re-experience their lives the way it happened when they were living it. For example, they may have become angry during their life and felt that someone deserved their anger, but in the *Life Review* they may see the same events, but without feeling angry. While they re-live that moment during the *Life*

Review they become aware that anger wasn't the best reaction. The way we feel about our lives can change when we see it again during the life review.

6 – The Transcendent Experience

An episode that's been called the *Transcendent Experience* comes after the Life Review. Again, it takes different forms according to the person's culture and their expectations about death. This phase isn't common, because NDEers are usually resuscitated before reaching it.

In the Transcendent Experience, a person can be granted access to 'higher truths' or 'planes of existence'. It can consist of discussions with angelic beings. One kind of Transcendent Experience is the visit to the Akashic Records[20], (sometimes called the Akashic Library). The Akashic Records are said to be an archive of all knowledge, including the kind that's usually only available to God or the Gods. In Thailand, they appear as a tour of heaven with teachings from Brahma or Indra, the King of the Gods. Like the other stages, the Transcendent Experience has a function that can be performed in many different ways, shaped by many mythologies. It never seems to occur exactly the same way twice.

If you think of a question during a visit to the Akashic Records, a book might appear, open to the page where the answer can be found. It may be a vision or a journey to see something from the past or future. It could also be a place filled with scrolls. You might just think of a question, and instantly know the answer.

The Akashic Records seems to use the mind's capacity to create information from within itself, much as it does in dreams. In fact, many people have had dreams of being in the Akashic Library. In traditional cultures and religions, the highest wisdom is always seen as coming from outside ourselves, like from a God, a Buddha, or a spirit. People aren't accustomed to thinking of their own minds as the source for deeper explanations of things, nor for their understanding of the meaning of life. Today in the West, many people feel that the truth 'lies within'. Some believe that the loftiest knowledge is closer to metaphysics, where there are no final or absolute truths.

Here[21], a Buddhist monk tours the heaven of Indra (Indraloka). Seeing heaven is a common third phase (entering the land of the dead) in NDEs from the West, but when it happens in Thai NDEs, it usually appears in the seventh phase (Transcendent Experience).

In the Thai episodes, the person has a conversation with a God, who explains how to be reborn there. There are several heavens in traditional Buddhist cosmology. Only two, the heaven of Brahma, and the heaven of Indra, appeared in the translated Thai NDEs.

In other cultures, people might find themselves on a tour of a crystal palace or a city made entirely of light. Whatever knowledge a person wants is given to them while on this tour. "Higher" questions are answered, fulfilling the common belief that all mysteries are revealed at the time of death.

One well-known NDEer, Mellon Thomas Benedict, had a Transcendent Experience. Whenever he thought of something he wanted to understand, a geometric shape would appear. Its form and movement would convey the answer to the question in his mind. He asked some very profound questions, such as 'How can we heal a human body?' He also wanted to know the reason for the Holocausts that claimed the lives of 6 million Jews, 2 million gypsies, and 5 million Russian prisoners-of-war during World War II[22].

The functions of the phases in the death-process.

Each phase of the death-process conveys a message to the person having the experience. Its function is fulfilled when the person understands the message. Our next step is to look at the messages each phase conveys. This will help us see the function of the whole process. As in all our discussions of the death-process, we're going to over-simplify it a bit, and the reader should remember that very few, if any, NDEs match the 'ideal' model we're working with. Some Western NDEs are very unpleasant. Some have had visions of hell. These are a small minority, and NDE researchers don't agree about what percentage of NDEs are 'hellish'. We are using Thai NDEs for comparison, though there are also NDEs from other cultures.

Usually in western NDEs, the first phase is the *autoscopic* out of body experience. An autoscopic OBE is an out of body experience in which you see your own body. The function of seeing your body during an NDE OBE seems to be to show you that you've died. Nothing that follows will make sense if you don't know you're dead. Otherwise, you could be filled with questions, like: 'What's going on here?' 'Is this is a hallucination?' 'Did someone slip something in my tea?' You might feel that you're caught in a strange dream, and try to force yourself to wake up.

If your death begins with an out-of-body experience, and you look at your own corpse, you'll know your time living in that body is at an end. If you hear mourners, or a priest saying that you've died, or perhaps ambulance or intensive care unit workers saying that they've lost the patient, you'll be even more certain. There have been cases where people who had OBEs seemed to accurately see the resuscitation procedures. When some of these cases were examined closely, it turned out that the people weren't quite right in what they saw. It may be that they had a hallucination with a very accurate, but not flawless, vision of the scene in which they died. I would suggest that the reason so many people have this vision is that it makes it clear that they're dead. It's not merely a perception of the scene around their body; it forces them to see that life is over.

The first common episode in Thai NDEs is being taken to the underworld by a servant of Yama. As it begins the Yamatoot says something like, "You're dead. I've come to take you to hell." The person may ask: "What's going on?" The answer would be something like, "Your body is now a corpse, and you're coming along with me." The Yamatoot will brook no argument; you *have* to go with him. In several

Thai NDEs, people were *told* they were dead. The servants of Yama are authorized to inform you, and they don't take bribes. The OBE tells you that you're dead, and the Yamatoot tells you the same thing. The both appear in the same phase, and they both do the same job.

The first phase of NDEs, whether in the form of an OBE or a harbinger of death, seems to make the person understand that they have died and the death-process has begun.

The next phase is the Tunnel, the Void, the trip across the river Styx or a walk down the road, either with a Yamatoot, or on your way to meet one. You begin the transition from this world into another. It's now apparent that you're leaving the world of the living, and entering the world of the dead. It's not enough to know that you are no longer in your body. It also helps you to understand you're going to another place, so you know in advance that the rules there are very different from those 'on earth'. The experience of moving from one place to another, down a road or through a tunnel, helps convey this. If you were to find yourself there suddenly, without anything leading up to it, you'd be likely to think that it's a dream or a hallucination, and not the death-process. Any of these ideas may prevent you from trusting your perceptions as the experience unfolds. Being in the place where the dead go when their lives are over is easier to accept if you see people being tortured in hell, or meet your dead friends and relatives in heaven or perhaps encounter angels. The scene's consistency helps you to trust your perceptions, and believe what you are told.

The next phase, being in *the place of the dead*, appears differently in various cultures. Having entered another "reality" makes it easier to accept that the rules have changed. When you've accepted death and you find yourself in either heaven or hell, face to face with God or Yama, the apparent reality of the situation helps you to surrender and accept it.

It's reasonable to expect fairness and your right to choose when you're alive. When you're dead, you take what you get. The knowledge that you are no longer in this world makes it easier to accept that a different set of rules applies. One doesn't resist as events unfold in this new existence. There's no point in saying that something isn't fair, and there is no appeal.

The *Being of Light* and the Being of Darkness are both dominant, alpha males. Both Jehovah and the wrathful Gods[23] are powerful. No one argues or disagrees with them. Their authority is absolute. It doesn't make any difference whether you were a General in the military, CEO of a large corporation or president of your country while you were alive. When you reach the other side, someone else is in charge, and you do as you are told. Accepting this makes it much easier to accede to the death-process and allow it to fulfill its purpose.

Arriving in heaven or hell, entering the spirit world or some other *land of the dead*, conveys that you are in another reality, dimension, or world. Of course, a brain-based model will say you are actually in a deeply altered state of consciousness. Things are very different than they were when you were alive. You accept a new set of rules and when you meet the ruler there, and you cannot help surrendering to his authority. You realize that your preconceptions are irrelevant, and you become aware of either feeling powerless or being overpowered. It takes the strength out of any other emotions you may feel. In the *place of the dead,* you are put in a subordinate role. Everyone has the same social rank when standing in front of such an absolute authority.

The function of the Transcendent Experience may come from that fact that many of the world's cultures and spiritual traditions tell us that all mysteries will be revealed when we die; there'll be no secrets, and somehow you'll receive a "higher" understanding. Some people long to understand the fundamental truths of this world, in much the same way personal details are understood during the *Life Review.* The Life Review doesn't answer questions like "What does it all mean?" It only looks at you and your life. I suggest that people who believe that revelations and access to "higher wisdom" are part of the death-process may well resist its end if they don't get the kind of information they're expecting.

If you believe that death will reveal the hidden mysteries of psychic skills, the origins of the universe, angels and other spiritual matters, you may resist "moving on" until they have been explained.

The *Transcendent Experience* is not very common in NDEs. The only ones to experience it may be those with a driving curiosity and interest in philosophy, religion, art, the sciences or other intellectual pursuits.

Summary of the Functions of the stages in the Death-Process.

1) The OBE or being taken by a harbinger of death.

     This convinces people that they are, in fact, dead.

2) The tunnel, the void, a landscape, or being taken to heaven or a walk with a harbinger of death.

     This shows people that they are leaving the reality[24] they knew during their lives, and are entering (or going to enter) a different one.

3) Meeting dead friends and relatives or seeing the tortures of hell.

     This make people accept that they are *supposed* to be in this 'other world', as well as putting them in a state of acceptance or 'surrender'.

4) Entering the light, or entering the underworld.

     This shows people that they have come to a place where new rules apply.

5) Meeting the *Being of Light* or the *Lord of the Underworld*.

     This convinces people that they have no power in the 'other world', and accept that the way the 'Lord' sees them and their behavior supersedes their own view of themselves. Their psychological defense mechanisms are abandoned.

6) The Life review.

     This categorizes our behaviors into two groups: Good (or 'virtuous') and bad (or 'sinful'). The theme here is of understanding one's self and one's behavior. We'll discuss function of the Life Review separately again, a little further on.

7) The Transcendent Experience.

This satisfies the common belief that all one's questions will be answered, and all mysteries will be revealed at death. The theme here is of understanding the world, not one's self. It prevents resistance to the next stage.

8) The point of No Return.

This seems to symbolize the cessation of the neural mechanisms that support the sense of self.

The Evolution of the Death-Process

Each feature of our species, whether recent or ancient, is a result of an evolutionary adaptation. Humans have the ability to use tools requiring finer control of our fingers and hands than any other species known. The opposable thumb gave us the ability to hold either a hammer or a scalpel. Our brains are much more complicated than those of our predecessors. The many folds on the surface of the brain give it more surface area. The deeper structures have more nuclei and layers, making them more complicated than those of other species[25].

When our species emerged, two parts of our brain underwent major changes. These were the frontal lobes, just above the eyes, and the temporal lobes, above the ears. The language centers situated in and around the left temporal lobe provided new language abilities. Our memory skills were amplified, and we became much more social. We had more to remember, especially what we said to others, how they spoke to us and how we related to them, more than before. Our memory got an upgrade, and so did our social skills. We became much more intelligent. We learned to make bows and arrows, fire, and to tell long and complicated stories.

Our frontal lobes may not have gotten bigger, but they became more complicated. It had more peaks and valleys (sulcus and gyrus), giving it greater surface area. This increase in cortical 'real estate' gave the frontal lobes (social skills & "executive functions") greater overall functionality. We got smarter, and we applied our superior mental kung fu to relating with others.

Some human males have achieved an ability that takes far more intelligence than making either a stone tool or a new computer program. They leave home; say they'll be back in half an hour, but come home at two o'clock in the morning, drunk, with lipstick on their collar. When they get home, and find their partner is waiting up for them, they manage to lie their way out of trouble and avoid a fight.

Human intelligence is put to its greatest test when we relate to others. Having an enemy is easy; having a friend is complicated. Someone agreed to publish this book. We made a deal, a contract, and agreed upon terms and conditions, making what anthropologists call a 'social alliance', leading the publishers to do what they do, and me to do what I do. This leap forward in intelligence enabled us to relate to one another in more ways. It was one of the decisive changes that made us human.

It seems likely that the death-process in humans originated as a part of a more general upgrade of our brain. Every phenomenon occurring in NDEs has been elicited through stimulation of the temporal lobe. Our capacity for such things as memory skills, complex culture, sophisticated tool making[26] and language (with nouns, verbs, grammar, syntax, idioms and profanity) are believed to have all appeared at the same time, as our temporal lobes became more complex[27]. The human death-process most likely appeared while these changes were happening. Reincarnation didn't start by itself. The 'manner of our deaths' changed as our whole brain changed. It's more likely that we started reincarnating during a much larger process that culminated in our appearance as Homo Sapiens.

If reincarnation is an adaptation that appeared alongside our increased language skills and our ability to live in our complicated cultures, then we shouldn't expect that it has a specific genetic basis any more than there is a gene for language. Rather, many other genetic changes enabled human speech. There may be no reincarnation gene for the same reason that there is no 'culture gene'. The ability to learn may have a genetic basis, but there is no gene for learning geometry.

The Life Review

We've left the function of the *Life Review* for last because it's the most important phase of the death-process in our model of reincarnation. The entire death-process could even be seen as little more than the context for the life review.

What's the point of reviewing your life when you're no longer alive? Our positive actions can't be repeated once life is over. The only place to apply the lessons learned in the Life Review is in another life. This invites us to look at NDEs as contributing to reincarnation. You can't use what you've learned when you're dead. You can't mate when you're dead. The idea of survival of the fittest implies that some people are more fit than others, and the dead are not fit to survive at all.

As I said earlier, people have emotional responses to being confronted with their own behavior during the *Life Review.* I suggest that this separates our behaviors into two categories; those to repeat and those to avoid. You want to repeat the behaviors you feel good about, and avoid the ones you feel bad about.

Remembering everything you did that didn't work out too well in this life would create a heavy burden of memories to carry into your next life, and in fact few people even claim to have past life memories. We don't need to remember our behaviors in order to make use of Life Review lessons. A record of the states of consciousness that motivated your behavior is quite enough to guide you in the next life.

Everyone has personality traits and behavior patterns they act out repeatedly. Identifying the *states of consciousness* that inspired your more frequent negative behaviors (and tagging them for avoidance) can rule out hundreds of maladaptive, counter-adaptive or just plain bad behaviors without needing to remember them all. If all behaviors inspired by anger, fear or sadness are suspect, then there's less chance of acting out these emotions irresponsibly. Most maladaptive behaviors consist of nothing but talk. Sticks and stones can break people's bones, but your words can *really* hurt them.

All the enduring adaptations that appeared during our evolutionary history served a purpose, especially language. It's the basis of our communication with one another, and it binds our cultures together.

We survive because of our reliance on our 'complex cultures', a survival strategy unique to humans. We stay alive by staying together, and anything that keeps us together helps us to survive.

We understand the reasons for the primary human behaviors like hunting, mating, raising children, religious ceremonies and rituals. Another consists of doing nothing as we sit around enjoying one another's company. Simply being sitting with other people helps us survive. It may well be the greatest momentum to our evolution came from sitting around talking to each other, for no particular reason (non-goal oriented speech). The continuous flow of speech between our earliest ancestors no doubt included a lot of nonsensical and useless thoughts. However, if 99% of all conversations are forgotten, and only 1% of what is said is remembered and passed on, these memes could become a vast cultural memory of jokes, proverbs and wisdom in just two or three generations.

Once, tribes that live with simple economics and technology were considered primitive. Over the years, anthropologists have come to recognize that they preserve subtle and highly nuanced hymns, epic stories, poetry, jokes, chants and songs. Complex culture demands that people use, or be able to use, the most sophisticated language they can. It helps us to gain respect and achieve and maintain a high social rank. Language increases our reliance on our cultures, and in turn, complex culture increases our reliance on language.

Language and complex culture developed around the same time, and reflect the same neural changes. The increasing complexity and sophistication of language allowed people to use it to show off, displaying their intelligence, and helping them gain social rank. Well-spoken people usually achieve higher social rank than those who are less articulate. Those with a ready joke offer more enjoyable company than people with no sense of humor. In our very early evolutionary history, the more pressure for people to show off their intelligence by speaking well, to compete for respect, popularity and influence, especially in tribal councils, the faster we our cultures and languages would have developed.

The Life Review emphasizes social behaviors; how we acted while relating to other people. Dead friends and relatives are sometimes seen in NDEs; as well as the appearance of an authoritative being.

The behaviors that appear in the Life Review are also mostly social, reviewing things we did while relating to others. This suggests that the death process is driven by social concerns. The death-process in humans is intimately related to our reliance on complex culture as our strategy for survival. It probably appeared around the same time as language and the kind of culture we still see today in many aboriginal peoples. I suggest that culture and reincarnation reinforce one another, just like culture and language.

Information from past lives regarding which states of consciousness to avoid or embrace would primarily be applied in social situations. We're a social species, and we relate to different types of people in different ways. It's fine to express sadness when talking to your mother, or anger when talking to your friend, but usually, acting out our emotions responsibly means paying attention to who you're with. Being aware of your own angry feelings, which can escalate into trouble at times, can prevent them from becoming a problem. It's easier to be aware of your anger overall than to control it in each and every situation. Knowing that it's best to be careful when you act out anger, sadness, self centeredness or fear can increase the success of your actions, for yourself and for your social group.

(Silverback gorilla. Image from Wiki commons, public domain)

When a gorilla becomes the leader (the alpha male) of his troop, the hair on his back turns silver. When one silverback male dies, the next senior ranking gorilla will find himself growing silver hairs on his back. Thereafter, the others acknowledge him as the leader. The societies of most primate species, including humans, depend on having a leader.

Acquiring social rank is very important in all primate species, including ours.

Becoming the alpha male can involve considerable struggle. However, aggression is perhaps the single most destructive kind of behavior. The states of consciousness that inspire it are potentially some of the most destructive a person can experience. Gorillas growl or posture aggressively, while humans mostly argue with each other. We become violent much less often. In our early history, actual violence between individuals may have been less common than today, because its consequences could affect more of the population. If a tribe consisted of only a few clans, fights between their members could impact a large percentage of the population. Schisms and feuds can break up a tribe, making it harder for each clan to survive.

Among humans, the dominant male achieves his position by showing better social skills, and outclassing his competitors. *Remaining* the human alpha male involves other skills. Human leaders are better off dispensing favors to make those around them feel good, and give them reason to continue their support for him. The alpha male may have to struggle to get his position, but once he has it, the need to struggle diminishes. Among humans, alpha males who avoid struggle and conflict have a better chance of remaining the leader. "Alphas" who achieve their position without visible strife with their competitors are more likely to find support than those who create trouble as they vie for the coveted higher positions in their tribe.

Caveat - The Origin of War Among Humans

To understand the purpose of war; and why our evolutionary path didn't rule it out, we need think about it in the context of our earliest cultures; nomadic tribes and people who live by simple horticulture. In these cultures, war doesn't usually take many lives. In some cases, nobody is hurt at all. Among the Plains Indians of North America, warriors often only *counted coupe* against their enemies, striking them with a stick to humiliate them, without actually trying to kill anyone or even inflict serious harm.

War between belligerent tribes usually meant that two groups of warriors met, spent some time shouting at each other, brandishing their weapons and making insulting gestures. The battle usually ended after only one or two died. Obviously, the most aggressive warriors were the ones most likely to be at the center of the battle. They were the ones most likely to kill someone, as well as being most likely to be killed. They wouldn't live as long, so their violent behavior would have less impact on their group.

Usually, young unmarried males don't spend much time taking care of children. In the kind of wars probably fought by the first humans, the males most likely to bring aggressive behavior to their community were the ones most likely to be killed in its wars. If the most aggressive males had children of their own, they would tend to copy their father's aggressive behavior. Killing them off in war might be the way we humans once limited the aggressiveness at work among our people. Today, we still use war – and prisons.

In many tribal cultures, young men are required to prove themselves in battle, either just before or just after their initiation into manhood, or before they could marry. This meant that there was a good chance that the most aggressive males would die in battle before they could raise children. As we know, children copy their parent's behavior. If their father was aggressive, there would be a higher possibility of the child learning the trait over time. This in turn, would increase the overall amount of aggressiveness in their society.

War, with its violence against other tribes and groups, may well have reduced the amount of violence within our earliest tribes and nations. Today, violence only seems to create more violence. The creation of disciplined armies around 500 B.C. (the time of the first Persian Empire) imposed a new character on warfare, and made it an instrument of politics. After that, warriors became soldiers. They attacked when they were ordered to; not when they chose to. In our early history, wars were often fought to protect individual homes and hearths (or acquire more resources for the warrior's tribes), giving honor and social standing to those who fought and survived the battles. The ones who survived were also going to be the ones who approached battle circumspectly, and who thought before they acted. The ones who acted out their bravado and took unnecessary risks were more likely to die. It's a good way to remove dangerous people – mostly men - from both the gene pool and their behaviors from the meme pool – by getting them killed.

War may be an evolutionary adaptation that actually reduced the amount of violence people lived with, day-to-day, by killing off the most violent people in the human populations and by allowing those who stayed out of the fighting to survive.

Karma

A single karma, as we are using the word, is a record of a state of consciousness, together with a record of how desirable other people's responses to it will be (and, to a lesser extent, from nature) when its acted it out. Most Karma would be expected to be social. Nearly every negative behavior is harmful because of its impact on other people, not because it's intrinsically good or evil.

Nearly every formal moral code ever known has had prohibitions against violence. If you kill a member of your tribe or nation, you're a murderer. If you kill an animal, you're a provider. If you kill an enemy attacking your people, you're a heroic warrior. A behavior that might offend one group of people like tribal or village elders can present no problem with another group, like young male warriors.

Our view of Karma is very different from the one traditionally found in Hinduism and Buddhism. It's also at odds with the classical view of sin in the Judeo-Christian and Islamic traditions, where things are good or bad because God decrees it. The willingness to live according to a formal moral code (like the Ten Commandments, the laws of Islam, the Hindu Laws of Manu, or the precepts of Buddhism) may reflect a subconscious perception of adaptive and maladaptive behavior, and the states of consciousness that inspire them.

These codes have always judged some types of violence as being far worse than others. When two warriors of the same tribe get into a fight with each other, it may not be considered very serious. An attack on an infant or elderly person is much more odious. To a large extent, this kind of innate morality can also be observed in other primate species. Infants, nursing mothers, the sick and the elderly seem to be entitled to special protections in all cultures.

Human culture can change too rapidly for us to be able to use instincts to guide our behavior. What is adaptive at one time can be bad for us in another. This means that instincts, being hard-coded, can't be the basis for our ever-changing morality. Social rules can change when the economics, military situation or religion of a society changes.

Learning from past lives gives us subconscious information that can guide our behavior without using instincts. Karma (our feeling for positive and negative behavior) can change in one generation or in one rebirth. Karma, which can be conceived of as a set of flexible social instincts, can itself be adapted when the needs of a society change. Prohibitions against some types of violence (murder, rape, theft, vandalism) are found not only found in every culture, but also in other primate species.

In contrast, the prohibitions against sexual behavior vary quite drastically from place to place and from epoch to epoch. In one culture, a man may have several wives. In another, he must content himself with only one. At one time, all sexual behavior between men and women carried the risk of pregnancy. In today's world, changes in sexual taste and the development of effective birth control allow people a degree of sexual freedom unprecedented when our traditional religions were created. At one time, homosexuals were killed when they were discovered. Nowadays they are slowly acquiring freedom and protection under the law. As it's no longer universally condemned, its associated Karmas can change to make it an 'allowed' behavior.

At one time, very early in our evolutionary history, thinking of one's own children as personal possessions was probably frowned upon. Within a tribe or village, children were often considered as everyone's privilege and responsibility. Being possessive about one's own children may have looked self-important. Of course, a child's chances for survival to adulthood increase when they have many caretakers and protectors. Today, your children are 'your' children, with the parents having sole responsibility for their protection and upbringing. Sometimes, it even can even be a bad idea to bond with other people's children, unless their ideas about raising children are the same as yours. The Karma (the right and wrong) of childrearing has changed. If we related to our children through instinct, our ways of raising our kids would have

43

become 'locked in', and we could never have gone from tribal families to extended families, and from there to today's nuclear families. The economic structures that today's families depend on would never have appeared.

We can think of Karma as a set of flexible social predispositions that can change with each generation. Some moral ideas are all but absolute and very unlikely to change. Others are subject to change in almost every generation. The Karmas that might guide people in their choices about food, like how and when to share it, will change as food supplies change, when the climate, food supply or population numbers - and other factors - change.

Karma and Biological Success

Being born with an innate sense of human social rules makes us less resistant to the rules we learn in childhood. The better you understand the social rules, the more effectively you'll relate to others. This understanding will, in turn, increase your chance of achieving a high social rank. In every primate species, including human beings, the higher a male's social rank, the more mating opportunities he'll have. The more he mates, the more his DNA gets passed on.

For females, the higher social ranks make it easier for them to find help in raising her children, and that can often mean getting extra food for them. This increases her chances for seeing her offspring grow to adulthood and pass on their DNA. Social rank offers advantages that help those who enjoy it, both to have more children, and to see those children grow to adulthood.

Helping the children of higher-ranking females tends to gain her approval. The "great mother" of her community is always someone with the intelligence and foresight to identify the needs of others, plan ahead to meet those needs, and then inspire others to support her in the work; a task that needs real intelligence and skill. Such a woman will be one of the last to starve to death should the food supply run out. Her children will be among the first to be whisked to safety when the group is attacked by predators or an enemy tribe.

For primate males, the higher his social rank, the more the mating opportunities are available. This applies in every primate species without exception. Mating is more than just passing on our DNA and an act of pleasure; it can also show one's social status. A young man brags about his sexual experiences ("conquests"). An older rich man marries a 'trophy wife'. A younger woman is kept by a 'sugar daddy'. New brides show off their husbands. In all these ways, sexual and romantic relationships can enhance and show off one's social standing. Marriage shows that people are no longer children and have reached sexual maturity. They can now demand the respect shown to adults.

The dominant alpha males and females both need a full repertoire of social skills. Yes, males have to be able to fight, and females have to be able to argue, but more importantly, they have to know how to negotiate, persuade, make peace, speak in public and act as teachers. They need to be articulate; to have a full command of their language. These may seem like truisms today, but at the time when we first appeared as a species, none of these skills could be taken for granted. Males could compete with each other peacefully by speaking in councils and vying to see who could offer the wisest opinions. This would have pushed our languages to ever greater sophistication. In this way, competition for social rank within human cultures contributed to the development of human languages. Reincarnation, as we understand it here, would raise a person's chances for achieving and maintaining a high social rank, and that cannot happen without language skills or intelligence. Language, intelligence, complex culture and reincarnation would all reinforce one another as each person tries to achieve the highest social rank they can.

The more a person is able to live by the rules of their culture, the better their chance to become an alpha or beta individual. Karma, in this view, helps us live with other people, and prepares us for social success in our cultural environments.

For humans, biological success is only one of our needs. We live under the rule that the fittest are more able to survive, but for us, survival isn't enough. We also have to try to get as much respect from other people as we can. We have to try to become a chief, a shaman, a respected warrior, a popular storyteller, or a wise woman whom others seek out for advice. We have to talk to our children with wisdom and insight. We have to have compassion. We have to be able to make jokes. Each of these skills, and a host of others, increases a person's social rank. The higher one's rank in our earliest history, the more offspring they saw living to adulthood. Among humans, biological success depends partly on social success. The connection between the two would have been amplified until a lack of these uniquely human traits would make successful parenting much more difficult. Women without social skills would be more likely to miscarry or die in childbirth as they received less help during pregnancy. Men without social skills would be less able to find partners. The past-life learning conferred by reincarnation would make these biological and social failures much less likely.

Those who reached the upper social ranks through this kind of past-life learning would eventually fill the entire population. A consequence of their higher rank is that, over time, they would replace those without this larger portion of social skills.

Those with past-life learning would have extra social skills, higher social ranks, greater mating opportunities as well as better chances for raising their children to adulthood. Gradually, over several generations, those without past-life learning would have been bred out of the population. As time passed, the tendency for reincarnation to confer social success, with all its benefits, would have been strongly amplified. There are anthropologists who believe that once human beings began to appear within the population of their immediate predecessors, there may well have been a split, where newly-evolved humans left their communities, and began new societies for themselves. Some believe the newly-emerged Homo sapiens began to exterminate their predecessors, eating them, and eliminating competition for food supplies, campgrounds and other natural resources. If this is so, then those with past-life learning might have filled our populations from the start.

Some spiritually-minded people have wondered if it's possible to reincarnate as an animal. Some like the idea of being a house cat in their next life, because such animals have an easy time in life. Another might want to be an eagle, because in this life, the eagle is a spirit guide for them. Can such people reincarnate as animals? For us, the answer must be that past-life learning would only be useful in a cultural context. Human beings are the only species that relies on spoken culture as our evolutionary strategy. Our past-life learning would be absolutely useless to anyone who reincarnates as a salamander. Salamanders don't live in complex cultures, and would not be able to make use of the information and learning from past lives. If this model of reincarnation is valid, then it's not likely that people can reincarnate as animals, but that doesn't mean that people can't see desirable traits in animals and learn from them. An eagle can still be a powerful symbol of awareness. A bear can still be a symbol of gentle strength. The lion remains a symbol of leadership.

A female of high rank has a better chance of getting her young raised to adulthood, because the other females and some males in her group want to curry favor with her, especially if the culture did not demand monogamy. The women share the food they gather with her, to stay in her favor. One family can only eat so much, and some of the extra food can be passed on to the alpha woman, after some has been shared with close friends. It doesn't matter whether she is already overstocked, because as the alpha female, she can decide who to share it with. By doing this kind of favor, she re-enforces her leadership. The alpha male has to be wise and gentle to maintain his power. Therefore, he doles out a more masculine kind of social favor. Power in many, if not most, early cultures was a matter of gentleness, generosity and concern for others. It may be that our evolution found a way to maximize our social intelligence by making use of learning accomplished in previous lives. The more learning this included the more capable and sophisticated our leadership could become, and the healthier our social groups would be. It would not only raise the quantity of DNA passed on to the next generations, but also the desirability of the traits it preserved.

There are several ways to become the alpha female. One of the most important is to be the mate of the alpha male. Another is to be so skilled at social manipulation that she is able motivate other women to assist her, not only in providing for her own family, but also for the less fortunate ones in her group. The alpha female, usually being more intelligent than other women, is better able to see the needs of the group, and plan ahead to meet them. An alpha female usually has more intellectual and emotional intelligence, as well as the ability to read the feelings of others and respond to them. The traits you need to be a female deserving an alpha position often cross the lines of division for power among males. She must be wise, but not necessarily as wise as the shaman, or in the same ways; and she must be able to give appropriate suggestions, though always recognizing the authority of the chief, the shaman and the tribal councils. She can show her anger when she is offended, but with far more self-restraint than young warriors need.

It's easy to understand the point of reincarnation, even if our hypothesis here isn't the final word on the subject. It helps us pre-adapt to living in a cultural environment[28]. This gives us a better chance of getting to the top of the social ladder, where we have better chances of passing on our DNA, and then seeing our children grow up and passing on their DNA. In this sense, the point of life may be having grandchildren.

Past-life learning is part of the price of admission to the human species. Those with past-life learning succeeded at the expense of those without it. Here's a brief look at a likely sequence. In the first generation, half the young didn't have the past-life learning and none of them got to the top of the hierarchy. As a result, they were not able to reproduce themselves to the same extent as those who did. In the next generation, more youngsters were born with past-life learning, and maybe only 25% didn't have it. After that, the number of those born without past-life learning would slowly taper off to zero. However, gene packages without the codes for picking up past-life information could have lingered for a very long time, continuing in an ever-shrinking minority. Remember that the frontal lobes are the "seat" of both social intelligence and intellectual prowess. This implies that the extra measure of social intelligence may have helped us to become more intelligent overall.

The Four Primary Social Rules

The most important, and perhaps the only, context in which we have to conform to social rules is among our own people. The concept of 'our people' implies the need to be nice to them, and may also grant permission for antagonism with competing tribes and hostile nations. This means there is a basic division between 'our people' and 'other people'. You have to be respectful, pleasant and conforming with your own people, while hostility toward the people of other nations carries far fewer consequences than it does toward your own group.

In the past, bad behavior within one's own social group was much more likely to be punished than the same behavior towards other people. Racism and religious intolerance are now seen as an absolute evil. In some times and places, however, aggression towards competing tribes and nations was seen as a good thing[29]. In today's world, the concept of 'our people' has expanded to include everybody on earth. The pollution in the air we breathe is partly produced on the other side of the world. Now, all people are 'our people'.

The basic bad behaviors are much the same in nearly every culture. There seem to be four primary types of negative behavior; stealing, sexual offences, violence, and defying the culture's religion. Other people will see a different set of fundamental rules, and some of them may be right, but these are enough for us, for now.

Stealing hurts the whole social group. Depriving others of their possessions without their agreement is immoral in almost every culture. A man who works hard to raise his sheep does it to provide food for his family or group, and to steal them is unacceptable. If something isn't yours or isn't given freely, you can't just take it. Everyone is motivated to provide the best they can for their family. For the earliest cultures, that meant food. Working hard and producing a store of wealth is fulfilling and gives one self-esteem. When that produce is stolen, the motivation to do it again is diminished. If people don't have faith that the wealth they accumulate will be theirs to use, they won't make the effort to acquire it. Any loss of motivation to produce has a negative impact on the whole community. Giving food to others builds and strengthens social alliances – friendships and bonds that mean that others will help you when you need it. However, you are entitled to decide who you'll help, and who you want to bond with. Even the food you give to others is, in some sense, yours, especially if you think they'll "owe you a favor" for giving it. There is an Eskimo saying that the best place to store your extra food is in your neighbor's stomach. Just because you have to give to others does not mean they can take from you without your agreement.

Sexual offences are another kind of unacceptable behavior. To have sex with your partner is acceptable, but sex with someone else's partner is offensive, and makes for trouble within the tribe or group. We are not a strictly monogamous species[30], but even when we cheat, we try to make sure we don't get caught. We take steps to ensure that no one has to hear about it from an abused husband, wife, parent or angry elder brother. By trying to avoid discovery, we are not only saving ourselves from a divorce, a beating or being stoned to death[31]; we're also minimizing the impact on our social group.

Earlier in human history, there were probably times when sexual fidelity didn't matter much, because every child was raised by the whole group, so no one was concerned about paternity. When inheritance rights appeared, involving land, titles, herds, thrones and financial portfolios, fidelity and compliance became important. A prosperous man had to decide what his son will inherit when he prepared his will. He certainly didn't want a strange young man to come along claiming to be his oldest son, and demand to inherit his herds. At one time, the only way to avoid this possibility was to restrict his sexual relations to his legitimate wife only.

Apart from inspiring jealousy and rivalries, extra-marital sex disrupts the life, not only of the family, but also of the community. Sexual offences could have profound economic consequences. Having sex with the wrong person can create a lot of trouble. "You shall not commit adultery". "You shall not covet your neighbor's wife ...[32]"

The origin of private property demanded the creation of the family. This, in turn, helped motivate the creation of states which protected inheritance rights, especially of its kings. As with so many other social conventions that began before writing was invented, the prohibition against sexual misconduct, in whatever way the culture defines it, may have emerged from economic realities. Changes in our societies demanded the creation of moral rules. These are more effective when people believe they come from the gods or God. The overwhelming majority of the world's people still live under laws that were originally inspired by codes of religious morality.

Another example of improper behavior is to defy the religion found in one's social group. Religion is a powerful force. It keeps cultures together by uniting the whole community in worship, through song, dance and the spoken word. Every culture has ceremonies where people gather together in a place they consider sacred. This gives the group or tribe something they do communally, which tends to bind them together. It helps ensure sure that people who may be only distantly connected will still have some kind of bond. In the event of some tragedy, epidemic, or a war with a neighboring tribe, they will see one another as members of one people. Not because they are related by blood, but because they speak the same language, and appeal to the same gods, united in both their understanding and purpose. It's not enough for only two farmers to agree about the planting when it's a religious ritual. They also do well to make the same assumptions about its religious meaning, both to themselves and the community. It maintains cohesiveness within the society, so the potential for cooperation can remain high, even under difficult circumstances.

The social group is united when everyone congregates to worship together. When someone undermines the authority of the communal religion, it undermines the integrity of their society. In many parts of the world, it's a matter of deep shame for a person to have a relative who rejects the religion of their family or nation. Jesus' rebellions against Mosaic Law created unrest in Jerusalem. The Prophet Mohammed's (blessings be upon him) rebellion against Arabian polytheism created a profound division in his home city of Mecca. The Buddha's teachings rejected the caste system, and weakened the basis of Hindu culture.

Maladaptive behavior is seen as negative or bad because of its impact on others. Bad Karma; the absence of inhibitions preventing negative behavior, is also anti-social. The main advantage of reincarnation is that it subtly guides behavior in a way that's not unlike having social instincts. It instills awareness of which states of consciousness to seek out and which to avoid, and in what circumstances. If you fight an enemy, it's good. To fight your brother is bad. The circumstance determines the social impact of our behavior and with it, the associated Karma; our flexible social instincts.

But Karma, as we understand it here, does more than just help maintain our evolutionary strategy as it reinforces our cultures and use of language. It also offers advantages to each individual.

Evolutionary Pressure

There must be an evolutionary pressure in order for an adaptation of any kind to appear. Evolutionary pressure refers to a condition that poses a threat to those who lack a certain trait, but not to those who have it.

Some adaptations among humans don't help individuals survive, but rather help them achieve social rank and prestige. For example, abilities such as language and empathy promote more effective interactions in social situations, rather than mere survival. Consistently losing out to one's social rivals can mean fewer opportunities for passing on one's DNA. The newer adaptive trait, spreading throughout the population, eventually means the older gene packets are extinguished. An evolutionary pressure can operate by slowly and gradually steering a population, without ever actually threatening its survival.

Language, complex culture, reincarnation and most likely, a new kind of religion may have all appeared at the same time. They were all part of one sweeping change. The evolutionary pressure possibly lay in the huge amount of learning required to live in a community with others. This social learning is essential, whether the person lived in an early society of hunter/gatherers or in a modern country.

A great deal of learning happens in childhood, but our species is already overburdened with childhood. Anthropologists believe that when our species originated, the life expectancy was about 45 years or possibly even less. It's a long time between birth and sexual maturity. Usually, adolescents are sexually mature around the age of 13 to 14 years. Considering that a typical life expectancy was only about 45 years in our early history, 14 years of childhood means that almost a third of our lifetimes were dedicated to preparing for the business of reproduction. The biological purpose of each and every human life is to make *sustainable* copies of their DNA and in this way, win the evolutionary game.

In our early days, it may not have mattered whether adolescents were emotionally ready for parenthood, because others in the tribe would take responsibility for the children. This was considered not only normal, but a pleasure. There are tribal peoples who still hold this view today. Child-raising was the communal responsibility of the entire village. Everyone helped to raise and protect everyone's children. Larger tribes meant more hands to help, and more hands meant more food. Tribes with many sons also enjoyed more meat, and greater protection from predators and hostile tribes. Tribes with many daughters could look forward to more babies being born, and so more people overall. Two sayings come to mind. "Many hands make light work" and "It takes a whole village to raise a child."

A newborn wildebeest can run at its top speed within 10 minutes of being born. This ability can make the difference between being a survivor and a lion's lunch. Some humans can't walk until about 10 months, and then only a few very shaky steps at a time. Many take 2 to 3 months longer. Speech and the willingness to share are essential for reciprocal relations and developing the friendships that pull people together. The time taken to master the art of speech takes more than two years, and learning to share with others takes even longer.

If we remember that it takes about a third of our lives just to learn the arts of social interaction and prepare to have young, we can see that adding any more learning to childhood could be bad for our survival. It can't be extended any further. As life expectancy has increased through history the duration of childhood seems to have lengthened, so that today in most places, people have wait until they are about 18 before their religion and laws allow them to legally have kids.

In our early evolutionary history, there was probably no waiting at all. People would have probably begun having sex as soon as they could. Indeed, the signs that one's body was able to have sex were probably interpreted as the right time for young people to become sexually active. Of course, in those days, early sexual activity probably didn't conflict with the tribal religion, so a young person would not be scorned or reprimanded for sexual behavior. Quite the opposite, in a society concerned with keeping its population as high as possible; the earlier they bore children, the better.

Today, in most parts of the world, early sexual activity is not just an offence against morals, cultures and laws, but also disrespect for the religion and its morality. Sexual precocity remains taboo in almost every culture. While it may be true that the invention of effective birth control resulted in the relaxation of many of the rules governing sexual behavior in some areas, most of the world's population remains unchanged by it. This discussion may offend some readers, but we need to see the crucial balance between how soon young people can produce children, and how long before they die. Longer childbearing years mean a larger population. Larger populations meant more hunters; a larger group of warriors; more women rearing children; more elders with wisdom and experience, giving their tribe a wider range of viewpoints from which the population could learn.

Pregnancy is also somewhat overburdened. Human pregnancy is already long enough that many women once died in childbirth, because the infant's heads were sometimes too large to pass through the birth canal. The ratio of brain size to body size in humans is one of the largest known in nature. Any increase in cognitive skills that meant a larger brain might have reduced our populations over time (not all cognitive skills would demand more brain mass). Adding past-life information would have added social and cognitive skills without adding any brain tissue. Past-life information would allow some of the learning required to live in a complex culture to happen in the womb - without extending pregnancy.

In our hypothesis, past-life information doesn't need to guide our behavior in specific ways. It only needs to give a sense of which states of consciousness, and in which contexts, lead to behavior that will be rewarded, and which motivate behavior that will be condemned or punished.

In evolutionary terms, lengthening either pregnancy or childhood would be very expensive and probably cost lives. The evolutionary pressure comes from the advantage in maximizing the amount of learning an individual needs to empower them to achieve social rank, but without making childhood longer. We needed to maximize our intelligence without making pregnancy longer, and to achieve this without resorting to inflexible instincts for use in flexible cultures.

Reincarnation relies on a complicated biological system, and one might wonder how this adaptation occurred. Some anthropologists believe the drive to achieve the highest possible social rank may be a true instinct, inherited from our primate ancestors. The lessons we carry in our karma may be an extension of it, serving us in our more complicated, constantly changing, cultures, giving each person a chance to climb the human social ladder.

A precursor for the death process

In the west, the death-process commonly begins with OBEs, followed by the Tunnel or the Void, where we sometimes encounter dead friends and relatives. These are followed by entry into the spirit realm, and then a meeting with the Being of Light. The Life Review comes next, sometimes followed by the Transcendent Experience and then the Point of No Return. The specific phenomena in the individual experiences can vary radically, according to the person's age, ability to anticipate their death, culture, religious beliefs, etc. The death-process is so flexible that no two individuals have probably ever had exactly the same experience.

In order to be fully prepared for the Point of No Return, one has to go through most or all the stages. This makes for such a complicated system that one might naturally wonder about its origin.

I suggest that the precursor to the human death-process lay in a process already in use – sleep, which also involves multiple states of consciousness. We go through several stages in the course of sleep in much the same way as we go through several stages in the course of dying. There are actually five stages of sleep. Dreams are not the only one we can remember. The other one is twilight sleep; when you've *almost* fallen asleep. Evolution is stingy and efficient. It doesn't waste resources. Rather than develop a new process to meet a new need, it will give existing processes new jobs instead. The chance that a mutation will affect an existing process is much higher than for creating a completely new one.

Most spontaneous OBEs occur during twilight sleep. The beginning of the death-process is often an OBE, and this makes twilight sleep the most likely precursor for its first phase. The crucial part of the death-process is the Life Review, where the events of our lives are reviewed. The stage of sleep when the most learning takes place is dream sleep. In the Life Review, we review the events in the course of our life. During dream sleep, we review things that happened in the course of the day or previous days. The Life Review and dream sleep both involve reviewing behavior to learn lessons, which are largely absorbed and acted upon subconsciously. Both the *Life Review* and our dreams access our memories in unusual ways. Dreams present our memories symbolically. Many Life Reviews, especially those found in pre-literate cultures, seem to be symbolic[33]. Evolutionary adaptations have precursors, and the death-process is no exception. Dreams are the most likely precursor for the Life Review, and sleep the best candidate for an immediate precursor to the death-process overall.

Nietzsche said "He who would learn to fly one day must first learn to stand and walk and run and climb and dance; one cannot fly into flying". Likewise, we couldn't reincarnate into reincarnation. It needed a mutation in an existing mechanism. Although there other processes involving several states of consciousness, sleep fits the bill very well. Eating is one example. To eat, you have to feel hungry, think about what you'll eat, get the food and prepare it, and only afterwards sit down to eat. Afterwards, there is a feeling of satisfaction, and we want to relax while we digest the meal.

Thirst offers another good example, although with fewer states of consciousness involved. Our state of consciousness shifts when our bodies are low on fluids and changes again when we drink something. The same applies to sex, where there is arousal, sex, orgasm and the relaxation that follows. Those with an amorous disposition can get along without mating, but they will go into sexual desire more and more often.

Series of states of consciousness for specific purposes are very common in human experience. The idea that several states of consciousness are involved in death and rebirth isn't really too farfetched. Of all the processes that could have been adapted to develop the human death-process, sleep with its multiple phases, and inner imagery has the greatest resemblance to the death-process, making it the most likely immediate precursor. Just as dreams can be either literal or symbolic (or both), so can Life Reviews.

Transmission of information

How does the information from a dying person in one place get into a fetus somewhere else? The signal needs a carrier. In an elementary school telephone, made of two tin cans with a tight piece of string between them, the string is the medium. Air is the medium for smoke signals. Electromagnetic radiation is the medium for radio and television. The earth's magnetic field appears to be the most likely carrier for information that passes between lives.

The brain has constant electrical activity, and it follows certain patterns. In one state of consciousness, the brain produces one pattern of electrical activity; in another state, it produces a different one. Each state of consciousness depends on its own pattern of electrical activity. All the magnetic patterns following our brain's electrical activities are broadcast into the earth's magnetic field. It cannot be otherwise, because magnetic insulation is against the laws of physics. Where there is changing electrical activity, there are changing magnetic fields. It's a law of physics. The electrical activity is unique in each state of consciousness, and the state following the Point of No Return, when there is no longer any possibility for someone to return to the body, is no exception. Its pattern could be the trigger for karmic information to be expressed into the earth's magnetic field.

I don't believe that we're "all one". If I stub my toe, I feel the pain, not you. I wouldn't want to impose my stubbed toe on the whole world. Of course, we don't want to feel pain from everyone around us. Otherwise, we'd all be in constant pain. Nevertheless, because our brains are all immersed in the earth's magnetic field, and all electrical activity is accompanied by magnetic activity, we *are* all connected.

There is even reason to believe that psychic connections between individuals work through the geomagnetic field. As we'll see later on, the earth's magnetic field can transmit information, and act as both the carrier wave and the signal.

A study published by Dr. Michael Persinger[34] seems to support this idea. In this study, he found that people prone to common altered state experiences (complex partial epileptic signs) were more likely to have OBEs (elicited through magnetic brain stimulation) when the earth's magnetic field was elevated. In other words, OBEs are more likely when the earth's magnetic field was busier than usual.

Some people don't have specific ideas about what death will be like, and their deaths don't seem to have the kind of symbolic and mythical themes found in Asia and tribal cultures. Unless their culture leads people to expect something different, OBEs seem to be the most common first phase of NDEs, and these are more likely to occur when the earth's magnetic field is in a certain state. This makes the earth's magnetic field a probable carrier for information from one person's past-life to someone else's future life.

For such a large body of information to pass from a dying person to an infant or fetus, it might well have to be packaged into something like the 'zip' files used to compress several large computer files into one smaller one. This mechanism would require a structure capable of bearing information, like radio and television carrier waves. The carrier wave would have to preserve information without corruption. If it were embedded in the earth's magnetic field, then we'd have something that could function as an intermediary between lives; a physical basis for reincarnation. There is no reason why such an information packet could not contribute to more than one individual, explaining how the number of people can keep growing. The reason why reincarnation seems to be at odds with the fact of our growing population is that the question assumes that *souls* are what reincarnate. If *information* is what takes rebirth, then many people might benefit from a single bundle of past-life information, just as a single computer file can be downloaded many times.

Let's take a brief look at a hypothesis that explains how this might be possible.

Photo by Piotr Pieranski[36].
A pair of solitons in water.

There is a kind of wave that could function in this way. These are called *solitons*. A Soliton is a "self-reinforcing solitary wave that is not connected to groups of other waves". A soliton "maintains its shape while it travels at a constant speed". Waves on the ocean come one after the other. Solitons travel alone.

Magnetic solitons have been observed, together with their movement in non-uniform magnetic fields (the geomagnetic field is a non-uniform field)[37]. In fact, gravitational and magnetic fields can and do move.

The most efficient way to preserve information within a wave form is to use two signals that interact with each other[38], a hologram. The points where those waves meet and interact are places where information can be embedded. Huge amount of information can be embedded in just one pair of waves. In fact, any fragment of that wave pattern is enough to reconstruct the information in all of it.

Photo of a Soliton[39]

If we had two solitons capable of bearing information in the same way as a hologram, which uses two lasers, a single pair of solitons could behave as a single wave, and preserve a great deal of information within the earth's magnetic field.

We must presume that the 'rebirth' soliton has a characteristic signature, shape or set of frequencies. If the brain activity of a fetus used a matching pattern, it would be a case of simple physics to transmit the information to the fetal brain through sympathetic resonance[40]. Once the information has been received, the fetus or infant would then possess past-life learning. In the chapter on psychic skills, we'll see that although its mechanism is not yet understood, there actually is a mechanism in place for the brain to receive information carried by the earth's magnetic field.

We now have the means and mechanism for reincarnation, as well as an evolutionary pressure favoring its adoption, and an understanding of how it contributes to our survival. The result is a scientific hypothesis, which holds together well enough to be published in at least one scientific journal, making it a scientific idea, however controversial.

Notice that we have not used any traditional beliefs as building blocks for this theory. Only the initial postulate is inspired by traditional spiritual teachings. It assumed that reincarnation is a human behavior in which adaptive information derived from a human mind is recruited by another during gestation or infancy.

It's all science, with varying degrees of certainty appearing at different points in the discussion. Primarily, it draws upon evolutionary biology, with a little bit of physics and some anthropology thrown into the mix. It involves the recognition that we're not just a social species; we're also a hierarchical species.

One question remains. Just what is it that reincarnates? Our Karma reincarnates. This is a record of our repertoire of states of consciousness, which acts to guide our behavior in productive and adaptive ways. It gives us information that facilitates social success, which in turn makes biological success more likely.

We *may* remember things from past lives, but, we don't need to say that memories are preserved in order to build this theory. It is said The Dalai Lama's past lives are continuous with his present life. Once, he was asked "Do you remember your past lives?" His answer was brief. "Remember my past lives? I don't even remember what I had for breakfast." Can you remember things from past lives? It's not impossible. However, in this model, such memories are not the foundation of karma.

Perhaps, after a number of generations, it became possible for memory skills to be added to the body of reincarnation information, allowing some people to have actual memories of past lives. Nevertheless, 'marking' or 'tagging' states of consciousness for repetition or avoidance would preserve the crucial information more efficiently than past-life memories, because this would need fewer resources, less information, and the information it does use can be applied in more contexts.

It's not impossible that we preserve more information than just what came from our immediate past lives. Still, it's unrealistic to think that after hundreds of thousands of years, information from many past lives (which we aren't aware of and never use) could be still available to us. If it's data, like our DNA, dreams, or even just ordinary moments of living, then a great deal of that content could be garbage. How many times have you brushed your teeth? Do you remember each specific time you did it? Of course not. Such memories would be useless. Even if you pay attention while you're doing it, you'll probably forget it. Memories of tooth brushing aren't likely to be useful. Likewise, a lot of what may have been retained from past lives may not have any practical value. Memories of some events may not have been created in the first place.

The idea behind karma here is that it allows us to succeed in our social hierarchies even when our cultures change. In one life, food is plentiful, so it can be shared with others freely. Over time, the environment can change or dry out, so that everyone would have less to eat, and the karmas associated with sharing food would have to change. Both sharing food and hoarding it can have social effects. Give food away, and your social status can rise. Get caught hoarding it and it can plummet. If the food supply changes enough, then, in principle, related karmas from time a when food was abundant would become obsolete. Such Karmas could senesce (suddenly atrophy), or become garbage data.

Two big questions are: do *we* reincarnate? and will '*I*' take rebirth? In order to answer whether your self – as an individual – will reincarnate, we need to have a concept of what the 'self' is. We can't address the question without first becoming clear about this. It's possible to say, "Of course, I'll live, but then I *know* I will survive. I will go on. I'm actually my own eternal spirit. I'm not this mortal coil. *I* will live forever." "Whoever shall believe on Jesus shall not perish, but have eternal life[41]" "The imperishable self is transcendental because of its beginninglessness" (Krishna)[42]. However, this could be an illusory perception that guides us towards adaptive behavior. It's a healthy thing to have faith in it, but that doesn't mean it's true. We need to have an idea about what the 'self' is before we can think about whether or not it reincarnates.

No hypothesis, including this one, can reach the status of a theory unless there's a way to try to falsify it. Only a hypothesis that survives the falsification process can become a scientific theory. To make this hypothesis real for many scientists, a way of testing needs to be offered, but right now, no such method exists.

Perhaps one day we'll be able to read information embedded in magnetic fields surrounding intensive care units. When that day arrives, we might expect to see a change in the finest structure of the magnetic fields in a room when someone dies[43]. If not, then everything here might be proved wrong. In order to do the best job of presenting a theory, one has to include a way to try to falsify it. This cannot happen now (that's why I'm calling it a hypothesis instead of a theory), but eventually, it will. I will be the first to admit that Evolutionary Reincarnation is speculative, but speculation is okay, so long as the one doing the speculating knows it for what it is. I have had critics say the idea wasn't supported by evidence (!) as though they had unmasked some kind of conspiracy. But then, skeptics live by the straw man fallacy, and the idea that I believe this idea to be a theory, instead of a hypothesis, is a straw man[44].

Inevitably there will be skeptics who will dismiss any science of reincarnation as pseudoscience, but that won't really apply here. Having been published in a scientific journal makes it science – there is no other authority, and no pope of science to make a final judgment. Skeptics who disparage the journal where controversial ideas are published aren't actually saying anything about the ideas. When a skeptic says that something isn't science, they presume an authority that no one can claim.

Speculation[45] is one of the many methods used in science. Almost all widely-accepted theories began as speculations. An idea has to be proposed before its proofs or falsifications are found.

CHAPTER 3

Some Brain Parts

This book is about the brain's role in religious and mystic experiences. To approach our subject, we'll have to learn something about the brain and some of its parts. The next two chapters will be a bit more technical, and a lot less spiritual than the ones that follow, but what we'll learn in them will be important as we go along. The reader can skip them, but that can make most of this book more confusing. We will review the functions of these brain parts again at several points, so don't be concerned if you don't absorb it all now.

For several reasons, we'll be speaking about brain parts in rather simple terms. Science knows that remaining conscious (or not-being-unconscious) is a function that belongs to the reticular formation, in the brain stem. If it's damaged enough, the person will lose consciousness and can never regain it. However, the reticular formation does lots of other things, too. It has a structure, and a form that follows its function. It has several types of brain cells, and each of them has a different job to do. There's a lot we don't know about what they're all doing, but if we're only talking about not being in a coma, we don't really need to know. This is how we'll look at 'our' brain parts; thinking only of how they relate to spirituality, and there's a lot we don't need to know in order to do that.

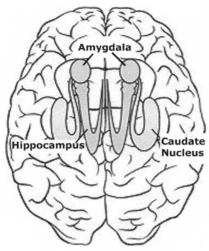

The brain's limbic system

This means we'll have to bypass a lot of fascinating information. This will make it easier for us to think about these brain structures, but it also makes their functions look simpler than they really are.

There are two kinds of brain parts we need to look at. The first group includes the frontal and temporal lobes are on the surface of the brain or its *cortex*. Deeper down we find the *limbic system*, including the amygdala, hippocampus and caudate nucleus.

The Cortex

There were significant changes in the cortex when we appeared as a species. The temporal lobes developed as it took on more functions, especially language and memory. The frontal lobes expanded, giving us the skills we need to live in complex cultures. Both regions acquired more folds and fissures, given them more surface area.

The Frontal Lobes

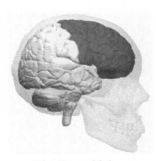

The Frontal lobes.

The frontal lobes help us plan things, anticipate possibilities and maintain our expectations. They're also deeply involved in our ability to relate to others, to care about the consequences of the events around us, and the results of our actions.

Although we think of human intelligence as the source for our technologies and the ability to produce art, music and literature, it actually finds its greatest expression in the way we relate to one another.

By mammalian standards, you have to be smart to produce a wooden spear. It requires a stone point lashed into place with a strip of wet rawhide, coated with dried tree sap, and then left to dry. However, true human intelligence is best seen when a person has a problem and needs help from those around them. As a species, we're able to anticipate the needs of those around us, and devise ways of meeting them. We need to be able to understand other people's interests and figure out what's good for them, to help us get the things we want and need.

Here's a simple example. I might want to borrow a few dollars from you to pay a bill. To do that, I'd have to explain why I need the money, and do my best to imply that it's in your best interests to make the loan. I'm probably not going to do that very well if I don't know what your interests are. In fact, if I don't get it right, my bill might go unpaid and I'd be stuck with a problem.

Suppose I wanted to marry your daughter. How do I persuade you to give your blessings to our marriage? To be able to respond to your view of the situation, I need some idea of how you think. You, in turn, must be able to judge my character, and make a reasonable guess about how my life will turn out, because that will affect your daughter. Will I become an alpha male? Will I be rich enough to support you in your old age? Am I an honest, pleasant, kind and compassionate man? Will we fight too much so she runs home to mama? Such decisions, crucial for maintaining one's social rank, are the domain of the frontal lobes. The frontal lobes are concerned with the future consequences of our actions - for ourselves and for others. Any form of relating to others always involves the frontal lobes (especially in the context of the complex cultures we live in).

The frontal lobes also exert control over other areas on the surface of the brain. When they're very excited, they can inhibit the temporal lobes, and vice versa. They exist in a kind of mutually antagonistic relationship. When one of them dominates the moment, the other withdraws from control. The frontal lobes exert a high level of control, and the temporal lobes give in to it.

The Temporal Lobes

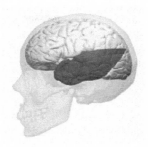

The temporal lobes

The temporal lobes of the brain have long been known to be involved in religious and mystic experiences (visions, epiphanies, apparitions, etc.), though more recent research has narrowed it down to the temporal lobes deeper regions.

Although the temporal lobes work in tandem with the frontal lobes, its functions are quite different. The most important of these is memory. This is where memories are created and accessed.

Our language centers are in the left temporal lobe. One of them is at the back of the temporal lobe, and the other is just forward of it. On the right, like many structures on that side of the brain, they process nonverbal information. We may produce words on the left, but their connotations and subtle meanings are drawn from the right side. The areas that support the 'felt' aspects of language are located in the same place as the language centers, but on the opposite side of the brain[46].

The temporal lobes are more sensitive than the frontal lobes. There are even seizures that stay in the temporal lobes, without including other regions. This is because they take less electricity to get started than the surrounding areas. Because they're more excitable, they respond to nearly any stimulus, but by also being subordinate to the frontal lobes, they're also quickly inhibited.

The frontal and temporal lobes are on the surface of the brain, which is less implicated in spiritual experience than the deeper temporal lobe structures; The Limbic System.

The Limbic System

The limbic system is the name for a set of structures deep in the brain, functioning in our basic, survival-oriented behaviors such as our emotions, motivation, and emotional associations of our memories. It's quite primal, being the source of 'raw' emotion. It's also the location for many automatic functions like heart rate, digestion, breathing, salivation, perspiration, pupil dilation, urination and sexual arousal.

The limbic system works together with the cortex in almost everything it does that we can feel directly. However, in much of our discussions, we'll speak as though it works on its own. This is not to put the limbic system on a pedestal, or to give it more importance than it deserves. It's to keep the discussion simple enough for ordinary readers to understand. Of course, this also means that our treatment of the brain's role in spirituality invites its own elaboration, with more attention to the roles of other areas of the brain. The responsible thing to do is to point out directions for further research when they appear, and the role of the cortex in religious and mystic experiences is one of them. The fundamental jobs of the limbic system are much the same for everyone (with normal brains), and even very similar in different species. In contrast, the brain's surface is very different in humans, and its workings have a wide range of variation from one person to the next. Understanding how the cortex of the brain contributes to different spiritual experiences is one of the directions for further research. Very few new hypotheses in the history of science have answered all the questions that could be put to them when they're first put forward[47]. If I tried to address all the possible questions that every reader might think of, both scientific and spiritual, this work could never be completed.

The Amygdala – Right and Left

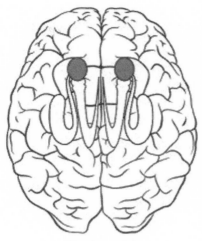

The Amygdala

The amygdala's main job is to assign an emotional response to the things we experience, moment-to-moment[48]. Working with other brain parts, it's the source for our emotions, but we should understand that all emotions appear in response to things, and never appear on their own. The events that trigger it might be from within our own minds, or from the world around us. We may not always be aware of them. The amygdala is fast. One research report suggested that "… the amygdala is part of an "impulsive," habit type system that triggers emotional responses to immediate outcomes.[49]"

The amygdala has a very quick response to nearly everything that happens, and they happen in very small periods of time. The amygdala doesn't stop to think.

It's what tells us when something *means* something to us, so that we know we need to respond to it. It's the most active part of the brain, based on studies tracking how much blood each brain part uses in relation to its size[50]. It's also the one most likely to be the source of epileptic events[51], though its neighbor, the hippocampus, is almost always involved whenever the amygdala is the source of a seizure. Few things in the brain happen to only one brain part.

The strongest emotions we feel usually appear when we're relating to other people. As both an emotional and social structure, it interprets the meaning of facial expressions, helping us see how other people are feeling. The prevailing theme of the amygdala is the emotions we feel when we're relating to others; a theme expressed with tremendous variation.

The amygdala responds when we see others gazing at us[52]; an important social cue. It also responds to gestures, body-language[53][54] and tones of voice[55]. It's involved with empathy, as shown by studies that find it doesn't work normally in sociopaths, who lack empathy[56] [57]. One kind of brain tissue (grey matter) is denser in the amygdala for people (and monkeys) with larger social networks[58]. This even applies to people whose social network is on the internet[59]. The left amygdala responds when we are gently touched[60]. One of its best-known social functions is how it responds to the facial expressions of others[61]. These amygdala functions are social; they have to do with relating to others. They're crucial in relating to others. A damaged amygdala can make it harder to know what others are thinking and feeling.

The right amygdala is more specialized for fear and anxiety as well as pain[62]. The left amygdala is involved with positive emotions,[63],[64] like elation and happiness, as well as the maternal happiness that comes with holding one's infant[65]. It recognizes positive emotions in others[66]. Although both amygdalas participate in fear and anxiety, the one on the left is specialized for positive emotions[67]. When neuro-imaging studies examine the amygdala, they find both sides responding to most emotions. When these studies distinguish between the left and right amygdala, it turns out they aren't doing the same things. There are differences between them. When only the left amygdala is stimulated using a magnetic signal that appears only from the amygdala, it often responds with a wave of strong positive emotions[68]. It may be that this mild ("weak") and non-invasive stimulation, which we'll look at more closely later on, is able to elicit effects that can't be achieved using other laboratory and clinical stimuli (like high-powered magnetic fields in TMS [transcranial magnetic stimulation] or stimulating the surface of the brain with an electrode) or stimulation-from-within (as in psychiatric disorders and most [but not all] seizures). Sometimes, with brain stimulation, "less is more". Despite a strong research bias in favor of examining the role of the amygdala in negative, especially fearful emotions, there is also ample evidence that the one on the left is involved in positive feelings. It even plays a crucial role[69] in the brain's reward system.

Most research in neuroscience has rightly focused on understanding psychiatric disorders. Investigating negative emotions is more useful for most neuroscientists and neurologists, who look for cures for ailing minds. For a long time, the bulk of medical amygdala studies gave the impression that it has no other role to play. However, looking carefully at research reports, we find this impression is mistaken; the left amygdala supports positive emotions.

The amygdala also has close connections to the olfactory bulbs, which is why different smells can have such strong emotional impacts[70]. Smells associated with our childhood can conjure subtle moods which can be almost impossible to put into words.

There is a story about a Sufi master who always used a certain perfume; one he made himself. Because it wasn't available anywhere else, the only place his friends and disciples ever smelled it was in his company. Before he died, he prepared a large batch of this perfume, and gave it to his closest devotees with strict instructions not to open it for 10 years. When those years had passed, they took it out and gave a bottle to each of his disciples. When the disciples received the vials of perfume, opened them and smelled its contents, each one felt their master's presence. They immediately remembered why they had followed him, and the disciplines he taught.

Each remembered his teachings and the states they achieved under his guidance. The master did this because he knew that smells are intimately associated with a sense of a person's presence. Lovers smell their pillows after their beloveds have gone. Mothers smell their babies' clothing. In Southeast Asia, many people prefer to smell their lover rather than kissing them. In Thailand, the word for this is *to 'hohm'*, which also means *fragrant*.

The human amygdala isn't an artifact of an earlier mammalian or reptilian brain. It's uniquely human. It's a very social structure, and our very different societies, much more complex than any other species, made new demands on it, so that it has more parts than those of other species. Interestingly, the amygdala also responds to images of animals, suggesting that in some ways, we look at animals the way we look at humans[71]. This may explain why so many are willing to treat their pets they way they treat people.

In spite of its being one of the most important brain parts for our discussions, the amygdala, with only 21 nuclei, is not one of the most complicated. For comparison, a chimpanzee amygdala has 12 nuclei, and a cat only 5. A working amygdala is the basis of our ability to recognize other people's moods and the meanings of their facial expressions, as well as its primary function, assigning emotions to events. It knows when to be happy and when to be scared. The amygdala's range of emotions includes all the ones come into play when we're relating to others, and sometimes feelings that go past that. Under exceptional circumstances, the amygdala can attain peaks of joy and fear beyond anything we would experience ordinarily. Its functions are very much concerned with 'self and other', and it plays a role in those profoundly altered states of consciousness where we experience 'other beings'. In these cases, they might be spirits, 'presences' demons, 'entities' God, angels or even aliens. We'll come back to this theme again in later chapters.

On the left, the amygdala is specialized for positive emotions, including happiness[72], bliss, joy and love. It works with other, surrounding areas[73], some of which may be may be more important for different positive emotions, but the left amygdala seems to play a role in all of them. The amygdala reads the amount of threat in something, and in some cases, assigns other brain areas to respond to it. When either amygdala sees a threat that's less than zero, it becomes a reward. All perceptions are first checked to see what they offer, first to see if they're threatening ("vigilance"), and only then 'allowed' to become a reward. As this happens, other brain areas become involved. Most rewards are social. Looking at it one way, we can say that *all* rewards are social. Even the 'primal' ones – food, sex, water, sleep and a place by the fire are acquired socially. Most people eat food that others have cooked. We might take plants and meat from nature, but doing it well usually means doing it with others. We need a partner to conceive our young. Our early ancestors often went in groups to get water, and later, our wells were put in the center of our villages whenever possible. Even getting water is a social act (Have you paid your water bill?). How much you can sleep can depend on your social obligations, and when you have to be up early, whether to catch fish or get to your office. For humans, there are few rewards that come only from nature. Mostly, they come from other people.

Another significant amygdala function is the experience of meaningfulness[74]. Certain things fill us with joy, fear or any other emotion. We identify with them ("I feel ..."). When we feel pain, our emotions change, even if only for a moment. The loss of something that gives meaning that creates trauma[75]. Our sense of well-being depends on the feeling that our lives are meaningful[76]. The absence of meaning leaves us feeling bored[77]. This amygdala job – meaningfulness – is defined by our emotions. If something has no meaning to *us*, it has no meaning at all, and we won't have any emotional response to it. When the sense of meaningfulness runs amok (when it's very disinhibited), common events can seem like omens, and people can find themselves thinking: *This Means Something*, even if the event is trivial.

In humans, positive emotions are wired into social functions. Look at what fills you with joy. It will almost always come from a social bond (or the prospect of one). Even if the source of that joy is God (as *you* know him), it feels like its coming from outside yourself, from another being. Look at what fills you with love. Mostly, we love other people. However, joy and love are very different emotions. Love is usually much more calm and relaxed (when it goes well). Naturally, in spite of their similarities, these two emotions will be supported by different areas in the brain, but both depend on the absence of fear. The network for processing emotions on the left is more complicated than the one on the right, which underpins our negative emotions. The right amygdala is only fearful, while the left amygdala can add either fearful or blissful feelings to our experience of an event.

The left amygdala is also involved with anger[78], although anger needs more participation from other areas, especially the left frontal lobe[79]. In social situations, the right amygdala, specialized for fear and anxiety[80], seems to contribute to nervousness, hesitancy, shyness[81] and the low self-esteem[82] that goes along with these traits[83], as well as stress, and even PTSD[84] [85]. The theme of the right amygdala is vigilance, the awareness of threats. Life is either neutral or unpleasant much more often than it's joyous, an imbalance people redress with religion, often with great success. Our brains are quicker to interpret things as neutral or negative than to see them as positive, because the left amygdala 'does' both positive and negative feelings, while it's counterpart only 'does' negative ones. We appear to be hardwired to worry and be disappointed or fearful, as well as wired for their antidotes, such as religion, spirituality, love and friendship.

The two amygdalas both speak the same language, even though they create vastly different experiences when they're operating at high levels. They share an internal language.[86] Some output from the two amygdalas might just be noise to other brain parts, but a signal from within the brain that means something to one of them will usually mean something to the other.

With its emotional and social functions, it works in the context of our hierarchical and linguistic relationships. It's running whenever people use words to relate to each other, interpreting the emotion behind the words[87], while leaving their meaning up to the language centers on the left, and their subtler connotations to places across the brain, on the right.

The amygdala is the most sensitive part of the brain. It fires more easily than any other part of the brain. It uses more blood than any other neural structure and it's the most common source for epileptic seizures[88]. It's the brain's most sensitive and active structure. Like many other brain parts, it never shuts down completely. Compared to most other neural structures, the amygdala uses more blood and responds to less electrical input.

The amygdala has very social functions. It helps us see what the facial expressions[89] and body language of other people mean, so we have a sense of how they're feeling. It responds to tones of voice, too[90]. We don't have to look at someone to know what they're feeling. Hearing their voice can be enough. Most mood disorders are accompanied by changes in the amygdala's size[91].

Almost every emotional disorder, if it goes on long enough, will either over-exercise the amygdala or atrophy it, making it larger or smaller on one or both sides. Sometimes, these differences can be quite dramatic. Bipolar disorder can make the amygdala larger or smaller[92]. Depression can make the amygdala larger on the left[93]. It's able to remember things that spark strong emotional responses within us ('emotional memories'[94]). Other memories are embedded, retrieved, preserved, consolidated, and created in different areas of the brain.

The Anterior Commissure

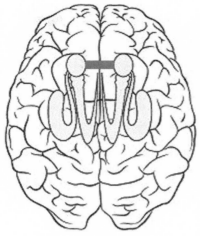

The Anterior Commissure

The anterior Commissure is a bundle of nerve fibers that connect the left and right amygdalas, to each other. It's the main channel they use to talk to each other[95], and give each other instructions, although there are also significant connections between the two amygdalas, running through the frontal lobes[96]. We will hear a lot about this structure in later chapters, but for now, we only need to say that its function is intimately related to the amygdala.

The Hippocampus

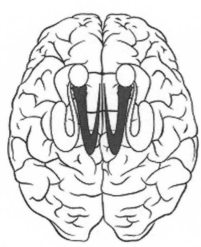

The Hippocampus

The hippocampus is a *cognitive* structure, meaning that it supports various kinds of thinking. It puts things in context[97], makes associations, and helps us to solve problems. Above all, it works with memory and inner imagery. It's also crucial in all kinds of spatial perceptions. It even has a slightly different shape in those with higher IQs[98]. Its best known functions are memory, and perceiving space; like spatial reasoning and the perceiving distances.

In many places in this book, we'll discuss a group of brain areas in and around the hippocampus as though they were one structure. In fact, hippocampal functions rely not only on the hippocampus itself, but also nearby areas on the surface of the brain[99]. A few people may find this to be an over-simplification, but without it, most readers would be overwhelmed with detail.

The hippocampus is more complicated than the amygdala. Depending on who's doing the counting, it has twelve layers and four different kinds of tissue. It has vast connections to both the amygdala and the cortex, especially the frontal lobes. A great deal of information runs directly through the hippocampus on its way to deeper structures. The hippocampus is more connected to the frontal lobes than any other part of the brain's surface, though the route between them[100] is a long one.

It consolidates our experiences in the present moment into memories we can remember later. The hippocampus recognizes things and is able to recall them from other contexts. When something reminds you of something else, that's the hippocampus in action.

The left and right hippocampus each have different functions. The one on the left works with verbal information and our memories of specific episodes and stories in our lives[101], and the one on the right works with non-verbal information. There are even differences in the kinds of connections found in them[102,103]. Schizophrenia makes more changes to the left hippocampus than the right[104], while post-traumatic stress disorder makes more changes to the right hippocampus than the left[105].

The left hippocampus weighs heavily in the ordinary operation of our minds, because it's instrumental in recalling words, and verbal thoughts tend to shape our perception of the world. We'll look at this again when we look at the human sense of self. With the help of other brain structures, the left hippocampus seems to support anger [106,107,108], although the full circuitry is not well understood[109]. The left hippocampus processes verbal memories, and some basic arithmetic skills[110]. Sometimes it remembers what someone said, but not their exact words. This says it remembers more than just the words[111]. It remembers what they mean. The left hippocampus is specialized for verbal memory, whereas the right is specialized for nonverbal memories[112]. It's also the source for the images that fill our dreams, and the inner images that come with memories. Its role in pictorial memories makes the right hippocampus the primary source of inner images of any kind.

"The concept of 'sleeping on a problem' is very familiar to most of us. With myriad stages of sleep, forms of memory, and processes of memory encoding and consolidation, to sort out how sleep contributes to memory has been anything but straightforward. Nevertheless, converging evidence, from the molecular to the phenomenological, leaves little doubt that offline memory reprocessing, during sleep, is an important component of how our memories are formed and ultimately shaped.[113]"

Of course, retrieving memories and seeing associations between what happened in the past and what's happening in the present is part of the reasoning process, so the hippocampus contributes to our ongoing thoughts as well.

When artists think in terms of color[114] and form[115], they're thinking without words, which implicate the hippocampus on the right. The same is true for musicians working with pitch[116], rhythm[117], the mood of music[118] [119], even bad music[120], and anyone else when they're remembering it[121]. Interestingly, when the mood of music is exciting, and the rhythm is fast, other areas of the brain replace the hippocampus' role in music appreciation.

When you use your mental map of the area around your home, you use one part of your hippocampus, but when you're learning your way around a new place, you use another[122]. Remembering how to get home is a hippocampal function[123]. Learning a new route to get to work also relies on the hippocampus[124]. It helps us know how far things are from us[125]. It helps us remember where things are located in space[126]. Taxi drivers, having passengers who go all over town, have more grey matter in their hippocampus than bus drivers, who drive on fixed routes[127]. The right hippocampus is also involved when navigating by a vector, which involves a bit of unconscious math[128].

The hippocampus is involved in our sense of balance[129], too[130] [131]. It knows how our body is oriented in space.

Theta states rely on the right hippocampus. These are states of consciousness that show theta activity on EEG readings. Some examples are meditation, trance, deep relaxation[132], and twilight sleep. These can happen naturally, as when people stare at a fire. They can be created by outside influences (like hypnosis), as well as created deliberately, through trance or meditation. The right hippocampus is the main (possibly the only) source for theta activity in the brain. The hippocampus is involved in meditation[133] [134]. Not only is it larger in people who've been meditating for a long time[135], but its tissue is different[136] [137], too[138]. Theta activity also appears in other hippocampal functions, like navigation, a spatial job[139]. Theta rhythms also appear from movement itself[140], a theme we will return to later. This makes it easy for meditation to include hippocampal themes, like space and spaciousness, a sense of movement, as well as time and timelessness. Meditation, like twilight sleep[141], can elicit inner imagery, a hippocampal behavior. Any specific 'hippocampal function' might be very minor, but there will always be a few people whose meditation experiences will be filled with it.

For us, spatial perception in the right hippocampus[142] is among its most important functions. It's an important part of the vestibular system[143], a widely distributed group of brain parts that helps us to stay in balance and perceive our location in space. It also plays a role in estimating distance and periods of time[144]. Something damaging the brain's ability to do the one may also interfere with its ability to do the other. It seems that in the brain, as well as in the physical world, time and space are interconnected. Anything to do with space seems to point to the hippocampus as its source, or one of its main sources. How we're oriented in space, which way we're going in space, seeing things that have space between us and them, movement through space, and thinking of spaces as well as where we want to go in them – all involve the hippocampus, especially on the right. You can't reach out across a space, move through it, or stay upright in space without balance. Not surprisingly, the hippocampus is crucial there, too[145]. Without it, we don't produce theta rhythms properly, and that influences a host of functions we all rely on. Balance is also an important theme in many spiritual traditions. "Thou art weighed in the balances, and art found wanting.[146]" "Walk in Balance on Mother Earth."

"Countless words
count less
than the silent balance
between yin and yang" – Lao Tzu, *Tao Te Ching*

One researcher has proposed that

"...the hippocampus may have developed a special
dependence upon the vestibular (balance) system during
evolution, since it was the first sensory system to reliably
indicate gravitational vertical.[147]"

Perhaps the ancient Taoist philosophers were right when they said
that balance (and the ability to perceive it, as well as imbalance) exists
prior to all other categories of experience, except consciousness itself.
Without it, our eyes could not tell horizontal from vertical. Our ears
could not locate the source of sounds. We wouldn't know where we
are or where our food is.

The right hippocampus seems to support mental calm and a positive
mental detachment. It may do so by inhibiting activity in the right
amygdala, its immediate neighbor, as the hippocampus is more active
during both anxiety and relaxation[148]. It also seems to be involved in
depression[149], which takes contributions from other brain structures. The
hippocampus on the right also supports inner imagery. It's important
in our ability to imagine the future[150] and to imagine objects[151]. It's the
main source for the imagery that appears in our dreams[152],[153] and our
pictorial memories. Interestingly, the older memories from our lives
rely on the right hippocampus more than our more recent ones[154]. Also,
'odor images' in the minds of perfumers also involve the hippocampus[155].

Its production of theta and low theta waves, linked with its ability
to elicit inner imagery, imply that the right hippocampus is involved
in psychic phenomena. Let the skeptical reader take note that we're
talking about the *subjective* experience of psychic perceptions, without
regard for their validity. In another chapter, we'll take the position that
psychic perceptions are often valid. However, we don't need to believe
in the validity of psychic perceptions in order to ask what brain parts

are at work when a person has them. The right hippocampus plays an important part in psychic flashes of images[156], as well as putative[157] telepathy[158] and enhanced intuition[159].

Caveat: Sacred Space

> "… how should man be just with God … Which maketh Arcturus, Orion, and (the) Pleiades, and the chambers of the south…"? (Job 9:1 – 9:9)

The right hippocampus is instrumental in meditation, trance, and hypnosis, and it's also heavily involved in the perception of space, which brings us to the idea of 'sacred space'.

Architecture can help elevate common religion to the level of mysticism. There seem to be two kinds of sacred spaces. Firstly, there is the small space, mostly used for very personal practices, such as the Catholic confessionals, sweat lodges, igloos, Japanese tea ceremony rooms and the caves once used in prehistoric Europe and still used today by many aboriginal tribes. In Hindu and Buddhist cultures, small shrines are often seen both in people's homes, and even in the street.

Then there are the large structures, such as cathedrals, the huge basket-like chambers of the Zulus, the sanctuary buildings in Buddhist and many Hindu temples and even the open sky. A circle of stones can be very large, with the sheer size of the sky seeming to define its sacred space, especially at night. Many sports arenas also have this effect and these also involve ritual and social behavior. The Greeks and Romans treated sports competitions as religious rites and dedicated their games to the Gods. Their arenas were also temples, where athletes performed for the Gods, and people were allowed to watch. At least, that was the official belief.

Theoretically, when a person enters or confronts a small sacred space, their awareness shrinks down to fit the space, and everything outside that space should be forgotten. As a person enters a larger sacred space, their awareness expands and they are impressed by the sheer size of the place. The sense of being in a sacred space is easier to create when the space is large enough. The hippocampus has to work a little differently there than in other spaces, and that keeps the place both unique and spiritual for the person who enters it.

It's important to remember that most of the larger sacred architectures developed at a time when all but the rich lived in quite small homes. Churches had the largest room most people ever saw and the act of entering such a place was both novel and somewhat awe-inspiring. Over time, churches became large enough to have good acoustics, and eventually the architects designed them with that in mind. Sound and its echoes help us to locate things in space. Good acoustics can make sound feel as if it's coming from many directions, evoking a sense of omnipresence. The combination of the sheer magnitude of the building and the sound within it could overawe the congregation. The act of entering a sacred space, large or small, activates those parts of the brain mediating spatial perception, which are on the right side of the brain, including the hippocampus and the temporal-parietal-occipital region on the cortex (where your antlers would be rooted – if you had antlers).

As we've seen, the hippocampus is very much involved with cognitive functions. It's been called the brain's 'contextualization engine'[160]. The role it plays in spatial perception may predispose it to perceive infinite space. It's ability to take any perception, emotion or sensation and put it into context[161] makes it a good candidate for explaining the feeling of all-knowingness that can happen during an epiphany, such as an LSD experience, an NDE or even a revelation. As every context interfaces with many others, a seemingly infinite chain of information can open to a person if their right hippocampus is freed of its usual inhibitions. It also plays an important role in our perception of time[162].

There are many ways to define a sacred space, and architecture is only one of them. The architect's style may define the building, but the *sense* of space, the most crucial element, comes from much more than that. The words and music, the special company and the pictures decorating it, all combine to create a set of associations in the minds of those who enter it, making them aware that the place they've entered is sacred.

Just entering such a large, magnificent chamber, resplendent with images of God, can bedazzle people. The soundscape would often be filled with sacred music, at one time the best and most-practiced music heard by the majority of people. People knew that strict but sacred rules apply in such places, inviting them to enter the state of prayer. If the person is not entrenched in another state, such as worry, fear, sexual desire or anger, you have an excellent setting for spiritual experiences. A sacred space doesn't create epiphanies, rather, it makes them just a little easier to achieve.

The example set by sacred spaces was not lost on many non-spiritual professions. A teacher standing behind a desk on a raised dais, or a king sitting on an ornate, bejeweled throne in a great hall, is redolent of a church with its altar. The only difference is that normally, common people didn't have access to the great halls of throne rooms and higher learning.

However, when they went to church, both the aristocracy and the peasants received the same blessings and sacraments, watched the same ceremonies and listened to the same sermons. For most of the citizenry, entering the presence of the rich meant entering a sacred space. In this way, the things that define a sacred space go beyond the architectural and neural aspects. It has a heavily social role, contributing to a person's feeling that the sacred place they visit is "*my* church". It was the only place where they could be in the presence of both God and their lord or even their king, and this also helped to made it sacred. When you enter a temple, you bow to the deity. When you enter a church, you genuflect.

At one time, though perhaps only once every few years, it was possible for anyone to see the King in a church. In Thailand, the King performs a ceremony in the Temple of the Emerald Buddha twice a year, where he is visible to everyone. Similar occasions occur in other cultures. As archetypes, kings and/or queens are powerful and evocative images filled with subtle connotations. For an ordinary man to be in the company of his king is a sacred occasion. At least in part, we can define sacred space as social space.

One of the best examples of a "sacred" space was also one of the most reprehensible in its purpose, no matter how well it utilized our ability to be moved by spatial perception. Albert Speer, the chief architect for the Nazis, designed the amphitheater for one of the Nuremberg Rallies. He set a circle of searchlights around it pointing at the sky. This created a space that began with the people below, and seemed to end only at the infinity above. Speer called it 'the Temple of Ice'.

The first public buildings in Washington DC, in the USA were erected when the Federalist school of architecture was emerging. It was intended to impress foreign dignitaries with American power. It came from a Greek temple design combined with the biggest surplus of wood any European had seen since Roman times. Federalist architecture says, "America is a nation of rational religious men", in much the same way a beer advertisement might seem to say "Buy our beer, and you'll get a date with a Japanese cheerleader".

Nazi architecture offered a similar subliminal message. There, the Roman motifs were designed to evoke a sense of strength. Hitler surrounded himself with architecture that he felt 'expressed the spirit of the Reich'. We shouldn't overlook the Stalinist style. It was designed to express a specific social ethos, but it also was intended to overawe people with Soviet power. In other words, each one tried to hijack a divine attribute to serve their ideologies. *Sacred space* has been commandeered for some very profane ends.

The Caudate Nucleus

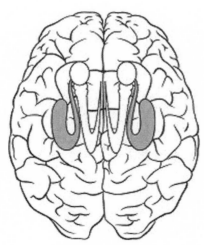

The caudate nucleus

The caudate nucleus has fewer functions than either the amygdala or hippocampus. It's a somatic[163] structure. Another name for it is the 'visceral emotive integrator', which is one way of saying that it keeps the connection between our emotions and our body's state of tension and relaxation. The left Caudate Nucleus supports arousal[164], including sexual arousal[165], and the right one supports more relaxed states, including some aspects of romantic love[166].

Interestingly, it was found that the size of the right caudate nucleus increased[167] in people with depression who had been treated successfully, but who found that the *physical* symptoms of their depression (lethargy) didn't improve even after the emotional and cognitive symptoms did. I suspect the lethargy appearing in depression relates to right caudate nuclear functions. The right caudate nucleus is involved in the recognition that one has been deceived and in its forgiveness[168]. It's also involved in romantic and maternal love[169].

Our understanding of the caudate nucleus is not yet as clear as that of the amygdala or the hippocampus. Although it doesn't play as big a role as the amygdala and hippocampus in spiritual experiences, understanding its various functions on the left and right sides of the brain will help us to see how spiritual experiences usually include a body-state that fits with the rest of the experience. Left hemispheric spiritual experiences tend to be exciting, and right hemispheric experiences tend to be relaxed and calm. The lack of clinical data on the caudate nucleus and its functions on the left and right may mean that there is less difference. In other words, the left and right caudate nucleus might not be as different as the left and right amygdala.

It's important to be clear that this idea, that the idea that the left caudate nucleus is involved in arousal and excitement, while the one on the right is involved in relaxation, is an hypothesis based on reports from people who stimulated their brains with a magnetic signal derived from the caudate nucleus (using a technology not unlike the "God Helmet"). It awaits confirmation from more standard clinical laboratory investigation; the published literature has little to say about its hemispheric specializations (the different jobs it does on the two sides of the brain). A few studies have shown small effects consistent with this hypothesis, but there are too few, and the effects are not robust enough to prove it. It's also possible that the caudate nucleus is less specialized than other structures in the limbic system, or that its specializations can change according to circumstances. Further research will tell.

Brain communication – chemical, electrical, and magnetic.

Some people will wonder why this book emphasizes neuroanatomy – brain parts instead of brain chemicals. There are several reasons for this. One is that neurochemistry hasn't really explained much about religious and mystic experiences – as they happen naturally. There are similarities between some mystic experiences and some drug experiences, but with a few exceptions, drugs, even hallucinogens, don't elicit the kinds of experiences we'll be looking at in this book or they do so only rarely. They rely on different mechanisms, so this comes as no surprise. The brain communicates with itself through its chemicals, but neurochemical responses are limited by the time required for their transmission across synaptic gaps, (0.5 to 2 msec)[170]. The brain's electrical responses happen many times more quickly than it's chemical ones[171]. Like any other flow of current, the brain's electricity is accompanied by magnetic fields, which pulse whenever the current changes. This means that there are magnetic signals going through the brain at all times. The brain's fastest internal communication is magnetic, and that makes it an efficient way to communicate with itself, including about which state of consciousness is best for each moment. Because altering states of consciousness is crucial for survival (you can be killed if you don't shift to 'flight or fight' mode fast enough when you need to), the mechanisms that determine our state of consciousness are almost certainly the fastest ones. These are electrical and probably magnetic, not chemical.

Our brains have over 5 million magnetite crystal per gram[172]. Nobody knows exactly what they contribute to our minds. These magnetite crystals are very small and very densely packed. It seems likely that they act as a system, like the brain's electrical and chemical systems. Magnetic fields would move through the brain in vanishingly small periods of time, much faster than neurochemical or electrical pulses.

We look to brain parts (and not brain chemistry) to explain spiritual experiences because neuroscience has seen a lot of new evidence over the past few years that point to changing activity in brain parts accompanying spiritual experiences. We're more able to look at what the brain is doing during mystic experiences. We can now see that it changes in specific ways that explain both spiritual practices and profound spiritual moments. Looking at brain *parts* has yielded more discoveries in recent years than looking at brain *chemistry*.

CHAPTER 4

Some Principles of Neuroscience

The Neurophenomenological Principle
(Mental Forms Follow Neural Functions)

One of the ideas we'll be working with has been called the *neurophenomenological principle*. It tells us that the content of our minds reflects the activity in our brains. In simpler terms, mental forms follow neural functions, (or neural functions *accompany* mental forms). The phenomena we experience, moment to moment, reflect the activity in the most excited areas in the brain in each moment, though at times; they can be busy keeping themselves and other structures quiet.

We'll be working with the assumption that everything that happens in the mind can be explained in terms of the brain. This is an *operating* assumption; a *postulate*. We don't know if it's true in any 'absolute' way. An operating assumption is a tool that guides us to discover something; an idea we use until something better appears. When we assume that all mental activity comes only from the brain, we're also deciding that we won't look for explanations from any other source. If the mind and its activity come from anywhere else, our approach will eventually break down, and reveal the point where mind is-more-than-the-brain.

Although it's possible this idea won't ever be proven, it's also possible it will never be abandoned. Of course, not being able to show that a belief is wrong doesn't prove its right. If human consciousness reflects the presence of a "divine spark", that spark must be present in the brain, or the brain will have a way it 'plugs in'.

This book is written with two types of readers in mind, scientists and people who want to understand spirituality, especially their own. Today, nearly all scientists will agree that mental forms follow neural activity, and nearly all spiritually minded people and religious believers feel that something above and beyond (and more godly) than our ordinary minds is at the heart of consciousness.

When we speak of activity in a structure supporting a particular experience, it might be more excited than usual. It might also be busy inhibiting conflicting phenomena. The same structure will also do many other things, and these functions might have to be inhibited. When you watch TV, you'll be tuned to one station, and that means tuning out the others. For example, imagination and memory are based on activity in many of the same brain parts. In order to remember where your keys are, you have to hold your imagination back. You have to inhibit it. Imagining your keys is not the same as remembering them. 80% of the connections in the brain are inhibitory, and these can create activity that doesn't elicit any experiences at all.

Two structures can be 'antagonistic' to one another, meaning that when one of them is active, the other is quiet. When one of the two supports a specific experience, the other has to be muted. It can take a lot of activity to stop excitement in the brain.

Imagine a brain part is busy doing one job, and that job only uses a small percent of its volume. The whole structure could be active, but most of the activity will be to inhibit the sections that aren't being used, with only a small part actively doing that job. Most activity in the brain actually *closes* connections between its cells. The brain has huge numbers of connections, letting it perform all sorts of functions, but it never uses all of them at once. The rest have to be kept still, and that can need even more activity than 'busy' parts require. If someone is good at a mental skill, the pathways that support it may not need much activity. A lot of the activity in the brain is dedicated to keeping other tasks from competing for attention.

Spiritual experiences are rare in our ordinary lives, because the neural pathways that support them are usually inhibited. The larger brain activity that supports them will inevitably include some disinhibition or excitement. The principle that mental forms follow neural functions will still apply. Just as a general is only one person, but still directs a whole army, the neural function behind a mental form might be a very small part of all that's happening in the brain. Andrew Newberg's studies of monks in meditation[173] found that one area was much *less* active while they were in meditation, while others were *more* active (based on how much blood they used). To use the same metaphor, he could have seen the movement of battalions in an army, but not the general himself. However, just as battalions can be held in reserve to support soldiers assaulting a main objective, muting the areas that compete is as much a part of the process as the meditation object itself. The general (remembering that the command keeps changing) could have the highest metabolism in the brain, using the most blood, and firing out the most electricity, but it also could be so small an area that it wouldn't show up when the area is seen on PET, MRI, CRBF (Cerebral Regional Blood Flow analysis), or EEG. A few neurons can be enough to organize the whole brain, especially if they are dedicated to a specific job. Newberg illuminated several brain changes that accompany meditation, and that's a good thing. He may not have seen the source, but he also didn't claim that the changes he saw *caused* the meditative state.

All scientists know that just because one thing accompanies another doesn't mean either one caused the other. An experiment can show that two things happen together, or that one thing always happens before another. Science uses theories and hypotheses to explain how one thing causes another. However, in the precise language of science, nobody ever says anything *causes* anything. Instead we say, one thing *explains* another, knowing that causality can be almost impossible to prove. You can prove aspirin helps with pain, but you can't prove that *your* headache was cured by *that* aspirin. There is always a chance that it was something else.

Uphill and Downhill in the Brain

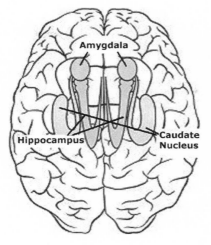

One of our principles is that neural activation will tend to move from less sensitive structures to more sensitive structures. In other words, excitement moves from less excitable structures to more excitable ones more easily, just as fire moves from wood to straw more easily than from straw to wood.

It's a bit like the way water flows downhill. It's also a similar to osmosis, where chemicals flow from areas of high concentration to areas of low concentration. Although the differences in their firing thresholds are small, the amygdala has the lowest thresholds in the brain. The hippocampus has slightly higher thresholds; it's a little less sensitive. The caudate nucleus is next in this list, and although still quite responsive, it's not as sensitive as the hippocampus.

This doesn't mean that electrical activity in the caudate nucleus will flow to the hippocampus easily. The amygdala stands between them. Just as two rivers, each flowing to the sea, may not flow into one another, the caudate nucleus and the hippocampus don't connect to each other as much as they each connect with the amygdala. Most (but not all) communication between them must pass through it.

In many places in this book we'll be looking at very intense and very rare experiences that involve high levels of excitement in very small portions of the brain. Sometimes, these can flow outside the usual channels between brain structures. Figuring out which direction that activity will flow will mean looking for the pathways of least resistance. The amygdala, the most sensitive structure, is a kind of sinkhole for most brains. Electrical energy flows in a little more easily than it flows out.

It doesn't matter how sensitive the structures are for well-exercised and habituated pathways, because some of the pathways we'll look at are almost never used, and the experiences they support are extremely rare.

Water may always flow downhill, but it's still possible to put in pipes and pumps and get it to go uphill. For the pathways supporting religious and mystic experiences, such plumbing usually isn't there. However spiritual practices, like prayer and meditation, can create them. When we stop to think how small a percentage of the population go deeply into these practices (becoming absorbed in meditation or lost in prayer), it's easy to see that for most people, it will take something unusual to override the usual inhibition of the pathways involved in spiritual experiences.

The Two Hemispheres

The brain is divided into two hemispheres, left and right. Throughout most of this book, we will gloss over the bulk of their differences and specializations. A comprehensive treatment of this very intricate subject would require a book as long as this one and there are already several such books. We'll be focusing only on the differences between the hemispheres that relate to spirituality, the theme of this book. Even within these limits, there's a lot that has to be left out, and some statements about the two hemispheres make it look like they are more separate than they actually are. However, if we were to clarify every point fully, this work would become very difficult to read for some people, making it difficult for it to fulfill one of its purposes: to allow spiritually-inclined people to understand more about spirituality without reference to religious traditions.

The brain is so heavily interconnected that talking about its parts in the context of just one of its jobs always tends to over-simplify things. This can't be helped, but if the reader knows in advance that things are always more complicated and intricate than they are presented here, they'll be prepared to learn more, if they feel they need to know the whole story. Of course, for the brain, the whole story is an epic. Here, we will only tell a few of its episodes.

In a way, there are no such things as parts of the cortex as far as their functions are concerned. They may be clear in anatomy books, but when they're working, they are not so much parts as places in a network where similar kinds of information is routed, with lots of different networks running through the same areas. Interestingly, the right side of the brain has more connections within it than the left side. This means that any brain part we speak of on the right is more likely to recruit (or be recruited by) areas around it than the same place on the opposite side would. On the left, operations are more focused, and they're more diffuse on the right.

Vectoral Hemisphericity
(Left and right sides of the brain always work together)

This principle tells us that both hemispheres contribute to all or almost all brain functions. There aren't any processes that are completely left-brain or completely right-brain. Instead, they draw from both sides of the brain. This means that most of the brain's functions are *vectors*[174], combining activity on both sides, even though most of it may arise from only one of them. The left hemisphere dominates the sense of self most of the time, a theme we'll return to several times. This means that 'you' are primarily a left hemispheric process, drawing from the right hemisphere almost constantly, maintaining *your* existence.

Language areas are on the left

The two major language centers are both on the left side of the brain's surface. One of them creates the words we think and speak, and the other understands the words we hear. Although language is processed in the left hemisphere, it needs input from the right hemisphere to provide its 'unspoken' or *prosodic*[175] components; the *feeling* for the meaning of words, their connotations, and an idea of what's between the lines. Words often mean much more than their definitions. The nuances of context and the subtle implications of words come from right-brain structures. We can say that the definitions for words are on the left and their connotations are on the right. A good example of language that's far from a left-brain process would be song lyrics. They may be handled in the language centers on the left, but the meanings, moods and associations evoked from the sounds, rhythm and formation of its lines arise in the right hemisphere.

Language is a left hemispheric function, but it draws from the right whenever it needs to. When it's well written, poetry is probably the most right hemispheric kind of language. It relies on the language centers on the left, the same as any other form of language, but it needs lots of contributions from the right side of the brain in order for it to evoke any sentiments.

Appreciating music is a right hemispheric function, but as soon as we start to analyze it, count its beats, or work out its structure or counterpoint, then the left hemisphere, with is more linear thinking and measuring, is drawn into the process.

The altered states appearing in devotional ceremonies are often dominated by the left side of the brain, but like poetry, it can take a lot from the right. Psychic readings, prayer, ritual devotion and spirit mediumship can reach their peak as they become as intimate as possible. The height of prayer is unity (*contemplatio*) with the god to whom you pray. In Hindu ritual worship, (Pujas), incense, lights and flowers are given to the deity, who may also be drenched with milk, honey, water, yogurt or clarified butter. Some say they achieve real devotion when they feel that the statue or picture of the God they worship is a living being; that it has a *presence*. This happens when the devotee starts to cultivate the same kind of emotions felt for their own mother, lover or child. In another example, a psychic must 'get into' the other person during psychic readings, prayer, ritual devotion, religious ceremonies or in spirit mediumship. The spirit medium tries to allow the spirit they're channeling to enter their mind, and they surrender their own sense of self to the spirit's control.

These are all very loving techniques. Prayer works best when you learn to love the god you pray to. Some, but not all, psychics work best when they cultivate the ability to love their clients. A Catholic devotee can cultivate a love for a statue of The Blessed Virgin that's as powerful as their love for a real person.

Love relies on both language and silence. The neural basis of love involves structures on both sides of the brain. However, the fact that love and prayer both use emotionally charged speech of one kind or another implies that they all rely on excitement in the left amygdala. Prayer is a social practice, in which you act as though a deity or spirit is another person, though it exists above and beyond ordinary relationships. It will involve using the same pathways our brains use when we relate to others. Dreaming of an event will involve the same pathways excited by the real event. A spiritual practice in which we feel something is a conscious entity will include the same pathways that operate when we're actually with another person. In these practices, a person will still be able to communicate with those around them. The devotee chants, but can stop long enough to say something to people nearby. The medium talks to those around them, passing on messages from the spirit they channel. The psychic can receive their impressions and still speak to the person receiving the reading. In contrast, talking during meditation will disrupt it.

Practices that create right hemispheric states, like meditation or shamanic journeying, need training. Language, and other left hemispheric phenomena, can interfere with the practice until the person becomes proficient.

Interhemispheric Intrusions
(The neural avalanche)

There are two sides to everything where the brain is concerned. No matter how much a process may be focused in one hemisphere, it will still maintain an outpost in the other one. This enables a kind of control valve system to operate. A good metaphor would be a system of pipes or wires connected across the center of the brain through which current can flow both ways. If activity exceeds a structure's capacity, then it shunts the energy to the most accessible place. In special cases, this turns out to be the corresponding structure on the opposite side of the brain, especially if the structures nearby the first one are already very active. The thresholds at which this happens differ for each area within that brain – and of course, for each person.

When the 'pressure' of excitement in a structure reaches its maximum, the accompanying experience will be among the most intense that specific brain part can produce. Their thresholds, and their connections across the brain, vary from one person to the next. This means that altered state experiences are extremely hard to predict or control. Mystic visions are more likely when the structures with the lowest thresholds, the most sensitive brain parts, are over-excited and dump their electrical loads. Structures with higher thresholds are more likely to dump their load into a nearby area with a lower threshold. The metaphor is of water, which always flows from the top down. When a river flows into a lake so it overflows, the uncontrolled flooding can change landscape surrounding it. When such electrical activity overflows and is dumped into another area, the connections between brain cells (synapses) that usually inhibit such activity can be stripped away in the process, like trees uprooted by a flood. When such an overflow happens, the person's inner landscape will also change. Sometimes, the personality changes that follow can last for the rest of their lives.

The amygdala has the lowest activation thresholds in the entire brain. It uses more blood than any other area, and it's the most common point of origin for epileptic seizures. This means that it's the structure most likely to build up activity on one side of the brain and suddenly transfer it to the other side. If the right amygdala, with its specialty in processing fear, becomes extremely active while it's left, bliss-supporting counterpart, stays quiet, the person will feel very frightened or extremely anxious. If this right side activity reaches a specific tipping point, it will redirect its activity to the quiet left amygdala. It's quiet, so it's primed and ready to receive this energy. Because of the positive emotions 'seated' in the left amygdala, the result can be happiness, joy and bliss. It can also be anger. The amygdala's deep involvement in relating to others means it can easily create a hallucination of another being. It might simply be sensing a presence or it could be a vision. If the experience is powerful enough, or if someone is unusually sensitive to it, it could appear as an angel or even God. The result would be a spiritual experience filled with elation, bliss or ecstasy, along with a powerful sense of meaningfulness[176]. The right (fear-processing) amygdala becomes quiet after dumping its load, leaving the person completely free from fear or anxiety.

Brain activity during sex is relatively more complicated than ordinary mystical and religious experience, because several structures operate in concert at the same time, from a slow build-up of excitement, sensation and tension to a sudden release at orgasm. The left hippocampus becomes quieter as talk becomes pointless, although, simple language (short phrases, for example) may still be available. At the same time, the right hippocampus becomes more active. Both amygdalas become less and less active as orgasm approaches. In the moment of release, they can switch off altogether. After orgasm, at least one of them stirs back into activity and the left hippocampus is available once more. Before orgasm, the left caudate nucleus becomes increasingly active until the moment of release, after which there is a sudden relaxation and it becomes quiet. Then its counterpart on the right re-asserts itself, and the person relaxes.

Both mystic experiences and sex involve activity building up in one place in the brain and spilling over into another one on the other side of the brain. From fear to joy in mystic experience and from intercourse to orgasm; both involve excitement building up and then being released. This mechanism, known as *interhemispheric intrusion*, underlies many of the most powerful human experiences. We can also call it a "neural avalanche".

Another form of interhemispheric intrusion happens when extreme fear leads to a type of psychotic breakdown. In the midst of battle or natural disaster, people sometimes have totally inappropriate fits of laughter. In such a case, the fear has built up to a point where the right amygdala can no longer contain it, so it bursts across into the left amygdala and other structures, especially the nearby left insula,[177] and initiates laughter[178] [179]. Of course, laughter will rely on different pathways when it's provoked by humor or comedy.

Intralimbic Intrusions

Intralimbic intrusion is an idea[180] that refers to what happens when activity is very high in one structure, but not high enough to break over to the opposite side. Instead, highly active structures in the limbic system, overflowing with energy, can abruptly spill activity into nearby structures on the same side of the brain.

An example of an Intralimbic Intrusion is seen when fear builds up to the point where it seems to drive words out of the mind and leaves a person speechless. Activity from the right amygdala, specialized for fear, will have moved into the right hippocampus; specialized for nonverbal kinds of thinking.

Sometimes, happiness can become too much to bear, and a person might not be able to stop talking and expressing their joy, or they might begin to cry. In this case, activity will have spilled over from the left amygdala to the left hippocampus, and excited the nearby language centers on the surface of the brain.

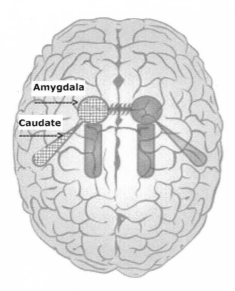

Activity abruptly spilling over from the Caudate nucleus to the amygdala can make you too excited to sit still when you're happy.

Bad news can be so devastating that one may sit down and stare, open-mouthed, off into the distance. Good news can be so exciting that one can't stand still. In both cases, activity will have moved from the amygdala to the caudate nucleus, so that in one case, the body turns limp, and in the other, it becomes very aroused. Children often jump up and down uncontrollably when something excites them, and adults might walk around gesturing and talking to express their happiness. It's even not uncommon for people to enjoy being angry. Anger, a left hemispheric phenomenon, can feel good when it includes enough left amygdala excitement.

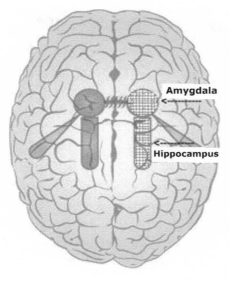

Depression involves the right hippocampus[181] [182]. Depressed thoughts are often disjointed or incomplete, and seem to spill over from the right hippocampus into the right amygdala, specialized for fear. Some people are actually afraid of the thoughts that appear when they're depressed.

An Intralimbic intrusion (a sudden burst of activity from one limbic structure to another on the same side of the brain) may happen during dream sleep, when the right hippocampus is already active (producing dream imagery). If it becomes active enough, as often happens during nightmares, activity in the right hippocampus can spill over into the right amygdala.

The right amygdala's role in fearful vigilance makes it impossible to go on sleeping, because one can't be asleep and vigilant at the same time. This explains how people often wake up nightmares just before something really horrible happens in them.

Times when people let off steam after a hard days' work offer another example. The need to suppress one's sense of fun while at work inhibits several sets of neural pathways. Once the day is over, these pathways can burst into excitement. Unless someone is very tired and wants to go home to rest, going out and having a bit of sociable fun after work looks very inviting.

Imagine the following scenario. You've not been feeling well, so you decide to visit a doctor. While anticipating the appointment, all sorts of worries start to build up. Is it cancer? Are you going to need surgery? Is it going to kill you? The fear and anxiety can build up to a crescendo while you wait to see the doctor. Finally, you're in the office and after a thorough examination, he diagnoses a minor problem that can be fixed with a few pills. Suddenly you feel completely relieved, your worries dissolve instantly, and you feel a whole lot better.

At the height of your anxiety, the amygdala in your right hemisphere was working overtime, but the moment you got the good news, the activity moved over to the right hippocampal area, and you have a feeling of wellness. This creates a strong sense of calm and relief. At the same time, activity in the right amygdala naturally crosses over and excites the left amygdala, creating joy, happiness or even bliss. In this case, we see intralimbic intrusion in the movement of activity from the right amygdala to the right hippocampus, and perhaps a right-to-left movement between the two amygdala. The result is a sudden and dramatic mood change the instant you hear the doctor's mild diagnosis.

Of course, worrying about your health and feeling relieved at good news are ordinary life events within the range of normal states of consciousness. This is not the stuff mystic experiences are made of. Nevertheless, these hypothetical cases allow us to see a mechanism behind many otherworldly experiences.

Such activity usually builds up slowly, sometimes without our being aware of it. It stays in one area of the brain for a while and then suddenly and dramatically transfers into one or more other brain parts. This mechanism is not limited to epiphanies and peak experiences, it happens all the time in our ordinary day to day lives.

In ordinary circumstances, most intralimbic intrusions relate to tension and relaxation. Something similar happens when one has been hungry for a while and can finally sit down to eat. The same goes for fatigue. Someone who is utterly exhausted will fall asleep faster. Once the brain stops keeping you awake, it dumps the energy into those brain structures that become more excited when you're falling asleep.

Not only is a greater amount of activity moved during tension and relaxation, but there is also a sharp and rapid change in the center (or focus) of neural activity. It's almost like a kind of hydraulic mechanism, operating with neural (electrical) excitement instead of air or liquid (of course, this is a metaphor). The current pushes brain activity around, with switches and valves going off when the pressure reaches certain points. When the pressure is lower and reaches lower trigger points, the activity might shunt within the same side of the brain. When the pressure goes above a certain (higher) level, the activity is more likely to shunt over to the opposite side of the brain.

Watching a movie and being drawn into the story will engage the temporal lobes. Our imaginations are pulled into the imagery of the film. We forget the events of the real world for a while. Our emotions and feelings are largely manipulated by the filmmaker. When the film finishes, the temporal lobes stop processing the movie's world, and the frontal lobes takes control again and steers our states of consciousness. The emotional residue from the film can still set your mood for some time after it's over. Of course, everyone responds differently to what's on the screen, but a well-made movie will shut down several brain processes while you're watching it. The parts that would normally process the day-to-day realities of life become quiet, allowing the mind to concentrate on the virtual world in the film. When the movie ends, one suddenly comes back down to earth and those same areas have to start working again.

A very familiar "higher" state of consciousness occurs when we hear stirring music. This engages the right hippocampus, responsible for processing non-verbal information. When the music reaches our favorite part, we often feel emotional thrills, chills and tingly feelings running through our bodies. The right hippocampus is not the only area affected. The temporal lobes on both side of the brain are also excited. When we're taken over by the music, the focus of activity is in the cortex, where it shifts; moving into or expanding towards the parietal lobes (bringing chills or "parasthesias"). When this happens, the movement of activity would very likely be accompanied by a change in the focus of activity deeper down in the limbic system, towards the caudate nucleus, integrates our emotions with our body's state of relaxation or tension.

Another example of intracortical intrusion can appear during a long telephone conversation. Usually, when we are interacting socially with another, we can interpret their facial expressions and body gestures. These give added information about the other's feelings, but on the phone, we can only relate using words. Brain activity is focused in the language centers while they try to glean information that would otherwise come from looking at the person. This means that there is less activity in those other areas and the amygdala is quieter than it would be when talking to someone face to face. One can feel somewhat alone and 'out of it' at the end of long personal conversations. A moment of inner quiet can descend on us immediately after hanging up. Sometimes, if the conversation was especially meaningful, it can feel like a loss or even abandonment. This slightly altered state of consciousness can feel rather uncomfortable, as the language centers shut down and the areas that were subdued while we were talking and get busy once again when the conversation is over.

The creators of our traditional religions were ancient cognitive scientists and they knew what they were doing. There are many traditional techniques used in religious practices, for both solitary and group rites, ranging from music and mantras to fasting and sexual abstinence. These were developed over many centuries to activate or deactivate specific areas of the brain, giving us effective ways to achieve spiritual experiences.

Interhemispheric intrusions and intralimbic movement are the basis for *episodic visions*. These visions are more than simple pictures, and when they have more than one phase, we should expect them to recruit several brain structures, one after the other.

The most powerful kind of mystic experiences are surely the episodic kind (where it's not just a single vision, but an experience with several episodes). They're the most likely to have impressive, long-lasting after-effects, because they can make small changes in many different areas. They also seem to be the most memorable visions, and the most worthy of reverence. They're highly valued in many cultural and religious traditions. In later chapters, we will discuss several of these more involved visions at length, including the Buddha's enlightenment, the visions of Saint Teresa of Avila, the God realization of Ramakrishna Paramhamsa and a few others.

When we look at NDEs (near death experiences), we'll see that the experience called *The Light* follows the *Tunnel* or dark *Void*, and the experience of meeting a being or several beings follows the Light. The shift from one episode to another involves a change in the focus of limbic activity from one brain part to another, but most spiritual experiences don't have so many or such clear episodes. They may be driven by only one or two brain parts but, like all other neural processes, many other brain structures will be involved.

If an altered state experience has only a single phenomenon, then the focus of activity is probably located in only one area or brain structure. If the experience changes in time and has more than one episode, the focus of activity will change when one episode ends and another begins. It's a case of mental forms following neural functions. If the mental forms change, the "neural focus" will also have changed.

Visions of the Virgin Mary offer good examples of this. More often than not, they begin with someone seeing her in the sky. Here, it's irrelevant whether the Virgin's appearance really was in the sky or in the minds of those who saw her (because the real and the illusory can have much the same neural bases). The focus of activity would be in the left amygdala, although many other brain areas would also be involved. In the next phase of the vision, the Blessed Mother speaks, as the language centers on the left side of the brain on the surface of the temporal lobes begin to contribute. It's a simple example of an episodic vision, but the same principle applies to more extended visions, like those that might take hours to unfold under the influence of hallucinogenic drugs.

Phenomena and States of Consciousness

At first glance, a spiritual experience *is what it is*. If an angel or a spirit visits you in the night, and seems to speak to you, you'll feel that it's a living being. It might use words, just as a person would. It might have a face, and seem to have a personality. It will 'feel' human, or "made in the image of man". The same neural architecture can also be expressed in another, very different experience, demonic visitors, for example. To use a metaphor, the same blueprints can be used to build several different buildings. They could be different colors. They might look completely different, but really be two different versions of the same house. They might have very different details, but the shape of the building will still be the same. So it is with spiritual experiences and the brain.

This became clear in a well-known experiment, done in the 1970s[183]. The experiment consisted of keeping track of what a group of patients experienced when they had temporal lobe epileptic seizures. They had several electrodes embedded in their brains. These were connected to a portable EEG that could record their electrical activity. They were also connected to a device that could use the same electrodes to *stimulate* the brain from within.

The electrodes recorded the seizural activity, and the patients made notes of what they saw, heard, or felt. The epileptic hallucinations that appeared were the same with each seizure. The patients had very different experiences when the same electrodes were used to stimulate the brain from within (with very faint electrical currents). In fact, what they saw in their hallucinations usually followed the theme of their "mental content" before they began. This conflicted with an earlier theory that said that hallucinations were expressions of single neural pathways. Each memory we have was also thought to be represented by a single pathway (an "engram"). Instead, it turns out that *all* the pathways that support memories contribute to each memory. Hallucinations are 'based on' states of consciousness, and these states are based on specific pathways, *not* the hallucinations that appear in them.

The same study also found that the hallucinations elicited through this stimulation were never repeated, even when the stimulation was exactly the same. The stimulation created an altered state of consciousness, and the phenomena that appeared in that state was different every time.

This will be important later on, when we see that the same spiritual *state* can bring up different spiritual *experiences* in different people, and may not even be the same each time for the same person.

This landmark study (because it revised the "engram" theory of memory) also found that some hallucinations had nothing to do with anything in the person's experience. Most importantly, some hallucinations *did* recruit memories of images, especially if it had a symbolic importance. Religious symbols, of course, play a role in many spiritual experiences.

Everyone can have the same pathways, so everyone can experience the same states, though not everyone is equally prone to all of them. The very different experiences that can happen when two different people take the same hallucinogenic drug appear because the drug creates a similar state, but the bringing up different phenomena. Thus, a 'bad trip', in which the drug experiences turns frightening, can be just as powerful as a good one. Both are emotional. Both are meaningful (one with a malevolent, and the other with a beneficent meaning). Both might include intense sensations in the body, with one being horrifying (like bugs crawling under the skin) and the other being ecstatic (every sensation feels blissful). One can involve heavenly perfumes, and another filled with an awful stench. These are opposite, but still similar, states of consciousness.

We should be very clear that spiritual experiences are not seizures. Instead, we will take the view that seizures can activate any part of the brain, including those pathways that create spiritual experiences at death naturally. When a seizure spreads to include one of these areas, a seizural spiritual experience *can* happen, but usually, temporal lobe seizures are not spiritual at all. In fact, most of them are unpleasant. It's not possible to say what percent of temporal lobe seizures are spiritual, because people who enjoy them are very likely to interpret them as spiritual events, and nobody sees a doctor to stop something that feels good.

Unusual patterns of activity involving specific neural pathways are the foundation for altered states, and altered states are the foundation for spiritual experiences.

CHAPTER 5

The God Helmet

Thousands of monks and nuns have prayed, asking to meet God face-to-face, and most of these prayers have gone unanswered. On the other hand, thousands of people have died and come back to life talking about having met God, without ever consciously wanting such an experience. NDEs can provide real clues that help us understand visions of God. That makes them a better place to look for evidence about them than the world's religious traditions.

NDEs may be the natural context for visions of God, but such visions have also been created artificially. A laboratory procedure that has induced visions of God offers another source for evidence about the neural basis of these religious experiences. The experiences reported by the subjects in these experiments who saw God are similar to those occurring in NDEs.

The God Helmet is a popular name for an apparatus invented by Dr. MA Persinger, and engineered and built by Stan Koren of Laurentian University. It's been used to study religious experiences for over a decade. It was used in the "God Helmet" experiments in which a small number of people saw God in the laboratory. In fact, the "God Helmet experiments" consisted of a large number of small experiments, and the ones who saw God were special cases in studies with more ordinary subjects, like depression (the God helmet worked as well as well as other therapies[184]), apprehensiveness (more likely for women than men[185]), and hypnosis (you can make hypnosis easier if you stimulate just the right side of the brain with the God Helmet[186]).

One of the most common results obtained in the so-called God Helmet experiments was the *sensed presence*. This is where you feel that someone or something is standing behind you, when there's actually no one there. In the God Helmet experiments, simple sensed-presence experiences outnumbered visions of God by eighty to one. However, both experiences were produced using the same procedure. This suggests that both of them have the same underlying neural basis, and the difference between those who had a simple sense of a presence and those who saw God was that the second group was much more sensitive to the stimulation. These experiences seem to be based in the brain's limbic system; the deeper structures with a primal range of functions.

In psychiatry, disturbances in the sense of self are accompanied by changes in the limbic system and in the temporal lobes. In some cases, the temporal lobes on one side actually start to shrink, because they're used less and less as the disorder progresses. There's a rule of brain operation called "use dependency." Everyone knows it: "Use it or lose it." In schizophrenia, the hippocampus on the left (language) side can be a different size than the one on the right[187], because it works harder. This inflicts a disturbance in the sense of self and explains the amazing and florid outflow of language schizophrenics display.

As far as the surface of the brain is concerned, the sense of self is a temporal lobe phenomenon; with substantial contributions from the frontal lobes (we'll see later that it's largely a deep brain phenomenon). Further, the sense of your body's location in space (which contributes to the self − you have to be *somewhere* in order to exist at all) comes partly from the parietal lobes. When the temporal lobes on each side start working differently, the chances for a sensed presence experience go up dramatically.

The temporal lobes, especially their deeper parts, are the primary source for religious and spiritual experiences. Dr. Michael Persinger has studied the temporal lobes and their role in spirituality extensively, and published many papers on the subject[188]. One of the most important of these is "Religious and Mystic Experiences as Artifacts of Temporal Lobe Function"[189]. This paper states his hypothesis most explicitly.

Religious and mystic experiences correlate with brief electrical events involving small areas, deep in the temporal lobes.

The amygdala is involved in personal meaningfulness, the sense that something *means* something to you. Usually, our sense of meaningfulness is perfectly valid. We may feel an event has significance for us or we might feel that it's more for one's social group, like their family, or even the whole world. When we hear words that present us with either a threat or an opportunity, they will mean something - to us. When this same *meaningfulness* happens without the usual controls from within the brain, it can make anything seem terribly important, even profound. The amygdala can make it seem much more important that it actually is, if it appears while you're in an altered state of consciousness. A simple word or number can become a sign of God's will, or a message from the spirit world. If you're a poet and you're ever short on inspiration, just find a schizophrenic, keep your pen and paper handy, and you'll soon have lots of material. I once had a next-door neighbor who had a schizophrenic episode. I was leaving my apartment and had just got into the hallway when I heard him call out: "'Get out, you ruffians,' said the princess to the waffle vendor on the horse." This made no sense, but the neighbor's tone and emphasis made it sound significant, as though it carried a profound meaning.

My favorite story about meaningfulness comes from a scientist who woke up from a dream in the middle of the night. His dream revealed the secret of the universe. Whatever he had encountered in his dream had given him a magic formula. He felt that it contained a profound and deep truth. He had the presence of mind to write it down, and then he went back to sleep. When he woke up in the morning, he remembered the note on his nightstand. There it was; the content of God's mind, at the moment of creation, the thought that explains the fabric of the universe. He picked it up and read it. It said, "A strong smell of turpentine pervades throughout." It wasn't meaningful because of a strong smell of turpentine. It was significant because, in the moment when he got it, he was filled with a sense of deep meaning so powerful that he felt it had to be important. It couldn't have been anything but the secret of the universe. Nevertheless, it meant nothing at all.

People can get locked into strings of words, especially when the left hippocampus or the left temporal lobes are 'stuck', working too hard[190]. Abnormal speech can imply an abnormal personality, even insanity. Once, while working in a nursing home, one patient continuously repeated the same chant all day long, in every waking moment. When she was eating, she would take a bite, swallow it and then repeat her personal chant, slowly and clearly. She chanted, "If I have to live in this world, Lord, if I have to live in this world, let it be on toasted eggs and toasted eggs and toasted eggs until the world is gone; until the world is gone." Obviously, something was going on, even if it meant nothing to anyone but her. She was utterly unresponsive to all conversation, and never even looked at me when I entered her room. Her language centers worked, producing nonsense words that seemed to have a deep meaning, even when 'she' was all but gone.

The structure that supports the positive feeling of meaningfulness is the left amygdala. Dr. Persinger has elicited same sense of meaning by stimulating it in his experiments. One would expect a similar activation of the right amygdala to provoke a sense of doom, foreboding, or danger. Most dreams are negative. Many people wake up from their dreams with just such feelings. This could be because our evolution found greater adaptive value in dreams that alert us to danger than in dreams that seem to foretell of rewards or opportunities.

Next, we see some lyrics and an illustration[191] that show how a musical chord can be filled with meaning one moment, and be nothing more than a sound in another. This is actually part of a set of Victorian postcards that illustrate a song called "The Lost Chord." Someone plays a chord, and feels a divine benediction. They felt the presence of angels, or even God, from a single chord. The person looks for that chord later on, but never finds it. The Lost Chord became a metaphor for the longing to be in God's presence. It's an auditory and emotional hallucination, combined with a very positive sense of a presence, and a powerful feeling of meaningfulness. Hallucinations can happen in any of our senses, including our sense of what means something to us and what doesn't.

THE LOST CHORD

The Lost Chord, lyrics by Adelaide
Anne Procter, 1858 [192]

Seated one day at the Organ, I was weary and ill at ease,
And my fingers wandered idly Over the noisy keys.

I do not know what I was playing, Or what I was dreaming then;
But I struck one chord of music, Like the sound of a great Amen.

It flooded the crimson twilight, Like the close of an Angel's Psalm,
And it lay on my fevered spirit With a touch of infinite calm.

It quieted pain and sorrow, Like love overcoming strife;
It seemed the harmonious echo From our discordant life.

It linked all perplexed meanings Into one perfect peace,
And trembled away into silence as if it were loth to cease.

I have sought, but I seek it vainly, That one lost chord divine,
Which came from the soul of the Organ, And entered into mine.

It may be that Death's bright angel will speak in that chord again,
It may be that only in Heaven I shall hear that grand Amen.

Hallucinations are also temporal lobe phenomena. In one of the first hallucinogenic studies, done soon after it was invented, LSD was given to monkeys. The most obvious result was that the experimenters could see the monkeys hallucinating; they were clearly "tripping." Afterwards, they opened the monkeys' brains, removed certain sections, and closed them up. Once their brains had healed, the monkeys were given LSD again. No matter which part of the brain was removed, the monkeys still "tripped." Removing the temporal lobes was the only thing that stopped the LSD from working. This part of the brain is instrumental in maintaining the sense of self, our awareness of others and our feelings for them. I apologize on behalf of all neuroscience for the animal vivisection, but let's not have our respect for Brother Monkey keep us from learning something from the experiment.

Another example of how the temporal lobes are the source of hallucinations, this time without monkeys, was the case of a woman in her mid-30s who had hallucinations of music almost constantly, usually repeating the same music[193]. Try listening to "Happy Birthday" for about five years, and see how you like it. An angiogram revealed the source of the problem as two aneurisms in the right temporal lobe which, as we've seen, is where music is processed and appreciated. After recovering from surgery to remove the aneurisms, the patient found that her musical hallucinations had stopped.

The recognition that hallucinations emerge from temporal lobe activity is strengthened by the God Helmet experiments that produced the sensed presence experience using magnetic signals applied over the temporal lobes. Dr. Persinger was able to induce visions of God, using equipment called the Koren Helmet. (It was later nicknamed the 'God Helmet' by a journalist who wanted to add a bit of sensationalism to his article about Dr. Persinger's work). Although only a small percentage of Persinger's subjects saw God while wearing it, the 'God Helmet' has induced many spiritual and mystic experiences[194]; Visions of God are only one of them. Understanding how the Helmet works will help to understand how such visions, including visions of God, can appear. The 'God Helmet' applies a theory that allows us to understand how religious and mystic experiences occur, and to create them in laboratory settings.

God Helmet Theory and the Sense of Self

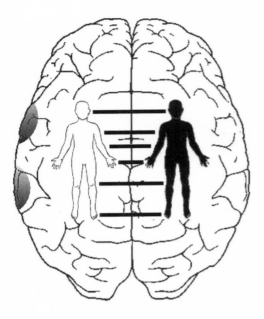

The God helmet experiments are based on Dr. Persinger's "Vectoral Hemisphericity[195]" hypothesis, which says (among other things), that we have two selves or 'senses of self' – one for each side of the brain. The self on the left side is dominated by the language centers and 'houses the linguistic sense of self, which thinks in words. The sense of self is a single function, involving both sides of the brain, but not equally. The left side dominates in most of our waking moments.

The two most important brain areas involved in language are Broca's and Wernicke's areas, which, broadly speaking, produce and understand speech, respectively. The corresponding areas on the other side of the brain also participates in our speech, adding *prosody*[196], the rhythm, intonation and stresses that add the emotional content and the other components of language we feel more than hear.

We are both a social and linguistic species. With some exceptions, we relate to other people using words. We have a constant stream of inner monologue supporting our self-image, expressing the assumptions we make about ourselves. Speech may not be the most spiritual form of relating, but it's the most common, and one that defines us in many ways. We use it when applying for a job, when saying "Hello!" to our neighbors, and our ordinary, day-to-day connections with people.

Every time we use language, whether running our inner monologue or actually speaking with others, we identify with this 'self'. The self on the right side of the brain is much more silent, because there aren't any language centers on the right side of the brain. When we're in normal states of consciousness, when our linguistic skills are helping us to relate to other people, this silent, non-verbal self goes on working behind the scenes.

Our sense of self isn't completely seamless. There are moments when we have to grope for it. If you're sensitive enough, you might even feel your sense of 'self' being interrupted from time to time, though you probably wouldn't call it that. However, both selves continue to operate even when the communication between them is disrupted. Both too little and too much communication between the hemispheres can disrupt the communication between them. In these moments, instead of having a dominant and a subordinate sense of self, we have two separate selves capable of working independently. We continue to identify with the linguistic left one; we continue to be the *self-that-talks,* and we sense the presence of the other one.

Our sense of self is integrated with our capacity to use and understand language. In order to maintain the linguistic sense of self, (dominated by its left hemispheric components), our speech and our sense of self have to stay available to one another. They 'work' as the "self" we identify with most of the time. It keeps us identified with the words "I" and "me". It's hard to imagine anyone being unable to use to use these two words correctly. If you were to meet someone who couldn't use the words that identify themselves, you'd think something was wrong with them. You wouldn't want them to be the chief of your tribe, and you wouldn't want them to marry your daughter.

We have to be 'in' our linguistic selves and able to use speech to relate to other people at (almost) all times. Like a car that's left running to save time in getting on the road, our unending stream of inner monologue keeps us ready to relate to others, because that's the only thing that can give us the rewards we crave. The way we talk to them shows our intelligence, social skills, and personalities. Without these traits, people can't win the respect of those around them and avoid the lower social ranks. It's a lot easier to get into positions of responsibility and respect if you're intelligence, articulate and have good social skills.

We build and maintain a self image throughout our lives. It's largely based in how we imagine we're presenting ourselves to others[197], so our social selves and our self-images reflect one another. Our perception of ourselves is shaped by the way other people talk to us. To some extent, 'linguistic self' is also the 'social self'. In either case, our species is completely reliant on language. We react immediately to what others say to us or about us. When I say 'self' in this context, I mean it also in the same sense as *self-esteem*. Our self-esteem can rise and fall according to the words we hear, and to a discerning ear, the way people talk reveals it.

Not only do we have language skills, such as grammar, vocabulary, and syntax, but we also use language to express our emotions. Even more importantly, we have emotional responses to things others say to us. The emotional aspects; its 'affective components' are as intrinsic to human language as nouns and verbs. Understanding why we get angry when someone insults us involves looking at more than just words.

Our sense of self, which includes our self-esteem, changes with what people say to us. If someone says, "You're beautiful", we feel good about ourselves. If our banker says, "You're broke", we feel awful. If another one says, "we'd love to lend you money", we feel great, at least for a while. Few things can loom larger in human consciousness than our emotions, and they can change radically according to the words we hear.

Sticks and stones may break your bones, but words can *really* hurt you.

The Sensed Presence

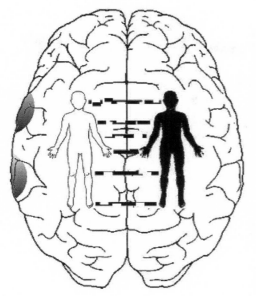

The left and right senses of self work together seamlessly most of the time. However, sometimes communication between the two hemispheres can break down; as though they've fallen out of phase with one another, or the information being passed between them is incoherent. One hemisphere or the other can stop working properly. For that moment, we can find feel that we are not quite 'all there'.

Each different state of consciousness includes a slightly different manifestation of the sense of self. The pathways that support it act a little differently in each (normal) moment, and act very differently in very unusual ones. When we're lost in reading a book or watching a movie, for example, and someone calls us, we have "pull ourselves together" before we can start interacting with them. It's not just a change in our attention; it's also a change in our 'self'. We're slightly different people when we first wake up in the morning than we are just a few minutes later. Certain brain structures support the sense of self, and when their activity changes, our sense of ourselves changes, too. When we've been alone for a while, and someone enters the room, we have to adjust our state a bit. We have to become our social selves once again. Monastic solitude; the Hermitage, seems to apply this idea successfully. By starving the cloistered one of normal socialization, the only being for them to relate to is God.

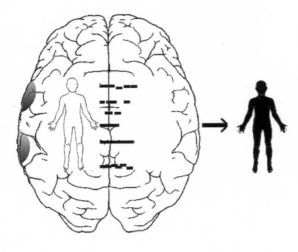

Non-physical beings are explained as the illusory perception of the right hemispheric sense of self, projected into the space around us.

This is the basis for a whole class of experience, known as 'visitor experiences'. This refers to those episodes when we see, communicate with, or are visited by a "spirit being" or feel a presence that seems to lack a physical form. These include angels, demons, aliens, ghosts, spirit guides, and 'channeled' beings. In these moments, we perceive the right hemispheric sense of self as a being that exists outside of our body's space.

The 'sensed presence' is the mildest form of 'visitor experience'. When you sense that presence, what's actually happening is that your subordinate sense of self has come into the awareness of your dominant sense of self, and you're experiencing it as an entity outside your body's space, though you still feel yourself as being one person. In that moment, you're two beings at once. A few people have this experience almost constantly; a few never have it, and most have it from time to time.

The 'God Helmet' has induced a wide range of visitor experiences, running the spectrum from a subtle sense of a presence to powerful visions of God, and from demons to angels. It relies on the same mechanisms that produce any other visitor experiences, which happen when the two sides of the brain are partially and temporarily disconnected from each other. Most importantly, the senses of self on each side of the brain are disconnected in such moments.

The *God Helmet* was built by Stan Koren, who works with Dr. M. A. Persinger in the Laurentian University Behavioral Neurosciences Program. It uses magnetic coils (electromagnets) to apply magnetic fields that get stronger and weaker every few milliseconds, in very specific patterns. In this way, these magnetic fields are also magnetic signals. One magnetic signal, with a pattern that mimics burst-firing in the amygdala, is also a tool to stimulate it, because it recognizes and responds to its own patterns. This procedure elicited visions of God in one or two percent of the subjects. Although this number isn't high, understanding how the God Helmet works allows us to understand much of what happens in the brain when people feel connected to God.

Dr. Persinger's research techniques are different from those of other neuroscientists. His work has shown that the left and right amygdalas are more highly specialized than was believed in decades past, though other researchers have recently confirmed this result. Persinger and others have found that the left amygdala is specialized for positive emotions. It gives us feelings like elation, happiness, joy, and even produces the kind of bliss associated with religious ecstasy. It also participates in the experience of fear, but seems to dominate when we feel positive emotions, as well as our ability to recognize and respond to the positive feelings of others.

On the right side of the brain, it produces fear. When the right amygdala runs, unchecked by the other brain structures that usually limit its activities, it can produce a state of fear so intense that people sometimes describe it as a 'feeling of impending doom'; as if death is just inches or seconds away. On the left, it can put us into joy or bliss.

The 'God Helmet[198]' has been able to produce a wide variety of experiences, including some oft-mentioned visions of God, out of body experiences, as well as the sensation of seeing into a black inner space (the 'Void'), which also appears in NDEs. Others results have included visions; some of angels, and a few of demons. There have been moments of bliss, and of terror. Some subjects have seen lights, including both little floating lights and powerful effulgent experiences of "The Light".

Others have felt very powerful tingly electrical sensations running through their bodies. Some of these experiences came about using procedures that were different from those which elicited visions of God. Phenomena appearing in NDEs also appear in response to God Helmet stimulation that targets specific brain parts[199].

It applies magnetic copies of EEG traces (or "brain waves"); signatures coming from specific brain parts. When a structure is excited, it can produce a specific irregular wave form − one that only comes from that structure. When the same irregular pattern is fed back into the brain, only the part it came from responds at first, and then other, connected, pathways begin to respond, too.

In Dr. Persinger's procedure, signal-bearing magnetic fields are directed through the Helmet. First, one type of signal is applied to the right temporal lobe and then another signal that uses a pattern taken from the amygdala is applied to both sides at once. The 'architecture' of this neural stimulation is very precise. The patterns that determine how the magnetic fields change their strength are derived from EEG monitoring of specific structures. The right electrical signal is found from a specific brain part, and then played back to the brain as a magnetic signal. The brain part it came from responds by producing the original electrical pulses again. Because the right signals only come from one structure, stimulation using them will only affect its "source" structure, and to some extent, other structures directly connected to it.

God Helmet Session Design

The God Helmet stimulates the temporal lobes with fluctuating magnetic fields. In the laboratory, these are controlled by software, which must be run only under DOS[200]. Outside the lab, there is a commercial version that runs under Windows, using PC sound devices. The program reads a waveform and sends it out to a box connected to an array of magnetic coils attached to the helmet. Every few milliseconds, it adjusts the current to the magnetic coils attached to the Helmet so the magnetic fields keep changing their strength, matching the waveform. The Helmet places the coils over the upper temporal lobes[201], the source for most spiritual, religious and mystic experiences. Evidence supporting this continues to mount, although there are theories that emphasize other neural systems. Of course, other areas of the brain participate in these experiences. Some of these become active in spiritual moments[202], and others become quieter[203].

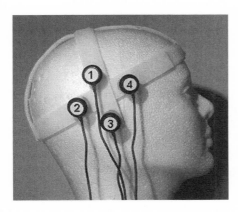

This is the version of the God Helmet, available to the public, developed by the author[204]. The magnetic coils are activated one at a time, cycling from one to four, counterclockwise. Four more coils go on the other side of the head, also cycling counterclockwise. It's an 8-channel system.

One journalist sat with some of Persinger's graduate students while researching a book on modern neuroscience[205], who told her things like:

"I heard someone say that she sensed her cat was in there (the chamber where the sessions are done)".

"Some people have terrifying experiences, while others say it's wonderful. White light and that sort of thing".

"Once there was a Japanese lady who sat there with tears running down her cheeks, jabbering away in Japanese. She said it had been sublime".

Another subject, writing about his use of the commercial version (The Shiva Neural Stimulation System) in an online forum, said:

"... for the first sequence, I felt nothing except relaxation and a tingling, numb feeling in my left leg.

But for the second sequence: I felt a whole-body "whooshing" sensation, like I was traveling very fast straight upward, then a distinct emotional impulse, growing intensity of feeling, culminating in the following - I felt myself questioning "how do I know it'll be ok?" (meaning: everything) and then the distinct answer returned: "I got this" (implication: don't worry).

I wouldn't call it a sensed presence, but it was definitely a Maslovian peak experience. I've had them before (sometimes even stronger) on my own, but very rarely, like a handful of times in my life.

It was lovely. I shed uncontrolled tears. I felt free and relieved and happy. I was on a bit of a high that whole evening afterward[206].

The journalist Jack Hitt, writing in *Wired* magazine[207]:

"During the 35-minute experiment, I feel a distinct sense of being withdrawn from the envelope of my body and set adrift in an infinite existential emptiness, a deep sensation of waking slumber. ... Occasionally, I surface to an alpha state where I sort of know where I am, but not quite. This feeling is cool - like being reinserted into my body. Then there's a separation again, of body and soul, and - almost by my will - I happily allow myself to drift back to the surprisingly bearable lightness of oblivion." "... I did have a fairly convincing out-of-body experience." (Strange to relate, but this same writer rated his experience as four out of ten – one must wonder what he was expecting)

The 'God Helmet' doesn't produce visions of God; it produces altered states of consciousness, and only some of these manifest as God experiences. Not everyone is equally sensitive to the Helmet's effects, but 80% achieve an altered state of one kind or another[208]. One needs the right conditions to use this, or any other technology, to produce an experience as dramatic as a vision of God.

Dr. Persinger does the Koren Helmet sessions in a completely soundproof Faraday Cage. The soundproofing achieves acoustic (complete) silence, and the Faraday Cage blocks out all *electromagnetic* influences. It doesn't block magnetic fields, like that of the earth. A compass will point north in such a chamber, but a cell phone won't work. One of the temporal lobes' functions is to monitor ambient (background) sound. Even a little noise can be a distraction. A silent environment increases the subject's chances for a spiritual experience under the God Helmet's influence[209]. The subjects were told they were participating in a "relaxation" experiment[210]. This helped subjects to relax, and that helped them avoid moods that can prevent the God Helmet from working.

'God Helmet' sessions have specific designs. There are several signals, derived from the amygdala, hippocampus, and a 'chirp' signal, which has been found to elicit activity in larger areas, but isn't derived from an EEG trace. During most sessions, two or more signals will be applied to different areas of the brain. The coils can be applied to several areas, although the 'God Helmet' experiments only used the temporal lobes. The length of the session also forms part of the design.

Several session designs have created spiritual experiences in Dr. Persinger's lab using the Koren Helmet. Here, we'll look only at the most successful; the one used in the so-called 'God Helmet' experiments.

God Helmet session designs have three crucial features.

1) Which signals are used, and in what order (often one signal over one side, followed by another signal over both sides).
2) The length of the session (40 to 60 minutes)
3) The location for the coils (over the temporal lobes)

Low voltage electric signals are fed to magnetic coils that produce magnetic fields, so the coils put out (low frequency) magnetic signals. No EMF emissions are used[211]. The electromagnetic outputs from a microwave oven, or a cell phone, for example, are completely different.

119

This technology isn't like putting a microwave oven on your head. It's more akin to putting on a pair of stereo headphones. Besides the music, stereo headphones also output magnetic fields, which rise and fall with the music, in approximately the same intensity as the signals used in the laboratory (about 10 to 50 Milligauss). However, the signals used in the lab have neural patterns, whereas the ones coming through the brain[212] when listening to headphones don't. They have whatever patterns come from the music.

As the procedure gets underway, a 'chirp' signal is applied over only the right temporal lobe. A chirp signal has a rapidly rising or falling pitch. As it starts, a "chirp" can be several octaves above middle 'C', and then it might quickly drop down to several octaves below that. One could also say that its *frequency* modulated, but with frequencies that change constantly. This signal repeats for about half an hour, with silences (latencies) between each instance. The silences can actually be longer than the signals themselves.

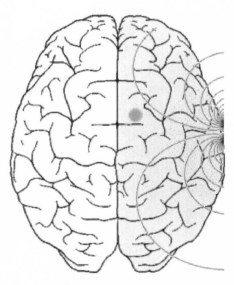

In this first of the two phases for this procedure, only the right side of the brain receives stimulation. The two sides of the brain stop working in tandem, making it easier for them to function independently. This alters their communication somewhat, muting the connections that keep the limbic system and the sense of self on each side integrated with each other. This is one of the pre-requisites for visitor experiences, whether they're a simple sense of a presence, or a striking vision of God.

The right amygdala responds the most because it's the most sensitive structure in the right hemisphere. The result can be fear, anxiety or just an uneasy feeling of apprehension, though others reported that they felt no negative emotions at all, and instead, found their minds filled with rich inner imagery. As the right amygdala becomes more active, activity in the left amygdala subsides. The first phase can be seen as suppressing the left side activity as much as raising the right side's excitement.

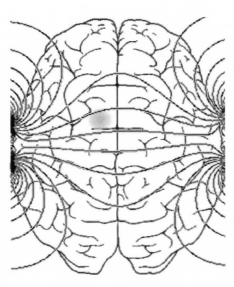

An EEG signal that appears when the amygdala is busy was sampled (using depth electrodes) and turned into a magnetic signal – an amygdala signal. In the second phase, a signal derived straight from the amygdala[213], is run through the coils placed on both side of the head.

Other structures on the right can remain active, because the signal isn't talking to them directly, so to speak. The left amygdala shows a rebound effect, becoming exceptionally active, after being 'drowned out' into silence in the first phase. This second phase can be blissful, as the left amygdala responds to its own signal. Its activity overwhelms it's counterpart on the right, as the "key" of this very specific signal opens the "door" to the structure.

During the first phase of these God Helmet sessions, the right amygdala became more active, and the one on the left became quieter. The stimulation in the second phase is designed to help the left amygdala burst into activity, dramatically outweighing the one on the right, eliciting bliss, joy, elation and so forth. In Persinger's lab, one of the most common results is a *Visitor experience* with a very positive feel. Not all brain parts are equally sensitive in all people. If a person's left amygdala is sensitive enough, they may actually find the experience unfolding into a vision of God. Other phenomena associated with the presence of God have also appeared in this phase. These include the sense of being loved, ecstasy, and the experience of being surrounded by, or filled with, light.

Many religious traditions depict God as being made of light. In Western tradition, God is seen as a radiant, effulgent, and resplendent being. As the Christ in Heaven, He is glorious, illuminated with an aura and/or a halo, and seems to glow. The word glorious means surrounded by light, and comes from an Indo-European root *"div"* meaning *brightness*. It's the source of the word Deva (Sanskrit for 'deity'), which shares a common (Indo-European) root with the Latin word for God, *Deus,* as well as the word *divine*. Historically, the word God implies light.

The following is from a brief email from Dr. Persinger, in reply to a question asking how many people, (what percent of the total subjects he worked with), experienced God in his laboratory using the God Helmet.

> Thus far, about 20 or so people *(out of about 2000)* have reported feeling the presence of Christ or even seeing Him in the chamber. *(The acoustic chamber where the experimental sessions took place)*. Most of these people used Christ and God interchangeably. Most of these individuals were older *(30 years or more)* and religious. One male, age about 35 years old, an alleged atheist but early childhood RC *(Roman Catholic)* training saw a clear apparition *(shoulders and head)* of Christ staring him in the face. He was quite 'shaken' by the experience. I did not complete a follow-up re: his change in behavior. Of course, these are all reports.
>
> What we did find with one world-class psychic, who experienced Christ as a component of his abilities, was that we could experimentally increase or decrease his numbers of reported experiences by applying the LTP *(a signal that associates with long-term potentiation, which happens while memories are being consolidated)* pattern *(derived from the hippocampus)* over the right hemisphere *(without his awareness)*. The field on-response delay was

about 10 to 20 sec. The optimal pattern, at least for this person, looked very right hippocampal. By far, most presences are attributable to dead relatives, the Great Forces, a spirit, or something equivalent. The attribution *(appearing)* along a devil to angel continuum appears strongly related to the affect *(bliss-terror)* associated with the experience. I suspect most people would call these 'vague all-around-me' sensations 'God', but they are reluctant to employ the label in a laboratory. The implicit is obvious. If the equipment and the experiment produced the presence that was God, then the extra personal, unreachable and independent characteristics of the God definition may be challenged" (Italics and parenthetical notes ours).

Let's return to the neural process involved with visions of God using the Koren Helmet. It begins by focusing activity in the right amygdala. By itself, activation of the right amygdala can lead to a feeling of dread, terror or even the feeling that death is imminent. This can happen during first phase of these experiments, though its a far from common effect. When only the right side is stimulated, some people do go into fear, though not as intense as it would be if the right amygdala was entirely active, and all nearby structures were shut down[214]. However, some subjects felt anxious, scared or apprehensive. These negative emotions stopped when the second phase of the session shunted the brain's response to both sides.

The sudden activation of the left amygdala in the second phase of the session produced the experience of God in about 1% of the subjects. In his email, Dr. Persinger said that this was from a total of about 2000, which is a small number when compared to the 80% of his subjects who sensed a presence of some kind; one that *wasn't* God. The more common experiences created by the God Helmet are not as intense. Most subjects felt the presence of a friendly spirit, an angel, or just a benign sense of someone being there. Had they looked around, they would have found no one there. (Of course, because most subjects wore blindfolds, they couldn't have looked anywhere.) A full range of visitor experiences;

God, angels, sensed presences, and evil demons, have all been produced using this technology.

In one of Dr. Persinger's case histories[215], who was haunted by a ghost, went into the chamber, and the helmet was placed on his head. The appropriate signals were applied, and he felt its presence again in the laboratory. It certainly wasn't a comfortable experience, but it reassured him that he was not cursed by God, or being chased by demons. Needless to say, the session was a great comfort to him. It showed him that his experience was a projection from his own mind, and it was much easier for him to live with his ghostly experiences after that.

Some people have a very deep and heartfelt religious faith in God. For such people, no amount of discussion or scientific evidence could ever prove that God exists only in the brain. There are others, who believe that God is nothing but a reflection of brain activity or a psychological delusion. To be even-handed, I have to point out that there is nothing in this line of evidence to prove that God exists, and nothing to prove that He doesn't.

If there is a creator of the universe; one who exists outside of me, and I feel His presence, is God working through my brain so I can feel him? Or, is my brain working to produce my sense of God's presence as though from outside myself? We have no proof in either direction. If you believe in God, you can consider the scientific evidence without compromising your faith. This book isn't going to suggest you give up your religion or spirituality. If you don't believe in God, and you're reading this to reinforce your atheism, you'll find it isn't going to tell you anything that will either strengthen or challenge your position. There is no proof that there is a God and none that there isn't.[216] I hope that everyone who reads this will take that point seriously, and won't feel that what I have to say offers a challenge to their religion.

My hope is that neuroscience will help enrich spirituality so that its benefits become more accessible. I'm not here to prove that anyone whose happiness is based on their belief in God is wrong. On the contrary, if anything, I'd rather try to prove that belief in God is a good thing. From my perspective, it doesn't really matter whether there is a God or not. Prayer certainly shapes the mind, even if it doesn't always seem to change the world around us[217]. If there is a God, and it's only in your brain, it's *your* God. You're free to work out your own spiritual beliefs; to engage whatever is most beautiful, compelling or uplifting about God, as you understand Him, regardless of whether it's from within your brain or from the universe at large.

Other research has revealed that the specific temporal lobe structure most likely to be the source for religious and mystic experiences is our friend, the amygdala[218]. Its social functions help us relate to other people, and they're also at work when we only imagine or dream of relating to others, or when we feel we're in God's presence. Persinger's success with the signal derived from the amygdala in the God Helmet experiments supports this idea.

Why, if we are the product of evolution, are we able to have the experience of seeing God or sensing His presence? Why would evolution provide us with such an unlikely potential, or one so rarely used?

If the capacity to experience God first-hand, face-to-face is a human behavior, how did it get wired into our brain? If it appeared during our evolutionary history, where, when and why could it have occurred? I believe the answer is in the role it plays in the experience of death. The experience of God plays a crucial role in the death-process, an evolutionary adaptation that contributed to our success as a species.

A few Lab reports

Let's look at some examples of dialog (from audiotape) of subjects participating in God Helmet experiments[219].

Subject 1

A Middle-aged professional journalist. Chirp signal applied over the right side.

> "I see shadows along my left side . . . there is someone touching my left side . . . there is a flash of light . . . a tunnel experience. I feel as if I am shrinking and expanding. There is a tingling inside of my thigh

. . . sexual excitement. There's a cold rush (subject shivered; EEG showed paroxysmal activity). I see a visual . . . it's an apparition."

Subject 2

A 21-year-old female with history of diabetes. Amygdala signal applied over both sides.

"I felt a presence behind me and then along the left side. When I tried to focus on its position, the presence moved. Every time I tried to sense where it was, it moved around. When it moved to the right side, I experienced a deep sense of security like I had not experienced before. I started to cry when I felt it slowly fade away" (the field parameters had been changed).

Subject 3

A 30-year-old woman. Chirp signal applied over the right side.

"I feel detached from my body. I am floating up . . . there is a kind of vibration moving through my sternum . . . there are odd lights or faces along my left side. My body is becoming very hot. . . . tingling sensations in my chest and stomach . . . now both arms. There is something feeling my ovaries. I can feel my left foot jerk. I feel there is someone in the room behind me."

Subject 4

A 25-year-old man, childhood history of three "mild" head injuries. Chirp signal applied over both sides.

"I feel as if there was a bright white light in front of me. I saw a black spot that became a kind of funnel . . . no, (a) tunnel that I felt drawn into. I felt moving, like spinning forward through it. I began to feel the presence of people, but I could not see them; they were along my sides. There were colorless, grey-looking. I know I was in the chamber but it was very real. I suddenly felt intense fear and felt ice cold."

Common Themes in God Helmet Reports.

"The most frequent themes and events reported or displayed by subjects who were asked to press one of two hand buttons when they felt a presence while being exposed to successive sequences of different magnetic field patterns over the right hemisphere or periods of no field. These themes occurred when the fields were present.

1. A dark, ominous force looming right above the person (as if it was going to descend).
2. A feeling of suffocation or pressure on the chest.
3. The sensation of "blacker than black" during brief periods within a minute of the onset of a specific pattern.
4. Re-experiencing previous altered states, such as haunts, kundalini, and psychotropic drug experiences. (These individuals had not experienced the unusual events again until they were exposed to the fields.)
5. About 20% of the participants clicked one or two buttons indicating they were experiencing a sensed presence but had no memory of the experience about 15 to 20 min later.
6. Religious figures, images of 'priests', and human skeletons, [which] occurred as "flickering" but repeated phenomena."

CHAPTER 6

The Stages In Near-Death Experiences

Near-Death experiences (NDEs) are stories about dying and coming back to life told by people who went through a temporary clinical death. Most people have heard about them, but I'll give you a typical one here. It's not a real NDE; it's intended to be typical, and no single NDE is ever exactly like another. NDEs are different in different cultures, and this one is typical only of those found in Western countries.

> "I was in a car accident. As soon as the other car hit me, I left my body and I could see the accident scene as I floated above it. I watched the ambulance crew try to bring me back to life, using those electric paddles that can restart the heart. After that, I found myself in a tunnel, flying or floating down its length. Eventually, I saw a light, and as I went towards it, I came to the end of the tunnel. I went into the light, where I found several people who had died before me; people I knew. Of course, I was overjoyed to see them, and found that I loved them much more here, surrounded by light, than I did when they were still alive. I'm not sure where they went, but eventually I realized I was in the

company of just one being, who was made entirely of light. He was brilliant, but his light didn't hurt my eyes. I was encompassed by waves of love and joy beyond anything I had ever experienced before. I knew it was God. Standing before him, I knew that God understood everything, not only about the world, but about me. He knew why I was who I was, and he knew why I was the way I was. I felt no judgment or disapproval from God, and I knew that to him, everything was going exactly the way it should, for everyone and everything on the earth. All of this understanding and all the things God said to me were transmitted instantly into my mind, without a word being said. God beckoned me to look off to one side, and as I did so, I saw my whole life happen again in front of me, as though it was a high-speed movie. It took just a few seconds, but I saw every moment of my life. I asked God to explain to me why the world was so difficult to live in, and for an answer he pointed towards a pedestal with a book on top. I went over to the book, thinking of how difficult life had been, and as I opened it I came to a page that explains the reason for human suffering. I wondered if this could apply to war as well, and the next page I looked at told me why human beings fought wars, and why God did not stop them. I asked a lot of questions. The book showed me anything I wanted to know. I remember being surprised at some of the answers. I thought how wonderful it would be to live my life again, knowing what I knew now. I also knew that if I did return to the earth, I wouldn't be able to remember what I had read. At one point, I knew it was time to stop reading, and looking up, I saw an open door. I walked towards it, and as I came to the threshold, I knew that if I stepped through the doorway the experience, and my life, would be over. The next thing I knew, I was in the emergency room, with tubes in my mouth, staring into a painfully bright light bulb. I had come back to life, and I wished I hadn't. It was so peaceful on the other side. It was also exciting. It hurt to return to my body, but I have the sense that everything in life has a purpose, including my survival in this injured body."

Remember our explicit assumption – that Near-Death Experiences are memories of experiences of the human death-process. This is a controversial assumption; one that some researchers will disagree with, but we won't look at the pros and cons here – there are plenty of books that do that. The evidence for our position isn't complete, but it helps us see how the brain creates religious and mystic experiences. If this assumption is wrong (which will be hard to prove either way), we'll have to go back to the drawing board – but probably not today.

Our evolutionary history found advantages in having certain experiences when we're dying. They occur consistently[220], and they have a function. This suggests that our brains changed at some point in our history in order to include these states of consciousness within its repertoire. This change probably occurred at the same time as the brain underwent other changes, to accommodate language, the complicated social skills needed to live with others, our longer childhood, our ability to plan for the future, and all the other traits which, taken together, make us human.

The death-process has seven common stages or episodes. Each state of consciousness creates an experience, which has specific functions to perform. There is always a reason why a specific trait is preserved, even if we don't see it. Of course, we openly agree with the Darwinian view that tells us that the death-process must be a product of natural selection, where adaptations confer an advantage at the time they appear.

Not all phases appear in every NDE. Some never go past the early phases. Although many appear to skip some of them, the episodes nearly always appear in a specific order. If an NDE contains both the Tunnel and the Life Review, the Review will usually come after the Tunnel. It makes sense to suppose that the earlier stages facilitate the later ones.

If an individual NDE lacks a specific stage, it may be that its function wasn't needed to complete the death process for that person.

If we believe there are seven stages to near-death experiences merely because seven is thought to be a sacred number, how do we explain those that have only have six? We accept biological evolution, so we are compelled to see the death process as a part of our evolutionary heritage; a process that's either biological or has its roots in our biology. The same holds true for its individual stages[221]. The death process is a biological process, and these are always efficient. Instead of having a specific number of stages, it may well fulfill its purpose with as few stages as possible, with seven as the maximum. We'll also take a deeper look at the way the peak experiences that happen during spiritual practices like prayer and meditation can match phenomena happening in NDEs. NDEs in different cultures have very different *episodes*, but as we'll see, we find the same *phenomena* (and therefore, similar states of consciousness[222]) in all of them.

Experiences Leading Up To Death

The death-process can be seen as beginning, not with death, but with the perception that one is going to die. When people know they're dying; when they can anticipate it, they can often go into *states* that echo NDE phenomena. People's moods often become incredibly warm and loving as they begin to die. An example appears in the story of Ms. Olga Berggolts[223]. It's from an account of the World War II Siege of Leningrad, when Nazi Germany tried to starve the city into submission.

> "Somehow she felt ready for death – or if not for death, ready just to sink down in the snow in the great drifts. Everything began to seem soft and tender. It was a mood, she later knew, which lay very close to death, the mood in which people began to speak very quietly, very gently, to suffix all their nouns with "chka" or "tsa" – that is to turn them into loving diminutives – "a little piece of bread", a "dear little drop of water.

This may not be the total love appearing in many NDEs, but to have genuine affection for a drop of water shows an expanded ("wider") love; one that can also appear in NDEs.

Here's a strange one. In the *premortem* phase, one woman said she saw and felt herself to have shrunk to a very small size. "The bed seemed huge to me, and I remember thinking, I'm like a little brown bug in this big white bed[224]."

There are many accounts of people experiencing visions when they think they are about to die. One such report was published by a rescue worker stationed at the base of the Matterhorn[225]. Part of his job was to help climbers who fell off the mountain. He collected a number of stories from people who thought they were going to die, but actually survived their falls. Many told stories of seeing their lives flash before their eyes, hearing music and feeling time stretch out, and other experiences. These people weren't dying – they only thought they were – but that can be enough to trigger death-process experiences[226].

People in the final stages of terminal illnesses have reported visitations by angels and the 'spirits' of people they knew who had died. One goes like this:

> "She was carrying on a conversation. I looked at her son, who was sitting by her bedside, and he said to me, 'She thinks she's conversing with my father who has been dead for seventeen years.' The patient's eyes were open, but she seemed to be in a trance. She spoke in a monotone: 'The children are fine – we have grandchildren[227].'"

On September 11, 2001 when the World Trade Center in New York was destroyed, those close to its base watched as people fell to the ground. They said it seemed as if the bodies had already gone limp before they struck the pavement. Perhaps this was because, by then, many of them had already begun their death-process.

Phenomena from almost any stage in the death-process can appear as a deathbed vision. It's possible that the states of consciousness that happen during death appear when conditions are right, and the conditions don't depend on death itself.

The death-process is a biological process with a function. It may be that deathbed visions 'prime' the process, getting its pathways ready to go ("potentiated"), so to speak. The episodes in the death-process have functions, and they will probably be the same when they occur as deathbed visions; visions that come before death begins.

Very few NDEs in India and Asia begin with OBEs. They commonly start with a visit from a servant of Yama, the Lord of the Underworld, and a walk down a road to the realms of the dead.

As in Western NDEs, the experience is one of movement from one place to another, recruiting those brain parts involved in spatial perception and mental mapping, especially the right hippocampus.

Harbingers of death are not veridical ("real"), but they can appear in a world that looks just like the real one. One Thai NDE found a Yamatoot waiting for him at the bottom of his stairs. NDE OBEs find the person moving out of their body, but they often stop in the space around their body for a time. Harbingers of death commonly walk down a road with the person they have come to take; a road leading to the underworld. Again, the theme is one of movement from one place to another.

The death-process in the West and Europe may have once begun from a visit by the Grim Reaper. He was the personification of death, and a ubiquitous cultural icon, (as well known in the middle Ages as Mickey Mouse is today). People in medieval Europe probably expected the Grim Reaper at the moment of death, in much the same way as people expect Yamatoots and Yamdoods in Asia and India today. It was the most common image of the arrival of death at that time, and everyone saw pictures of him many times during their lives.

During the medieval and Renaissance period, even after the Protestant reformation, preachers of all denominations regularly reminded people of their inevitable personal deaths. They quoted things like, "O son, observe the time and fly from evil" and "Ask not for whom the bell tolls." Western culture and its laws have sanitized death. It's literally a crime for dead bodies to appear in most places. We've lost the common familiarity with death we once had. In India, to this day, groups of mourners carry dead bodies through the streets on biers, making their way to the burning sites. Passersby stop, and make the Namaste (hands folded in prayer) gesture. I'm not sure if they are showing respect to the dead person, to the mourners, or offering their own prayers to God. It may not matter. It's enough that they respond to the fact of death with a religious gesture.

In India, funeral processions are an everyday sight. When I was there, I once found myself in a taxicab held up by a funeral procession, where they carried the body on a bier, wrapped in saffron cloth. As I looked out of the cab's window, it was only about 18 inches from my face. I asked at the driver, "How long will we be here?" The driver's philosophical answer was: "However long it takes." "That guy is dead, right?" I questioned. "Oh yes. What's the problem?" he said. "No problem. It's just a new experience for me." The driver turned around looked at me, and gave me a big smile, saying, "Yes. In India, dying is part of living. No problem."

The image of the death-process learned from your own culture will be the most convincing message for getting you to understand that you've died when your turn comes. If the most pointed image of death is that of your dead body, then it helps to leave your body, taking the time to see your corpse. Yamatoots, the Grim Reaper and the out of body experience all serve the same function. They show the dying person that their death has begun, and they are very convincing.

These are all very different experiences, but they have a great deal in common. Both begin with the person seeing the environment they were in when their death-process began. As we saw before, a hallucination can be filled with the images in the person's mind just before it began. As the death-process begins, we move from a world created through outward ("exogenous") perception to an inner ("endogenous") world created in our minds. This includes our perception, emotions, and our sense of our bodies. This second phase of the death-process seems to the point where our perceptions (perhaps remembered from scant moments before) are replaced by hallucinations. It offers an example of what it feels like (the "phenomenological correlate") when the focus of brain activity moves from one group of brain areas to another.

Countless reports of NDEs refer to a sense of understanding something deep and meaningful. I suggest this feeling appears when the previous phase of the death-process is complete, and we understand that we've died. Even without having this realization appear in words, we will have understood something important. When we leave the "world of the living", we recognize that we've made a transition. That understanding feels deeply profound, and can make everything else that happens through of the death-process feel terribly meaningful.

Out-of-Body Experience

The first episode in NDEs found in Western countries is most commonly an out-of-body experience (OBE).

> "The next thing I knew, I was in a room, crouched in a corner of the ceiling. I could see my body below me. ...[228]"
>
> "... I went down almost in the middle of the lake...I kept bobbing up and down, and all of a sudden, it felt as though I were away from my body, away from everybody, in space by myself. Although I was stable, staying at the same level, I saw my body in the water about three or four feet away, bobbing up and down. I viewed my body from the back, and slightly to the right side. I still felt I had an entire body form, even while I was outside my body. I felt like a feather.[229]"
>
> One NDEer remembered waking up, 'and feeling that although my arms and legs were very heavy, I was floating above my body.' The entire room was very dark and she could only see her body below her, with her parents and the medics at her bedside. She denied being light-headed and said 'I wasn't really looking

down at my body, it only felt like I was floating above
my body.[230]'

Many OBEs feature a point where the person looks down to see
their own body. Sometimes they're shocked when they recognize
themselves. The experience says something to those who have it during
the death-process. It says, "You're dead, but you still exist".

> "She was aware of light, and then she was above the
> scene, looking down, as the doctors struggled to find a
> heartbeat. The activity around the table was interesting,
> but she didn't really care about it. When she realized
> that they were working on her body, apparently dead,
> her attitude didn't change markedly. She saw the event
> as interesting, in a detached sort of way. Although she
> realized that she was dead, that didn't concern her either,
> because there were other things happening around her.
> There was a bright light in the distance[231]."

I don't know of any NDE account where a person had an OBE, saw
their own body and felt they were still alive. The OBE conveys the fact of
death directly, with an immediacy that seems to break through any hopes
or denial. The message is especially clear it follows a trauma that's serious
enough to actually threaten a person's life. OBEs happen in other contexts
(like during meditation), but they don't seem to convey the same message.

One of the most common questions about OBEs is whether they
are 'real'. Creating a bit of vocabulary to dodge the issue of what 'real'
means, researchers use the word 'veridical' roughly meaning *really* real'.
If you are having an OBE, are you out of your body or not? The word
to re-define here isn't 'real', but rather 'you'.

Here's a conversation I've had scores of times.

> "Are OBEs real?"
> "Of course they're real. They're experiences - real experiences."
> "No. I mean are they really real?"
> "Really real?"

"Yeah - Like, are people really out of their bodies?"
"Do you mean in *ALL* OBEs?"
"Well, maybe not all of them, but are any of them real?"

To answer, I sometimes tell them the story about "Maria", a patient at a Connecticut hospital, who found herself outside the third floor of a hospital during an OBE. She noticed a tennis shoe on a ledge. She noted that one lace was underneath the heel and the toe was somewhat worn. She begged her nurse to go to where she'd seen the shoe, and if it was there to bring it back to her. The nurse found the shoe and gave it to her. The shoe was proof *for her* that what she had seen while she was clinically dead was real[232].

The story doesn't end there. Later on, skeptical researchers found that the woman could have seen the shoe as she went into the hospital, and if she wasn't aware of it, it's not impossible that she saw it subconsciously.

There have been other such cases. Patients have described the doctor's clothing at the time of their admission as D.O.A. and described their own resuscitations. Even children with no knowledge of emergency room methods have been able to describe their doctor's actions.

These cases are hard to dismiss, especially because medical workers, doctors and respected researchers collected them. While it may be easy for scientists to avoid spending any real time on astrology, Atlantis or numerology, the numerous peer-reviewed medical reports of valid perceptions from out-of-body perspectives call for an interpretation. One possibility is that OBEs – most of them, at least – are hallucinations of the actual environment; including the person's own dead body. In this scenario, the mechanisms of hallucinations are set in motion, allowing people to begin their death-process, from within their own minds, before their bodies begin to die. This lets the OBE perform its function, before the person feels they have left the "this reality".

There are also many cases where people's out-of-body perceptions were inaccurate. It may be that OBEs are hallucinations or it may be that the person is 'really' out of their body. For most of the ideas in this book, it doesn't matter very much. The OBE is the typical first phase in Western OBEs, and whether it's happening *in* the brain or *through* the brain, the brain remains the origin of this, and all other, subjective experiences.

It's easy to accept that emotions reflect the activity of specific brain parts. Most people understand that changes in the brain, like head injuries, can create changes in a person's emotional life. Moods that are common for a person during their lives may not appear during their NDEs. Interestingly, the full range of emotions happening when we're in the body also occurs when we're out of it[233]. If experiences depend on brain function, then something of the brain must exist during OBEs whether we are in the body, having hallucinations, or we're 'really' out of it.

There are several kinds of OBEs. In some, the people see their bodies, and in others they don't. Some experiences *called* OBEs are actually closer to 'astral travel' – where the person feels they are in another world, real or not. If they're in another world, they're not in this one, where their bodies exist. They may call it an OBE, but astral travel is different, because it takes place in a (perceived) different environment. Those who think OBEs aren't 'real' would classify them as illusions. In an OBE, you're seeing the same environment, but from another perspective. Assuming that astral travel and Shamanic journeying are different names for the same thing, they are more like hallucinations than illusions[234].

In Shamanistic 'spirit journeying' a shaman mentally journeys into the earth or the sky, usually to find a cure for a sick person[235]. Such visions may take the shamans into world's that aren't 'real', but they come back with information that 'works'. The techniques of shamanism have answered a wide range of human needs for hundreds of thousands of years. If we assume that the experience of being in the spirit realm enhances the ability to use intuition to meet the needs of a person or a tribe, then shamanic journeying would add a significant cognitive skill to human intelligence, and increase our chances of survival. Not everyone needed the ability to do it. If just one member of each social group had such shamanic skills, the whole group could reap its benefits. The fact that Shamanic journeying differs from an OBE doesn't mean that it's any less powerful or spiritual.

There's an interesting variation of OBEs found in NDE reports - the 'partial' OBE. In this experience, a person is both in their body and having an OBE at the same time.

"... I discovered a most remarkable thing: I could be in two places at once. I could exist physically in my father's arms as he carried my terribly injured body ... at the same time, I could be above us, watching the whole scene as if I were a detached observer." [236]

"I was conscious of being two persons - one lying on the ground in a field where I had fallen from the blast, my clothes on fire, waving my limbs about wildly, at the same time uttering moans and gibbering with fear... The other 'me' was floating up in the air, about twenty feet from the ground, from which position I could see not only the my other self on the ground, but also the hedge, the road, and the car, which was surrounded by smoke and burning fiercely. "[237]

"I was about eight years old. I had to have some teeth pulled under anesthesia, and as I was put to sleep, I seemed to be two people. One of me was lying on the operating table and another was rolled up into a ball being hurled very fast through a long tunnel. The doctor said later that he had given me too much ether, and my heart had stopped. I guess that's when I split in two. It all seemed very simple."[238]

There is evidence that both sides of the brain are involved in OBEs[239]. A published EEG recording taken during an OBE showed that the same brain waves appeared in both sides of the brain, but in different regions, while the subject had an OBE. If these brain waves happened on only one side, a 'partial' OBE might well be the result. Partial OBEs might happen when only one hemisphere is involved. It may be that the basis of OBEs lies in right-hemispheric excitement, together with inhibition of some left hemispheric activity. If that inhibition (or at least some of it) fails, the neural activity behind OBEs will stay exclusively on the right side, and the left hemispheric sense of self will not be affected. These 'dual' OBEs seem to suggest that both sides participate, and occasionally they don't connect the way they normally do when people are out of their bodies.

In NDEs from other countries, some OBEs occur in the beginning phase, but often lack the autoscopic feature where the person sees their own body. If this phase is to make the person aware that they're dead, then we would expect that some people wouldn't fully realize their death has happened until after the next phase. Many NDEs with this theme feature a harbinger of death, which might be an angel, a servant from the underworld or perhaps in earlier times, the Grim Reaper. Such harbingers of death appear to the person, and make it clear that they're dead.

From a Thai NDE:

> I came home from work feeling very tired and sleepy, after feeling run-down and fatigued all day. I lay down to take a nap, and when I awoke, I got up and found that, although I was standing up, my body was still sleeping. I went outside the house and stood under a coconut tree. I experienced a deep sense of beauty. I did not know where I was. Looking around, I saw a road, and wondered where it went. I walked along the road. Suddenly, I heard two people talking very loudly. I looked and saw that they were Yamatoots (servants of Yama, The Lord of the Dead). One of them spoke to me saying "we've come to take you to hell"[240].

The Tunnel, the Void, or a Spirit Walk.

Most often, the next phase of the death-process in Western culture is a dark tunnel. Often, but not always, the Tunnel has a kind of honeycomb pattern on the walls, though it can also take other forms. In some NDEs, this phase appears as a huge, even infinite, deep black space instead of the tunnel. Sometimes it has a brilliant point of light in the center that seems unimaginably far away. One name for this experience is "The Void". It's not just an empty space. It's more than just emptiness, blackness or blankness.

The experience is much more than that. It's a vibrant, alive, 'electric' place where you touch nothing, yet sense there's a texture. There's a sound, although nothing is heard. You understand nothing from it. It isn't talking to you. Nevertheless, to be in that place, and faced with this Void, creates a feeling of understanding something profound and at the same time, being in a larger realm.

The second phase of the death-process can appear as the Tunnel, and the person moves along its length. You're not just *in* The Tunnel, you go *through* it. When it's a journey to the underworld, it also means movement through space. In The Void experience, the point of light expands as the person moves towards it and goes into the next phase seamlessly.

This second phase of NDEs can take several forms. *The Tunnel* and *the Void* are both very dark, but they 'feel' like space. In the majority of cases, the Tunnel is dark and the Void is a place of utter and absolute blackness. However, both the Tunnel and the Void have an important feature. A tiny point of light usually appears. In the Void, it's very far off in the distance, and in The Tunnel, it's at the end. Here are a few examples of the Tunnel.

> "The next thing she was aware of was that she was moving through a 'dark railway tunnel'. Far off in the distance she could see a tiny point of light.[241]"
> I went in the tunnel as a child. I had a high fever, and was falling asleep. I went into the tunnel, Floating around, and spinning. I saw adults there. They said" You should not be here" and I went back into my body.[242]"

A tiny point of light often appears in the center of the Void. In the NDE Void[243] experience, you move through a vast, dark open space until you enter the light – the same light found at the end of the Tunnel.

> "She was sucked into a dark tunnel and was aware of others, human and animal, traveling with her. Again, she felt no fear, but seemed more interested in what experience lay in front of her. In the distance was a point of light.[244]"

Raymond Moody found NDE accounts that spoke of 'an utterly black, dark void' and one that referred to 'a deep, dark valley'. One subject "escaped" into this dark void[245]. One of Kenneth Ring's subjects [246] remembered "...total, peaceful, wonderful blackness. Very peaceful blackness..." I've heard people speak of the Void as though it had a texture. One told about a 'velvety blackness'. Another NDEer spoke of a 'shimmering Void'[247]

> "I had a heart attack, and I found myself in a black void, and I knew I had left my physical body behind"[248].
> "I was eight years old when I almost drowned in a swimming pool. I remember a deep black void. Then suddenly there was a bright light ...[249]"

In Buddhism, there are four levels of meditation called *Arupa Jhanas*, (formless absorption states). These states are "beyond the perception of matter". They happen in the course of concentration meditation (where the person concentrates on an object). They're said to be especially helpful in attaining enlightenment. The first is *The Realm of Infinite Space (Akasanancayatana)*. One Buddhist teacher says that all material and visual phenomena cease in this state and space is seen as the limitless source of all phenomena.[250] Achieving this state of consciousness is said to create "uplifting happiness, powerful enough to lift the body and make it spring up into the air." It can also create 'pervading (rapturous) happiness ... (in which) ... the whole body is completely pervaded, like a filled bladder; like a rock cavern invaded by a huge inundation'.[251] The process then goes on through three more states and after that, the teaching says, the next step is enlightenment.

Although the Void often occurs as the second stage in NDEs, the Tunnel may actually be more common.

> "I then entered into a dark round tube or hole. I could call it a tunnel. I seemed to go headfirst through the scene, and suddenly I was in a place filled up with love and a beautiful bright quiet light."[252]

The next thing she was aware of was that "she was moving through a dark railway tunnel. Far off in the distance she could see a tiny point of light.[253]"

A four-year-old child said:

> "When I died, I went into a huge noodle. It wasn't like a spiral noodle. It was very straight, like a tunnel. When I told my mom about nearly dying, I told her it was the noodle, but now I'm thinking that it must have been a tunnel, because it had a rainbow in it, and I don't think a noodle has a rainbow."[254]

> "I was playing golf as a storm was brewing when -wham- I got hit by a bolt of lightning. I hovered above my body for a few seconds, and then I felt myself sucked up this tunnel. I couldn't see anything around me, but I had a sense of moving forward very rapidly. I was clearly in a tunnel, and knew it when I saw this light at the other end getting bigger and bigger."[255]

The Tunnel is the most common second phase in Western NDEs. In Thailand, the most common second phase consists of a short journey, usually on foot, accompanied by a Yamatoot ("Yah-mah-TOOT"), one of the servants of the lord of the underworld. In one case, the person was already walking down a road when he met the Yamatoots. Although these two kinds of episodes are very different, they do have an underlying phenomenon in common - that of movement through space. In one, the Tunnel defines the space. In the other, as in life, the road defines it. As its name implies, The Void is made of nothing but space. Their similar phenomena imply that the parts of the brain involved in the Tunnel experience include those that mediate spatial perception.

Some Thai NDEs include both themes; OBEs and servants of Yama.

> I heard a voice telling me that I was dying. It said that I should go with him. I got up quickly. I turned to look at myself lying on the bed, and found that I could see my own organs. I then saw that the voice belonged to a Yamatoot, who told me "You must now leave your family". I cried for a long time. He took me to another world. The Yamatoot ordered me to lie down on a glass plate. He said that he would use it as a way to transport me to another world.[256]

Harbingers, those who come to take you to the 'next world', also appear in NDEs in the West. Here is one account:

> "A handsome man in a shining robe was my guide, and we walked in silence in what appeared to be a Northeasterly direction. As we traveled onward, we came to a very broad and deep valley of infinite length... He soon brought me out of darkness into an atmosphere of clear light.[257]"

Here, the deep and dark valley seems to have supplanted the dark void or a tunnel. It shows how there can be striking variations in the way a single primary theme or phenomenon can unfold.

Just as one moves through the Tunnel or the Void in the second phase of NDEs in the West, in Asia - you take a trip. The two experiences are very different, but they share the underlying phenomenon of movement through space, and both include an episode of movement from one 'plane of existence' to another. Other phenomena can appear in this, the second phase. In Japan, for example, many NDEs include walks through landscapes and gardens.

THE LIGHT - Entering the land of the Dead

The Light will be familiar to most readers because it's one of the most common NDE themes appearing in films about the afterlife. The Light, like the light at the end of the Tunnel, is important in the structure of the death-process.

In the west, this phase of the death-process is quite different from those found in Asian and Indian cultures. The Light never appears in the published accounts of NDEs from Eastern cultures, but that doesn't mean it never happens for Asians. It might be that the existing samples of Asian NDEs aren't large enough for the phenomenon to emerge. If something happens in 5% of all cases, and you have 10 cases, it might never appear in your data. The small size of the sample could lead to the impression that it doesn't exist. It's easy to be sure that something *does* appear with a small sample, but not to *rule out* something that doesn't.

While living in Thailand, I noticed that the Thai attitudes to death and dying were very different from those found in my own country, the United States. Their fundamental mythologies about death and dying are radically different. I wondered if NDEs in Thailand were as different as those in the West, and found they were. This was reflected not only in the local culture, but also in their NDEs. We will use them as a point of comparison in much of this book.

In the same phase marked by the experience of "entering the light" in the West, In India and Asia, one enters the underworld. In these countries, the traditional belief about the next world says that it's where people are tortured and punished for their sins. The underworld of Asian mythology, which many call hell, is a place of torture, but not a place of eternal damnation.

There is a special hell where sexual offenders are forced to a spiky tree while being tormented by demons.

A comic panel illustrates this[258]. In Thai mythology, trees are believed to have spirits. Here a sexual offender is climbing a spike-covered tree. The tree spirit tells him to 'get that out of my face'. Behind is Yama, the lord of the underworld, commander of the Yamatoots.

Motifs drawn from the traditional mythology of death and dying are common in Southeast Asia. They appear in posters, comic books and even cartoons. I once saw a safety poster for motorcycle drivers. It had two pictures. In one, a motorcycle was weaving wildly in and out of traffic, with a Yamatoot[259] riding on the back. In the other, the motorcycle was staying in line with an angel riding along. The poster's message was that if you drive dangerously, you're going to meet death and a Yamatoot, but if you drive safely, an Angel will protect you.

Interestingly, Thai NDEs usually have Yamatoots, but only rarely have angels. Angels are more common in popular cultural images from the West. They exist in many other cultures, but they are quite rare in NDEs in Southeast Asia, where they play no role in the popular mythology and beliefs about the death-process. In the West, where the belief in Guardian Angels is many centuries old, NDE reports show angels to be common harbingers of death. These reflect the memories, expectations and imagination of people in different cultural groups. The *content* may be an expression of suggestions from a lifetime of subtle death–related images, but the *form* is integral to the death process itself.

The Tunnel, the Void and the walk down the road with a Yamatoot all provide the experience of leaving one *realm* and arriving in another. Of course, we don't arrive anywhere, and we haven't really left anywhere. We've 'moved' from one state of consciousness to another, although it feels like one has gone through much more than that. It seems as if we have moved into 'another dimension', 'gone beyond the veil' or 'woken up' in 'another realm'. All of these phrases reflect a change from one state of consciousness to a dramatically different one. The working assumption for this book is that there are no 'other dimensions' or 'other planes of existence'. We'll be thinking of these as expressions of altered states of consciousness, reflecting changes in specific patterns of activity in the brain. In the second state, the content of our consciousness no longer reflects our senses. What we experience after this is 'endogenous[260]' (from within). The outer ("exogenous") world no longer exists for us, as our senses no longer carry information from it. Our minds are now filled with content only from within.

To be in the Light is bliss, ecstasy and joy. In the light, people find acceptance and happiness so great and so subtle that no words can ever express it. The sensation fulfills the expectations of those from the West, who traditionally believe that death means coming to the entrance to heaven, and then entering into God's presence. When you're in the Light, it's not just that you're dead, but you've also left the "material plane", and are now in the "realm" of the dead. First, one enters the light, where they might meet dead friends and relatives, or angels or spirits. This brings them to the realization not only that they're dead, but that for them, the living are gone. In order to have face-to-face meetings with the dead, you have to be where people go after death - because *they're* dead.

The 'Light' is one of the most compelling and emotionally intense NDE experiences. I once asked P.M.H. Atwater, author of several books on NDEs, if she had interviewed any NDEers who found themselves healed of the terminal health problem that brought on their clinical death after their NDE. Without hesitation, she replied "Oh yes - many!" When I asked what NDE phenomena were most likely to occur in these NDEs, she answered again without hesitation, "Bliss and The Light".

Bliss and The Light often happen at the same time during NDEs, implying that they are different features of the same state of consciousness, and supported by the same brain parts.

> "When I was in the Light, the pain was completely gone," said one NDEer.[261]
>
> "Two nights before surgery I was sleeping when I was awakened by a bright light shining in my eyes. I opened my eyes to see a large sphere of light floating about five feet in front of me. There was a light within it rotating slowly from left to right. This sphere spoke to me: 'You aren't afraid, are you?'
>
> Seeing the light made me fearless. In fact, I was filled with most incredible peace I have ever known. Whoever was speaking to me knew what all my problems and fears were. All of my burdens slipped away.
>
> Suddenly the light went through me. It didn't reflect off me or anything like that. It went straight through me. As it did, I was filled with unconditional love, which was so complete and powerful I would need to invent new words to describe it.
>
> I asked that my cancer would be removed. I prayed actually.[262]"

Dr. Melvin Morse, who published this story, also added the detail that the patient's cancer had disappeared after this episode.

... there was this burst of light. It was the brightest thing I had ever witnessed, but it wasn't blinding.[263]

"I came out of this tunnel into a realm of soft, brilliant love and light. It surrounded me and seemed to soak through into my very being.[264]"

"It was just there. I didn't move toward it. It didn't move toward me. It was just like someone had switched a light on right in front of me. It was a brilliant light, more like a sheet of light, than a single point.[265]"

Both in NDEs and out of them, The Light seems to appear along with bliss. The Light can also appear in other circumstances. The spiritual teacher, Adi Da, once known as Franklin Jones, and at different times in his career also known as 'Da Free John' and 'Ruchira Avatar Adi Da Samraj' wrote:

> From my earliest experience of life, I have enjoyed a condition that, as a child I called 'The Bright' ... Even as a baby I remember crawling around inquisitively with a boundless feeling of joy, light, and freedom...[266]

It may be that Adi Da, as his disciples know him, had an NDE at birth. He wrote that he could recall his birth, and that his own umbilical cord nearly strangled him. It's possible that this exercised NDE pathways and gave his brain easy access to death-process states for the rest of his life. If so, he would seem to have been all but born enlightened. His fascinating autobiography, 'The Knee of Listening',[267] has a detailed account of 'The Light' as an enduring feature of his life. This author, at least, has no trouble accepting that Adi Da is genuinely enlightened[268].

The Light seems to be an NDE phase all by itself, but it doesn't stop when the next phase begins. In fact, none of the NDE's phases end abruptly. Rather, there is usually a smooth transition from one phase to the next, and the themes of one phase can persist into the next one. Sometimes beings form out of The Light, bringing us to the next common phase in Western NDEs.

In The Company of the Being of Light

In the West, people commonly have an experience of Heaven[269], or (something like it) after "entering the light". They typically meet the *Being of Light* there, after the meeting with dead friends and relatives. (These meetings don't happen in all NDEs, but they never seem to happen after the meeting with the Being of Light). There are very few (if any) visions of a God-like, dignified person sitting on a marble throne at the center of heaven. Most often, there's nothing but bliss and a blast of light, revealing God in His radiant, resplendent, and glorious form. God, and only God, can be so effulgent. The experience of being with God goes beyond anything words can express. His glory, divine light, innate majesty, power, and the sight of Him in the center of heaven are indescribable. To be in this realm, it seems, is pure bliss. The experience of being close to God is ecstatic. In Christian and Jewish scriptures[270], the rapture of heaven emanates from His presence.

Several kinds of beings emerge from The Light. Often, they're people who've died, including beloved friends, relatives (even celebrities or strangers), or the 'Being of Light'.

> "Don found himself standing in front of a divine portal, surrounded by familiar faces. "I did not see a single person that I did not know," he says. "They were relatives, they were friends that died in high school, they were teachers - they were people I had seen and known all my life who had gone to glory (died – author). They were smiling; they were embracing me; they were welcoming me' they were in the process of taking me through the gate of heaven.[271]"

Sometimes the Being of Light is replaced by an angel or group of angels, but most often, people feel they're in the company of God. There are even reports of living people appearing in NDEs[272]. I know a priest who appeared to a woman during her NDE, and said that he has no idea what he was doing when it happened. He certainly wasn't aware of any "psychic connection" between himself and the NDEer, either at the time of their NDE, or at any other time. In an informal interview, the man said "for all I know, I was eating pizza at the time". However, in most cases, the people who are seen in The Light will have died before the person had their NDE. Here are two examples of the more common meetings that happen in *The Light*.

> "I was met at the end of the tunnel by a bunch of people. They were all glowing from the inside like lanterns. The whole place was glowing in the same way, like everything in it was filled with light.[273]"
>
> "I caught sight of Elvis. He was in this place of an intense light. He just came over to me and took my hand, and said, 'Hi Bev, do you remember me?'"[274]
>
> "In 1992, Matthew B. had the shock of his life. "I just felt something hot pierce in the back of my head and I was in a black cell," Matthew said. "It was void of all things good and went forever in all directions; then I saw a finger coming toward me and then a hand; it looked ancient like it was created before time. Then I heard, "It's not your time." ... "The hand that came toward me brought warmth and brilliant white light and I was being pulled upward...[275]"

Here, only the being of light's hand appears, yet still it came with the same brilliant white light. Images of hands are not uncommon in altered-states experiences. This may be because of the extensive representation for our hands in the surface of the brain. This one is from Melville's *Moby Dick*.

> "At last I must have fallen into a troubled nightmare of a doze; and slowly waking from it--half steeped in dreams--I opened my eyes, and the before sun-lit room was now wrapped in outer darkness. Instantly I felt a shock running through my entire frame; nothing was to be seen, and nothing was to be heard; but a supernatural hand seemed placed in mine. My arm hung

over the counterpane, and the nameless, unimaginable, silent form or phantom, to which the hand belonged, seemed closely seated by my bed-side. For what seemed ages piled on ages, I lay there, frozen with the most awful fears, not daring to drag away my hand; yet ever thinking that if I could but stir it one single inch, the horrid spell would be broken. I knew not how this consciousness at last glided away from me; but waking in the morning, I shudderingly remembered it all, and for days and weeks and months afterwards I lost myself in confounding attempts to explain the mystery. Nay, to this very hour, I often puzzle myself with it."

I'd like to thank Ken Vincent, author of "Visions of God from the Near-Death Experience". It's an excellent collection of simple reports of meetings with the Being of Light. Vincent's scholarship has been a great help in preparing this book.

"There was a person radiating a white light so bright I couldn't make out a body, but saw a face, also radiating very white light...[276]"

"I would say it was Jesus Christ; I mean it looked like him. He was dressed in a robe that was robin's egg blue, and a long flowing robe that wrapped around him, and he had this staff that was a bright gold. It must have been ten feet high.[277]"

"It was white, yet golden. For all its brilliance, it didn't hurt to look at it at all. It was pure, strong. It was truth, justice. It was Jesus. I knew this was Jesus the same way I knew I was dead... I saw all things. I was all things. But not me; Jesus had this. And as long as I was 'in him' and He was 'in me' I had this power, this glory (for lack of a better word).[278]"

"I was listening to a choir of angels singing. Angels were totally outside my reality at the time, yet somehow I knew these beautiful beings to be angelic. They sang the most extraordinary music I have ever heard. They were identical, each equally beautiful. When their song was over, one of their number came forward to greet me. She was exquisite, and I was mightily attracted, but then I realized my admiration could only be expressed in a wholly nonphysical manner, as to a little child. I was embarrassed by my error, but it did not matter. All was forgiven in this wonderful place."[279]

To be with the *Being of Light* creates a different mood from *The Light*. While The Light seems to appear with bliss, joy and ecstasy, the *Being of Light* brings love, acceptance and forgiveness. The man's attraction wasn't going to work out in a realm without bodies, but he saw that all was forgiven. He accepted himself without shame, despite his flaws. The meeting with the being of light makes one's shortcomings seem trivial, the way we look at children's misbehavior. This willingness to look at one's own mistakes, failings and flaws helps people in the Life Review, when people confront the bad behavior of a lifetime.

The Being of Light appears in the works of Carlos Castaneda[280] as "The Mold of Man", where it's a sort of template or mold, used to cast or outline normal human consciousness. In Castaneda's story, his teacher, Don Juan, could hit him on certain parts of his body and send him into other states of consciousness. Don Juan's explanation was that the blows weren't to Castaneda's body, but rather to his luminous being, which Don Juan, being a seer, could perceive and manipulate.

"He hit me on my right side, between my hipbone and my rib cage. That blow sent me soaring into a radiant light, into a diaphanous source of the most peaceful and exquisite beatitude. That light was a haven, an oasis in the blackness around me (note the dual themes of blackness and light, which also occur in the transition from The Void or The Tunnel and "Into the Light").

From my subjective point of view, I saw that light for an immeasurable length of time. The splendor of the sight was beyond anything I can say, and yet I could not figure out what it was that made it so beautiful. Then the idea came to me that its beauty grew out of a sense of harmony, a sense of peace and rest, of having arrived, of being safe at long last. *(The same sentiment appears in many NDEs – Author.)*

I felt myself inhaling and exhaling in quietude and relief. What a gorgeous sense of plenitude! I knew beyond a shadow of doubt that I had come face to face with God, the source of everything. And I knew that God loved me. God was love and forgiveness. The light bathed me, and I felt clean, delivered. I wept uncontrollably, mainly for myself. The sight of that resplendent light made me feel unworthy, villainous...

...As I gazed into the light with all the passion I was capable of, the light seemed to condense and I saw a man. A shiny man that exuded charisma, love, understanding, sincerity, and truth. A man that was the sum total of all that is good.

The fervor I felt on seeing that man was well beyond anything I had ever felt in my life. I did fall on my knees. I wanted to worship God personified, but Don Juan intervened and whacked me on my left upper chest, close to my clavicle, and I lost sight of God."

The Life Review

When Thais and Indians see the souls of the dead being tortured in hell, it's immediately apparent that they are in *the realm of the dead*; in the underworld; in the place where the dead go. In Thai reports, people saw others being tortured, but no one was tortured during their own NDEs.

A book[281] about European medieval NDEs book found the same thing. It supports the idea that the point of these tortures is not to punish sins; it's to tell you that you're now in the realm of the dead. Once you know you've 'moved on', and are now in Hades, it's possible to put the death-process experiences that come after in their proper context. One can surrender and accept what you learn from God, Yama, an Angel or perhaps a spirit who appears as the *Being of Light*. The apparent infallibility of the death-process makes it impossible to resist its messages.

There is a set of beliefs found all through Asia and the West, probably with antecedents in Dynastic Egypt. In this mythology, death begins with a messenger from the underworld who tells you you're dead, and then travels with you to the center of the realm of the dead, allowing you see the souls of others as you go. After that, you are judged by a fair but stern authority that rewards your good actions, and punishes your bad ones. If you're 'good', higher knowledge is given to you if you ask for it, sometimes even if you're only 'good at heart' without really having lived a virtuous life. The Epic of Gilgamesh tells of a nightmare of being snatched by a terrible creature with eagle claws (a harbinger?) and cast away to the underworld of death.

These episodes make up a story told with many variations in many lands.

Thai Near-Death experiences reflect beliefs found in a 12th century text, written by a Thai monk, Prah Malaya. It's uncertain whether he was born in Thailand, but his book is still in print there today. In this tradition, the underworld has a center, where Yama, who is not only the

Lord of Death, but also the ruler of hell, sits at his desk. Yama has power over the souls that stand before him. The people standing before Yama are always shown trembling with fear, unless they are monks or nuns.

Malaya's visions, like Dante's, were of heaven and hell. Heaven was paradise and hell was a place of torment, with different kinds of tortures for different kinds of sins. Drinkers suffered the hell of having to drink molten lead. Liars have their tongues torn out, and there is the hell of being chopped to pieces for those who butcher animals or kill people violently. In this vision, it's pretty easy to see that instead of being the place of maximum ecstasy, it's a place of maximum fear. In Thai tradition, judgment is based on where Yama's scales, which show if you have more Merit or Sin.

The judgment that follows this weighing of virtue against sins could mean being assigned to torture or receiving one's next (sometimes unfortunate) incarnation. Those who were very virtuous during their lives may even be allowed some time in heaven.

Here we see people standing before the imposing Yama, seated on his throne[282], supported on a dais of skulls, with one of his servants nearby, ready to read from The Book of Karma. Interestingly, only 1 of the 11 NDEs collected by this author in Thailand contained any reference to the Buddha, the primary deity[283] in the Thai religion.

The Yamatoot looked up at the sky and pointed. "That big star," he said, "is the Lord Buddha, and all the little stars are the other enlightened ones; those who have followed the Dharma to the end. I'm afraid you won't be able to see the Buddha in any other form. You are not pure enough…[284]"

Yama's judgment, based on the content of the Book of Karma, appears to be a manifestation of what NDE researchers have called the *Life Review*, the next phase in the death-process. In Western culture, the Life Review sometimes just appears for person undergoing it, without a Being of Light[285] there to guide people.

Yama giving orders to a Yamatoot[286]

In contrast to the Life Review in the West, where people see their own behavior, in Southeast Asia and India, others review your life for you, and judge your behavior as recorded in the *Book of Karma*.

The Book of Karma has records of your deeds, which Yama's 'accountants'[287] examine. If the person's name is not there, Yama tells the Yamatoot he's brought the wrong person, and orders them returned to the world. If the person's name appears in the Book, their sins are read out to them. Usually, the person's life is not reviewed in its entirety. It's often just a single episode, possibly representing the person's most salient sinful behavior pattern. If they are going to be condemned to the hell of being cut to pieces, then they only see the sins that call for that particular hell, even though they may have many other transgressions. Of course, no one in the collection of Thai NDEs was tortured – they were all ordered to return to life.

The earliest afterlife mythology in the Hindu and Buddhist worlds is The *Garuda Purana*, which tells about what follows the moment of death[288]. The *Shiva Puranas* also tell a similar story. It describes multiple hells where people are tortured for their sins, as well as the rebirths that follow from particular actions.

"Some of the sinful are cut with saws, like firewood, and others are thrown flat on the ground and chopped to pieces with axes. Some, their bodies half-buried in a pit, are pierced in the head with arrows. Others, fixed in the middle of a machine, are squeezed like sugar cane." (Garuda Purana)

In either case, whether it's the Western 'life flashing before one's eyes' or the Eastern Book of Karma, your life is reviewed. The difference in the kinds of two Life Reviews may reflect an important cultural difference. In the West, we now have a greater amount of autonomy in our own lives. During the past two or three generations, we westerners have become accustomed to making our own choices, and "doing our own thing", whatever that may be.

The slogan "live your dreams" has come to express the personal philosophy of many Westerners, whereas in much of Asia, things are still quite traditional. There, you don't live your dream. If you're a man, you live your father's occupation. Women follow in their mother's occupation, which is almost invariably that of mother and housewife and sometimes an unskilled laborer. Although it's officially banned, the caste system still has a very strong influence on what people expect from life. In Southeast Asia, there may be a little less pressure to follow your parent's footsteps, but parents remain close to the center of nearly everyone's social life, especially in the working classes[289].

In cultures where people are not accustomed to making their own life choices, people are told what their next existence will be like. This theme is less common in cultures where people are used to making their own choices (and where not everyone believes in reincarnation). In Asia, the person is told they must return to life, and that they were only brought to the underworld because of a clerical error. They weren't supposed to be in the underworld, because they weren't supposed to die. The person is given have no choice in the matter. Perhaps a lifetime of obeying instructions and following religious laws creates a death-process where taking orders seems natural.

In the West, it's somewhat different. NDEers are told, 'It's not your time.' They are advised to return to the land of the living. Sometimes

Westerners even argue with the being(s) who tell them that their time hasn't come. They want to stay in the place they find themselves after death and seem to feel they should have a choice in the matter. In Southeast Asia, no one asks to stay. Of course, Eastern NDEs are often fearful, so many wouldn't want to stay even if they could.

During the Life Review, the person reviews their actions during their lives. It involves more than just self-acceptance or abandoning denial. It includes looking directly at one's flaws. In some cases, the person accepts their failings through a sense of total forgiveness. In others, they accept their shortcomings because they feel so completely shattered when they confront them that any defense seems futile. In either case, they're prepared to review their lives and accept what they see.

The Life Review can take many forms, and it usually comes during or after the meeting with the *Being of Light*. In Western NDEs, a person will sometimes see their life re-played at high speed, or they may literally re-experience their lives in just a few seconds. It's often mentioned in books and journal articles on NDEs, but the person often says little more than "I saw my whole life pass before my eyes".

> "In a moment, in the twinkling of an eye, every act, every design of her past life, lived again, arraying themselves not as a succession, but as parts of a coexistence[290].

Like the other phases in NDEs, this simple theme has many variations. A person can also have a Life Review where they experience events in their lives from the perspective of other people, like this one by Dannion Brinkley.

> "The being of light engulfed me, and as it did I began to experience my whole life, feeling and seeing everything that had ever happened to me. It was as though it burst, and every memory stored in my brain flowed out. ... from Fifth to Twelfth Grade, I estimate that I had at least six thousand fistfights. Now, as I

reviewed my life in the bosom of the being (of Light),
I relived each one of those altercations, but with one
major difference: I was the receiver".[291]

Brinkley spent time as a military assassin during the war in Vietnam.
When his Life Review reached the point where it examined his wartime
experiences, he experienced a killing from the perspective of a North
Vietnamese Colonel he had shot.

> "I didn't feel the pain that he must have felt. Instead,
> I felt his confusion at having his head blown off, and
> sadness as he left his body, and realized he would never
> go home again. Then I felt the rest of the chain reaction
> the sad feelings of his family when they realized they
> would be without their provider. I relived all of my kills
> in just this fashion. I saw myself make the kill, and then
> I felt the horrible results."[292]

Other life reviews focus on positive actions, as in this example:

> "That was when the life review began. It was as
> though she'd suddenly stepped into an enormous movie
> screen on which scenes from her life were playing in
> three dimensions. She saw good things she had done
> and bad things, people she'd hurt and people she'd
> helped. Suddenly she was back in the parking lot ...
> It was night, the store was closing and she noticed a
> woman having trouble starting her car, the battery had
> died. Kathy watched herself give the woman a jump-
> start. Then, she saw something that hadn't happened,
> but would have had she not intervened. Kathy watched
> a man come up and approach the woman stranded in the
> parking lot with a car that wouldn't start. He threatened
> her and took her purse."[293]

I once met an NDEer whose Life review consisted of nothing but the good actions in his life. He said it was a very positive experience, and that he understood that each act of kindness ripples and reverberates outward, affecting lots of people.

In Thailand, life reviews tend to focus either on a few incidents in the person's life, perhaps typifying behavior patterns. Accounts of NDEs from Thailand include standing before Yama seated at his desk, while a clerk reads from the Book of Karma.

> I was taken to the house of Yama, the Lord of the Dead. Yama told me that I had committed many sins, especially in having butchered a number of chickens. I denied it. I said that I had not done that, not even once. Yama was surprised, and asked his records keeper. 'How old is he?' 'Thirteen years, Lord', came the answer. 'What's his name?' My name was read out. Yama said, 'You've taken the wrong man. Take him back. Quickly. You've made a mistake.'[294]

Here's another, much more modern, life review:

> Then I was instantly zapped to a domed room with square screens up and down the walls, on the ceiling – hundreds of television screens. On each screen was a home movie of one event in my life. The good, the bad, the secret, the ugly, the special. Everything was going on at once; nothing was chronological. All was silent. When you looked at one screen, and focused in, you could hear what was there. Not only words, but your thoughts, your feelings, everything; and when you look at the other people or animals, you can hear their thoughts, their feelings, too. You make the connection between these and the events that ensued. You are filled with, not guilt, but a strong sense of responsibility.[295]

In some cases, no actual events are seen in the Life Review. According to one NDE researcher[296], Life Reviews can take a symbolic form (especially for hunting and gathering societies), so that the person may see symbols instead of literal re-plays of events in their lives.

In the Life Review, we remember things involuntarily – even against our will. The experience of going through a Life Review and being revived afterwards can be shattering. An NDE can be so dramatic that it can change the brain, leaving people with dramatically different personalities and cognitive skills afterwards. The Life Review goes further than this. It forces people to look at their behavior, and when they come back from the experience, they often *want* to change it. They look at their lives and more often than not, they're unhappy with what they see. This doesn't always happen, but there are enough reports like this to show that the experience of examining one's life without any psychological defense mechanisms can be profound.

SIX – The Transcendent Experience.

The next stage of the death-process is the *Transcendent Experience*. It can take a number of forms. The most common in Asia seems to be a tour of heaven, and in the West, its seeing life's secrets revealed. In Gustav Dore's version of the Transcendent Experience[297] as Dante described in the *Paradiso*, he is standing before heaven, looking into hosts of harmoniously singing angels. The theme of being shown otherworldly mysteries looms large here.

Prah Malaya, who had visions of hell, also had a tour of *Indraloka*, the heaven of Indra. He found several heavens, each one arranged on top of the other. The highest is the realm of the Buddhas.

He also had a vision of heaven set in the future; the Time of Sri Arya[298]. If one's actions on the earth are virtuous enough, it's possible to reincarnate in the time of Sri Arya. Sri means 'the honored', and Arya means 'the noble' or 'the distinguished'. In the time of Sri Arya, there are Mani (wish-fulfilling) trees, whose branches offer a harvest of precious stones. There is no conflict, hatred, anger, envy or malice. Every desire is met, so no one is poor. Everyone is healthy. In other words, the 'time of Sri Arya' is heaven.

There are even romantic relationships, and everyone is happy all the time. Although the time of Sri Arya is well-known known in the folklore and popular culture of Thailand, it may or may not have appeared in the 11 Thai NDEs. Graphic images of this messianic kingdom could easily create expectations about what heaven would look like.

Most of the Thai Transcendent Experiences that have been translated into English consist of being in heaven and talking with a god – either Indra, or Brahma. Each has their own level of heaven. The World of Indra is 'Indraloka'[299], and the World of Brahma is 'Brahmaloka'.

In these heavens, people receive teachings from the gods, composed entirely of Buddhist admonitions.

In the West, the Transcendent Experience is usually different. People don't hear lectures from spiritually superior beings. Westerners usually experience access to something we can call "the Mysteries of Existence', where they ask their own questions, and receive the answers they seek. There may be a revelation or a trip to the Akashic Records[300] where people find they only have to think of something and instantly, they feel they know everything about it.

> "Before this happened I … had these millions of questions to ask and in an instant they were all answered. The meaning of life and all … and then I got this instantaneous … download that said 'Okay, if that's what's causing you to behave this way, here, bang, take this and now you don't have to do this' … I just didn't have those questions anymore. They were just gone. They were answered. I can't tell you the meaning of life. … then this presence told me very directly that 'life is not that serious'. It's not about that. Chill out.[301]"
>
> "This corridor was alive – it was a living room. It had walls that went up about ten feet and then there were upper wall panels that leaned in toward us. These panels seemed to be beaming down onto me. As I went through, all this knowledge was coming to me. Everything that was known to mankind was in these archives, and it was coming down into my mind. By the time I got to the end, I felt I knew everything. But now I can't remember it![302]"

In one reported Transcendent Experience, a man asked questions and immediately saw a geometric figure, whose shape would seem to answer his questions. Others have reported Transcendent Experiences consisting of discussions held with a being, or a council[303]. They talked about the life they had just lived, and even planned their next rebirth.

"It was absolute, total knowledge. I had direct communication with that light in a telepathic way. I had the opportunity to ask questions, and the absolute unequivocal answer would be emanated to me instantly... Needless to say, I had many questions answered, and many pieces of information given to me, some of them were very personal, some were religiously oriented. One of the religious questions was with regard to an afterlife, and this was definitely answered through the experience itself. There was absolutely no question in my mind that the light was the answer. The atmosphere, the energy was total knowledge, total pure love...[304]"

"There was a moment in this thing – well, there isn't any way to describe it – but it was like I knew all things.... For a moment, there, it was like communication wasn't necessary. I thought whatever I wanted to know could be known.[305]"

Other Transcendent Experiences happen in heaven. One of the more engaging stories like this come from a translation of a Thai NDE report.

"I found myself in another place, which was very pleasant. The weather was nice; I was no longer hungry. I saw a garden with trees all in rows. It was very beautiful, like the garden of a king or a millionaire. As I walked into the garden, I smelled some flowers. They were so very fragrant, with a scent I had never known before. Next, I saw some angels, both male and female. They glided through the air. They were dressed beautifully, and wore exquisite jewelry. Some had flowers in their hair.

I kept walking, and saw a pavilion with a roof like that of a palace. There was an angelic man sitting inside. His body was surrounded by a green halo. I approached the angel, sat down and made obeisance. I asked, 'Who are you? Where am I?' He answered, 'I am the lord of the angels, and this is the angelic world'. I then recognized that this was none other than Indra, the King of Heaven.

He said to me 'When you go back to your world, you should teach your fellow men not to commit sins, as it causes them to go to hell. If they do good, and behave in a moral manner, they will be reborn in my heaven. I will show you the mercy of teaching you the Dharma; The sacred law.'

He imparted this knowledge by opening my wisdom eye. I then saw all the truths of the universe. The future, the past, and the present. After six earthly days, Indra told me that he would take me to another level of heaven, The World of Brahma.

I saw Brahma, the creator of the universe. His face was similar to Indra's with a fresh, clean look about it that indicated mercy, compassion, lovingkindness, and equanimity (The Buddhist quadrivium of virtue). He had a golden halo. Brahma explained that the angels in his level of heaven were all on their way to take new births in the ordinary world. Therefore, there were many empty houses. He was waiting for those who had created a lot of merit during their lives to take rebirth there, but they were very few. Those who were there had mostly been monks who had been strict in their observance of the monastic rules.[306]"

Another person explained his experience as being like a download of information from a computer.

"I had these millions of questions to ask, and in an instant they were all literally answered. The meaning of life and all ... Before this happened I had all these burning questions and it's like someone said, 'Oh, I can handle that'. That was the sense of it by God, but not the words. And then I got this instantaneous, the best I can tell you, that I got this download that said, 'Okay, if that's what's causing you to behave this way, here, pain, take this and now you don't have to do this.

The flow of information continued. Immediately ... everything I was doing before ceased. I just didn't have those questions anymore. They were just gone. They were answered. I can't tell you the meaning of life ... it wasn't religious. I didn't need any religious people. I couldn't tell you that I saw angels or anything like that. It was like I met my uncle, who said, 'Okay ... these are the answers.[307]"

Other episodes include being in a vast library with cosmic information instantly appearing, giving an immediate understanding of everything. Others have experienced the 'Akashic Records', which Theosophists describe as the repository of all knowledge.

Of course, we don't take the insights and secret knowledge granted during such an experience as the truth, but rather as explanations that satisfy ("feel right") to the individual.

Seven - The point of no Return.

The final stage in NDEs has been called The *Point of No Return*. In this phase, a person comes to the realization that they must return to their body. They become aware that they won't be able to return at all unless they return immediately. In some instances, it comes like an understanding from within. In others, it's a voice from outside one's self. It could even take a more symbolic form, such as the sudden end of a path they were walking, or coming to a closed door. No matter what form it takes, the person somehow realizes that they aren't going any further and the experience is over.

This is last phase in NDEs. In one way or another, the person is told that it's over, and they must return to life, now or never. For some it's a portal, a gate, a wall of mist or a barrier.

> One NDEer "… was instructed by a deceased grandmother not to cross a line in front of her. The OBEer did cross the line, at which point the grandmother said 'I told you not to cross the line.' The older woman 'got right in [her] face' and said, 'You are to go back now!" [308]
>
> From a Thai NDE: "You have been separated from your body for 7 days", said Brahma. "If you don't return soon, you will not be able to.[309]"

It seems that there comes a point when the death process is over. The person, in a frame of mind where they're ready to understand much more than they could when they were alive, now "knows" that the experience can go no further.

Variation in NDES

Not all NDEs are the same. There are "typical" NDEs in both the East and the West, but very few match them exactly. The death process can be interrupted when the person is resuscitated, preventing them from reaching the later stages. Reports from the later phases are far less common than reports from the earlier ones. Some NDEs may skip a phase or two, suggesting that the message conveyed by the missed phase was clear already, and wasn't needed to carry the process from one phase (or state of consciousness) to the next.

In one study[310], the Life Review was more common in the NDEs of people who died suddenly, than for those who had time to anticipate their deaths. Perhaps this is because those people, aware of their imminent death, had reviewed their lives while they were dying, making this phase superfluous.

Not all OBEs are autoscopic. Some people don't experience either the Tunnel or the Void. Each phase can unfold with tremendous variety. In one NDE[311], the person did a memory exercise throughout their entire experience, which activated the part of the brain most involved with memory functions. His NDE had no other beings in it. There were no dead friends and/or relatives and no 'being of light'.

Some NDEers (those who have had NDEs) meet God face to face, and feel filled with bliss, joy, and acceptance as well as an awareness of their vulnerability, even as they felt very safe. They felt everything their religions led them to expect when they were in God's presence. Others were surrounded with light, entered into a state of ecstasy, maybe heard a voice or felt His presence and interpreted the experience as being God, without ever actually having seen Him. Some find themselves in the company of angels instead of God during the phase where He usually appears. Angels can act as God's messengers, just as Yamatoots can act on Yama's behalf.

As we saw before, the Life Review can take many forms. It can involve re-experiencing one's whole life in just a few seconds, or seeing one's life flash before one's eyes. In a few cases, the review has no personal memories that all, but shows symbolic imagery instead. Some have experienced how the impact of their actions affected others. Sometimes, those who hurt people will undergo the review with the feelings of fear and the horror of violence felt by their victims.

There are large enough numbers of published NDEs gathered in the West that researchers can investigate them using statistical methods. However, the number of NDE reports from other cultures remains small. In the 12th century, there was a cultural transmission from India to Thailand, so they share many ideas in common, including those about death. The common beliefs about the afterlife in Thailand today were probably imported from India[312], about 800 years ago. The collection of NDEs from Thailand, that we refer to so often, consists of only 11 cases. However, the similarity within this collection allows us to us make generalizations. The cultures of Japan, China, India, and Indonesia also preserve the belief in an underworld where one goes at death, and these include Lord Yama. They appear to constitute an NDE cultural group. If so, then a theme that appears in many NDEs in any one of these cultures may commonly appear in all of them, but may not appear in NDEs from the West. Further research will tell. The NDEs of hunting and gathering societies may constitute another cultural group, and another exists in sub-Saharan Africa.

At one time in human history, every major culture was united by its religion. Today, in the West, we find a very wide variety of religions. Many, perhaps most, people there are now unwilling to accept the teachings of their own religions as literal truth. This means that, whereas once almost everyone had the same expectations about what death would be like, today in the West, many people simply don't know what to expect. This may explain why imagery drawn from religion doesn't dominate the death-process in the West. The images and phenomena of NDEs in the West seem to reflect the 'raw' activation of primary brain structures. It's as though the pathways driving each phase of the process are activated without any culturally derived expectation, and can yield NDEs with far less complicated images than those from people in cultures where religious belief is still strong. Of course, this is a generalization, but any general theory about any aspect of human behavior, including death and dying, will involve generalizations.

Each instance of the death process is as unique as any fingerprint. No two are ever alike. The hypothesis here is that the death process involves the activation of deep brain parts in different combinations, so that death unfolds in a certain pattern, with each phase preparing each person for the next one. Each phase reflects a "core" state of consciousness, and the different instances of each of these states can create a wide range of specific experiences (phenomena, images, or presences). The states of consciousness in each phase may be the same, but those states can be expressed through a wide range of phenomena.

There are seven commonly recognized phases to NDEs.

1) OBE or harbinger of death
2) The Tunnel, the Void, or landscape
3) The Light (including meeting dead friends and relatives or seeing hell)
4) The Being of Light (or the wrathful Yama)

5) The Life Review
6) The Transcendent Experience
7) The Point of No Return

Not all of the episodes in NDEs are equally common. The early stages (OBEs, tunnels and light) are reported much more often. The process can be interrupted, if the person returns to life. In such cases, only a few of them will be in the person's NDE.

There is a great deal more variation in NDEs and the human death-process than this chapter has shown you, though it's enough to make the point that the death-process follows the same sequence in all cultures, even though it can be expressed differently; 'translated' into each person's own language of symbol, myth, religion, and legend. Usually, but not always, these will come from the person's culture, which usually, but not always, comes from its religion.

In our next chapter, we'll look at the areas of the brain supporting each of the stages of the death-process, and start using what we learned about a few brain parts earlier in this book.

CHAPTER 7

The Neural Bases for the Phases of Near-Death Experiences

N ow we'll look at examples of NDE phenomena coming from people with Temporal Lobe Epilepsy, receiving electrical brain stimulation, and a few other contexts. There are many scientists who believe that spiritual experiences should be explained as examples of Temporal Lobe Seizures[313], and by extension, that religious and mystic experiences cannot happen for people with healthy brains. Others explain them as pathological disturbances deep in the temporal lobes (TL)[314],[315] or as delusional subconscious attempts to find a father or mother figure. All these positions imply that people who have religious or spiritual experiences "aren't quite right in the head".

I believe that spiritual experiences are not epilepsy, and that NDEs are not an epileptic phenomenon. Rather, a seizure can follow any pathways, including the ones that support the death process. If a seizure includes pathways that support spiritual (NDE or death-process) experiences, then epilepsy can them out into the open. Epilepsy is one of nature's ways of burrowing into otherwise inaccessible brain areas and showing us the phenomena they can create. Whether you hear a note from a piano during a piece of music, or when a cat walks across the keys, the source of the sound will be the same. Just as the notes are part of the music, the pathways of spiritual experience are part of our evolutionary heritage. Like the cat that can step on any note, a seizure can 'step on' any pathway, getting them excited, so that the person experiences the phenomena they support, however disjointed or subtle they might be. Also, just as a cat can 'play' a sequence of notes that would never appear in any but the most abstract modernist music, a seizure can elicit experiences that have no natural context, creating moments so strange that nothing in life could ever remind you of them.

Temporal lobe seizures, also called *complex partial seizures*, don't spread throughout the entire brain. They remain in the temporal lobes, its most sensitive area. If the seizure has moderate intensity, it remains there, and doesn't move out to 'recruit' the rest of the brain. Temporal Lobe seizures don't cause convulsions. Among other things[316], they create altered states of consciousness, and these can unfold into the 'spiritual phenomena of Temporal lobe epilepsy'. Negative TL seizures are much more common than uplifting, spiritual ones, but the ecstatic ones show the temporal lobe's involvement in spiritual experiences.

This book proposes that spiritual and mystic experiences represent activity in the pathways that support the death-process, happening while we're still alive. Different kinds of mystic experiences are based on excitement in the separate neural foundations of the various phases in the death-process. Each phase is supported by different patterns of activity in the limbic system, and so we should look at them again, one at a time, this time to see which brain parts support which kinds of experiences.

One of our postulates is that NDEs make the death-process explicit. To put it another way, NDEs are not brain accidents or malfunctions. They reflect what it's actually like to die. They are the brain's organic, normal, and adaptive response to death. Whenever we speak of NDEs, the reader can substitute the phrase "death-process". The reader should understand that we equate the two, even though some NDE researchers will not agree. A common mechanism underlies the subjective experience of death in all humans. When taken together (and they happen with an almost bewildering variety), they express the range of possible death experiences.

The experiences fall into certain patterns. Near-Death Experiences, and so the death process, is not just a single episode. It has phases. In Western countries, the most common first phase of the death-process is the Out-Of-Body Experience (OBE).

Two emotions are most likely to appear when one feels death is approaching. Both appear through activation of the right hemisphere. One is fear, like the fear you'd feel when standing in the street, with a bus speeding towards you, when there's no way to avoid it, or the fear you'd be in if you fell off a mountain, but hadn't hit the ground yet – or the fear you'd feel if the grim reaper (or a Yamatoot) approached you in your kitchen.

When that happens, you know, without any doubt, that you are going to die. The emotion would be fear, if not mind-numbing terror. All your thoughts would be limited to how to try and escape your helplessness, and escape death. That is, of course, if you could think in words at all. The sense of impending doom that appears when death is moving towards us at high speed can stop to all verbal thoughts.

The other likely emotion is a calm state of surrender and acceptance. It's much more common in people who know well in advance that they're going to die. They could be in the final stages of an illness, lying in a hospital Intensive Care Unit. They've had time to reflect on their lives, and to engage the inevitability of their death. They begin to make peace with it, and often find a deep contentment as they await its arrival. Some go into *pre-mortem* altered states[317], where they might meet angels, "see the light" or encounter people they know who've died. They may even have out of body experiences, and there are reports of telepathic and clairvoyant perceptions happening to those in the final days and hours of life.

There comes a moment, which Elizabeth Kubler-Ross[318] calls 'acceptance'. The person accepts the inevitable, and from then on, they're at peace with it. Many people told Dr. Kubler-Ross, saying things like, "I finally understood something. I don't want my life to end, but the truth is that I'm dying and somehow it's okay." When the family visits the dying person, they find that instead of 'raging against the dying of the light', they've relaxed into its inevitability. They've begun to find something sacred in the promise of 'moving on'. Some even begin to look forward to it.

Once I had a job in an old-age home working around people who were extremely close to death. Their move into the home was the last life change they would experience. The inevitability of death was in the mind of each person, and I saw them many times while they were in the throes of coping with it.

One old man had days when he would jump out of his bed every few minutes in a state of terror, almost at a complete loss for words. I don't know where the words he found came from, but he would say, "Mommy, Mommy, put me to bed. Put me to bed, Mommy". I would take him gently by the arm, and lead him back to his bed, where he would lie down quietly while I rearranged his blankets, and then say, "Thank you, Mom". It reminded me of the stories of dying soldiers who call for their mothers in their last moments. Once, in one of his lucid moments, I asked him what he was afraid of, and he said it was dying. He couldn't keep it out of his mind, and it scared him.

Another patient sat in a wheelchair in her room all day, always in the same posture, with her hands folded, and one of the most serene expressions I've ever seen. My job included mopping the floor of every room, everyday. When I got to her door, I would have to stop and pause for a few seconds, and take a breath before going in. I paused, not because I might disturb her calm, but because I wanted to arrange my thoughts, and take in her serenity for myself. She was very old, and the only thing she had to look forward to was dying. It didn't seem to be a problem, though.

One day I spoke to her about it. "I come in your room every day, and I always find you in the same place, sitting in exactly the same way. May I ask what you're feeling?" A smile came over her face as she said, "Just calm. Just peaceful." I felt compelled to ask, "All the time?" She answered. "Yes. Sometimes they give me food I don't like, and that bothers me a little. Besides that, I'm just calm." "All the time?" I asked. Her answer was short and simple. "Yes, all the time."

States of relaxation, calm and acceptance depend primarily on the brain's right hemisphere. It's the main support for things like meditation, trance, and hypnosis. Terror comes from the right hemisphere as well, but from a different area. Fear and terror come from the right amygdala[319]. Calmness and acceptance are more suggestive of right hippocampal function[320]. In fact, the two structures are interconnected. The amygdala adjusts our emotions, and the hippocampus modulates cognition; thought. The strong interconnection between the two structures gives our thoughts and emotions some control over one another – a mechanism that breaks down in many psychological disorders.

Each phase of NDEs reflects the activation of certain brain parts, though we expect them to be in and through unusual pathways[321]. The first phase of the NDEs, in my view, is in the emotions we feel when death is approaching, and both fear and serenity are located in the right hemisphere. Most NDE researchers consider the next phase we'll discuss (OBEs, etc.) to be the first one.

The death-process involves specific neural events that would usually happen only at the time of death. These would involve ordinary brain parts, although perhaps being activated in an unusual sequence, or with unusual intensity, or using rarely-accessed pathways at the time of death. There are hundreds of parts in the brain. The potential connections between the cells that make them up can number in the trillions. One would expect only a few of these to act in support of the death-process. The rest serve much more ordinary functions. These brain parts do ordinary things when they're activated in ordinary ways and extraordinary things when they're activated in extraordinary ways. There is a brain process called "dynamic stabilization[322]" in which rarely-used pathways are activated to ensure that they don't atrophy. It's been suggested that they are the source for some unusual dream experiences, like dreams of flying. This same mechanism might keep the death-process pathways active and available. If the dream happens in the middle of the night, it's less likely to be remembered, and could keep our death-process pathways ready without us knowing anything about it.

Altered states of consciousness are triggered by unusual circumstances, like seizures, drugs, head injuries, going without food or water, etc., and these unfold into individual experiences. Two people in similar states of consciousness can have very different experiences. Each phase of the death-process appears to differ widely according to religion, age, and other factors, but each will reflect expectations about death usually, but not always, derived from their culture or religion. They also reflect the differences in each person's brain. However, even within a single culture, each part of the death-process can take many different forms. Individual neural histories and life experiences, as well as a person's private imagery and symbolism, will also shape their experience.

Like any fingerprint, each death process is unique, though they all have similarities. Each person can see different expressions of these same states of consciousness. A good metaphor may be that each phase of the death-process is a template that each person fills in with their own colors and designs. To use another metaphor, the neural molds for death are the same for everyone, but no two people ever pour exactly the same material into them.

Different people can have different experiences[323] arising out of the same altered state. Each phase of the death-process performs the same function for everyone, even though they take on different forms for different people, and they each have a function to perform. For example, the emotions happening just before death can be very different (fear or acceptance), but they all seem to activate areas of the right hemisphere, especially in the deeper structures of the limbic system. These emotions may ensure that the focus of neural activity is in the right limbic system when death actually begins, giving it more direct access to the states of consciousness that come next[324].

The states of consciousness most common at the end of life will integrate seamlessly with those at the beginning of death. In my view, life begins to end before we actually start going into biological or clinical death. The beginning of the death-process may lie in the emotions that appear just before it begins. Different emotions are based in different brain parts. If it's strong enough, the emotion, no matter what it is, will be a function of one of the busiest pathways in the brain at that moment. Brain areas supporting other emotions will be relatively quieter.

If we accept that the various states of consciousness in NDEs are the result of excitement in specific brain areas, then stimulating those parts should eventually elicit phenomena that also appear in NDEs. A seizure can excite specific areas of the brain. So can stimulating the surface of the brain with an electrode. So can schizophrenic brain

177

activity. Phenomena appearing in NDEs have also appeared from the God Helmet's magnetic stimulation.

We'll use several kinds of evidence to see which brain parts stand behind the various stages of the death-process.

Experiences before Death begins

To me, it looks like the death process can actually begin while we're still alive. The *pre-mortem* phase can include almost any phenomena that can happen during death. These can be visions of angels, hearing a divine voice, OBEs, seeing dead friends or relatives and other variations on these themes. These states involve many structures, widely distributed throughout the brain. However, the structures that 'drives' the most common states that appear when a person begins to die (fear or calm acceptance) are in the right hemisphere.

There are spiritual traditions that tell us that a fearful death reduces our chance of a fortunate rebirth. More time for exploring the space between death and the next birth, we are told, makes for a better reincarnation. However, we see the death-process as an algorithmic (automatic, and following a predetermined sequence of events) brain process. It probably won't be equally efficient in all circumstances. Paradoxically, the worst ways of dying may make the entry to the death-process; quite different from what the eastern traditions tell us.

Remember that life was far more dangerous when the brain first evolved than it is today. Many deaths in our early evolutionary history were sudden or violent and terrifying. At that time, fear was probably the most common state just before death. In such cases, the most active structure, just as the death-process began, would have been the right amygdala, which 'does' fear. However, many deaths were also slow and gradual. There is evidence that our early ancestors nurtured those who couldn't take care of themselves[325], including the weak and the sick. After a battle or accident, they took the wounded and injured back to the tribal village whenever possible and nursed them, so although it's possible that most deaths were traumatic, many were still slow and comparatively gentle.

Several studies tell us that fear alone can be enough to trigger the death process. People who survived falls that should have killed them have told stories about leaving their bodies before they hit the ground. Apparently, the death-process for them began when death seemed inevitable, not when they were killed. These and other tales of similar trauma suggest that being convinced that death is imminent can be enough to trigger the process. On the other hand, one can speculate that it can also begin when one of the body's vital systems fails. A failure one of the brain's critical homeostatic mechanisms, monitored and controlled in the hypothalamus (and from there, directly connected to the amygdala) might also trigger the start of the death-process.

In any case, fear is the state most likely to precede sudden deaths, making the right amygdala the structure that's most active just before it begins. It's the most excitable structure in the brain, making it an easy starting point for the death-process (as well as lots of other, more mundane neural responses).

The amygdala is also instrumental in visions involving angels or demons, and in some cultures, the death-process often begins with a visitor experience like this. In Southeast Asia and India, the death-process may begin with a visit from a Yamatoot, a servant of Yama, Lord of the Underworld. They're quite threatening creatures. Angelic visitors seem to get their sacred quality from the left amygdala. Demonic visitors, like the Grim Reaper or a Yamatoot[326], get their fearful and malevolent quality from the one on the right. In Asian cultures, where the experience of death is very different from that of the West, it often still commences with a right amygdala (scary) episode, providing an ideal jumping-off point for the following phase in the process (Tunnel, Void, Road), also in the right hemisphere.

However, it's become more common for people to die slowly, undergoing fewer sudden and traumatic deaths than in our earliest evolutionary history. In today's world, people often die in hospitals, and even when illnesses are incurable, there is an arsenal of medications available to try to make them more comfortable. I wasn't able to authenticate a Hindu tradition I heard of, but it says that when people die naturally, they know about it three days in advance. In either case, people who die slowly often have visitations[327]. Mostly, they're visions of a being or entity. Sometimes, the visions are of someone they knew who has been dead for some time. For others, it might be an angel or even Jesus. The visions usually convey the idea that there is no reason to fear death and sometimes they even encourage people to embrace it. Some people go into states of poignancy, sentimentality and nostalgia, or feeling love for everyone around them. Naturally, not all deaths are preceded by such powerful altered states of consciousness. Others die in quite normal states of consciousness. Perhaps the wide range of experiences appearing before death reflect the fact that some people have altered states all the time, others have them occasionally, while others never have them at all. The triggers for pre-death experiences might be the same for everyone, but we should not assume that everyone is equally sensitive to them

Instead of dying in a state of fear, which suggests right amygdala activity, some die in a state of bliss, indicating the one on the left. In other words, the same brain structure is at work, but on the opposite side of the brain. Some people who die slowly have out of body experiences, visions of people they've known who are now dead, or see their life pass before their eyes before death actually happens. In these cases, we expect the focus of activity (deep in the brain) to be in the right hippocampus. The right hippocampus can mute the amygdala excitement that often comes before clinical death, whether it's the extreme in sudden deaths, or as something quite blissful, like a vision of an angel. There are pathologies which escape these patterns, such as rabies, whose victims are in extreme pain until the last moment.

Most likely, the phenomena that appear in the pre-mortem phase reflect the most excitable areas in the limbic system for that person. The brain sustains insults and injuries as it stops working. Just like injuries from without, those from within will break more connections that inhibit activity than those that excite it[328]. As this happens, the experiences that appear in the death-process are dis-inhibited. The pre-mortem phase sees NDE phenomena increasing, but (in principle) more for those people with more excitable death-process pathways (or more prone to spiritual states) in the first place. Because the death-process hasn't begun, there is no structure to guide pre-mortem experiences, so they can recruit experiences from any portion of the process.

Not all harbingers of death are like the imposing Yamatoots or the frightening Grim Reaper.

> "At the moment of death, say followers of the Jodo sects of Buddhism, the dying person is greeted either by Amida, the Buddha of Everlasting Light, or by Kannon, the Bodhisattva of Compassion and Love.[329]"

Some people have experiences that are clearly positive, but which they don't really describe. One of the most famous of these was Steve Jobs (founder of Apple Corporation) whose last words were "Oh wow. Oh wow. Oh wow". Another was Thomas Edison's last words: "It is very beautiful over there". Another interesting one was Victor Hugo's: "I see black light" – which reminds us of the Void experience.

Albert Speer, Hitler's architect, was gravely ill with a pulmonary embolism, and lay close to death for nearly a month. He had an experience that might have been a premortem NDE episode, or perhaps a fever delirium – or both.

> "… I myself was feeling a remarkable euphoria. The little room expanded into a magnificent hall. A plain wardrobe I had been staring at for three weeks turned into a richly carved display piece inlaid with rare woods. Hovering between living and dying, I had a sense of well-being such as I had only rarely experienced.[330]"

Some pre-mortem experiences show phenomena that don't appear in NDEs. In the pre-mortem phase of the Betty J. Eadie's NDE[331], she saw and felt herself to have shrunk to a very small size. This experience, called *macropsia* (where things seem larger and farther away than they actually are, or you seem smaller), is a disturbance in spatial perception, which suggests that its foundation is in unusual excitement in the right hippocampus[332]. It's a known feature of hippocampal seizures[333]. It's common in epilepsy, but hasn't been reported from any NDEs I know of. Pre-mortem experiences don't seem to be limited only to pathways that support the death-process.

The hippocampus is strongly implicated in macropsia (where things look closer and small than they actually are) and micropsia (its opposite). In these experiences, you, or the things around you, seem larger or smaller than their real sizes. They might seem to be stretched or shrunk. This appears out of the same parts of the brain as OBEs, the hippocampus on the right, in connection with other areas. Electrical stimulation of the same region has elicited both.

> When the surface of their brain was being stimulated with an electrode, one of Penfield's[334] patients reported "that everything …was magnified". Another patient told his doctor "wait a minute! You are getting bigger. The nurse is standing beside you. She is getting bigger[335]".

This was during electrode stimulation of the surface of the temporal lobes, rather than during a seizure, but the same thing seems to be happening. Micropsia and macropsia are related to the normal brain function functions of spatial perception and the perception of movement in space. Just as you can have a hallucination of smell when the olfactory portions of your brain are misfiring, you can have a hallucination (or an illusion) of space when the spatial parts of the brain are busy in unusual ways. Micropsia and macropsia seem to rely on the hippocampus, especially on the right. It's as though spatial illusions can presage OBEs, 'warming up' the parts of the brain[336] they both rely on.

> Macropsia can also happen in epileptic seizures. One such patient told about a seizure in which he…
> "… stared at my food while my depth perception distorted gradually. I stared at my food quite closely while everything else seemed to have a different size and was clouded in a weird haze.[337]"

In NDEs, *The Tunnel* and *The Void* appear to be almost interchangeable. OBEs, the tunnel, the void, macropsia and micropsia, and the movement down the road with one of Yama's messengers all involve either changes in perception of space, changes in location in space, or distortions of spatial perception, and that means that they all appear to depend on the same structure, the right hippocampus, according to the rule that mental forms follow neural functions.

Lewis Carroll, who had temporal lobe epilepsy[338] (TLE), had experiences of the "Tunnel", which probably inspired the rabbit-hole episode in "Alice in wonderland".

> "The rabbit hole went straight on like a tunnel for some way, and then dipped suddenly down, so suddenly that Alice had not a moment to think about stopping herself falling down what seemed to be a very deep well. Either the well was very deep, or she fell very slowly, for she had plenty of time to look about her, and to wonder what was going to happen next. First, she tried to look down and make out what she was coming to, but it was too dark to see anything ...."
>
> "What a curious feeling", said Alice. "I must be shutting up like a telescope".
>
> Some of Alice's experiences also seem evocative of macropsia.
>
> "... as nearly as she could guess, she was now about two feet high, and was going on shrinking rapidly: she soon found out that the cause of this was the fan she was holding, and she dropped it hastily, just in time to save herself from shrinking away altogether." ..." and things are worse than ever", thought the poor child, "for I never was so small as this before, never!"

Alice wasn't dying, but her experiences are similar to those of people who are. Lewis Carroll is thought to have had TLE, and the parts of his brain that were affected by his seizures seem to be the some of the ones that are also involved in the death-process. This is why tunnels appear in both near-death experiences and in "Alice in Wonderland". Betty Eadie's[339] feeling that she had shrunk down to the size of a bug just before her NDEs began, seems to be made of the same "stuff" as Alice's (actually Lewis Carroll's) shrinking and getting larger. This is an example of phenomenological thinking – seeing the same phenomena in two different contexts, and inferring that the same brain areas are involved in both (in this case, the right hippocampus). It lets us cut through the ambiguities of mental phenomena to see the core neural processes, without having to decide if any specific phenomena are caused by excitement or inhibition, or by too much or too little activity. Most brain imaging only shows us which areas are busy, but not what they're doing (one exception is EEG, but it can't read activity deep in the brain). Just as a person yelling "shut up!" to a group of people is busy keeping things quiet, a busy brain part can put quite a lot of neural activity into inhibiting functions. An "active" brain part can be caught up in inhibiting some parts of itself, while leaving other areas excited, in order to let specific functions 'get through', so to speak.

ONE – Leaving the world – The Hippocampus on the Right.

For our early ancestors, what came before death most often was probably fear. To go from fear to an out-of-body experience, the focus of activity in the limbic system has to move from the right amygdala to the right hippocampus. In many pre-mortem altered states, the left amygdala (visions of angels, seeing God, hearing voices) is excited. In others (OBEs, visions of landscapes, the halls of heaven, etc.), the focus is in the right hippocampus, making it primed and ready to go.

OBEs have happened in operating rooms during surgery, when the surface of the brain was stimulated using an electrode. It isn't a practical way to achieve OBEs, but it does implicate specific locations in the brain.

> While Dr Wilder Penfield was stimulating "the superior surface of the temporal lobe, within the fissure of sylvius" ... one of his patients "exclaimed 'Oh God! I am leaving my body.[340]'". Another said "she felt as though she were floating away"[341]. In another case, a patient said "I feel as is I'm floating"[342].

As we mentioned before, the hippocampus is a very cognitive structure; it works with information. It's specialized for verbal information on the left and non-verbal information on the right. Some of its other right-sided functions include spatial perception and reasoning, the images that appear in dreams, accessing and maintaining the states of consciousness that come up in trance, meditation, hypnosis, and other "absorbing" states.

OBEs can happen to people practicing yoga or meditation, as well as seeming to happen spontaneously. In fact, they've been reported during and shortly after (God Helmet) stimulation of the temporal lobes using magnetic 'copies' of the electrical signatures that show up in EEGs when specific brain structures are active[343]. They have been reported by people using a home version of the technology[344] used in the God Helmet.

> "Last night - the 2nd evening after the session - I had an OBE. It was wonderful. I am not sure how long it lasted, but I knew it was going to happen because at first I had very vivid visions.[345]"

Dr. Olaf Blanke published a report[346] of an OBE after stimulating the Right Angular Gyrus of an epileptic woman (all patients who received Blanke's stimulation were epileptic - the surgery they were undergoing is exploratory; it helped doctors pinpoint the location where their seizures began). During this stimulation, she said:

> "I see myself lying in bed, from above, but I only see my legs and lower trunk". "...she (also) reported seeing her legs 'becoming shorter'. If the patient's legs were bent before the stimulation... she reported that her legs appeared to be moving quickly towards her face, and took evasive action" "When her eyes were shut, she felt that her upper body was moving towards her legs, which were stable..."

The patient's perception of her arms changed in similar ways, but only on the left (her seizures and the stimulation were both on the right side). The experience of her legs becoming shorter looks like a limited example of micropsia, with only part of the area of the brain where we perceive our bodies involved, and only part of the body affected by the experience. Of course, stimulation with an electrode isn't a natural way of activating the brain, so effects can appear from it that would usually be all but impossible. Eliciting these two effects (micropsia and an OBE) while stimulating the same area suggests they each rely on some of the same brain areas. These are the hippocampus on the right, and the surface area above and behind the ears (the angular gyrus - where your antlers would be rooted if you were a stag deer)[347].

OBEs can happen in many contexts, including the seizures of temporal lobe epilepsy (TLE). One epileptic[348] said:

> "During my life - since early childhood, I've had many conscious "out of the body" experiences, when I could travel about in the so-called "Second Body" or "astral body" to familiar (and sometimes unfamiliar) places on earth."

It may be that Penfield's and Blanke's results represent only two of many places that contribute to the experience. Blanke's observation received a lot of attention after its publication and journalists were quick to interpret it as the discovery of an out-of-body 'center' in the brain. None of them seemed to know about Penfield's report, where the same result followed stimulation of completely different spots on the brain's surface. There is also evidence that suggest that OBEs may rely on having the same brain waves appearing in the frontal lobe of the *right* side of the frontal lobe, as well as the temporal lobe on the *left*[349].

Out of body experiences are the most common first phase in near-death experiences in Western countries. They involve a dramatic change in our perception of our location in space. In the limbic system, this is primarily supported by the hippocampus on the right.

The hippocampus plays a role not only in spatial memory and perception, but also plays a role in our sense of balance, and our sense of our body's orientation and location in space. In two studies[350] [351], lesions anywhere in the vestibular system, the brain's system for balance, degraded the hippocampus's usual output of theta activity, and its ability to learn and remember anything that depended on spatial perceptions or memories[352].

Harbingers of death are the most common beginning for the death-process in some Asian cultures. These visitors are 'sent' by the lord of the underworld, and their frightening character suggests that they are the 'very coinage' of the right amygdala, a structure specialized for both fear, and relating to others[353]. Just as dreaming of doing something excites the same brain parts that support doing it in real life, visions of frightening beings involve the same brain parts that become excited when we are actually with someone we're afraid of. That implicates the right amygdala, as we saw earlier. When it's a servant of Yama, or a grim reaper, this first phase isn't over until the right hippocampus has gotten involved, as you go down a road with the deathly messenger – by moving through space. It also happens in Greek mythology, where you meet Charon, the ferryman, who moves you across the river Styx. You don't suddenly find yourself in the 'other world'; you have to *travel* to get there. This movement through space implicates the hippocampus on the right. You can't have an experience of moving through space, real or illusory, without its support.

Dr. M.A. Persinger found that OBEs are more likely at times when the earth's magnetic field is stormy[354], showing an interaction between OBEs and the earth's magnetic field. He offered an "exploratory hypothesis" in which "the neurocognitive processes which are associated with the generation of the sense of self are coherent with or intercalated with some unspecified feature of the steady-state or quiet component … of the geomagnetic field."

In other words, the brain processes that make the sense of self may be bound to some part of the earth's magnetic field. This will become important to us later on, but for now, let's look at the magnetic side of the brain.

Our brains have over 5 million magnetite crystal per gram[355]. These very small magnets aren't shaped like the magnetite formed in the earth. The ones in the brain have their own unique shape, so they probably have a specific function. Nobody knows exactly what they contribute to our minds, but they may be part of the basis for consciousness and changes in our states of consciousness. These magnetite crystals are very small and very densely packed. It seems likely that they act as a system, like the brain's electrical and chemical systems. It could even allow consciousness to have a component that operates outside the brain, from within the Earth's magnetic field, as well as letting the brain communicate with itself. Magnetic signals would move through the brain in vanishingly small periods of time, much faster than neurochemical or electrical pulses.

Two - *The Tunnel, The Void,* or a walk down the road with a harbinger of death.
The hippocampus on the right.

In the next phase in the death-process, a person may feel they are traveling through a dark tunnel or a black void. The tunnel is sometimes so dark that the person going through it often cannot see the walls, but rather "feels" them. Sometimes it's light enough to see the walls. There can be a honeycomb pattern on them, or sometimes a textures or images. At the end of the tunnel, there is a light, which becomes very bright as one approaches it.

The void is described as a very dark and infinitely large space, but there is much more to it than that description implies. Often, it will have a texture, even though you don't touch anything when you're there. It's more than just darkness. It's a blackness that seems vibrant, or filled with energy; it shimmers with darkness instead of shimmering with light. It seems to say something very important, but one cannot understand it. Because the void is a right hemispheric experience, and language is left hemispheric (language centers are on the left side of the brain), its meaning never unfolds into words, so you really can't know what its saying. If and when the experience begins to move into the next phase, a tiny but brilliant point of light appears in the center.

This kind of darkness has been artificially created through the God Helmet. One reporter[356], who visited the laboratory where it's used, had this to say (during a God Helmet session):

> "At some point I say, in almost incomprehensibly muffled words, "There's kind of a roiling darkness, like a battle of darkness; it's off to my left. ...
>
> Persinger observes, excited: "You've just reported the actions on your left. And now you are beginning to experience — and my compliments to you — what is called 'The black,' or 'The dark of the dark.'"

The fact that the darkness is on the subject's *left* is significant — it indicated that the experience was coming from the *right* side of her brain. One of Penfield's patients[357], describing her seizures, spoke of a "Mental darkness", accompanied by a threatening figure gesturing with a long sharp implement. Penfield successfully removed sections of the deeper portions of her right temporal lobe to stop her seizures. Another epileptologist recorded a case where the patient said that during a seizure:

> "One side of my mind was racing from scene to scene while the other was whirling and gnashing in dark chaotic colors moving in total clear blackness ...[358]"

This isn't the same as the void or the tunnel, but the 'total, clear blackness' is also found in *The Void*. This seizure almost certainly affected pathways included the ones that support *The Void*, but involved more pathways than it takes to maintain it, so that the shapes and movements could also happen at the same time, but the underlying phenomena is much the same in both.

Another seizure report said ...

> "For me, it[359] was a smell of bananas. When I smelt that, I'd just sit down wherever I was before the blackness came.[360]"

The association between blackness (or the lack of light) and the hippocampus is supported by lab experiments, where rat studies have found changes in the hippocampus from light deprivation[361] and where the hippocampus responds to changes in melatonin levels, which rise when it gets dark outside[362]. Other studies have also found a hippocampal contribution to our daily (circadian) rhythms[363].

Here's an interesting example of a Tunnel episode (where Buddhist teachings are mentioned in the NDE of a contemporary American Indian Woman). The important detail is at the beginning, where she goes through a tunnel, moving toward The Light.

> "Passing through the tunnel and going toward a very bright light, she was stopped by the Buddha. He told her he was the Buddha of Infinite Light. She asked why she met him and not Jesus, or one of her spirit guides from her native (American Indian) spiritual tradition. He told her that he was all of them; he was the ground of existence. She said that they talked for a while and that he spoke of emptiness, impermanence, and conditional arising. She didn't know what he was talking about. When he told her that it was time for her to go, she said she wanted to stay with him; he told her it wasn't yet time and that she had to go back[364].

Tunnels have appeared in the phenomena of TLE. One epileptic had seizures that started ...

> "...with a dreamlike state going on around me, but no matter how hard I fight it, reality is like a tiny, tiny tunnel that is directly in front of me. I usually can't move and try very hard to keep this tunnel in front of me, but it's almost as if the dream is pulling me in[365]."

Like other NDE phenomena appearing in epilepsy, it's more than the bare, essential experience. It's 'colored' by phenomena from the other areas involved in the seizure. The death-process follows a natural (algorithmic) progression, and appears to follow a "hard wired" sequence of pathways. When these pathways are involved in a seizure, they can be combined with other pathways and won't be limited to death process phenomena. Here's another example, *not* taken from an epileptic's report. The fear the person mentions twice suggests that it comes from the right side of the brain, and the fact that being in *The Tunnel* involves looking down its length, suggests that it's a right hippocampal experience. However, as with any phenomenon, it involves other brain areas. Just as <u>moving</u> into a tunnel-shaped space (or a space defined by a tunnel) will at least partly rely on the right hippocampus, <u>seeing</u> *The Tunnel* implicates the visual cortex[366].

> I've always been afraid of water, deep water. Lately, I've been practicing putting my face in the water in the shower. When I wipe my face off with the wash cloth, while my eyes are closed and looking into the dark of my closed eyelids, a light appears. If I keep looking at it, it gets brighter, turns to a perfect "wide" circle, with edges that look like I'm looking through a tunnel, and then the colors start to vibrate. Once (I stay with it as long as I could without getting afraid, (not sure what's happening. I have had eyes checked, they're healthy.) The longest I've stayed with it, the light vibrations began to turn into a lavender colored light, vibrating, in the center of a golden white light[367].

Complex magnetic signal stimulation (a category that includes the God Helmet) has elicited *The Tunnel*. Here are three reports from magnetic stimulation not unlike the God Helmet:

> "I did a one hour session and after about 20 minutes I felt something. It felt good. ... I was sleepy afterwards and started having some intense dreams where the visuals were very real. I was on a mission, entering a

tunnel that was a time warp allowing me to travel from the year 2100 something back to around this time[368]."

"The tunnel geometries and continual motion of the psychedelic 'visualization' display felt unusually intense[369]."

"I have had OBEs in the past, only recently after using the headset. Another one I had (experienced) was the flowing of my consciousness down a long tunnel, like a wormhole effect you would see on star trek, the vibrations of this particular incident were intense, but without …(any) accompanying negativity…[370]"

Like other NDE phenomena, the "Void" has happened during epileptic seizures, though, interestingly, the tunnel is not as common. Here is one account from what was probably a seizure (triggered by sleeplessness):

"There was no light. It was the clearest and most lighted (sic) black … Not the color black we think of, more than that. It was like the color orange/yellow vs. seeing an orange/yellow sun at sun rise. The color itself being the same, but to compare it to the sun, not too bright to look directly at, it has that luminous, shiny, alive thing going on. This black was as luminous but without light. I wish I could explain better. I don't want to say it was alive of course – but although it was nothing, empty…it was not. It was so very much… I'm sorry. There just aren't words to describe it[371]."

A few NDEs tell of having both blackness and The Tunnel happen in the same experience.

"Her heart stopped. (She) says that was where the journey began. "I went up. It was very, very, very dark. There were no stars. And I don't know if there was wind, that I cannot tell you. But before I became

192

frightened, there was a tunnel there. She was carried toward a place she says was real and heavenly. "I went through the tunnel like 'shwoosh,' and at the end of the tunnel was a light. I followed it. I had no choice. I came out by the light. There was no sun. It was all in a golden, warm, loving light," she says.[372]"

We can see the connection between *The Tunnel*, *The Void*, and darkness in a published case history[373], about the hallucinations of a pool hustler, who had LSD flashbacks of a "black hole" that appeared in unexpected places, like the street, in parks, and in a newspaper. These were terrifying experiences, which suggests they have a right limbic basis (because the right amygdala is specialized for fearful emotions).

"I kept calling his name and asking him to describe what he was seeing. After five minutes, he could talk again [his inability to speak also suggests a right-hemisphere base for his experiences – language centers are on the left]. The black hole was gone, he panted, but he had seen it clearly for the first time: a giant funnel about 16 feet in diameter. The outside of the funnel was covered with a black lacework, while the inside was lined with geometrically arranged girders. There was a bright light in the center of the hole."

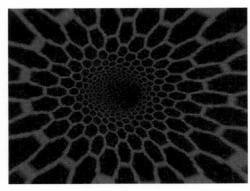

The Tunnel, with a lattice pattern along its walls.

The description for this 'funnel', including its geometric patterns, is an almost perfect match for some descriptions of the Tunnel found in NDE reports. The light in the center of the hole is almost certainly the same phenomenon that appears as the point of light in the center of *The Void*, and the light at the end of *The Tunnel*. Geometric patterns often appear on the walls, but so do Tunnels with pictures and images.

Like any NDE phenomena, *The Tunnel* can appear differently in other contexts. We work with the idea that the death-process appeared during our evolutionary history, and each of its phases has a job to do. It can start doing that job because of an epileptic event, a magnetic signal, a hallucinogenic drug, or a surgeon's electrode. These can activate its pathways, but when it happens outside of the death-process, they're activated along with other pathways that add things to the experience, making it very different from the NDE experiences we read about in books, even though they retain the core phenomena.

Here, the core phenomenon is the sense of being in a space unlike anything one could normally encounter. The hippocampus plays a crucial role in dreaming, as well as in the perception of space. It might create an environment we could only encounter in a dream, or in the experience of "astral travel" or it could create another reality where we move through a space; like the tunnel or the void. In the phases of NDEs that come later, the hippocampus will still be active; providing images that fill out their states of consciousness with imagery that matches the *state*.

In India and Southeast Asia, this same phase of the death-process finds the person walking down a road accompanied by a messenger from Yama (sometimes flying with them) until they come to the underworld. Instead of floating or being pulled along through a tunnel or an infinite void, the people are walking. The simple phenomena they share in common, of movement through space, dominate the action. In each case, the person is going somewhere. This phase makes it absolutely clear that they are moving out of the world of the living. An out of body experience can convince you that you are not your body, allowing you to accept its loss more easily. Going through the tunnel or the void and into the light, or down a road towards the *land of the dead* can show you that you have left this world, and you shouldn't resist moving into the next one. However, our attachments to the people we love can remain, so some people resist the death process. In Thailand, some people may try to fight it off from sheer fright.

From a Thai NDE:

> I said (to the Yamatoot) "I'm not going", and I tried
> to escape. I turned and repeated that I was not going to
> go to the house of Yama. I soon realized that I could
> not escape[374].

Many NDEers have said they came back to life to take care of the people in their lives. We are a social species, and our bonds are emotional. We're reluctant to leave behind the people we care about. The realization that we're really saying goodbye to our children, or that we'll never again see those we love, can inspire strong resistance. The next stage in the death-process can make it okay, either by filling us with bliss, or by putting us in such fear that we accept death without resistance.

Three & Four - Being in The Light - the Amygdala on the left.

The next phase of the death-process has two smaller phases. In the first, you "enter the light". In the second, you encounter dead friends and relatives. People you knew while they were alive, but who died before you did.

Dr. M.A. Persinger[375] reported that *The Light* has appeared to some subjects during the second phase of God Helmet sessions, which targets the left amygdala in the roundabout way we described in chapter 5.

Reports from users of a neural stimulation device[376] similar to the God Helmet include one where the person was doing a visualization exercise and felt "...a sense of overwhelming ecstasy will develop till there is a sense and experience of an implosion (or) explosion ... of Light." Another said he: "was in an open space and ... (saw) ... thousands of very small colored lights.[377]"

Visions of God and of light at the same time are common in NDEs. Their common phenomenology ("God is Glorious" meaning *surrounded by light*), as well as the emotions both inspire (bliss, joy and ecstasy),

195

suggest the same pathways are involved in both. Persinger's results imply that the left amygdala, whether artificially excited in the lab, or during the death-process, is the primary source for the phenomena that appears in this stage of the death-process.

Although the God Helmet has created visions of God, it's done so in only a very small percent of the subjects. It's not called the "God helmet" because it produces visions of God, but rather because visions of God have been produced using it. In any case, the name was given by a journalist, and not by any of its inventors.

The appearance of light in God Helmet Sessions is a matter of exciting one of the brain's recondite functions; light, or at least, inner light. Of course, the appearance of light is accompanied by phenomena from other parts of the brain. One example is the moment when someone sees the light at the end of the tunnel. However, when the person is seeing *The Light* and the tunnel at the same time, the left amygdala (light) and the right hippocampus (tunnel) are both contributing at once. The same thing happens when someone sees the light on the other side of "the void". The transitions between stages in near-death experiences aren't abrupt, so the focus of neural excitement moves smoothly from one area to another. The overlap between the succeeding phases shows that they each taper off only after the next one begins, and there is a gentle change of focus of excitement moves from one set of pathways to another.

The amygdala is a very social structure, it mediates the emotions we feel when we relate to others, and it also helps us with a kind of emotional memory and intelligence (as, for example, when we are able to tell what other people are feeling). The amygdala on the left must step up its participation when dead friends and relatives appear in the death-process. Before, it only needed to produce light, now it manifests both The Light and visions of people; sometimes, many of them. Then, there is the meeting with them. This very unusual social group typically greets you as you step in among them.

It's a social occasion – a reunion, and the left amygdala's contribution to loving relationships comes into play as it interacts with the caudate nucleus and the insula (an of the cortex that's 'tucked' deeply below the surface). The insula is heavily implicated in the experience of romantic love[378] [379]. Maternal love affects both the caudate nucleus and the insula[380]. Both structures have extensive connections to the amygdala. One end of the caudate nucleus directly connects to it, while the insula has connections to at least six parts of the amygdala[381]. Both the left amygdala and the insula appear in several neural brain circuits[382], including some that support reward mechanisms[383].

In Western cultures, the meeting with loved ones who've passed on before us is a joyous one. They're happy to see us and we're happy to see them. You're dead, but by this point, it feels good. If you reject or resist the fact of being dead, or you try to return to life, you'll have to part with many loved ones. You want to remain.

In NDEs from India and Southeast Asia, the meeting with other beings takes a very different form. There, you see people you know are dead, but the meaning is anything but joyous. People see hell, with all of its tortures. Meeting your dead uncle and having a happy reunion can help you to accept that your death. In Southeast Asia, seeing the dead being tortured, and knowing what it means, is enough for people to accept that they are no longer in the land of the living. The tortures of hell are horrible. Resistance is futile.

The next part of this phase of the death process is the meeting with the *Being of Light*. It's no longer a vision of several people at once. The focus is now on a single sacred *Being*. Most people unhesitatingly identify the Being of Light as God. Sometimes, it appears as an angel. In many cases, the person doesn't see the *Being of Light* at all. Instead, they only feel its presence. Apparently, those who don't actually *see* God don't miss much. The sense of love, compassion, understanding, and forgiveness is so overwhelming that it doesn't matter whether they *see* God or not when they stand in his presence. Many people, telling about their NDEs, have said that they had a sense that God knew everything about them. He saw all their imperfections and flaws, and accepted them lovingly, without judgment of any kind. God, it seems, loves you no matter who you are, where you've been, or what might be wrong with you.

In Southeast Asia, the Being of Light is replaced by another central figure; Yama, the Lord of the underworld. He too looks into the center of your being, and knows all about you. However, he *does* judge you, and is *not* indulgent. His job main is to punish, which he does by sending people to be tortured, or by sentencing them to a reincarnation where what they have done to others is done to them.

The Being of Light is part of the spectrum of "visitor" experiences, in which people see beings that seem to be non-physical. These have appeared also appeared in epilepsy[384]. The 19th century neurologist Hughlings Jackson recorded a case in which the patient regularly saw a "little black woman who was always very actively engaged in cooking; the spectre did not speak"[385]. Wilder Penfield mentioned a patient who once saw Jesus coming down from the sky "as though in a picture"[386].

Like all the other core phenomena in the death process, meetings with other beings have been created through neural stimulation. Some of that stimulation has been with electric probes, touching the surface of the brain[387]. Olaf Blanke, the Swedish Neurologist, published a report of a "Shadow Being" elicited through electrical stimulation of the brain's surface. It has also appeared through stimulation with the God Helmet[388], and through epilepsy.

Being in the presence of someone who sees your flaws and either accepts them completely, or makes you completely ashamed of them, makes it easier for you to see them without denial or resistance, which brings us to the next phase in the death-process - the Life Review.

Five - *The Life Review,* the Right Hippocampus and Both Amygdala

The *Life Review* is the stage in the death-process were you see your life pass before your eyes, you re-experience your entire life in just a few seconds, or perhaps just see an example (or a symbolic representation of) a behavior that dominated your life. Some people face the "Book of Karma". The Life Review can take many forms. One of them even consists of seeing your life displayed on a large number of television screens. In near-death experiences from tribal (pre-literate) societies, the Life Review appears to be entirely symbolic[389].

The brain part most likely to produce this exceptional example of long-term memory is the hippocampus on the right side. The hippocampus is crucial in the consolidation and retrieval of memories. The one on the right specializes in the kind that doesn't use words. Unquestionably, the Life Review depends on other brain parts involved with memory; one of them being the area of the cortex closest to the hippocampus (the parahippocampal cortex). As with any other experience, it makes use of areas on both sides of the brain, even though it's dominated by a specific region on one side.

The Life Review commonly happens in the presence of the *Being of Light*, or the Lord of the Underworld. This implies an amygdala involvement in the Life Review, because the amygdala is instrumental in relating to others, including beings that exist only in our minds. The fact that the Life Review displays our behavior with respect to other people also implicates the amygdala, with its social functions.

Remember that karmas are almost exclusively about social behavior. The Life Review is a rare kind of memory retrieval, so the structures that normally support memory are sure to be involved. So is the limbic structure that supports relating to others, and assigns an emotion to everything that happens– the amygdala. When we see something in our life review we feel good about, the left amygdala will be included, and when we see something we feel bad about, it will be the right amygdala. The phenomena of (primarily) non-verbal memory and the production of both inner images as well as the phenomena of being with other people implicate the right hippocampus and both amygdala.

Whether you meet the Being of Light or the wrathful lord of the Underworld, or you meet one of the less common deities (if you meet any of them at all) depends mostly upon your culture, and your own expectations about death. During this meeting, we accept our behaviors just as the Being of Light or the Lord of the Underworld sees them, as sins that have been forgiven or acts that must be punished. Many Life Reviews don't involve the *Being of Light* (or of darkness) being present, and happen as a series of flashbacks[390]. In this case, flashback doesn't mean that they repeat (as with LSD flashbacks). Remember that we are taking a phenomenological approach, which means that we look at the phenomenon (involuntary memories). The context is much less important.

Brain stimulation has elicited 'flashbacks' in several ways. The neurosurgeon Wilder Penfield[391] had a patient who had a traumatic childhood experience when a man holding a bag filled with snakes in it approached her and asked if she wanted to climb in. She re-lived the episode in her dreams, and when she developed temporal lobe epilepsy, her seizures often included re-experiencing it. Penfield was able to elicit the experience by stimulating the surface of her temporal lobes with an electrode. He also elicited less dramatic memories, like hearing music or names being called[392].

Memories have been elicited through complex magnetic stimulation. Here are three interesting examples from reports by people using a home version of the God Helmet[393]:

> "A few visuals came but the most noticeable thing was the childhood memories presented, at which point I could freely explore many memories." And another - "The next day was a 'day of meaning and profound insight'. The world around seemed a bit like a fairy tale and a bit like it was all eternity. Some childhood memory would rise up to the surface and blend with the present-day memories". One reported "hypnogogic (twilight sleep) type images, (and) fleeting remembrances of childhood memories..."[394].

In one lab study[395], Dr. M.A. Persinger found that the God Helmet brought up 'old memories' for women and 'dreamlike' states for men.

Caveat – 'Repressed memories'.

One issue surrounding childhood, 'old', 'buried' or 'repressed' memories is that one can never be sure if these memories have any basis in events in the past. It's all too easy for the mind to create memories of things that never happened. Memories of childhood abuse, especially sexual abuse, memories of being abducted by aliens, or memories attributed to past lives all have a way of appearing without ever having been accessed before. The common interpretations of these memories ('buried', 'suppressed' or 'blocked') may sometimes be valid, but certainly not always. Most new-age counselors believe they aren't remembered because the events were too dramatic or too traumatic for the person to "handle". Remembering such events is thought to be so painful that the person sequesters them, cutting them out of their thoughts. I would suggest that most such memories are "state specific". This means that if a memory was created in a very unusual state of consciousness (or the event put you into such a state), you won't be able to access it when you're in normal consciousness. The way you felt when you laid down the memory and the way you feel when you try to retrieve it can be so different that the memory just won't "come through".

A memory of a painful event can help us avoid feeling that same pain again. As the saying goes, "Once bitten, twice shy". If the painful event happened during childhood, it would have occurred before the brain had finished growing. Most people don't remember much from when they were three years old. They often won't remember their toys, games, or bedtime stories. They will also not remember beatings, abuse, and trauma. By the time they reach adulthood, their brains will have been rewired more than once. They won't be able to get into the same state of consciousness they lived in as a small child, and won't be able to retrieve many of the memories laid down at that time. Such memories could well be state-specific (only available while the person is in a certain state of consciousness), and the states they belong to may be very rare for adults.

When a person accesses a "repressed" memory, sometimes it's a real memory, but it can also be a *false memory*[396]. Interestingly, it seems that people are often more convinced of the truth of their false memories than their real ones[397]. One can never take for granted that such memories are either real or false. It doesn't matter whether these memories come up spontaneously, through hypnosis, or appear during spiritual practice. While the person who has such memories should be taken seriously, the memories themselves should be questioned.

Almost all memories that reappear after they seemed to have been "buried" are memories of traumatic experiences. I've never heard of anyone unearthing a "buried" memory of a joyous moment. It might be that such memories, carrying no pain, have no reason to be buried. In any case, we've lost many memories of our childhood by the time we become adults. The right hippocampus, with less access to words; can create a memory that *symbolizes* an event, even if that event only happened in the brain – or *to* the brain.

The person who experiences an upwelling of repressed memories will have emotional needs that should be met, whether the memories are real or not. Still, too many child molesters have been allowed to repeat their abuse because their victims did not remember what happened, and too many innocent men have been falsely accused on the strength of false memories that were taken at face value, when the memories actually reflected events in the brain, and not events in the past.

False memories are far more than merely delusions. Instead, they are created in extraordinary mental states. They reflect states of consciousness, not events. They symbolize, express, and give shape to an event in the brain that's so far outside of normal states of consciousness that it must be presented to the mind as a very powerful event. At one time in western culture, there may have been false memories of meetings with Satan or demons. Today, in the West, more people believe in aliens than believe in devils, and like the demons of hell, they can be very cruel to the people they meet. They also come from "another world".

I'm not saying there are no such things as aliens who violate the people they abduct, only that most meetings with them happen in the mind. "Buried" memories of childhood sexual abuse also reflect a sense of being violated. The hippocampus, the source for much of what we experience in our dreams, is also the place where our memories are formed. It can create false memories, just as it can create dreams of things that never happened. The hippocampus uses symbols in creating memories[398], so such memories can be symbols of events that only happened in (or to) the brain.

We're looking at false memory syndrome because it helps us understand the wide variety that the *Life Review* shows. Memories, like locks, can be opened by the keys of specific states of consciousness. A false memory gives context to an event that harms the mind from within the brain (like the neural traumas that can come with seizures, high fevers, drugs, excessive alcohol, or head injuries). Remembering an event that never happened in the world can symbolize something that actually did happen - in the brain. In the same way, behavior patterns can be represented in the *Life Review* symbolically. Doing so would tend to make the Life Review more efficient, as large numbers of behaviors could be symbolized by just a few images. It may be that at one time in our evolutionary history, all Life Reviews were symbolic; just as many dreams are symbolic. The language of symbols, their meaning and their contexts, involves processing nonverbal information. In the *Life Review*, our memories can be retrieved and presented to us in a way that almost never happens when we're alive. This implicates the right hemisphere in general and the right hippocampus in particular.

There may well have been at time at the dawn of our species when our neural hardware was in place, but our languages were not complex or sophisticated to use all the resources it gave us. To this day, there are languages that lack many words found in the world's major languages, like English, Chinese, Hindi, and so forth. According to one source[399], the Lakota language does not have any words for: admit, assume, because, believe, could, doubt, end, expect, faith, forget, forgive, guilt, how, it, mercy, pest, promise, should, sorry, them, us, waste, we, and weed. It may seem impossible to think and speak without using these words, but there is a novel, "Hanta Yo", which was written in English, and then translated into Lakota, and then translated back into English. The final novel contains no words that aren't in the Lakota language. Instead of saying that someone 'assumes' something, they might say that someone 'understood' it. Anything we can say in English can also be said in languages with less complicated grammar and syntax, but we must change the way we think in order to do it.

At one time, our spoken language used simpler grammar, smaller vocabularies, and was augmented with gestures. It seems reasonable to suppose that symbols could have augmented the words in our internal dialogue. If this were so, then our memories may once have been far more symbolic than they are now. Because one symbol can represent many different things, symbols, both in dreams and in the Life Review, could use of our memory mechanisms efficiently. In more linear kinds of Life Reviews, we can see our lives pass before our eyes, or re-experience our entire lives from beginning to end in just a few seconds. This could reflect a modern variation of the Life Review that accommodates our tendency to think in words, as well as our reliance on linear and logical thinking. Readings from both the book of Karma in Asian Life Reviews, and the symbolic ones found in near death experience reports from hunter/gatherer societies, may both be examples of nonlinear Life Reviews. These could be reflections of the larger differences between the 'mindsets' of North America and Europe and the rest of the world. It seems possible, even likely, that the symbolic Life Reviews found in near death experiences from less complex cultures were once the only kind that happened to anyone. In the literature of near-death experiences, linear and literal Life Reviews are the most common, but they may have been quite rare until recently. Perhaps someone should write a book: "The Origin of Memory in the Breakdown of the Bicameral Mind".

Remember that the *Life Review* often takes place in the presence of the being of light. When this happens, the dominant structures would be the amygdala on the left, and the hippocampus on the right. To summarize, the *Life Review* is an unusual kind of non-verbal memory, implicating the right hippocampus as its main source. Interestingly, I've never read any accounts of discussions during the life review, although they do appear both before and after it. The fact that people have emotional responses to what they see in the *Life Review* implicates the amygdala, with its very emotional functions, but either or both amygdala(s) can participate, according to whether or not the emotions we feel during a *Life Review* are positive or negative. The right hippocampus will always be involved, because of its crucial role in non-verbal memories.

Six – The Transcendent Experience

This typically comes close to the end of NDEs, so it won't happen if the person is resuscitated. In the Transcendent Experience, the person might tour heaven and hell, have "the mysteries of the cosmos" revealed to them, or be shown "God's plan". They might enter the "Akashic records", where all knowledge, past present or future, about anything, is made available to them. One near-death experience from Southeast Asia included visiting the realms of Indra, King of heaven, and Brahma, creator of the universe.

'I found myself in another place which was very pleasant. The weather was nice, I was no longer hungry. I saw a garden with trees all in rows. It was very beautiful, like the garden of a king or a millionaire. As I walked into the garden, I smelled some flowers. They were so very fragrant, with a scent I had never known before. Next, I saw some angels, both male and female. They glided through the air. They were dressed beautifully, and wore exquisite jewelry. Some had flowers in their hair. I kept walking, and saw a pavilion with a roof like that of a palace. There was an angelic man sitting inside. His body was surrounded by a green halo. I approached the angel, sat down and made obeisance. I asked "who are you? Where am I?" He answered "I am the lord of the angels, and this is the angelic world. I then recognized that this was none other than Indra, the King of Heaven. He said to me "When you go back to your world, you should teach your fellow men not to commit sins, as it causes them to go to hell. If they do good, and behave in a moral manner, they will be reborn in my heaven. I will show you the mercy of teaching you the Dharma; The sacred law." He imparted this knowledge by opening my wisdom eye. I then saw all the truths of the universe. The future, the past, and the present.[400]'

This kind of experience is not common, and most near-death experiences don't include it. I suspect that there are people who want to learn more from their death processes than usual, or who also believe that "All questions will be answered" when they die. They might resist the final phase in the death-process until after their expectations have been fulfilled. This is speculation. Nevertheless, I cannot help comparing the transcendent experience to the Life Review. It's as though the *Transcendent Experience* is a Life Review that "widens" beyond one's life experiences to encompass the purpose for man's existence, the "meaning of life", and "why we're here".

There don't seem to be any reports of transcendent experiences from open-brain stimulation with an electrode, or reports of it happening during seizures. But it has been observed in a few subjects, when God Helmet stimulation was applied over the right temporal lobe, using a signal taken from the hippocampus[401]. One had an episodic vision in which he was shown the structure of human relationships, another 'understood' that all things were vibrations. Another had a vision of a crystal city[402].

The *Transcendent Experience* comes after the *Life Review*, and both seem to be based on hippocampal excitement. Both the Life Review and the Transcendent Experience rely on the production of large numbers of meaningful images or insights. The *Life Review* may make the *Transcendent Experience* easier to achieve. Moving from one to the other would mean changing the way the hippocampus is operating, but without changing the focus of excitement from the hippocampus to another structure. They may be two forms of the same experience, with the Life Review being about one's own life, and the Transcendent Experience being about *all* lives.

Seven – The Point of No Return

The point of no return seems to be the end of the death-process. In it, a person might travel down a hallway, and find it blocked by a door. They will "know" that if they pass through it, they will not be able to return. One spoke of being confronted by a wall of fog, and knowing that if they entered it, they would not be able to come back[403]. Some NDEs include stories where people tried to pass the Point of No Return, but were told that it wasn't their time, and they had to go back. In one Southeast Asian near-death experience, the God Brahma told the person that they had been out of their body for so long that if they waited any longer, they wouldn't be able to return to it.

The sense of self is supported by specific neural functions, which apparently cease at the end of the death-process. According to Persinger[404], the sense of self includes the amygdala and hippocampus on both sides, and these may be some of the last pathways in the brain to shut down completely during the death process. I suspect that the point of no return is the subjective experience of cutting the power, so to speak, for the sense of self.

The point of no return may represent a breakdown in the integration of our perceptions, including our perception of time and space, a thing that happens in the thalamus. Once these stop operating, our sense of self, based in structures with heavy inputs from the thalamus, would also stop. The thalamus seems to function as a neural oscillator[405], not unlike the piece of quartz that keeps a good wrist watch accurate. It sets our brain's "absolute" clock. Because its oscillations help us perceive the passage of time, shutting down of the thalamus would mean that for us, time would stop. Once someone had entered such a state of consciousness, they might not be able to return. All of the previous states of consciousness in the death process have primarily been based in the limbic system, with each one dominated by a specific structure. The Point of No Return would involve a structure below it.

If the focus of activity is in the thalamus at the end of the death process, then the process could continue without any input from the limbic structures. If anyone had gone beyond the point of no return, and was then resuscitated, they wouldn't be able to remember the experience. People who've died for just a moment or two and been resuscitated afterwards have reported near-death experiences that seemed to go on much longer. It's possible that the thalamus might speed up its oscillations (like changing from 8-bit to 256-bit) so that time would seem to slow down, though it hasn't been observed so far. Of course, any imaging technique that could detect it would have to have a very high sampling rate and it would have to be imaging a thalamus at the time of death – an unlikely scenario at present. However, this speculation does explain how very quick deaths might still yield death processes that seem to last a long time.

The neurological basis of mystic experiences

We've looked at the neural bases for the successive stages of near death experiences and the brain parts that support them. Now we can discuss the model we use to understand religious and mystic experiences in terms of brain function.

Each of the states of consciousness in the death process reflects the activity of recondite pathways involving specific brain structures. Our brains are hard-wired with an adaptive mechanism that produces these states of consciousness at the time of death.

In my view, almost all religious, mystic, and spiritual experiences are death-process phenomena that appear while we're still alive. These phenomena are manifestations of states of consciousness that primarily occur in the death-process. When one of the pathways that functions in support of the death-process is activated in another context, the result will be a religious or mystic experience.

The death-process appears to have seven distinct phases, suggesting seven core states of consciousness, supported by seven primary groups of pathways. The exact pathways can be different, sometimes very different, for different people, though the larger structures (amygdala, hippocampus, etc) will be the same. To use a metaphor, there are many roads you could use to go from Paris to Warsaw, but everyone will have to travel through the same countries to get there. These groups of pathways can be activated in other contexts (outside the death process), but they will still create the same state of consciousness. The experiences they create will unfold with different phenomena; because the different context can leave some pathways running that would keep still during death. The things that happen in mystic experiences during people's lives are different from death process experiences, even though the underlying neural pathways (and the states of consciousness they create when they're active) will be the same.

An OBE during meditation can be different from one that happens during an NDE. The person isn't dying when it happens. Their expectations are very different. These influence its manifestations, making it feel quite different. An NDE OBE can involve powerful emotions[406]. In contrast, a strong emotional reaction to an OBE during meditation will tend to pull you out of it, and stop the OBE. OBEs during the death process will have a different emotional tone than the ones that happen during meditation. The core phenomena will be the same, but its secondary sensations might easily be different. For example, what the person feels when they leave or return to their body, their sense of having a 'subtle' body, or the emotions they feel.

If there really are seven phases to the death-process, it implies that it can supports seven primary or 'core' states of consciousness which can be projected onto the screen of our awareness. This projection can be filtered by what other brain parts are doing, and it can be fed by what was happening just before the experience began.

Different limbic structures (alone or in combination with groups of pathways spreading out to include several brain areas) play decisive roles in the various core experiences. Each deep brain part can create different experiences when it's connected to different areas on the surface of the brain. A single deep structure, working in tandem with three different surface structures, can produce three different kinds of experience.

> "If structure dictates function ..., then one would expect (specific) classes of experiences to be associated with specific regions of the brain..." – MA Persinger.

The temporal lobes[407] are believed to be the heaviest contributor to near-death experience phenomena - from the *surface* of the brain. A single deep (limbic) area, when working in connection with the frontal lobes, produces one kind of experience. The same structure will produce other kinds of experiences when operating together with the temporal lobes. Other variations will appear if it's working in tandem with the parietal lobes. When the pathways crucial for the death-process are active or excited, we expect them to create similar experiences, varying according to which of the many other possible areas are involved, following the rule that *mental forms follow neural functions.*

In some cases, the neural structures that support the death–process can be so active that they take over a person's consciousness completely. They can also operate much more quietly, so that instead of dominating an experience, they may just contribute an indefinable spiritual quality to an otherwise ordinary moment. Not only can these groups of pathways vary in the degree of their activation, but they can do so with their neighbors either quiet or active. If a group of pathways supporting a mystic experience is active while the rest of the brain is busy, the experience will be different from the one that would appear if the rest of the brain was quiet.

We don't know whether children will have the same experiences as adults when given access to the Akashic records, because no one has studied the phenomenon. Likewise, no one has studied the kinds of mystic experiences appearing to those who live in solitude, as compared to those who live in monastic communities. We also don't know how much the content of seemingly spontaneous experiences differs from those who attain them through long spiritual practice. There are many factors that can influence a mystic experience. They show tremendous variation across cultures, religious traditions, and individuals. Strange as it may seem, these seven core states, together with all the things that can things influence them, are actually enough to account for the overwhelming majority of mystic experiences, in spite of the fact that each one is unique. A good metaphor might be that the crystalline pattern of ice can explain the structure of all snowflakes, even though they are very rarely identical.

If someone is dying and has an OBE, it's not necessarily a mystic experience, (the way most people usually use the term); it's the death-process. Naturally, one doesn't have to be a mystic to die. But if you see God while you're still on this earth, then you'll be a mystic in the classical sense of the word.

The Life Review can help to make sense of the life you've just lived, the world you lived in, or the cosmos it seems to be a part of. If the same core state appeared while you're still alive, it might easily appear as a moment of profound and insightful self-examination. Afterwards, you might become be more interested in learning things you can apply to the life you're living now. The context for your spiritual learning will change according to what you want to learn, and this can influence the outcome. The very different contexts make it hard to recognize that today's transforming insight[408] about yourself is akin to tomorrow's Life Review.

The same or similar states of consciousness can have completely different meanings and manifestations outside the death-process. The hippocampus supports both the experience of space, and the experience of inner imagery. During the death-process, The Void, for example, feels meaningful. For some psychics, experiencing it during psychic readings, it can offer meaningful images that appear superimposed over a dark space. The void is infinite, implicating the brain's spatial perception and spatial reasoning areas.

It's not likely our evolutionary heritage would've provided us with one neural basis for 'Being in the Light' when one is dying, and another neural basis for the same experience during intense prayer or in response to a crisis. Almost certainly, the same mechanisms are at work in both cases. Having two structures doing the same thing would be inefficient, and evolution favors efficiency. Our evolutionary heritage has provided us with a ready-made set of sacred pathways supporting the death-process. If the same pathways are activated during one's life, the result is a religious or mystic experience[409] of some kind.

They are also many labels for the experiences. A person might think they've had a moment of God-realization, illumination, self-realization, 'union', 'grace', or cosmic consciousness, to name only a few.

An ideal example of the point is this picture[410] of the vision of Baha'u'llah, the founder of the Baha'i religion, who had been locked up in a completely dark dungeon.

There are three elements in this illustration. The first is the light streaming down on the man as he has his experience. It appears to be another form of The Light that appears in the death-process. It tells us that to be dead is blissful with nothing of which to be afraid of. You've come home - everything is just as it should be.

The second element is the group of shaded spirit beings behind the man.

In the death-process, these beings may appear to be friends, relatives or acquaintances who have died before you. The pile of books at the man's feet is the third element. Books can appear during the Transcendent Experience phase, as one form of Akashic Records. The books will reveal any mystery[411], however subtle or secret. Here we see a different form of something that happens as part of the death-process, which marks it as depicting an authentic mystic experience.

Another experience is Astral Travel, often confused with OBEs. Astral Travel usually doesn't involve 'leaving the body'. Astral travelers find they're already out of it. Instead of seeing the same place their dead body would be (assuming the OBE is part of a death-process and not a meditation experience), they find themselves in another 'plane' or 'dimension'. Astral travel or being in other dimensions has a lot in common with OBEs, but OBEs involve being in *this* dimension. During astral travel, one also has the experience of not being in the body.

They may have the same neural foundations as The Void or visions of landscapes[412]. The "Astral Plane", can be seen as an inner world with the same basis as the inner worlds some people encounter in dreams, making them not unlike a transcendent experience.

The *Being of Light* takes many forms in NDE reports. The manifestations of this experience that happen when a person is still alive also take many forms. Taken together, they're *Visitor Experiences;* encounters with non-physical beings[413]. The explanation of how the brain produces the experience of God will also shed light on visitor experiences of any kind, whether positive or negative, subtle or intense.

Visitor Experiences include angels, gods, spirits, spirit familiars, guardian angels, protective spirits, Apsaras, Gandharvas, the manitou, fairies, muses[414] and Iktomi (the Lakota Indian 'trickster' spirit) to name but a few. They also include much more negative things like a child's monster in the closet, demons under the bed or frightening ghosts. Some people wake up in the middle of the night seeing these (sometimes only half-formed) apparitions out of the corner of their eye, with a feeling of unpleasant foreboding. Monsters in the closet and guardian angels are both created through similar states of consciousness, and reflect similar patterns of activity, but in opposite sides of the limbic system. The Angel is a sensed presence that seems to offer protection only to you. The other is negative, and feels like it threatens you. The experiences are the same, except that the angel recruits the amygdala on the left, while the demon recruits the one on the right. Of course, the fact that we see things all through the death-process implicates any one or perhaps several pathways that contribute to vision.

CHAPTER 8

The Sensed Presence and Visitor Experiences

– A more informal chapter –

D o you ever get the feeling there's someone behind you, but when you turn around to look, your find no one is there? This is a common experience, known as the *Sensed presence*. A few people have never had this feeling, most people have it occasionally and some have it very often. You might be able to tell when someone is really standing behind you or perhaps staring at you, but that's a different experience. Here, we're only talking about the *illusion* of feeling something or someone behind you.

Dr. Persinger has done careful and rigorous studies of the Sensed presence experience, and these have followed several lines of research. One consisted of looking at the neural profiles of those who have the experience often, in comparison to those who have it rarely or never. In another, the God Helmet induced the sensed presence experience in about 80% of Persinger's subjects. Another line of research consisted of looking at how these presences make people feel when they happen, and how the brain activity on each side changes when it happens.

We've already been over Persinger's explanation for the Sensed presence. In brief (again), it starts with the premise that there are two senses of self, one on each side of the brain. The left one is the dominant, linguistic sense of self. The right one is the subordinate self and it has few language skills. Ordinarily, both work together, producing a seamless focus for everything you experience and a fully integrated "self". When the communication between the pathways connecting the two senses of self break down, becomes hyperactive, goes out of phase or loses its coherency, the right hemispheric sense of self changes its role. It moves out from the "shadow" cast by the left hemispheric self (so to speak), making it possible for the left hemispheric "self" to perceive it directly. It manifests as the feeling of a non-physical being, like a spirit, deity, ghost, doppelganger, etc. Together, these are called *visitor experiences*. The most common is a simple sense of a presence.

We can say that the right hemisphere's sense of self is working with different information and emotions while the experience is happening. The two hemispheres don't need to be *completely* disconnected during a Visitor Experience. There are several sets of connections between the hemispheres, and only one of them needs to be disturbed. The anterior commissure, connecting the two amygdalas to each other, is the one that is most likely to be disturbed during such an experience. Its job is to connect the left and right amygdala to one another. When the connections between them aren't working together they way they usually do, a 'social hallucination' will appear; the illusion that you are in the presence of another being, even though you're actually alone. The idea that there are 'social' illusions and hallucinations[415] is not at all strange when we stop to think that disturbances in language centers can create auditory hallucinations. Disturbances in the very close connections between the amygdala and the olfactory bulbs (where the brain connects to the nose) can lead us to smell things that aren't there, and a blow to the head that affects the visual cortex can create visual hallucinations; seeing stars and so forth. We have places in the brain that are crucial in relating to others, and when they work in odd ways, we have odd perceptions of others. We might, in such a moment, feel that everyone is lovable, forgetting that people can sometimes offer threats. We might feel that everyone is out to hurt us. We might think that everyone hates us, or we might perceive people that aren't there at all.

The sensed presence is a portion of our total self, projected outside of ourselves where we can see, hear, or feel it. Our left-hemispheric sense of self keeps its role, allowing us to have the experience. Its capacity for relating to its right hemispheric counterpart is normally somewhat limited. The two hemispheres aren't actually very good at understanding each another. The left is happy or angry, while the right is fearful or calm. One thinks and the other feels, so to speak. You could say that each one makes up for the shortcomings of the other, usually by inhibiting pieces of it. You might think that encountering yourself in such an unusual way would tend to be a transforming experience, but it doesn't seem to be so. Actually, when people talk about encountering themselves, seeing themselves, becoming themselves and so forth, they're using metaphors. These have nothing to do with the self as we understand it here.

Many people can create a *sensed presence* simply by imagining it. In one study[416], people who had NDEs were able to re-create fragments of their experience simply by imagining a presence behind them, and to their left. The technique is simple. First, close your eyes and spend a moment just paying attention to your breathing. Then, you imagine that someone is standing behind you and to the left, where you wouldn't be able to see them even if your eyes were open. Just try it. If you're like most people, the presence will feel good on the left, and uncomfortable on the right.

Most readers will be familiar with the idea that the right side of the brain controls the left side of the body, and the left side of the brain controls the right side of the body. It's a simple case of left-brain/right-body and vice versa. It's more complicated than that with regard to sensing a presence. We're already accustomed to evoking presences with our imaginations, prayers and reminiscences of others. Visions of other beings are perhaps the most common kind of hallucinations, but we also try to evoke them deliberately at times, through our imaginations and memories. The disciple who misses their guru, the lover separated from the beloved, or people who visit graves, are all trying to evoke a presence for themselves. Prayer is a way to try to create a presence. Prayer that makes you feel like God is hearing you is more fulfilling than simple inner talk. Just talking - to no one at all - is stark and futile. The sense of meaning (or *meaningfulness*) is much more likely to appear if you feel someone is listening.

It's easier to feel our words go beyond ordinary speech if they're directed to a deity that we believe exists above and beyond this 'mundane world'. It helps us to have faith that our prayers will be answered. As we'll see later on, this reduces stress, so there is an advantage in keeping the ability to pray intact in our species, even if everyone doesn't have the same aptitude for it. The same structure that responds to the feelings of others, the amygdala, also infuses our moment-to-moment experiences with meaning. We should expect that the most meaningful moments in our lives are those we share with others, and that truly meaningful prayer depends on having a sense of God's presence; relating to him as though He were in the room with us.

When the presence comes, not from imagination, but from a hallucination or brain stimulation, then the sides reverse. Imagining a presence on the left feels good, but when it's hallucinated and appears on the left, it becomes unpleasant. The *sensed presence* experience can have an emotional impact. It's very social character (self-and-other) is explained as an unusual pattern, not only of communication between the two hemispheres in general, but also specifically between the left and right amygdalas. You can use your imagination to *create* the experience, applying your intention and willpower to *force* it to happen. This suggests that the surface of the brain as the main source for the experience of *imagining* a presence. However, when it happens through a *hallucination*, the amygdala is its most likely source. When the sensed presence experience begins deep in the limbic system, the presence on the left will be negative[417]. When its source lies close to the surface, the presence on the left will be positive.

The Sensed presence experience relies on a disturbance in the communication between the two hemispheres, and this calls the 'split brain experiments' to mind. Actually, these weren't so much a series of experiments as an attempt to treat otherwise incurable epilepsy. The two sides of the brain were split by cutting the *corpus callosum*, the largest bundle of nerve fibers connecting them. After surgery, the patients suffered from a strange but subtle defect. When given an object, they would know either what it was for or what it was called, but not both at the same time. In most cases, the patients were unaware that anything was wrong. We're not going to go into the details of these studies. Several popular books about the brain describe them very well. In much the same way as the 'split brain' patient has their mind cut in two, a person having a sensed presence experience has their sense of self cut in two, even if only for a moment.

In these moments, the left hemispheric sense of self can perceive its right hemispheric counterpart directly. We might sense it, feeling that someone is just behind us, or we might actually see it. We might hear a voice within our head, or one that seems to come from outside us. It might even seem to touch you. Like a servant, who remains discreetly behind the master whenever he is at work, but is free to roam around when the master is asleep, the right hemispheric self projects outside of the mind and appears as a presence somewhere around us. The 'self' on the left is programmed to make it function as the *only* self, and it continues to operate as the focus for our experiences. Because that job is already taken by the left-sided 'self', there is nowhere else for the right hemispheric sense of self to appear, except outside the body's space. To use a technical phrase, it feels like an *ego-alien* presence.

The most intense forms of these experiences appear when activity in the amygdala is first inhibited and then excited so suddenly that much more excitement moves between the right and left amygdalas than would ever happen ordinarily. It can sometimes be enough to overload synapses that would usually inhibit this kind of movement. This process combs out some of the synapses that usually hold back activity in only one direction (from right to left for positive experiences, and the opposite way for negative ones), a bit like a comb that easily moves through straight hair, but pulls out knotted ones.

There is a related experience, where people have half an out of body experience, or feel that they are half in and half out of their bodies at the same time. I also experienced this as a child suffering from temporal lobe epilepsy. I once interviewed a woman who had just such an experience in adulthood and remembered it very well. One of her bodies, the physical one, was able to think in words and was quite detached about the whole thing. The other, floating below the ceiling, could not think in words and was in a state of fear. It was an OBE, which began in the right hemisphere, but didn't quite reach over into the left.

The most fearful structure in the brain, the right amygdala, is a next-door neighbor to the right hippocampus, which appears to play a role in OBEs. In her case, the self that was out of her body was in fear. The self that remained in her body was able to go on thinking in words, because the language structures remained available to it. Having no direct connection to the right amygdala – the *self* on the left felt no fear at all. It may also be that, just as the sensed presence appears when the two amygdalas are disconnected, these dual-OBEs happen when the two hippocampuses are not communicating as they normally would.

Very often, people who have sensed presence experiences also have other common altered state experiences[418], like déjà vu or the feeling that their bodies are moving when they're actually keeping still. Such people often have tingly sensations while listening to music (together, these are called *Temporal Lobe Signs*). They are also more likely to be poets, psychologists, artists, musicians and abstract thinkers, who all have a common need to articulate aesthetic perceptions and ideas; the need to integrate information from both hemispheres. In addition to being creative, they are also more likely to be suggestible, anxious and emotional. In general, women experience the sensed presence more often than men. This is probably due to women's extra connections between hemispheres. It also happens more often to people who meditate, and those caught up in otherworldly ideas, whether they're about religion, metaphysics, aliens, or reflect the delusions of mental illness. The sensed presence experience can seem to offer proof for their beliefs to a person who fits this last profile ("I feel the spirit, so I know it's the truth").

The emotional impact of the moment plays an important role, too. Of course, it determines whether the experience is positive or negative[419], but the intensity of the emotion determines the intensity of the experience. Any powerful emotion can leave one side of the brain more active than the other, and this can have a brief but profound impact on communication between the hemispheres. As a result, sensed presence experiences are more common during times of fear and anxiety, when the most sensitive structure in the brain, the amygdala, is more active on the right side than on the left. It also means that the sensed presence experience is more likely during the *aftermath* of intense left-hemispheric emotions, such as anger or joy, and this leads us to our next theme.

The Visitor Experience

The Visitor Experience is a spectrum – actually three spectra - of experiences. The first runs from very mild to very intense. The second ranges from deeply blissful to unspeakably hellish. The last applies to the entire human race, running from people who never experience such visitors, to those who experience them constantly. The first two relate to individual experiences, while the third relates to the entire population.

Several studies have been done using questionnaires that looked at how often people had religious experiences and altered states of consciousness. They asked about experiences like déjà vu, the *sensed presence*, tingly sensations, feeling one's body moving when it's actually at rest and seeing points of light at the edge of one's vision. There were also questions about dissociation, the autokinetic effect (where things seem to move if you stare at them long enough), and some other more intense experiences, such as feeling the presence of the God they pray to, out of body experiences, and the sudden and random experience of bliss. Taken together, these sensations are known as *Temporal Lobe Signs*. Over several years, over 2000 psychology students completed the questionnaires. Of course, psychology students don't represent the whole population, but there's no reason to think that their brains, as a group, are much different from any other group.

The studies found that the number of people experiencing these sensations almost constantly was about the same as the number who never had them at all. The number also equaled the number of people having an *average* number of experiences. In other words, there was an even spread of sensitivity to these altered-state experiences throughout the population. The result *wasn't* a bell curve. A bell curve is the curve that appears when you describe the frequency of random events. It has the highest numbers in the middle and the lowest numbers at each end. Bell curve mathematics applies only to *random* events. A spectrum is very different, because what you find in the middle is very much like what you find at either end, suggesting a nonrandom, functional arrangement.

The wide range of sensitivity to altered states, without any one group dominating the population, makes our evolutionary strategy, our uniquely human formula for survival, more effective. Sensitivity to altered-state experiences is spread evenly throughout the population, and this also spreads out the personality traits appearing with them. In this way, the range of perspectives and personalities accompanying these traits will be evenly distributed, and every event, no matter how trivial, could extract a wide range of responses from the community, as they discussed it in tribal councils. This makes it possible for the social group to select the best responses to threats or opportunities.

CHAPTER 9

Out-of-Body
Experiences (OBEs)

I n the West, OBEs are the most common phenomenon at the beginning of NDEs. In other cultures, it may begin with a messenger from the underworld. Both experiences make the person realize that they're dead, but they express the point in very different ways. They seem to be two very different manifestations of the same state of consciousness.

The OBE is uncommon, but not unknown, in the NDEs of Asia and India. This may have to do with how the popular cultures in these areas recognize OBEs as a sign of progress in meditation, a skill belonging to holy men and women, or perhaps a moment of "divine grace".

In many, if not most, OBEs during the death-process, the person sees their own body. Some researchers call these autoscopic OBEs (AOBE). *Autoscopic* means to see yourself.

OBEs in NDEs often involve the person leaving their body, and looking down to see their own corpse. This perception forces people to understand that they've died. You can leave your body under other circumstances and think it's a very unusual dream, or the experience of Astral Travel. In an autoscopic OBE, however, you look down and see your own body, with all your body's traits, like your hair color, hairline, skin tone and any identifiable scars. When that happens, and you think, "My God, that's me!" you know you're dead. If you add the anticipation of your own death, whether suddenly in terror, or after some time fighting a terminal disease (during which, hopefully, you have come to a sense of surrender and acceptance), it would be easy to recognize this OBE as the beginning of your death. Understanding that you're dead, while having an OBE, should be even easier if your corpse is damaged, surrounded by people in grief, or very old.

What Brain Parts Are Involved In OBEs?

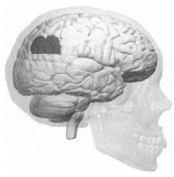

The Right Angular Gyrus[420]

Several areas of the brain are implicated in OBEs.

In 2002, a Swedish epileptologist, Dr. Olaf Blanke, stimulated an OBE from a thirty-four year old female epileptic patient[421]. He was performing surgery to locate the starting point of her epileptic seizures. When he touched a spot on the right side of her brain with an electrode (*the angular gyrus*), the patient had an OBE.

He repeated the stimulation and he found that he got the same result every time. This implicated the angular gyrus on the right side of the brain as a 'center' for out of body experiences. He also elicited several "sensed presence" experiences. Interestingly, she only had OBEs when her eyes were open. When they were closed, she only felt her body had changed position, but didn't have an OBE[422]. There appears to be a connection between vestibular sensations, where your body feels like it's moving even though you're staying still (as in vertigo), and out of body experiences. Some teachers who guide people to have out of body experiences begin by encouraging them to allow such sensations whenever they appear.

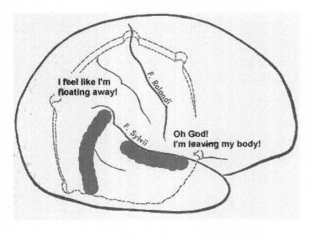

When Dr. Wilder Penfield stimulated a spot forward of the right temporal lobe, just below the *Sylvian Fissure* (F. Sylvii), one of his patients said, "Oh God, I'm leaving my body"[423]. He stimulated another OBE by putting his electrode on the area shown in this Illustration[424], towards the back of the brain. When this area was stimulated, one of his patients said, "I feel like I'm floating away"[425]. Interestingly, another researcher's patient, stimulated in the same area, reported being in two places at once; both in their body and out of their body at the same time[426].

Recently, Persinger did an experiment[427] in which a subject had an OBE while they were being monitored by EEG, while their brains were being stimulated with a certain pattern of magnetic stimulation. That single experiment uncovered a possible characteristic EEG 'signature' for OBEs, in which the right frontal lobe became synchronized with the left temporal lobe.

The most common question about OBEs is "Is the person really out of their body?" There is very little solid scientific evidence, but not everyone who asks this question is a scientist. Some scientists dismiss stories about paranormal phenomena as 'anecdotal'. If they are unable to attach any numbers to the stories or reproduce the events, they may disregard them completely.

People who have had out of body experiences usually want to know what happened to them and how it happened. Those who are intrigued by OBEs, seeing them as deep and profound mysteries, will often ask the same thing. Some, especially in the Hindu and Buddhist worlds, want to see OBEs proven "real" to support and buttress their religious faith, including the belief that one is not one's body.

These people don't demand rigorous proof, and none of them are willing throw away their opinions until such proofs appear. Individuals, wanting to know if death will be the end of it all, don't need scientific proof to accept the veridicality of OBEs. The kind of investigations conducted in courtrooms, with its system of witnesses and corroborating evidence, would conclude that the sense of self exists outside the body in OBEs. The editor of a scientific journal might find that there is too little hard evidence, and too many less-than-formal stories, and conclude that it's not possible to draw a conclusion. They might even be hostile to such a "woo-woo" idea.

It would be a mistake to think that proof that OBEs are (or aren't) veridical would also prove or disprove the existence of a soul. The word 'soul' implies more than just a sentient entity. It also implies one that exists forever. It may be that the sense of self is maintained outside the body only for long enough to complete the death-process, and after that, it just no longer operates. If it isn't eternal, it's not the soul, at least as most major religious traditions use the word. This doesn't mean there is no such thing as a soul. If it exists, it will need a separate hypothesis to explain it.

OBE drawn by a seven year-old girl[428].

There are many reports of people having out of body experiences, and seeing things they couldn't have seen were they in their bodies. Children, who knew nothing about resuscitation procedures, were able to accurately describe them later on. Patients have mentioned people who had been in the room while they were unconscious. People who lost consciousness in an accident, and only awoke later in a hospital, were still able to accurately describe the paramedic's procedures immediately after the accident. All of these scenes were viewed and described as seen from an out-of-body perspective.

There are also several published accounts of people describing the scene around their body *incorrectly*. Obviously, having out of body experience doesn't always make you an accurate psychic, and not every out of body perception is valid. How do we reconcile the extremely accurate descriptions of resuscitation procedures with the mistakes that people who've had OBEs make when they described the scene around their body?

I think the solution to whether or not out of body experiences are "real" is that OBEs are hallucinations, but the hallucination is of their actual physical environment. They perceive the environment that surrounds them, but reconstructed from within their own mind. Even though the person is unconscious, some perceptions still get through, and shape the content of their hallucination. Even if they're unconscious, a person can still often react to the words spoken around them, and respond to being touched. Any information from the world around them will be incorporated into their hallucination, tending to increase its accuracy.

I will not go so far as to say that *all* OBEs are hallucinations. It's not impossible that the magnetic components of a person's consciousness could still exist outside the body, integrated with the Earth's magnetic field. We will return to this theme in later chapters.

CHAPTER 10

God and the Brain

L et's begin with the idea that there's a relationship between God
and our brains. When a person is eating, their brainwaves (EEG
patterns) taken will show certain patterns. Others will appear
they're when falling asleep, and different patterns will appear when
they're running uphill.

Each behavior, thought or feeling will create different "brain wave"
patterns. It's not a very big step to imagine your brain waves will have
unique patterns when you're on the top of a mountain, with your arms
upraised, enraptured in prayers of adoration. Others will occur when you
feel connected to God in any other way; through prayer, reflection on the
points of your faith in God, or while having a powerful vision of God.
They'll appear when you are praying, thinking of God, or even just hearing
words that remind you of Him. This brings us to our starting point, the
recognition that God, whatever that means to you, has either some place
in your brain, or some effect on it. Our relationship with God, whether
based on a spiritual truth or an illusion, happens in or through the brain.

According to many scientists, God exists only within the brain and
mind, whereas according to most theologians, God exists independently
of anything psychological. The lines of research behind this book offer
no proof for or against the objective existence of God. For those who
believe in Him, the experience of God, whether deep or superficial,
will involve your neural hardware. God may not exist only through
your mind and brain, but *you* do. Your ability to perceive God (no

227

matter how you understand him), as well as the book you're holding in your hands now; depend on *you* and your brain.

The understanding of the brain's role in the experience of God began with some observations by the famous Canadian neurosurgeon, Dr. Wilder Penfield, who did his best work between the 1940's and the 1960's. He stimulated the surface of the temporal lobes of some of his epileptic patients using an electrode[429], and some very interesting things happened. He elicited a number of what he called *psychical* (a term from an earlier era) experiences. These included out of body experiences, visions, depersonalization, and strange sensations that aren't easy to describe in words. He also reported a few of the spiritual experiences that some of his epileptic patients had during their seizures. Although he is more renowned for his discovery that the brain has maps of the body, the link he saw between the brain and spirituality would eventually help lead researchers to understand the role of the brain in mysticism and religion.

One of Penfield's published cases[430], showed an explicit link between the brain and spirituality. One epileptic patient had visions of God, seeing Him coming down from the sky, framed as though in a picture. He saw the link between spirituality and the brain, but neuroscience had to wait some decades before the connection was understood.

We'll take the stories of meetings with God as anecdotal[431] reports of real experiences. I'm not saying that they actually saw God. Likewise, I'm not saying they didn't. What I am saying is that they had an *experience* of God, whether real or illusory. Dreams are real experiences, but usually not experiences of reality. The subjective character of dreams hasn't stopped science from looking for explanations for them, nor will it stop science from looking at religious visions.

Dostoyevsky, for example, had seizures, that didn't include clear visions of God, but they did have experiences of bliss and ecstasy so intense that he couldn't attribute them to anything else. He wrote about just such an experience in *The Dispossessed*.

Although the temporal lobes work primarily to create and retrieve memories, they also have a number of other functions. The temporal lobes are the source for most religious and mystic experiences[432]. Several researchers have described how people with temporal lobe epilepsy are often prone to be deeply involved with religion and spirituality. Many of those suffering from this type of epilepsy have reported seizures containing spiritual themes, hallucinatory 'interior locutions'[433] (hearing voices), and visions.

The frontal lobes are concerned with the future, anticipation, extrapolation, and expectation, as well as planning and thinking about how to relate to other people. When we humans emerged as a species, our cultures became more complex and so did our frontal lobes, the basis of our ability to relate to others. One trait we probably acquired at this time was empathy, the ability to imagine ourselves feeling what others would feel in similar circumstances. This is different from being able to feel other people's emotional states intuitively. We can think about the consequences of our words and actions in terms of how they would make others feel. We can watch another person in a 'social situation', like undergoing a ceremony, coming home from a successful hunt, being shamed in front of the group, having a baby, or being seen in conversation with the chief or the Shaman, or any one of a thousand situations, and have some idea how the person feels. Early humans might have been forced to imagine themselves as dead when they tried to feel empathy for a dead person, but empathy fails us when we look at a corpse. It failed us in our early evolutionary period, too. Our ability to be aware of our own personal death necessarily grew at this time, but not our ability to understand the death-process. Thus, the lore about death has two contradictory messages, and these are found in almost every culture. One is that death is a mystery, and no one knows what it will be like until it happens. The other is that death is a continuation of life.

> "Death is just another path. One that we all must take. The grey rain curtain rolls back and all turns to silver clouds. And then you see it. White shores…. and beyond… a far green country under a swift sunrise."
> J.R.R. Tolkien *"Return of the King"*

Dr. Persinger suggested that the only way people can understand the fact of their own death is to think about it[434]. We're predisposed to harbor a healthy kind of denial about the fact of our own death, which allows us to live with constant awareness of threats to our survival (helping us avoid them and so, to survive), but without too much anxiety.

Nobody has first-hand experience of what death is like, because no one, except the few who've died and come back to life, has ever been dead. The only way we can understand we're going to die is to think about it, and arrive at the verbal construction - *I WILL DIE*. From that point, death demands a personal acceptance of the inevitable. The first intellectual understanding that each person's life ends in death for our species could have run something like this:

> This person got old and they died. Another person got old; and then they died. I look at my reflection in a stream and see my wrinkled skin and gray hairs, and think, 'Oh, dear! I'm going to die too.'

In another scenario, a person might begin to show symptoms of an illness that they know killed other people, and see that they, too, are not long for this world.

The knowledge (or "meme") that everyone has to die probably entered our cultures just as soon as the neural pathways needed to understand it appeared in our brains – possibly in the very first generations of Homo sapiens.

Of course, as soon as it became apparent to our newly–appearing species that each person is going to die, this crucial understanding would be encoded in myths, stories, or other memes. From that point on, people would be told, in one way or another, that they would not live forever. However, there is still a huge difference between knowing that people die, and having a real sense of your own mortality.

Understanding that living things die is very different from taking death personally; knowing that 'I' will die. We're not born knowing we can cease to exist at any time. All parents have a moment when their three or four-year old asks, "Does everyone have to die?" The reason it happens while a child is still learning to speak reflects something of our evolutionary history.

When we emerged as a species, our temporal lobes were able to remember more kinds of information, and the frontal lobes acquired a more extensive ability to extrapolate into the future; make plans, build expectations, and anticipate things before they happen, especially when relating to other people. The first questions about death appear during the 'preoperational' stage[435] in a child's growth, when children begin to use language to represent experience (both in their minds, and in the world around them), and to use symbols to represent objects. Early in this stage, they also personify objects (not 'the book, but rather 'Mr. Book'). Their ability to think about things and events that aren't immediately present improves. During this period, a child begins to make simple abstractions, allowing them to believe that the 'person' they knew is no longer in 'their' body. They can imagine that the 'person' has 'gone somewhere' more easily than they can imagine that they no longer exist. Contemplating our own non-existence involves very abstract thinking. It's a lot of work, and it means overcoming our natural denial about it.

One of the easiest ways to try to understand death is to imagine it's like something we already know. Dreams show each person that the mind and the body can be in different states at the same time, and provides a ready metaphor for death. In form only – not in content. True or not, young children have an easy time believing it, and early in our evolutionary history probably everyone else did too, because there were no ideas to compete with it. Dying is like entering a dream, and being alive is like being awake. Alternately, being alive is like being asleep, and death is a kind of 'waking up'.

The frontal lobes were able to extrapolate into the future, more widely and abstractly than before. The unlikely experience of personal death can be arrived at as a conclusion, even by a three year-old. People know they're going to die, but they tend to suppress such thoughts to avoid the stress and anxiety they create. This suppression[436] is one of the foundations for spirituality.

The belief that we're somehow going to live forever is found in all religions.[437] We don't die. We move on. Death isn't the end. It's an awakening. Death is a transition to the spirit world. Death is going home. Death is leaving to go and be with the Gods. Death is joining our Father in heaven. There doesn't seem to be a culture on earth without a religion expressing this idea. I'm not saying that we have souls or that we don't. The word soul doesn't have a scientific definition, so using it here will tend to move us away from science and into theology.

However, belief in the immortality of our souls seems to have played a role in our evolution, whether it's real or not. It allowed us to know that 'death is stalking us', without facing the fear, depression, hopelessness and despair that knowing this can create. The human brain is equipped with the ability to know that death is real, but without taking it seriously.

We can suppress our awareness of our own individual mortality, and reduce death anxiety, but we can't suppress it completely, and we can't keep it out of our minds all the time. We have no trouble presuming the possibility of our own death when our life is threatened, but it's easy to forget about it while we're comparatively safe. In small doses, death anxiety is a good thing. It encourages us to anticipate potential threats to our survival, and take steps to avoid them. As we walk through a jungle, we're much more likely to keep looking up to avoid becoming their prey when we know that jaguars high in the trees might jump down and kill us.

Our ability to anticipate various ways of dying and act to avoid them helps us survive, but always being aware of our own death can be very stressful. Try the following exercise if you think you can consider your own death without any stress or psychological discomfort. Pretend your doctor has just told you you've got a terminal illness. How do you feel? If you're feeling okay, it's probably because your religious faith (which means different things to different people) invoked the idea that you won't really cease to exist.

Spirituality extends our lives, helping us live without the stress that death anxiety creates. At the same time, beliefs about death make us aware of the fact and reality of death, which helps us reduce our chances of dying prematurely. They make life easier, and help it last longer. However, both being aware of death and in denial about it at the same time demands a special psychological defense mechanism. Human evolution has allowed us to make constant efforts to stay alive, without always being worried about dying.

In Hinduism, the name for a first-hand vision of God is *Darshan*[438]. Some Christians call it *contemplatio*. In discussing the direct experience of God, we'll start by accepting that it's a real experience; that most people who've said they've met God face-to-face aren't telling lies. Of course, many of them *have* lied[439], but if we accept that even a few of them are telling the truth, then we're presented with the challenge of explaining how these experiences appear.

One explanation is that there actually is a God; a creator of the universe. In this explanation, the creator of the universe has an individual relationship with each person, making his presence available to them, when he chooses to reveal himself. The one we're going to work with in this book is that our brains are able to create the experience. If so, a question arises. Why are we able to have a face-to-face meeting with what seems to be the creator of the universe, the source of love, bliss, knowledge, acceptance and all of God's other divine attributes? The answer is straightforward - we're wired for it. The brain mechanisms supporting our death-process include the ability to see God, though only under certain circumstances.

Another look at the limbic system

Visions of God depend on limbic activity, so we'll take a moment to review the limbic system once again.

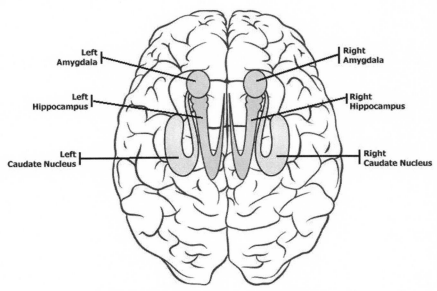

A simplified rendering of the brain's Limbic System[440].

In this review of the limbic system, we'll emphasize the differences between the functions of its parts on each side of the brain. This will help us to see how phenomena from a limbic structure on one side of the brain tends to happen along with other phenomena from other limbic structures on the same side of the brain. The simplest example we'll see is that right hemispheric experiences tend to be accompanied by relaxation, and left hemispheric experiences are more likely to appear with excitement.

In the illustration above, the two round structures at the top are the left and right amygdalas. The hippocampus and the caudate nucleus appear below it and are directly connected to it. The amygdala, hippocampus, and caudate nucleus seem to be the main 'centers' for the death-process, and the primary sources for mystic experiences. Other structures in the limbic system also contribute, including the ones that connect specific brain parts to their counterparts on the other side of the brain.

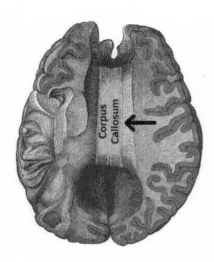

The fact that there are structures that function only to keep them communicating with each other lets us see how important they are. The connections between them, with their predominantly emotional and social functions, follow their own dedicated groups of pathways, rather than being shunted through the corpus callosum, which carries the overwhelming majority of communication between brain's two hemispheres. More importantly for us, the amygdala and the hippocampus each have other structures that keep them connected to their counterparts on the opposite side of the brain. For the amygdala, it's through anterior commissure and, to a lesser extent, the frontal lobes. For the hippocampus it's through two structures, the *fornix commissure* and the *dorsal hippocampal commissure*.

Looking at these cross-brain structures helps to illustrate how unique the functions of the amygdala and hippocampus are, as well as how separated their operations are from those of other areas.

Let's briefly review some of the functions of the amygdala, beginning with the one on the left side of the brain.

The Amygdala

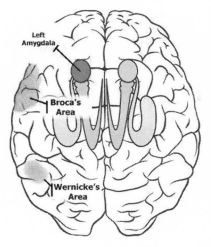

The left amygdala is specialized for joy, happiness, elation and bliss. It's probably the only driver for the raw experience of positive emotion[441], even though it can also to contribute to fear. In addition, it plays an important role in anger and irritability.

The left amygdala assigns a positive emotional tone to positive events, so we feel good when good things happen.

The left amygdala responds to positive facial expressions, according to the feeling they express, and becomes quieter when it confronts fearful faces.

The left side of the brain is also where the language centers (Wernicke's and Broca's areas) are found. The emotions that rely on the left amygdala, like happiness and anger, are more easily expressed in words than fearful feelings, because the left amygdala is closer to the primary language centers.

The right amygdala is specialized for fear and anxiety, and also

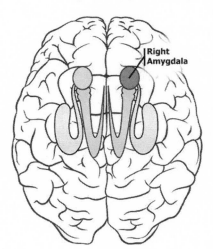

contributes to depression. It activates in response to fearful faces.

The right amygdala's emotions, located on the opposite side of the brain from the language centers, usually find us somewhat inarticulate, like when we're in fear, sadness, or depression. We have a harder time thinking of the right thing to say when we're scared or depressed.

The right amygdala is one of the most vigilant brain parts, always keeping us aware of potential threats to our social position and physical well-being.

The Right Hippocampus

The right hippocampus is involved with creating and accessing memories. It's also involved with music, especially rhythm, as well as spatial perception and reasoning.

The left and right sides of the brain "think" very differently. On the right, its activity is quite subtle and because it happens without words, it's hard to describe. For a musician, it can be pitch, tone, rhythm, harmony, melody, counterpoint and so forth. For an artist it can be form, colors, shapes, shades and so on. For a chef, it would be texture, taste and smell. This 'silent thinking' brain part contributes to all sorts of activities in conjunction with different areas of the brain's surface.

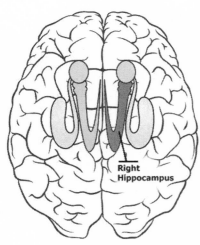

Right
Hippocampus

God Helmet stimulation with a signal taken from the hippocampus showed that activity in the one on the right is more pleasant than in the one on the left[442]. The right hippocampus is the primary source (If not the only source)[443] of theta activity in the brain; the brainwave patterns associated with meditation, hypnosis, trance and other 'inward' states of consciousness. It's also the source of mental imagery and the images that appear in our dreams.

The content of our dreams, it seems, is woven from episodes taken from our memories, including symbols, motifs, and allegories we've learned. This happens through hippocampal contributions to REM sleep[444]. It 'does' its thinking and cognition through contextualization, associations and extrapolations, all the while checking everything against our memories. It can take a single thought or perception, and infer all sorts of things from it, so its related themes can fill out our dreams. Most dreams reflect the person's ordinary life (with our experiences filling out of our dreams, often three days after the event[445]), but a few are strange spirit journeys to places the person has never seen. As both dream images and theta activity, (which has been associated with psychic perceptions[446]) depend on the same structure, the possibility of psychic perceptions may be stronger during our dreams, at least for those whose right hippocampus is more active than usual. The time it takes to forget an event is the same as the time it takes for the event to appear in a dream (about three days) – both memory and dream imagery are within the domain of the hippocampus and the nearby areas that support it.

Although the route is very circuitous, (via the cingulate gyrus), the hippocampus is more extensively connected to the frontal lobes than to any other area on the surface of the brain. Along with many other functions, the frontal lobes are specialized for thinking about ways to relate to other people. Many of our responses to other people happen intuitively. Choices about how to respond to people, according to whether or not they may be a threat, have authority over you, how vulnerable they are or how emotional they are at any given time, are made largely without verbal thinking. There are many kinds of non-verbal thinking, and these will usually involve contributions from the right hippocampus.

The Caudate Nucleus

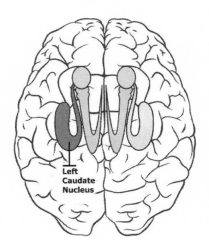

The next structure is the caudate nucleus, sometimes called the *emotive-visceral integrator*. It integrates our body's state of relaxation or tension with our emotional states.

On the left, it supports *arousal*; the body's state of excitement when in states of anger, sex, joy and excitement. Think of how little kids react when they get good news. They may jump up and down, and squeal with delight.

237

This image might almost symbolize the action of the left caudate nucleus. Working with other structures, the caudate nucleus is also involved in romantic love[447], as well as the kind mothers feel for their infants[448], and even "unconditional" love[449].

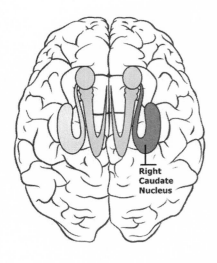

Right
Caudate
Nucleus

The right caudate nucleus supports relaxation. Depression nearly always involves relaxation, silent thinking and low self-esteem. These are all on the right. When a person gets depressed enough, they can relax to the point where they become lethargic, and have trouble dragging themselves out of bed. Some become so relaxed that the words needed to express themselves don't come easily[450]. When asked to talk about how they're feeling, they often reply with silence. The words may appear in their minds, but never coalesce into a coherent answer.

On the left, we have joy, excitement and verbal thinking. Really good news can make us so happy that our bodies are filled with energy. If the source of such joy or bliss is something spiritual, there may be an urge to "shout it from the rooftops"[451] or "Go tell it from the mountain. Over the hills and everywhere". It might be romantic, so you're unable to stop talking about your new relationship. Perhaps, at some point, you may have found yourself with a compelling need to talk about such an experience. People who have frequent spiritual episodes without experienced guidance sometimes fill reams of diaries and journals, just like schizophrenics. Schizophrenia has bursts of manic joy, rapid speech and episodes that feel deeply meaningful, even though they may mean nothing when the patient recovers. Indeed, the Caudate Nucleus on the dominant side of the brain (usually the left) has been found to be involved in schizophrenic hallucinations[452].

The *phenomena*; the main symptoms of depression are right hemispheric. The right hippocampus is the primary (and possibly the only) source of the theta activity[453] associated with the extreme calm and inner quiet appearing in deeper states of meditation[454]. The relaxation achieved in meditation implicates the caudate nucleus on the same side of the brain. In fact, the two are connected, but not as extensively as the amygdala and the hippocampus. When both the right hippocampus and the right caudate nucleus are working together at unusually high levels, they can 'crowd out' the right amygdala, responsible for fear and anxiety. This is why meditation, which can create a calm state of mind, and help achieve a relaxed body, makes people less prone to fear and anxiety[455]. The 'gut feeling' of fear has a harder time getting started.

Again, joy, arousal and thinking in words are all on the same (left) side of the brain. Fear, silent thinking, and relaxation are on the opposite (right) side of the brain. When any of these sensations are strong enough, it makes the others, on the same side of the brain more likely, and the opposite phenomena, on the other side of the brain, less likely. The silent thinking of the right hippocampus can drain (to use a metaphor) activity from its next-door neighbor, the fearful amygdala. Elation and happiness coming from the left amygdala can also drain activity from the other structures on the left side of the brain. When an experience drives a brain structure to high levels of excitement, its counterpart on the opposite side[456] can become quiet, and the structures that surround it on the same side can become more excited.

There's a kind of symmetry to this arrangement, and it's going to become important as we discuss how the brain creates the experience of God, and how that experience can change the brain.

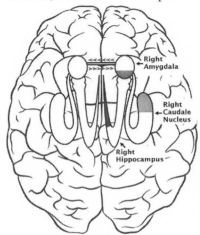

The *Vision of God*[457] usually begins with fear, depression or pain: right amygdala excitement. The other deeper structures on the right side of the brain are also active, but not to the same extent. The amygdala, the most sensitive structure of them all, dominates the experience. Other parts of the brain will be involved, but these will differ from moment to moment and from person to person. This is not the first phase of the God experience. It only sets the stage.

In this example, the right hippocampus and the right caudate nucleus are shown as being somewhat active. If the left caudate were active instead of the right, it would still be fear, but with the focus on either fight or flight. Here, it looks more like fear with a sense of hopelessness, high anxiety or perhaps sadness. Of course, this is an idealized image of the limbic system in a moment of fear. The actual picture would be much more complex, with lots of structures on both sides of the brain participating to some degree.

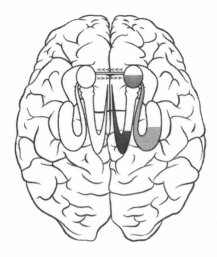

Here, right-hemispheric dominance of the moment is increasing, and (not shown) these same structures are becoming quieter on the left side of the brain.

As the process continues, we find that the right amygdala is 'filling up' along with the right hippocampus. The right caudate nucleus is becoming increasingly active. The person is not just feeling fear. Now, they are terror-struck and at a complete loss for words. If they were feeling depressed earlier, they are now in a state of total anguish or absolute despair. The right limbic system is now working almost to capacity.

These experiences can come from many places. They can be from within the brain, as may happen with a very powerful anxiety attack or from the "real world", when someone is in extreme danger, like when a bus is closing in on them at such high speed that there's no time to escape or when being attacked by a tiger, whose powerful jaws are starting to rip at their body. It doesn't really matter what the source of the terror is. The brain uses the same structures to create fear, no matter where it comes from.

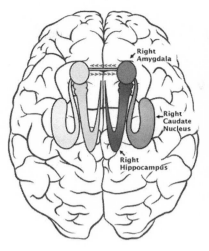

Now we reach the stage where both the right amygdala and the right hippocampus are working at their full capacity. There is real inner silence. The despair is total. The abject terror becomes stronger, turning into a sense of impending doom. The right caudate nucleus is now so active that the person is limp with fear, and the person might be speechless with dread.

Of course, this is hypothetical. In fact, the relative levels of excitement could be very different for others, even when they are confronted with the same external triggers. A lot depends on the person's individual neural history. Another person might need their right amygdala working to its maximum before their right caudate nucleus even began to respond. Each brain is different, and with those differences come differences in the way one brain part responds to activity coming from another. Different people can have very different 'thresholds' where specific brain structures become excited.

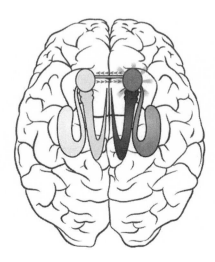

Here, the right limbic system is full to capacity, especially the right amygdala. For some, it will be terror, and for others despair. Of course, the surface of the brain will become involved in any process that makes the limbic system very active. The precise areas drawn into the process will vary for each person, so this intense activation of the right amygdala will never create exactly the same experience in any two people.

241

Now, we've arrived at the last part of the neural process behind visions of God.

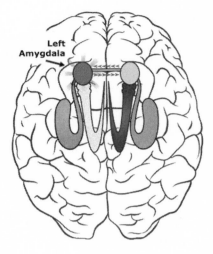

At this point, the right amygdala, the most sensitive structure in the brain, goes past the threshold where it dumps its activity over into the left side of the brain. Suddenly, instead of terror or despair, we feel bliss and contentment. Such a person might see *the light* and perhaps have an experience of God.

This process is called an 'Interhemispheric Intrusion' (see chapter 4). The threshold at which these happen is almost always reached in the amygdala before other nearby structures, because its activation thresholds are lower than those of any other part of the brain.

It doesn't take a neural avalanche of this kind for a person to see God during the death-process. In that context, the process happens naturally. Remember, we work with the idea that the death-process is intrinsic to our species, so the pathways that support the experience of God don't need higher levels of excitement to activate them when someone is dying. We might say that death holds to key to the experience, while an interhemispheric intrusion is more like breaking down the door.

There are four reasons why the overloaded right amygdala dumps its activity into its counterpart on the left instead of some other structure. First, the other structures on the right are already very busy, so pathways into the other side of the brain become the paths of least resistance. Secondly, the anterior commisure is dedicated to communication between the amygdala on each side, and provides a ready channel where activity can go. The third reason is that the patterns of information ("brain waves") within the right amygdala are also meaningful to the left amygdala. Finally, both amygdalas operate with approximately the same amount of electrical energy. In most cases, the right amygdala is a little more sensitive than the one on the left.

The hippocampus on the right, having slightly higher thresholds than the amygdala, isn't under the same pressure. Once the right amygdala has transferred its activity to its counterpart on the left, the entire right hemisphere becomes much quieter. Other structures, being less sensitive, are less likely to reach the high thresholds at which their activity is transferred across the brain. The right hippocampus can remain active even after the focus of amygdala activity has shifted from the right hemisphere to the left.

The fearful (right) amygdala sends a huge load of activity across the brain, and then quiets down. Once the overall pressure on the right hemisphere has been relieved, there is far less need to move large amounts of activity out of it, keeping an approximate dynamic equilibrium[458] between the two hemispheres. The right hippocampus can remain active even after the next-door amygdala has become quiet, because the hippocampus is not as sensitive as the amygdala. The left amygdala and the right hippocampus are the two structures most likely to dominate the moment immediately after a right-to-left Interhemispheric Intrusion. In simpler terms, the 'bliss' structure, and the 'silent knowing' structure are the deep brain parts most likely to be highly active during and after a vision of God.

The combination of intense left amygdala and right hippocampus excitement creates a moment where all kinds of non-verbal information are available to the person having the experience. At the same time, they may be filled with bliss, the presence of God, light, radiance and exultation. The left caudate nucleus can now become more active, and if that happens, the person feels fervent and impassioned, or may feel waves of love. In that state, nonverbal phenomena (from the right hippocampus) rapidly finds expression in words. They might start speaking or writing about their spiritual insights. Because the left amygdala also contributes the sense of positive meaningfulness, these insights will seem profoundly meaningful. Sometimes they really are – a detail that distinguishes mystics from madmen. If the right caudate nucleus remains active, the person might feel a deep relaxation, or a sense of calm relief, as their once-profound troubles now seem trivial.

They have "been there"; they have *seen*. God has visited them. They are now qualified to proclaim His message to the world at large.

They can write their own scriptures, and share them with the world. This sometimes really happens after people have these experiences. They have a sense that they have been given something important and precious. God knows everything, and the experience of God is often filled with all kinds of subtle, ineffable information from the right hippocampus. In the moment of meeting God, one can have the sense of revelation of all kinds of deep, unstated yet enduring mysteries of existence, the cosmos and of oneself. God (and the right hippocampus) will seem to know everything, but much of it is not in words. "The Tao that can be spoken is not the real Tao". "He who knows does not speak. He who speaks does not know." The right caudate nucleus may continue to be more active than the one on the left, though it would probably still undergo some kind of electrical "insult" (a change) when the Vision of God began, in which case, the experience would not be one of excitement at experiencing a revelation, but rather of deep calm and quiet, with an all-pervasive joy.

A first-hand experience of God can change someone's personality for the rest of their life. From that moment, they are one of the "Holy Ones"; sometimes becoming a religious leader or a spiritual teacher. They are never the same again. The same pathways involved with visions of God are also involved in maintaining the sense of self. The changes following a vision of God are so powerful that people feel as if they've been 'reborn'. The event can leave them feeling they have been chosen for a special task, or that God has given them a ministry. This compelling experience can often be the motivating factor for them to change their lives, putting their vision and its message at its center.

The feeling that they have been changed can all but force a person to convert to another religion. Among born-again Christians, the act of salvation, in which they admit they are a sinner, and ask Jesus to take control of their lives, can be enough to make a person feel they've been born again. That type of conversion is less spontaneous than others, because it relies on making a decision ("to be saved"), yet it's still enough to transform someone. For example Saul, a zealous Pharisee who worked to stamp out Christianity, became Paul of Tarsus after being struck blind by his famous vision on the road to Damascus. He became one of the most important exponents of Christianity in its early years, after working for the Romans to try and stamp it out[459]. Paul worked to reform the early Christian church, most importantly to include Gentiles.

Earlier, we briefly discussed the anterior commissure, which plays a role in visitor experiences, including visions of God. It connects the amygdalas to each another, working with pathways that run through the frontal lobes. When the anterior commissure changes, so does the person's personality, because it connects the two amygdalas to each other, and these have a powerful influence on personality and the sense of self. Interestingly, the anterior commissure is bigger in women (and gay males[460]) than in men. Let's look at how it changes when a person has the experience of seeing God.

Here, we see the anterior commissure connecting the two amygdalas. The arrows show that it has communication in both directions. Usually, it's not perfectly balanced, the way it's shown here. In most people, activity will flow in one direction more easily than the other, because one is usually more sensitive.

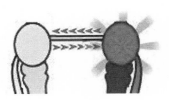

Here, we see the moment when the fearful (right) amygdala is running at its maximum, but hasn't spilled over to the one on the left yet. The negative emotions will be close to the maximum.

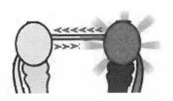

Now, the electrical activity is spilling over, stripping away synapses that *inhibit* communication from the right to the left. Overloaded, they 'drop out'. The more electrical current involved, the more synapses will be lost.

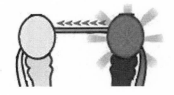

At this point, activity from the right amygdala has crossed the anterior commissure, reaching the one on the left. Synapses that inhibit communication from the right amygdala to the left one are now either gone or partly pruned away.

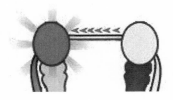

In the final moment of a vision of God, the left amygdala is suddenly activated, and the anterior commissure is now less able to activate the right amygdala, the fear structure, because the synapses inhibiting communication in the opposite direction have been stripped away. Activity flows from right to left easily, while activity flowing in the opposite direction encounters much more resistance. Fear and other negative emotions based in the right amygdala, now give way to the positive emotions supported by the left amygdala[461] easily. Because inhibitory synapses are more fragile (so to speak) than excitatory synapses, the overall effect of such a dramatic burst of uncontrolled electrical energy will be to remove inhibitions to emotional and cognitive functions. Emotions and thoughts find a new freedom in the mind of the person who sees God. Normally, neural activity doesn't always mean neural excitement, but when the levels of activity are high enough, and the movement of the limbic focus of activity is abrupt enough, they become much the same thing.

A similar mechanism probably works on the connections that run through the frontal lobes to the two amygdalas.

Before someone has a vision of God, there should be approximately (but never *exactly*) equal amounts of communication between the two amygdalas (assuming they don't have a psychological disorder). The amount of activity from left to right (and vice versa), varies from brain to brain. Happier people are expected to have more communication from the right to the left, through the Anterior Commissure, so that the left has more current going into it. Depressed people may have more communication in the other direction, though this hasn't been studied yet. For such people, the fearful, depressed and despairing right amygdala receives more communication. In fact, depressive brains have significantly more communication between their amygdalas than normal ones (and for a time, it looked like no such communication existed, though now we know differently)[462].

A vision of God involves a strong jolt of neurological activity from the right amygdala to the one on the left. Synapses that inhibited communication from right to left (from fear to joy or from 'dysphoria to euphoria') are overloaded and stripped away, both in the frontal lobes, and across the anterior commissure. Excitement in the left amygdala supports an equally wide range of positive emotions (cheerfulness, bliss, exultation, rapture, the sense of being uplifted, etc). Removing obstacles that reduce the flow of activity from the right amygdala to the left makes it easier for fear or sadness to fade into happiness, joy or even bliss[463]. Of course, fear comes in various hues and strengths (anxiety, nervousness, fear, terror, apprehensiveness, etc), and while some fears last only a few milliseconds, others endure for a very long time.

The amount of electrical energy in the right amygdala has to be greater than the amount only one of them can hold, or it wouldn't spill over to the other one. This amount will predictably be more than the anterior commisure can carry without also being overloaded and losing synapses. Some of these events are more powerful than others, and the more powerful the resulting experience, the more energy will be involved, and the more inhibiting synapses will be stripped out of the right-to-left amygdala pathways. This means those having the most powerful experiences will also have the most dramatic personality changes appear after the experience is over. The experience of God changes the person who has it in direct proportion to its depth. People who have less powerful experiences may also have personality changes, but these won't be as deep as the ones that happen to those who have intense experiences, and may not last as long.

Remember our starting point in this chapter, that spirituality offers an evolutionary advantage by helping people avoid death anxiety. A person whose brain is rearranged by a face-to-face meeting with God might start having positive responses to negative events. A person who has seen God can face the terrifying fact that they will die, and yet find no threat in it. Once that set of inhibitory synapses from the right amygdala to the left has been either totally shorn, or just somewhat pruned, it's no longer possible for a person to go into negativity the way they used to. There is a saying, 'it's always darkest just before the dawn'. Such people can find a light at the edge of any darkness. They can be a source of inspiration, optimism and hope to those around them, especially during times of hardship. Perhaps this is why our evolutionary strategy seems to include having a percentage of our populations prone to such experiences.

A religious experience of any kind will give its subject the strong *feeling* that religious truths exist (faith) and this cannot help but inspire religious beliefs; intellectual convictions. When a religious experience is mild, it's often easy to fit its insights into existing religious frameworks, beliefs or dogmas. On the other hand, a deep and profound religious experience will often come with radical insights that call for a rejection of existing religious ideas. A powerful meeting with God can even lead a person to come up with their own religious teachings. This happened to Moses, Jesus, the prophet Mohammed (*Sallallahu Alaihi Wa Sallam*), John Wesley, Neale Donald Walsch, St. Francis of Assisi, Chaitanya Mahaprabhu, and others. New religions or radical reformations of existing creeds are usually based on new points of *faith*, not theology.

One of the functions of the amygdala is to infuse events with a feeling of emotional meaningfulness[464] [465]. It responds to anything that happens, and tells us whether it offers a threat or an opportunity. The heavy involvement of the amygdala in the direct experience of God makes it feel important, even profound. This feeling of personal meaningfulness draws such mystics into a sense of faith. I say "sense of faith" because to me, the word faith means the *feeling* that something is true. Like many Christian theologians, I see a difference between faith and belief. To me, the word *belief* refers to an intellectual conviction that something is true. People learn religious beliefs during their childhood education, but acquire religious faith through spiritual moments and practices. These don't have to be profound, mystic experiences. More ordinary enhancements can be something as simple as becoming absorbed in prayer, or being moved by the poetry of their scripture.

The structures involved in such an experience also maintain the sense of self. When *they* change to allow God, *you* change along with it. We'll look at this more closely later[466]. Whether you believe God is to be found in the brain or in the cosmos, meeting Him face to face will usually create a radical change in your personality and outlook on life.

The experience of God seems to be driven by the amygdala, a very 'social' brain structure[467]. By itself, the one on the left can create bliss, light and love[468]. Disturbances in its connection to the olfactory bulbs, just behind the sinuses, can even create heavenly or otherworldly fragrances, the perfumes of heaven.

The hippocampus is a cognitive, 'thinking' structure. On the right side, it has an all but unlimited ability to find and create contexts for things (even fabricating them, as it does when it produces the images that fill our dreams), and plays a decisive role in retrieving memories and information. The seeming ability to 'know all' could easily appear through right hippocampal activity, even if the feeling of 'all-knowingness' is a rare illusion. This suggests that the belief that God knows everything may have had its source in visions that included an active right hippocampus.

The right hippocampus participates in creating the content of our dreams, where we sometimes create entire worlds for ourselves. This gives us firsthand experience, however indirect, telling us that worlds *can* be created. It's easy to project this subconscious experience onto God, giving us intimations that He created the universe. The right hippocampus creates the inner worlds we see every night, when we go to sleep and dream. The subtle and often unconscious knowledge that we can create worlds in our dreams is extended, and projected onto God, creating the intuitive and subconscious perception that he is the creator of the physical world. The fact that we can create whole worlds for ourselves in our dreams creates a kind of precedent for the faith that tells us that the universe was created by God.

I hope this discussion has clarified how the brain changes when someone sees God. Although the actual experience takes only a couple of minutes, the effects of meeting God can last the rest of one's life. Dr.

Persinger wrote "Religious and mystic experiences can be brief, very transient, lasting just a few seconds, focal displays deep in the temporal lobes"[469]. Those few seconds are life changing. Afterwards, you are no longer the same person.

I've given you the pattern: fear, despair, angst, terror, followed by bliss, joy, elation, love, light and God. If this really is the structure of the God Experience, then classical stories of visions of God from different spiritual traditions should show it. Obviously, we should expect variations according to the person, their time and place in history, their neural history, and the negative state that preceded their vision. Let's remember that that fear and despair can come from widely different circumstances.

The same brain processes that produce an experience of a spirit or angel can, if amplified, become the experience of God, with the same groups of pathways[470] supporting both. To understand how the brain produces the experience of God, we look at some of the parts of the limbic system. Some of these must be very excited, and to produce this experience, they must be activated in a specific order, as discovered in the God Helmet experiments. Visions of God and visions of angels, protector spirits, and ghosts who come to help us are all manifestations of the same basic neural process, happening with different intensities, and in different contexts.

Case Histories

Our first case history comes from Joseph Smith's (the founder of the Mormon religion) vision of God. Joseph Smith had a tremendous problem, one which may not seem like much today. To most people today, it certainly wouldn't be enough to go into despair, but it was deeply disturbing for him. He couldn't decide what kind of Christian he wanted to be.

He knew he wanted to be a Christian, but he was in a quandary as to which denomination to join. He looked at all the religions available in the middle of the 19th century in rural America. There were so many

– Roman Catholic, Presbyterian, and Episcopalian, to mention just a few. He couldn't tell which would suit him best. His indecision literally tore him apart inside, and brought him to a point of deep despair. He felt a powerful longing to feel God through his church and fellowship with its congregation.

Everyone in Joseph Smith's commu-nity lived on small farms, most of them cut out of the land with their own hands. Their only contact with others was when they went to church or into town. The importance of church fellowship in that time and place is beyond the understanding of many people today. For Joseph Smith, it was compelling.

An 1886 engraving of Joseph Smith receiving the golden plates and other artifacts from the Angel Moroni[471].

His despair reached its tipping point, and he had a vision in which he saw both God and Jesus, who told him that his sins were forgiven and that all existing religions were false.

Later, the angel *Moroni*[472] appeared before him, and explained Smith's role and work in the world. He told Smith that his purpose was to be a prophet, and that in a certain place (in Palmyra, New York), he would find a new scripture written on golden pages. Mormon history tells us that Joseph Smith found the book. After some time, and with Moroni's help, he translated it into English.

Ultimately, he was able to produce a translation of the book, now known as the Book of Mormon. After that, he was able to communicate regularly with God and angels, receiving the essential revelations of the Mormon faith.

251

Ramakrishna Paramhamsa[473]
(1836-1886)

Ramakrishna Paramhamsa, the famous Hindu mystic, offers a very different case. During his worship of the Goddess Kali, whom he called *Mother Kali*, he began to ask himself:

"If I am worshipping a living God, why does she not respond to my worship?" This question nagged him day and night. Then he began to pray, "Mother, you've been gracious to many devotees in the past. You've revealed yourself to them. Why would you reveal yourself to them, but not to me? Am I not also your son?"

"He would weep bitterly, and sometimes even cry out loudly while worshipping.

One day, he was so impatient to see Mother Kali that he decided to end his life. His despair was to the point of suicide. He seized a sword, (a ritual object belonging to the Goddess Kali), and was about to strike himself with it. Suddenly, he saw a light in the temple issuing from the deity, (also called the *Murti*). This light came over him in waves and they overwhelmed him"[474].

After that he was in regular, if not constant, contact with the Goddess Kali, his chosen deity[475]. He became one of the most famous spiritual teachers India ever produced. The Goddess Kali herself is a bloody deity. At one time in India, some Kali worship included drenching her image in blood, but for Ramakrishna, she was nothing but purity, light and love. He spoke of her as *Mother* Kali, because for him, her presence invoked the sacred mood of motherhood, and her, wrathful appearance shows the power she uses to protect her children when they are threatened.

In another example, Blessed Sister Josefina Menendez heard the voice of God chastising her regularly. She couldn't bear the thought that God was unhappy with her, and inwardly hearing His angry voice put her into a deep despair. She stayed that way until one morning, after one of her many nights of anguish; she did not just hear Jesus' words; she actually saw him before her - looking beautiful. He was standing in white robes, holding His heart in His hand, shining with radiant light. "His hair was like spun gold, and the wounds of His crucifixion shone like little suns". She also had visions in which an Angel led her on tour of hell[476].

Neil David Walsh's book *Conversations with God*[477] became a best seller all over the world. His tribulations began when he was hit by a car and forced to wear a neck brace. During his recovery, he lost his job and couldn't get another. No employer was willing to take a chance on hiring a man wearing a neck brace. Falling off his chair at the office could paralyze him for life. He became unemployable. Ironically, he was too sick to hold a job behind a desk, but not too sick to live in a tent in a park as a homeless person. He started collecting bottles and cans from the garbage for his living, and managed to do it without breaking his neck.

Finally, his neck brace came off and he got a job working each Saturday afternoon in a local radio station in Oregon. Slowly, he began to rebuild his life. After a while, he rented an apartment and had a roof over his head like anyone else. There was even a refrigerator with food in it. It wasn't always full, but he had food.

He had a new life, and was just beginning to enjoy its normal comforts again, only to find that the whole exercise was pointless. A normal life came with long work hours. His romantic relationships came with the usual struggles. He found he was entering the "rat race" once again, and the life he had worked so hard to create for himself seemed futile and pointless. He went into a state of despair. One night, after waking up at four o'clock in the morning, he found himself wondering "what does it take to make life work?" He sat down on the sofa in the dark, found a large pad of paper, and began to write an angry letter to God. While he was writing, he heard God speak to him asking if he really wanted answers to these questions, or if he was just venting his anger. Walsh said that yes, he did want answers, and all at once, a huge amount of information seem to download to his mind (remember the NDE "transcendent Experience" and the Akashic Records); information that answered his questions. Feverishly, he wrote down the answers, but they also inspired more questions. As these new questions appeared, more information seemed to flow into his mind. Along the way, he began to feel that he had been healed of the despair that threatened to fill his life. His conversation with God went on to become a whole new set of religious teachings – the theme that fills his book. It's probably one of the most subtle, original, and comprehensive works of modern theology. It embodies the experience of "all knowingness", projected onto an external presence. Walsh's right hemispheric ability to see meaning and find understanding was disinhibited, and so his God was omniscient.

Saint Teresa of Avila[478]

St. Teresa of Avila suffered from a severe illness throughout most of her adult life. Although the exact nature of her ailment is unknown, she was in severe pain, and was often unable to eat. There was an entire month where she could only move her little finger. At one point, St. Theresa of Avila's doctors gave her "purges" [479] every day for a month. It's possible that these were actually the cause of her illness.

During this time, she began to have visions of God, so exquisite she could hardly bring herself to describe them. One of her descriptions said "His soft whiteness (was) infused with a radiance which delights the eye".

Faustina Kowalska[480] (1905-1938)

Our next case is somewhat different. I include it here because it offers a rare exception to the rule. Sister Faustina Kowalska, an early 20th century Polish nun, today known as the Blessed Faustina, after being beatified[481] by Pope John Paul II.

Most of the time, visions of God come after something painful, and visions of God are a blissful, even ecstatic experience. The Blessed Faustina underwent the opposite. Her visions were very bleak, and they came when she felt cheerful and happy.

Instead of beginning with fear, anguish or despair, they began when she was happy and elated, an emotional state dominated by the left hemisphere. Her first vision began while she was out dancing. Presumably, this went above a threshold (probably unusually low in her case) in her left amygdala, and shunted the neural activity created by her dancing, over to her brain's right hemisphere[482]. She had a vision of the tormented Jesus - His body covered in wounds, the tortuous crown of thorns on his head, enduring unspeakable pain. After feeling so elated, she saw a bloody, tortured man, filled with pain. So for her, the pattern was reversed. However, it didn't stop there.

During her vision, she was in turmoil, because Jesus had said she was failing in her duty to God. She was filled with grief and despair, further activating the right amygdala. In this state of deep anguish, she went into a church and prostrated herself before the altar. She prayed earnestly, asking God to reveal His plan for her life. It was then she heard the voice of God telling her to go to and enter a convent in Warsaw. Without question, or any lapse of faith, she boarded the next available train to Warsaw, without any money in her pocket. Within a few hours of her arrival, she had found somewhere to stay, and within a few days was accepted into a convent.

The last example of such visions of God[483], are those experienced by Jesus while he was in the wilderness, fasting for forty days and forty nights. Towards the end of this retreat, he met Satan himself. He must have been extremely hungry after His long fast, and Satan said, "If thou be the Son of God, command that these stones be made bread[484]."

Jesus quoted[485] The Book of Deuteronomy:

> "... man doth not live by bread only, but by every word that proceedeth out of the mouth of the LORD doth man live."

Satan tempted Him further.

He took Jesus to a cliff, and told him to throw himself off of it. Satan quoted from the book of Psalms[486]. "For He shall give His angels charge over you, to keep you in all your ways. In their hands they shall bear you up, lest you dash your foot against a stone." Jesus' replied[487]: "Get thee hence, Satan: for it is written, Thou shalt worship the Lord thy God, and him only shalt thou serve." Jesus had met the 'evil one'; Satan himself, and it's very likely that the experience was negative, even if Jesus' words betray no fear. As soon as the meeting with Satan was over, Jesus had a vision of angels "Then the devil leaveth him, and, behold, angels came and ministered unto him[488]". The interhemispheric Intrusion principle says that, the chances for a positive vision are much higher after such a negative one. Excitement in the right amygdala (Satan) moved over to the one on the left (ministering angels). Thus, a vision of "The Evil One" can be followed by an angelic vision.

In closing this discussion, I recommend that those people who believe in God continue in that belief. Believing in God calls you to act with ethics and morality. In anthropological terms, it facilitates adaptive behavior.

For those who don't believe in God and believe that the experience of God is nothing but a matter of the brain, I would point out that belief in God and belief in prayer are two different things. Being an atheist means you don't believe in God. It doesn't mean that you believe that prayer has no value. Separating your two senses of self into discreet entities allows new insights, and creates an opportunity for your intuition to emerge[489]. It also creates a moment when your emotions lend themselves to the presence of the sacred, whatever that means to you. Some thoughts seem crude during prayer, and those that express anger, spite, greed or a willingness to do others harm will be excluded from our thoughts. This creates a context in which our own morality can appear, and our immediate desires and temporary expediencies seem less important.

Prayer invokes God, whether God exists inside you or in the universe at large. When you pray, you separate your two senses of self. At times, the separation can be deep, as when someone becomes lost in prayer. At other times, it can be quite shallow, with a person only mouthing words they have memorized. Prayer allows the self that you usually identify with greater access to the self that's usually quiet. This means that, whether from outside or inside, you open up a source of insight and wisdom that's usually less available. Prayer may be the single most effective psychological coping tool ever invented. Even if none of this were the case, prayers, like poetry, have a way of uplifting the person uttering them.

My personal belief is that humans believe in God because our brains are wired for it. Belief in God is part of our evolutionary heritage. I believe, like many Hindus and Buddhists, that if I ever come face to face with God, I'll be facing a portion of myself. My willingness to accept that "He" comes from my brain doesn't stop me from praying. Indeed, I find real fulfillment in it. Moments of prayer can grant new insights, hope, peace and all sorts of deep spiritual values, even without a traditional belief in God.

I can't tell you what my own private beliefs are. Partly because I can't put them into words, and partly because every time I find myself saying I believe something, I soon find I'm contradicting myself. For me, the only sacred thing is choice. The only sin is certainty. The only ethic is responsibility. The only morality is love.

My *belief* is that God is a matter of the brain. My *faith* tells me that there is a higher power that is concerned with my well-being and is pleased when I acquire wisdom or show compassion. I use the word faith because I have a *sense* that God exists, and not because I've been *convinced* of it. In fact, my conviction is that he does not. Some years ago, long after realizing that I was an atheist, I gave myself permission to have faith in God. After all, how can I write intelligently about faith if I haven't had the experience since I was a child? I soon found out that there is a reason why religion is found throughout history, and in every culture. It may have begun in order to close the gap between our thoughts (how to avoid) and our feelings (deep fears) about death. It may have spread throughout the human population because religious people often have helpful ideas that don't occur to others. But one question remains. Why do people feel that God is real? The answer is simple. It feels good, and people enjoy feeling good. It's fun. Children invent games, making up their own rules as they go along, and they feel good when they win. If you follow God's rules (as you understand them), you win. People approve of you. That feels good, too. There is also a kind of beauty to be found in religion that appears nowhere else. The music, the art, ceremonies and poetry are often exquisite.

In some ways, religious rituals are stately games; elegant fun that appeals to both our playful imagination and our higher aspirations.

Why, atheists ask, do people go on believing in God? Because there are feelings that appear through faith – good ones – that don't appear anywhere else, and feeling good is more important to humans than the truth is. It's often impossible to know the truth firsthand, so people often don't choose it. But we know what feels good, and what feels bad, and we choose to feel good.

So, in a choice that's so obvious and effortless we don't really see ourselves making it, we choose that agenda on which all religions may rely. We choose to try to feel good as much as we can. That may mean that we try to shield ourselves from the pains of this world using either the shield of delusion and/or the shield of St. Michael the Archangel, but what we shield is our ability to enjoy life.

I wonder if there are atheists who think that the need to enjoy life, and to stay away from pain isn't worthy of the word *sacred*.

CHAPTER 11

Romantic Love

This chapter will look at some similarities between feeling God's presence and being with one's beloved during the first and most powerful phase of intense romantic love. This will give us an opportunity to review some of the principles we work with as well as the fundamental hypothesis of this book.

Neurophenomenology

Our death process (as it appears in NDEs) is part of our evolutionary heritage. It's as uniquely human and as widespread among us as language.

There's a principle in neuroscience that what we experience, moment-to-moment, reflects the constantly shifting focus of excitement[490] and activity in our brains. "Mental forms follow neural functions".

As we have seen, the death process occurs in several phases. Less intense versions of the same experiences can also happen while we're still alive. Each phase is different from the one before it, and each is based on a different pattern of brain activity. When one of these patterns appears during our lives, it creates a mystic, religious, or spiritual experience. Imagine pathways that work only during the death process. The same pathways will also be able to produce a profound experience when they're excited in a different context (for example just after an episode of very high stress, deep in Yoga, or when absorbed in prayer). There are also spiritual states that don't happen during NDEs, such as the ones that appear when someone is absorbed in meditation. NDE pathways are probably very specific. There can be thousands of ways two brain parts might interact, but only a very few of them will support spiritual experiences. To my knowledge, no one has reported meditating during an NDE. Nevertheless, meditation can make experiences that use NDE pathways more likely, by exercising the pathways that support them. In other words, meditation prepares people for mystic experiences, just as its teachers say. However, it's also said that the best meditation avoids the more flamboyant mystic experiences, and focuses on simple mindfulness.

Anything that consistently excites one of the groups of pathways that operate during NDEs can make spiritual experiences more likely, even if it doesn't trigger them. As we have seen, the direct experience of God implicates a specific pattern of brain activity. The same experience can also appear with less force than it would during an NDE, but it will still show the same theme. A person might have a sense of God's presence, or hear his voice from within, or sense his will. They might find themselves overcome with a deeply prayerful mood, or might find themselves drawn to read and re-read scriptures. They might feel the presence of other beings, like angels, prophets, goddesses or the Blessed Mother, depending on their religion and culture. They might just sense a presence around them, without knowing who or what it is. Let's look at one example; the uplifting self-and-other relationships that appear in both prayer and the experience of love.

Love is an example of the self/other (I and thou) relationship. Even though it's really about ourselves, we experience it as having to do with another person. Let's look at the experience of 'the other' more deeply.

It seems that love is an instance of a larger group of experiences: relating to the 'other', and it looks like the 'other' is actually a part of one's self.

Let's remember The *Sensed Presence*. It's that feeling people get, most commonly at night, where they feel that there is someone or something in the room with them, perhaps an 'energy' or a 'presence'. They might simply feel that they are 'not alone' or that they're 'being watched.' It's an indefinable feeling that there's a conscious being of some kind in the room with them. To understand it, we need to look at the self, and not the 'other'.

To start, we need to see that the self is more than our ordinary experience shows us. Even in our most quiet moments, when we are still, it can be very hard to see our 'self'. Buddhism teaches that there is no such thing. If they're right, then looking for it is a wild goose chase. Other traditions say that the self is a manifestation of God. If these teachings are right, then our self is so elevated that we may have no hope of ever perceiving it directly. Fortunately, brain science is a bit more down-to-earth than religion.

Some 'teachings' from neuroscience tell us that we actually have two selves, one on each side of the brain. They're specialized. Like any other brain function, they each have specific jobs to do. One of them, on the left, is the one that experiences things through language. It's very social. Language is primarily a tool for relating to other people, so the 'linguistic' self is quite conscious of where it stands with others. It's very aware of its social rank, which it hears in the words of others. A simple string of words, like: 'you're fired' or 'I love you', can have an amazing impact on the person hearing them. People feel that 'they' are affected by these words. And as social beings, they have been. When we lose a job, our social rank is reduced. When we start a new relationship, or we feel more secure in a present one, our social rank – our importance to the people around us - is raised up a bit.

The right side of the brain has a 'self', too. It experiences the world in non-verbal ways. It's more introspective. It's silent. It's affected by music, art, pictures, and our perception of what other people are feeling; *how* people say things rather than what they say. It usually operates "behind" the left hemispheric one, so to speak. It takes this role because the linguistic self uses words to interpret the world and our experiences, all the time, and we identify ourselves as the source of our verbal thoughts.

We maintain an almost constant inner monolog. For most people, this keeps the silent self out of sight, so that it operates without our feeling it directly. The self that can be "self-aware" is the one on the left, with more subtle input from the one on the right. The one we feel is our 'real' self is the dominant one, on the left. The one that doesn't claim our identity, on the right, is subordinate.

The Sensed Presence experience happens when our two senses of self lose their normal connections to each other. In these moments, the subordinate sense of self comes into view for the (dominant) left hemispheric sense of self, so the left-sided self experiences it directly. We can't identify with two senses of self at the same time, so the intruding silent sense of self is experienced as an external presence, and feels like it exists outside our body space.

I believe that something very much like the sensed presence happens when we relate to other people. Some presences mean threats, while others imply support, comfort or safety. I suggest that we are projecting a part of ourselves onto real people whenever we're relating to them. The presences we experience in other people are the creations of our own minds, externalized and projected onto others. Each individual presence will call up a slightly different state of consciousness. From infancy onwards, we have acquaintances; people who are too socially distant to be called friends, but close enough that we pay some attention to them. The default settings for relating to acquaintances are derived from our experiences while we were with such people in the past. Other kinds of people are absolutely unique. Some of them catch our attention very sharply. We fall in love with them, or we come to hate their guts. These people are not mere acquaintances. Their presence comes closer to home. For whatever reasons their words can affect our self-esteem, our social rank, or both.

We are an intensely social species. Our self esteem is largely a function of how we think others value us. Most of the time, people speak to each other in ways that show their respect, or lack of it. Respect has a lot to do with social standing and rank. For the most part, we feel self-respect when we feel respected by those around us.

Our self-esteem changes almost constantly. We experience most of these changes through our emotions, although they also have a serious impact on the way we think. Our moods can be raised and lowered by the words we hear from others. Phrases like 'you're hired' and 'you're fired.' Or, '"will you go out with me?" And 'leave me alone.' "Get out of my shop and *never* come back again". Our moods reflect our level of self-esteem in each moment. In normal conditions, our experience of our selves changes according how others treat us. Especially how they speak to us.

Each normal, ordinary state of consciousness carries its own level of self-esteem. For example, we enter certain states of consciousness when we're in subordinate positions. These states call up sets of responses that minimize the situation's stress by helping us do what the dominant person wants. Other states of consciousness help us to avoid it. Each state has its own ways of thinking, feeling, speaking, and acting. Even for the most aware people, it's hard to see all these things happening at once. We live on autopilot, so to speak. Trying to make *conscious* decisions about how to act would crash the system. We have to be on automatic, for the most part, because there are so many controls to adjust for each state. When you're on the phone with your boss, you're in the subordinate role. If you hang up, and start talking with your child, you take on the dominant one. The way you think, feel, and speak will all change all at once.

We want to repeat positive states, and avoid the negative, unpleasant ones. This creates a tendency to bond with people that feel good to be around. Simple, eh?

Not really. We 'decide' who feels good according to what we project. We make these choices largely out of habit. It begins in infancy, when we first begin to experience ourselves as individuals.

There has been some research in pre-natal psychology that suggests that the fetus experiences its mother's states of consciousness as though they were its own. Sometime after birth, the newborn begins to experience its own states for the first time. Before birth, the mother gets angry; the fetus experiences the same state, although certainly it will have very different phenomena. After birth, when the mother gets angry, the infant no longer experiences it with the same immediacy. The infant must find the new boundaries of its "self".

In the womb, the fetus probably didn't distinguish between itself and its mother. She must now be experienced as an external presence. Its mother, now a separate being, becomes the source of all its physical and emotional needs, almost without exception. Many psychologists, commenting on the experience of romantic love, have argued that the experience of early childhood comfort and nurturing provides a template from which later expectations about relationships are drawn. We begin to feel that our lover ought to treat us they way our mothers did. Women, of course, have the additional process of mapping their sense of comforting, loving presences onto men.

Romantic Love

Searching for romantic fulfillment is also an attempt to find an experience that will change the way we experience ourselves. Not by looking for love within ourselves, as so many life coaches suggest, but by allowing a part of our 'self' to manifest through another.

For some people, or at some times in a person's life, 'true happiness' might be found *only* outside one's self. Our brains and minds are configured for relating to others in so many ways. Humans have a long childhood compared to other primate species, and most of it is spent relying on others to meet our most basic needs. Children are so engaged with the presence of others that they can usually play with anything and imagine it's alive. Their imagination imposes a presence on their toys, so that a teddy bear becomes 'Mr. Bear'. The Buddhist faithful feel that a Buddha statue has the presence of the Enlightened One. The disciple sees God in his Guru. These are projections. In the same way, lovers project love, *as they know it*, onto their romantic partners.

Falling in love may be the process of projecting one's right-sided sense of self onto one's beloved.

Because the same pathways that maintain the right-sided, silent sense of self are also specialized for negative feelings, our maintenance of this romantic illusion is delicate at best. It's easily broken, and rarely lasts for more than a few weeks in most cases and a few years in cases when it's accompanied by respect and a sense of responsibility. These relationships need to be based on more than just romance.

People often want to feel really passionate love before starting a relationship. But that kind usually doesn't last. When it fades, very few people escape disappointment of one kind or another. People are angered when their lover turns out to be who they are instead of who they were supposed to be. Sustaining romance past this point calls for either denial or skill with relationship and communication.

I can use a fancy neuroscientific phrase to describe the nature of romantic love (a sustained interhemispheric intrusion), but even I, your humble author, don't enjoy seeing my romantic side reduced to such a sterile set of words.

Lovers sometimes speak of losing themselves in the other, or that they can't tell where they end and their beloved begins. Like the sensed presence experience, being in love may happen when the silent sense of self comes out where linguistic sense of self can see it, except that instead of being sensed as a feeling that we're being watched, we project it onto the beloved. In the process, the normal division of other and self is blurred.

As long as one can sustain the illusion that one's partner will be the source of fulfillment, the projection can continue undisturbed. Inevitably, something happens to disturb it. It's been said that, when it comes to relationships, everybody is looking for a tailor-made fit, even though it's an off-the-rack world. The 'interhemispheric intrusion' ends. The honeymoon is over. These 'Hemispheric intrusions' are often very brief events. A vision of an angel might last just a few seconds. The first flush of 'true love' might continue for only weeks or months.

There was a study of the relationship between hemisphericity and self-esteem, and it found that the higher a person's level of right hemispheric 'dominance', the lower their self-esteem[491]. Right hemisphericity means that a person's experience of their self is dominated by their right side more than for (statistically) normal people. This is the side of the brain that's specialized for both negative feelings and non-verbal ways of processing our experiences. All other conditions being equal, the more intuitive and spontaneous a person is, the lower their self esteem will be. Of course, people compensate in various different ways, so 'all other conditions' usually aren't equal.

When a person is in love, their right hemispheric 'self' has access to the positive emotions on the left. Love feels good. However, after the experience is over, the person is more vulnerable to threats to their sense of self, so anxiety and sadness appear more easily. People feel bad when the relationship is over, and that leaves them feeling more sensitive. "Left hemispheric" people are much less vulnerable. They're better able to feel good about themselves even in the face of a romantic disappointment, but they're also less likely to fall so deeply in love in the first place.

The typical aftermath of a mystical experience also finds the person feeling somewhat shaky. They won't be able to cope well in many social interactions, and may avoid people with 'energy' that tends to 'bring them down.' They may even retreat into solitude, and avoid relating to others as much as they can. They tend to reject the mind-sets that support the opinions of those whose company they don't enjoy. Paradoxically, there can also be an almost obsessive desire to 'share' their experience with anyone willing to listen. They seek out validation in the eyes of those around them, making up for the fragmentation their sense of self sustained in an epiphany. They may cling to those whose company they find supportive. Less spiritual personalities are judged and labeled using such phrases as 'there are none so blind as those who will not see.' When others disagree with them, they may take recourse ideas about karma or Satan's influence to explain how 'some people just aren't ready to hear the truth.'

Someone in an unrequited love, or losing a lover they want to stay with, finds themselves in much the same position. They, too, are vulnerable. They also feel that others 'just don't understand.' Their self esteem falls. They may cling to those who are willing to support them, just like those 'processing' in the wake of spiritual experiences and awakenings. They may also feel that they are not the same person they were before they experienced their romantic disappointment, just as someone who has had a mystic experience is also a 'changed' man or woman.

In the Sufi tradition, God is referred to as The Beloved, and it preserves many metaphors that convey the idea that separation from God is as painful as separation from one's beloved. Union with God is likened to romantic fulfillment.

Romantic love may rely on some of the same brain mechanisms that support the experience of God. While a mystic experience is often short and intense, romantic episodes may last a long time. Both of them involve the silent, right-sided self coming being projected onto another being (real or not), along with intense positive feelings. The after-effects are based on similar neural and psychological mechanisms. The dark night of the soul and the despair of unrequited love are made of the same 'stuff'.

There is some truth in the sayings that the beloved is God, and that when we love God we love ourselves. I and thou are one. The other is the self. The point to this discussion is that these similar states of consciousness can create very different phenomena.

More On Neurophenomenology

When a pattern of brain excitement, even operating very quietly, becomes a constant feature of someone's mind, it takes a step from a state of consciousness to a personality trait. The person who has seen God might find that He, as they understand Him, fills their thoughts to the point where it may be difficult for them to talk about anything else. They might search out inspirational books and videos. They might spend time reading scriptures. For someone with this trait, which some psychologists call "hyperreligiosity", there's an imperative to be as close to God as possible at all times. In the death process, God's presence fills one with love, bliss, and acceptance. For those who are absorbed in their relationship with God, it becomes easy to accept the Christian teaching to love everyone. Of course, when we are kind and generous to those around us, they often respond with gratitude and leave us feeling loved, even if only for a few moments. In a very natural way, ongoing intimations of God's existence can make it easier for us to love and be loved. Of course this is going to inspire some very adaptive behavior. It will help people maintain their social connections, and cement their social rank; a trait that evolution would probably preserve.

I must ask my readers to forgive the masculine pronoun - no sexism is intended, but the fact remains that the overwhelming majority of such visions of God in any context find Him to be a male. Some have speculated that there is a cognitive template (an *archetype*), that helps us recognize alpha males. It also operates to impose masculinity on God, because the highest being in our experience, when our species was still young, was the dominant male, most often a tribal chief. God appears as a male because he is the 'most alpha' of them all.

The second phase of NDEs usually consists of a trip through a tunnel or a huge dark empty space, but in some cases, it can be a walk down a road accompanied by a spirit. These all share the experience of movement through space. Naturally, this will excite the portions of our brain that are involved in spatial perception. These are on the right. When the supporting brain areas are excited during life, they might give us an experience of being continuous with the space that surrounds us, an experience that might be described as being "one with the universe", which is actually one of the rarest types of mystic experiences[492]. When these brain areas are excited enough to dominate our experience, we might find that our inner monologue, the near constant flow of words in our minds, might slow down, become quiet, or even stop altogether. The experience would go 'beyond words'. This is because spatial perception is located on the right, and language is on the left.

Experiences involving spatial perception (including seeing into or sensing infinity) and inner silence are related – they are both 'hosted' by the same structures, so that having one makes the other easier to achieve. In a similar way, God and language are related (both rely on neighboring structures on the left). Rapture and sex are related. So are humility and introspection.

This book takes a *neurophenomenological* approach. This means that it tends to classify spiritual experiences according to the brain parts that support their themes. There are recurring themes, even though each person's experiences are unique. One of them is movement. Going through a tunnel involves movement, which recruits the brain's vestibular systems, which keeps us oriented in space. This implicates the mechanisms for spatial perception as one of the brain's bases for experiences of space, like tunnels, the experience of floating or moving through space or a sense of "the infinite". Of course, spatial perception and our sense of location (the "vestibular sense") are intimately related. Seeing things from a different location in space, and having an altered sense of *where we are* can combine in an out-of-body experience.

The hippocampus is implicated in out-of-body experiences. It may be that OBEs rely on heightened excitement in the 'spatial' parts of the brain (hippocampus and occipital-temporal-parietal area on the right, where your antlers would be if you had antlers), but a disturbance in one of these areas can also account for the phenomena. We take for granted that we are where we are, but this perception comes from ongoing activity in specific areas of the brain. When those areas stop working the way they usually do, we can experience ourselves as literally being somewhere else. Whether Out-of-Body Experiences are illusory or 'real', they will be accompanied by a change in the activity that supports our feeling for our location in space.

If we hear about a mystic who finds himself unable to remain indoors during an intense moment, and goes bursting out into the night (like St. John of the cross), we should understand that he or she has just changed the size of the space around them, and activated their right hemisphere-based spatial perception. If we hear about someone who has an experience in which their mind is "expanded", we're pretty safe in guessing that *something* feels like it takes up more space than it did before.

In the same way, the areas of the brain that support us as we relate to others (like seeing their moods and deciding how we'll talk to them) will also play a role in the experience of non-physical beings (like gods, demons, spirits, ghosts, etc). The context will be completely different, but the phenomena will be the same (self-and-other). Spiritual experiences are woven from the same fabric used in ordinary ones. The same *phenomena* can appear in both altered states of consciousness and more ordinary moments.

Two separate experiences that seem completely different can have the same *phenomenology*, and with that, the same neural basis. This will explain how so many different spiritual experiences can appear from only a few brain parts. Each brain is unique. The pathways of least resistance (or the most excitable pathways) are different for each person, and this allows even more variety. What your right-sided hippocampus creates for you when it reaches a new peak of excitement and what mine will do in the same situation will be different. Only the themes and motifs in our experiences will be similar. You might be in an empty space, feeling in love with infinity, while I might be on a vast plane with a glowing crystalline city before me. Both of them are going to use the brain's 'sense' of space – the one that tells you how far you are from a street where you want to turn your car. Extraordinary moments are made from the common stuff of the mind, excited in extraordinary ways.

Many people have spiritual experiences that involve the same structures, but those structures are also connected to other brain parts. The exact routes and the extent of those connections will be different for each person, making each related experience absolutely unique, even though they show the same motifs or phenomena.

The phenomena that appear in any specific spiritual experience will reflect the activity of specific brain parts. When those same brain parts are busy – even with the same pattern of activity – in another person, they might create a very similar *state*, but manifesting as a completely different *experience*. In this way, romantic love and the love of God have the same neural foundations.

CHAPTER 12

Enlightenment and the Self

You can't tell whether someone is enlightened by looking at them. The profound and spiritual moods that can come up in the presence of an enlightened person aren't proof of their enlightenment, because other types of people can also such similar moods. A mother can feel that she is in the presence of divinity holding her newborn infant, but that doesn't mean the baby is enlightened. You might hear of enlightened people performing miracles[493], but miracles can be faked, and many "holy ones", like Padre Pio, have reputations for performing miracles without claiming to be enlightened. There is no litmus test for spiritual liberation.

There's no way to prove whether someone has received enlightenment. Throughout history, the only basis for belief in a person's enlightenment has been their own claim to it. Brain images have been taken from people who practice advanced meditation, as well as monks and nuns practicing contemplative prayer. Some striking data has appeared, but no patterns of brain activity belonging only to enlightened people. After all, there is no laboratory criterion for enlightenment, so no laboratory can find proofs for or against its existence.

Stories supporting traditional ideas about enlightenment would probably stand up in a courtroom. There would be lots of eyewitness testimony and irrefutable first-hand accounts to support them. Such stories offer the only starting point we have, even though they might not be valid for a medical journal. If religious traditions didn't accept these reports, then there wouldn't be any need to discuss enlightenment at all. Therefore, we begin by postulating that a state of consciousness exists which corresponds to what Hinduism and Buddhism call enlightenment. This assumption (or postulate) could also be loosely expressed by saying that at least some stories about enlightenment are not fabrications. This means we will be starting off a definition for the word. Instead, we'll look at the attributes of enlightenment as we go along, and allow the definition to emerge.

The only way of seeing into the brains of enlightened people is by looking at 'enlightenment stories'. These come from both the Hindu and Buddhist traditions, and some of today's spiritual teachers. We can look for their patterns and form a hypothesis to explain them.

Enlightenment, as understood in its classical traditions, has several features. The most important is that it involves the experience of bliss. This bliss can take more than one form. For some, it might be constant or recurring exultant elation. For others, it might be a sense of imperturbable calm and a "peace which passeth understanding". Constant bliss does not mean that enlightened people are always in the same mood. Their level of happiness may well change moment-to-moment. Indeed, it would be surprising if it did not. The relative balance of thought and feeling will also change. We should expect that enlightenment consists of an end to all unpleasant states, or that positive ones appear (very) much more easily. We'll have to sacrifice agreement with some of the traditional teachings about it, or else we won't be able to stay on-topic. We apologize to those whose understanding of enlightenment is different from ours.

However, we're going to begin with one of the other commonly-held beliefs about enlightenment: that it involves a radical change in the sense of self. These two themes come together because, to understand enlightenment and how it happens, we have to understand something about the self. All the spiritual traditions that uphold the concept of enlightenment agree that it involves a drastic change in the self. After their awakening, the *enlightened one* is no longer the same person.

The Sense of Self

The obvious place to begin is with the question "What is enlightenment?" Three major religious traditions deal with enlightenment: Hinduism, Buddhism, and Jainism. The most important are Buddhism and Hinduism, though most of the ideas we'll examine about enlightenment actually come from the Buddhist tradition.

All the religions that uphold teachings about enlightenment agree that enlightenment is marked by constant or intermittent bliss. The most likely source for the experience of bliss in the brain is in the amygdala on the left side.

Hinduism and Buddhism view enlightenment somewhat differently. In Hinduism, enlightenment is called *Moksha*, which literally means *liberation*. Enlightenment has several meanings in the Hindu traditions. It could mean that your self has united with God or that your "true" self has emerged into your awareness ("been realized"). You've been illuminated and filled with light and knowledge. Perhaps your ego, your sense of individual existence, has been destroyed. It can be confusing. All these sound equally exalted in English. They seem to be different ways of referring to a group of similar, but not identical, experiences. Of course, enlightened minds can never be identical, if only because each enlightened person started off with a completely unique *unenlightened* brain.

Buddhism is much simpler and clearer. In Buddhism, enlightenment means that the illusion of self has come to an end. The word used is *nirvana*, which literally means "to blow out", as in extinguishing a flame. In Pali, the Buddhist language of Southeast Asia, the same word is used for blowing out a candle[494]. In Buddhism, the self is extinguished, revealing its illusory nature. Buddhism is very clear that there is no such thing as the self, an idea that we'll clarify, in our own terms, as we go along. Buddhism has a teaching called the doctrine of *no self*, sometimes called *anatta*. The word *anatta* means *no self*, "an" (no) and "atta" (self, related to the Sanskrit word *atman* or *soul*). One important difference between Hinduism and Buddhism is how the self changes after enlightenment. In Hinduism, enlightenment is usually (but not always – there are many schools of thought in Hinduism) seen as the self uniting with God. In Buddhism, it reveals it to be a fiction.

Many psychiatric disorders have been described as disturbances of the self or disturbances in the sense of self. A concept proposed by Dr. M.A. Persinger – that we have two senses of self; one on each side of the brain helped move the self from psychology to neuroscience. We have looked at this in previous chapters, but we'll review it again here.

He showed that the sense of self is primarily a limbic system function, with substantial contributions from the cortex, the outer layer of the brain. He studied the feeling that someone behind you when there's no one there. His model of *the sensed presence,* based on his research and experiments, play a pivotal role in our understanding of the self throughout this book. Many readers will know this experience first-hand.

Our Limbic Players, once again.

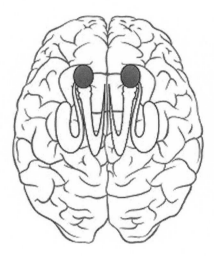

This illustration[495] will be a point of reference throughout this discussion. It shows the limbic system, deep in the temporal lobes. The sense of self is primarily a limbic, deep-brain function. Let's review the main parts of the limbic system, which we looked at in the chapter on brain parts, though now, we'll look at them with an emphasis on understanding the sense of self.

The round bits are the amygdala.[496]

The left one is specialized for positive emotions, such as joy, bliss, and elation (though it also contributes to negative emotions at times).

When the left amygdala suddenly becomes excited, it can feel as if you've just received good news, or that something happened that would create a feeling of elation. Left amygdala excitement supports a variety of positive emotions, from joy and bliss to energized happiness of any kind. Happiness, the kind with energy and excitement, is not the only "aroused" emotion supported by the left amygdala[497]. Anger also depends on it, although the left amygdala appears to support the feeling of anger only in combination with other structures[498].

The amygdala on the right supports the opposite feelings, being specialized for fear, angst, despair, a sense of impending doom, and anxiety. You don't feel good when it's excited. It's kind of a bad–boy structure. If you could directly control your brain structures, you'd want to keep turning down the right amygdala. The process of enlightenment does something very much like that, and we'll be looking at this soon.

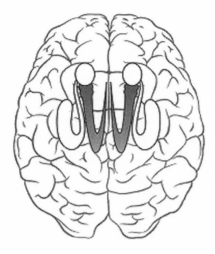

In this picture, the hippocampus is below the amygdala. Like the overwhelming majority of other brain parts, there are two; one on each side. The hippocampus is a cognitive structure. It associates seemingly isolated information and finds contexts for it in things we already know or remember. It's a "thinking" structure. It thinks by finding contexts for all kinds of phenomena, and even invents them when none exist. When new information doesn't fit any existing memories, it can create a false one to give it context, or integrate it into a dream. The human hippocampus differs substantially from those of other species, including other primates.[499] It works in conjunction with the cortex, especially the frontal lobes, where the executive functions that contribute to social skills, are carried out. Although the pathways between the two parts are somewhat indirect,[500] the hippocampus has more connections to the frontal lobes than to any other area on the surface of the brain. Relating to other people requires a lot of intelligence. How we relate with others can determine the amount of respect we get from others, and that can determine our social rank.

The left hippocampus remembers words and seems to have a pessimistic outlook.[501] It supports conscious thinking because such cognitions primarily happen in words. The left hippocampus responds to words and holds verbal memories, whether the words entered through the ears or one's thoughts, although other brain areas (on the surface) make bigger contributions to verbal thought.

The right hippocampus deals in silent, nonverbal thinking and memories and seems to have a relatively positive outlook. If something happens, and the right hippocampus dominates our interpretation of it, it will tend to look like good news. It's a forward-looking, positive brain structure. Its location on the side without language centers means that its cognitions; its 'thoughts', don't use words. These include the kind of thinking involved with colors and shapes in art, or melody, rhythm and harmony in music. It's also crucial in spatial perception. Its best-known function is its role in creating and retrieving memories. Of course, all these kinds of non-verbal thinking involve lots of other areas, mostly on the right side of the brain.

Our memories provide the raw materials for the images and episodes that appear in our dreams, no matter how fragmented they appear. Sometimes they are highly stylized and symbolic, and often involve new contexts for existing memories. These memories are often of other places, including those visited only in our childhood imaginations. The hippocampus is capable of creating entire worlds that exist only in our minds. It provides the most likely source for the images in religious visions, although the emotions people feel during such experiences come from a different brain part, the amygdala. The intimate relationship between dreaming and memories allows us, sometimes, to remember our dreams, as well as weaving dreams out of our memories.

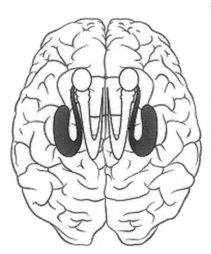

The Caudate Nucleus integrates our body's states of relaxation or excitement with our emotional states. It's also the most likely foundation for the lassitude and fatigue that goes with some negative emotions. It's important to understand that the side of the brain that produces happiness also produces excitement (left), and the side that's responsible for unhappiness is also responsible for relaxation (right). The caudate nucleus also contributes to some memory processes and even responds when a bilingual person switches languages.

These minor roles for the caudate nucleus are overshadowed by its other functions, which include both love, including maternal love, and sex. It may be that the caudate's role in arousal and relaxation is a sub-system of a larger "bonding system". After all, love can call forth both relaxation and excitement.

A couple of things distinguish the caudate nucleus from the other structures that we've been talking about. It seems to be more highly diversified. Nearly all functions known to belong to the amygdala are *affective* or emotional. Almost all functions belonging to the hippocampus are *cognitive* or reflect some kind of thought, in the broadest meaning of the word. In contrast, the caudate nucleus has a much wider range of functions, including memory, love, language, and motivation. While both the amygdala and hippocampus can be said to have central themes (or *neurophenomenologies*), the caudate nucleus has a much wider range of themes. Of these three limbic structures, the caudate nucleus is the one with the highest thresholds, followed by the hippocampus, with the amygdala having the lowest threshold, making it the most sensitive structure in the brain.

People who've been through times of depression know that it can make them lethargic. Nothing beats a soft chair and a television when you're depressed. Even if they can think of something to improve their mood, finding the motivation to get up and do it can be difficult. Depression involves an under-activation of the left hemisphere (especially the left frontal lobe), which allows the right hemisphere to determine the content of a person's mind, but without becoming more active than usual. An overly dominant right hemisphere will mean that the body has too little energy or too much relaxation. Depression leaves people feeling that their strength and energy have been sapped. I suspect that the right caudate nucleus is behind the feeling of lethargy, and that depression involves keeping at least some of it excited[502].

Only the left caudate nucleus is instrumental in both romantic love and sexual desire. A few unpublished reports exist where stimulation of the left side of the brain created feelings of expansive, undirected love. This love did not directly target specific people; it was just love, without an object. The best word for this is *Agape*. *Agape* is a Greek word defined as "unconditional love for everyone and everything." There are many varieties of love, and each one seems to implicate the left side of the brain.

I. The Self

Although you may experience your *self* as being one person, you have two selves, or more accurately, two senses of self. The left side of the brain generates one, while the right side generates the other. Although they aren't equals, they do work together seamlessly. The one on the left is more important in our daily lives, although the one on the right may well understand the world around us better[503].

In neuroscience, we know the left side as the *dominant* side, making it the source of both right-handedness and our dominant sense of self. The self on the right is the subordinate one. The left side is dominant because that's where the language centers are. Our normal sense of ourselves, with its constant stream of inner monologue, is largely woven around our inner speech. Because *we* are the field of play for language, both inward and with the people around us, our words continually reinforce our perception of our own existence.

Our normal inner chatter implies things about ourselves. Our perception of our worth is a reflection of our perception of our own social rank. For example, even if we don't actually ask for a raise, just thinking about it implies that we believe we may be in a position to get one. We might think we deserve it, or that our job is important enough that we can demand one. We might also decide not to ask for one. Perhaps we imagine the boss will think we don't deserve it. Thinking about asking for a date with someone implies a specific social position with respect to the person we're attracted to (or thinking that we're cool enough to ignore rank altogether). The shy guy is less likely to get his feelings hurt if he stays away from well-dressed rich girls named "Ashley" who ridicule boys, even though he may have a better chance with them than he realizes. Our bank balance can be a direct measure of our larger social rank - outside our friends and family. So can our credit scores. Usually, we feel bad about ourselves when we have no money.

Our thoughts, whether from our inner monologue or our imagination, reflect our assumptions about our social position. We are such deeply social beings that our social position is almost the same as our *selves*. When our social position goes up, our self-esteem goes up with it, but only for a short time. We soon become used to our new situation. When our social position goes down, our self-esteem goes down, and it can stay that way. Very few people can avoid a drop in self-esteem after they lose a fulfilling relationship or a prestigious job. As we saw in our discussion of reincarnation, humans seem to have an intrinsic tendency to try to achieve the highest social rank they can. Spiritual practice, such as prayer and meditation, can change the habit of seeing one's self through the lens of social rank, so that over time, we can redefine ourselves in terms of our relationship to God, the development of equanimity, mindfulness, or any other spiritual quality we cultivate. Not only do intense prayer and deep meditation change the self (by making changes to the neural pathways that support it), but they also change the way we see ourselves.

Our sense of self is a process, not a thing. We refresh it constantly, primarily through the words that we use in our minds. The word *self,* for us, refers to the same thing in the phrases: *self-esteem*, *self-image* and the phrase *sense of self.* Our sense of ourselves comes largely from our thoughts and the stories that we tell ourselves in our imagination. All of these depend on the near-constant stream of words we maintain in our minds. Without it, we can soon start to fall apart - or go through spiritual changes.

One of the core processes in many spiritual disciplines is shutting off the internal monologue. Doing this makes our sense of ourselves somewhat fuzzier, making room for other, special, perceptions to appear.

The stories that we tell ourselves in our inner monologue buttress our self-image, assuming one has a healthy self-esteem. Benjamin Franklin once said that he didn't understand the Christian condemnation of vanity and pride. He said he'd given himself many happy hours simply sitting in front of the fire, remembering all the good things he'd done in his life. He would tell himself that he was one cool guy, and this would boost his morale.

The dominant, linguistic, sense of self maintains itself in several ways. To have a self that functions well, you need language, with grammar and syntax, and a sense of the connotations of words. You'll do even better if you have an inkling of how they might be used poetically. You have to understand the different ways of speaking with one's social equals, one's social inferiors, and one's superiors. Earning respect among one's own people, whether they are family, tribe, or town, calls for more than one technique of speaking. Having good language skills is vital for full participation in any society. In many ways, social skills *are* language skills. The linguistic, dominant sense of self, maintained in the left hemisphere, is built on the foundation of our social self. Self-esteem may be nothing more than how we feel about what we believe other people think of us. The desire to achieve a high social rank stimulates the linguistic skills our societies expect. We develop our social selves with the intention of achieving some kind of success.

Many brain processes combine to maintain the linguistic sense of self. So many neural processes are involved that some spiritual practitioners actually get the feeling that their normal, ongoing sense of self is an obstacle or a burden, hampering their spiritual growth. A Carmelite nun once told me that she felt that her own individual existence was what kept her from being closer to God.

The self, the normal ongoing sense of self, can be a burden, especially for those who look to find something richer in their inner worlds. Many mystics have said that the "ego" is an obstacle to spiritual growth. In Buddhism, enlightenment is said to put an end to the illusion of self, which allows the truth (that the self isn't real) to be seen.

One of the most elegant statements of this sentiment I've seen comes from Rabindranath Tagore's book *Gitanjali*. Tagore wrote, addressing God:

> *Beautiful is thy wristlet lord, decked with stars and cunningly wrought in myriad-colored jewels.*
>
> *But more beautiful to me thy sword, with its curve of lightning like the outspread wings of the divine bird of Vishnu, perfectly poised in the angry red light of the sunset.*
>
> *It quivers like the one last response of life in ecstasy of pain at the final stroke of death; it shines like the pure flame of being burning up earthly sense with one fierce flash.*
>
> *Beautiful is thy wristlet, decked with starry gems; but thy sword, O lord of thunder, is wrought with uttermost beauty, terrible to behold or think of.*

The Buddhist Monk Buddhadasa Bhikku, a very popular Buddhist teacher in Southeast Asia, wrote this poem, offering it as the essence of Dharma:

> *Do work of all kinds with a mind that is void.*
> *And then, to that void, give all of its fruits.*
> *Take food from the void, as do the holy saints.*
> *And Lo . . .*
> *You are dead to yourself*
> *From the very beginning.*

Ordinarily, the silent self on the right hemisphere and the talking one on the left are seamlessly integrated. The sense of self on the left responds to the meanings of words (their denotations). It receives constant input from the one on the right, which responds to the mood and sentiment expressed in those words (their connotations). The right sense of self deals with aesthetics and any relevant nonverbal information, responding to things like poetry. In most conversations, words go beyond their dictionary definitions, and it also feels the difference between when a cute child says something and when an imposing adult says same thing. The left, linguistic, sense of self reaches over to its counterpart on the right to capture the meaning, emotion, and significance we need to fully understand the words. The left handles the words themselves, and the right handles our sense of what they *really* mean.

An inner silence can appear during the sensed presence experience. It's not always pleasant. Remember: the primary fear structure is also on the right side of the brain, so it can be scary, and in such a case, it wouldn't be right to call it a spiritual experience. When the left hemispheric sense of self is externalized, the person might hear the voice of God or an angel. However, the person might also hear a Satanic hissing or a malevolent, scratchy voice. In most visitor experiences, the silent sense of self, the silent one, is externalized, while the dominant one, the language self, remains *you*.

In one God helmet experiment, when researchers asked the subjects to focus on the presence they sensed, it moved[504]. They couldn't keep it in mental focus. The sensed presence is a manifestation of the sense of self, and it does the same thing when you try to focus on it. The more you try to look at it, the more elusive it becomes.

Who Am I?

There are a few spiritual traditions that maintain practices where people try to find the self through introspection. Inevitably, they fail. Looking within, they find that each thing they encounter turns out not to be the self. In pursuing the sensation that they exist, they always find that sense of self they feel vaguely seems to mislead them, moves, or dissolves when they try to focus on it.

The Indian saint Ramana Maharishi advocated a method that he called "Nan Yar?" In Tamil, this means "Who Am I?" In this method, one repeatedly asks oneself, "Who am I?" Under the guidance of an experienced teacher, the students are encouraged to reject the answers that they find. You are not your body. You are not your mind. You are not your tastes and preferences. You are not your personal history. You are not your peak experiences. You are not pure love because you still exist even when you're in another mood. You are not your eternal spirit because you don't remember eternity. You aren't your beliefs, because these can change. You aren't defined by what you've experienced, because experiences always end, and you're still there when they're over.

In Buddhism and some yogic Hindu traditions, there is the "neti, neti" (not this, not this) method of inquiring into the self. No matter what one sees while looking for the self in meditation, it isn't "this," and it isn't "that." In English, it might be more accurate to say, "It isn't *here* and it isn't *there*," but it would still mean about the same thing.

The self isn't available for scrutiny. In fact, according to Buddhism, it doesn't exist at all.

The situation isn't much better for those who believe that the self is a fragment of God (a "Divine spark", or "The God Within"). People in these traditions believe that searching for the self is the same as searching for God. God may exist 'within', but "he" isn't found by 'looking within'. Most mystic visions of God seem to happen to people who believe that God exists outside of them. However, some powerful Yoga practices have been designed to disrupt the self so powerfully that God can "come through". In these traditions, you don't look for God within, but prepare yourself for God to emerge by getting yourself out of his way.

It's impossible to focus directly on either the sense of self or the *sensed presence*. You can feel both vaguely, but trying to make them clearer in your own mind only makes them more obscure. The same is true for your self-esteem. You can't see it directly. You may recognize which of your thoughts denigrate yourself, or presume you are worthless, but you can't see where these thoughts come from.

The sense of self is not in your thoughts, nor is it made there. It is not in your feelings or in the things that make them. It's not in your body or the things keeping you connected to it internally. When you're thinking normally, you have a sense that *you* are where the field of thought is. When we're feeling emotions, that's where our self seems to happen, but when you try to see the self in them, they will disappoint you each and every time. Looking for your *self* within yourself is pointless.

The sensed presence moves when we focus on it[505], and the self is equally elusive. This should come as no surprise when we recall that the sensed presence is a manifestation of the right hemispheric sense of self. The same thing happens with hallucinations, especially in the most common context for them, which is the moment we're falling asleep. Twilight sleep, sometimes called *hypnogogic* sleep, is a time when people experience all sorts of illusions and hallucinations. Some people see vivid images flash through their minds, or feel their bed moving when they know it's perfectly still. These perceptions can also change when they focus on them.

The moment of twilight sleep, when the brain is shutting down, one part at a time, is the most likely moment for the connections between neural structures to step out of their usual grooves. This state creates an opportunity for hallucinatory phenomena to appear. I've seen faces, sometimes unspeakably beautiful women's faces, coming through my visual field one after another, even though my eyes were closed. I've also seen awe-inspiring landscapes. Sometimes, these visions have incredibly rich three-dimensional effects. Then I drop off to sleep, and the next thing I know, everything has re-integrated, and I'm in a dream or I'm awake. Twilight sleep is the time when you are most likely to spontaneously break up into your inner parts. Your body can fall asleep before your thoughts stop. If you have the presence of mind to try, you can confirm the Advaita Hindu statement: you are not this, and you are not that.

Twilight sleep is a theta state. The brain also produces theta activity in trance, hypnosis, and meditation. However, according to some recent work, the right hippocampus, the silent structure that thinks without words, might be the source of all theta activity in the brain. It's also the source of the imagery in dreams and the images that flash through our minds immediately before falling asleep. Hallucinations can appear to any of our senses, and I'm going to ask you to stretch your ideas about what a sense is.

There are olfactory hallucinations, which are more common than most people might think. You smell something. It might be a faint smell, lasting only a few seconds. Unless the smell is unusual, you might not give it much thought and decide, "The neighbor's cooking something," or "Someone's having a cigarette." However, sometimes, if you look carefully into the source of the smell, it turns out that there isn't one. Other olfactory hallucinations are more compelling. Some temporal lobe epileptics have smelled heavenly perfumes or awful, macabre rotten stenches or the stink of burning hair.

Occasionally, while meditating, I've experienced the smell of burning wood, which at times caused me to jump out of meditation to check. I would think, "Where is this smoke coming from? Is the apartment on fire?" No, it was the amygdala firing away with its immediate connections to the olfactory bulbs, conjuring up a smell.

Gustatory hallucinations aren't as common. When these happen, you can taste food or drinks that aren't real. I once spent six weeks with the most exquisite flavor of cappuccino in the back of my throat at all times. Tactile hallucinations are much more common. Almost everyone has experienced this at least once. You get the feeling that there is a bug crawling on your skin, yet when you look down, nothing's there. Some people, including schizophrenics and heavy drug users, can even feel that something is crawling *under* their skin.

All of these types of hallucinations have appeared in temporal lobe epilepsy. The sense of self arises out of the temporal lobes, especially from the deeper limbic parts, and this is the place in the brain where disturbances can cause hallucinations. These hallucinations inspire my understanding of the human sense of self, as well as explaining why Buddhism says there's no such thing. It's quite simple. It's because there isn't any.

The self is a hallucination.

Our idea is that the sense of self is a hallucination, a functional hallucination with a job to do. Its function seems to be to unite everything that happens to the organism we live in, both from within and without, into a single phenomenon that can communicate with the rest of our bodies and minds. The sense of self is both a phenomenon and a sense. It responds to other phenomena in much the same way as the standard five senses respond to input. You could say that the self responds to vision as vision responds to colors.

There are many kinds of hallucinations and illusions. One called *synesthesia* mixes up perceptions, so that sounds have tastes, textures have pitch, and thoughts might have smells. I suggest the sense of self is a *synesthetic* phenomenon, cross-matching all our other senses with the hallucinatory perception of "self." The resulting neural mechanism would identify with everything it perceived and experienced, whether from within the mind or the world at large. The self is what the synesthetic cross-matching of all perceptions[506] to a hallucination feels like. All other sensory, affective, and cognitive modalities (ways of feeling, sensing and thinking) come together in the thalamus, so we expect it would make a critical contribution to the sense of self.

If you stub your toe, it's not just *any* toe being stubbed; it's yours. Your toe has been hurt, and *you* feel the pain. The phenomenon of pain is imposed on the sense of self, which in turn responds with the perception that *you* are in pain. It unites your perceptions, thoughts, and emotions, and forces your body and mind to respond to them. This guides you to act in ways to preserve your body, maintain your self-esteem and your role in your social group. Both the social and linguistic 'selves' are essential for passing on your DNA, carrying on the cycle of life, and continuing to be a survivor (or even a winner) in evolutionary terms.

Which of your senses tells you what you're feeling, and which tells you what you're thinking? If I move my hand, you see movement; that's visual. You know what sense that is. If I make a sound, you hear it. You also know what sense that is. However, emotions are different. How do you know what you're thinking? Which of your senses tells you what emotion you experience in each moment? We smooth over this ambiguity with phrases such as: "I feel angry" or "I feel happy," but there seems to be a sense that perceives these feelings. I suggest that it's the same sense that hallucinates the *self* into existence. You know your own thoughts and feelings belong to you because they are self-evident ("immediate" or "immanent") to your sense of self. The sense of self is the sensory organ. The self is its hallucination. Our day-today existence is based on a fiction, as though we are talking to a ghost in all our thoughts

The sense of self may have another function.

When we feel the sense of a presence, we are projecting the right hemispheric sense of self outside ourselves. Our sense of self, I suggest, is also projected onto other people.

Our sense of real people and our experiences of nonphysical beings are made of the same stuff. This makes them real - to us. Projecting part of ourselves onto others leads to the belief that what is painful to us will be painful to them. This assumption is so fundamental that it's almost never spoken of explicitly, and no religion is without a statement that one should "do unto others as you would have them do unto you." To create and maintain social alliances, such as those with friends, lovers, co-workers, and business associates, one has to understand what the other wants or likes. We know this by mapping our experiences onto them. We like food; so do they. We don't need to ask. At times, we tend to forget that this egocentrism is central to human relating. It's a flawed assumption, but it adjusts and becomes more refined as we grow up. Boys and girls recognize that they don't all like the same things. Children learn that the noise that they love often annoys adults. Men learn that romantic feelings can more to women than they do to them.

When you're in love, your right hemispheric sense of self is projected onto your beloved. The right hemisphere deals in nonverbal perceptions and thoughts. As a result, your beloved will seem somehow beyond words to you. To an extent, the extreme emotions that we feel about other people—hatred, anger and love—are all manifestations of our own sense of self. When the mystic poets talk about "I and my beloved becoming one," they're alluding to something profound. The beloved, as the lover sees him/her, is actually a manifestation of a part of their "self." A romantic disappointment can wound "you" deeply.

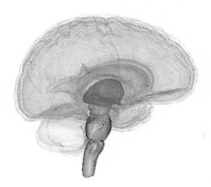

This[507] is the thalamus, the area where our thoughts, emotions, and sensory perceptions all come together and become equal players on the field of consciousness. The distinction between perceptions, thoughts, and emotions is somewhat artificial to the thalamus.

Most of our time is spent higher up in the brain, identifying with phenomena that arise in the limbic system and the cortex, but these are not the only structures that participate in constructing and maintaining the sense of self. We perceive ourselves only from the inside; through a glass darkly. Nothing we can look at introspectively will ever be the self, and the feeling that it exists is hallucinatory. The self is the process of cross-matching of all perceptions to a hallucination: the "sense" that one exists.

Pathways from all our different senses, including internal ones, need to be synesthetically bundled together, connecting to a single structure in order for them to all be happening to *us*; to our selves. The thalamus is not the center for the sense of self – there is no such center. Instead, the many pathways that support it all seem to be looped through it. Because the sense of self binds all of our perceptions together, it's a basic part of the mechanism of perception. This makes it impossible to perceive it directly; in much the same way as you cannot see your own eyeballs as you use them to look at the world around you.

In an earlier chapter, I tried to answer the question of whether the self can reincarnate. The answer would seem to be no, because it's not one of the materials that make up one's karma. It's a creation. If you take rebirth into another body and build up a new psyche, you'll create the neural substrates for maintaining the sense of self once again. Asking "Is the self reborn?" is like asking "Is vision reborn?" It develops, like any other sense, without having to be carried from one life to the next. You'll re-create yourself at the inception of your next life, just as non-reincarnating species (and I have no idea which they are) create their very different sense of self during pregnancy and infancy. The process is partly shaped by the content of your karma; your catalog of states of consciousness that are tagged "to be repeated" or "to be avoided" in your next life. Your karma would then impose personality traits, emotional patterns, and behaviors on you. These will develop as you share the moods of your mother while in the womb, as your DNA expresses itself in your brain's growth, and as you grow up, learning the ways of your culture, and undergo ordinary life experiences.

II. Enlightenment

The normal states of consciousness for enlightened people include considerable bliss. Like anyone else, the enlightened ones are not always in their normal state, so their bliss may not be constant. Several spiritual traditions believe that that it's the pinnacle of spiritual growth, and purpose of life is to attain it, after going through our cycles of lives.

The belief that we exist in order to eventually attain enlightenment is a *teleological* view. Teleological thinking assumes that things are designed for, or directed toward, a result or purpose. Scientific explanations are about how things happen, not their destinies. Language appeared because it helps us live in groups. It didn't appear in order to culminate in either poetry or computer programming. Reincarnation, as we saw before, moves us away from social failure, not toward enlightenment. There isn't any scientific basis for thinking that enlightenment, or any other state of consciousness is everyone's destiny. Of course, even if it were, science would have no way of seeing it, because destiny isn't a scientific idea.

At the outset of this discussion, I should point out that we won't be looking at enlightenment in terms of classical spiritual teachings. I don't want to offend anyone by this approach, but the scriptures that describe enlightenment can't be used as a basis for a scientific hypothesis, if only because they're written in vocabulary that lacks scientific definitions.

One feature of enlightenment all traditions agree on is that it involves either ("euphoric") bliss or an absence of ("dysphoric") negative emotions. There are other traits that can appear with enlightenment, but it appears that few, if any, enlightened people have ever enjoyed them all. It's been said that no one but an enlightened person should speak about enlightenment because they are the only ones who can understand it. This view amounts to a ban on all scientific investigation of the phenomenon. We'll risk the wrath of the gods and begin our discussion.

I'll try to answer four questions about enlightenment:

1)   What happens in the brain when people attain enlightenment?
2)   How does enlightenment change the self or the sense of self?
3)   How does enlightenment create bliss?
4)   Why is enlightenment different in different people?

Some enlightened people seem to have psychic skills, while others don't. Some of them teach elaborate systems of psychology. Others just go into silence and say nothing, becoming silent (or *mauna*) Buddhas. Some enlightened people are thought to perform miracles; some aren't. Interestingly, the kinds of miracles the Buddha performed are different from the ones attributed to Jesus.

19th century image of the Buddha's miracle at Shravasti.

A rival teacher once challenged the Buddha to perform a miracle to prove his enlightenment. In response, the Buddha made multiple copies of himself. One minute, there was only the Buddha himself standing there. In the next moment, four other Buddhas surrounded him, each lying in serenity and silence. The rival guru instantly became a disciple of the Buddha, bringing all of his students with him. There are many such stories in the life of the Buddha. Other "enlightened masters" say that the greatest miracle is not to do them. Zen Buddhism seems to look down on miracles, saying that it's better to cultivate awareness than miraculous powers.

Meditation as preparation for Enlightenment

Because many spiritual practices, especially meditation, depend on the right hippocampus, they sometimes involve a sense of spaciousness and relaxation. In Southeast Asian Buddhism, seeing a vast inner space is a mark of entry into advanced ("formless") meditative states. The Buddhist teacher Chogyam Trungpa encouraged his students to find an inner spaciousness. Spatial reasoning and inner quiet depend on the hippocampus on the right side, where the caudate nucleus tends to support relaxation. In meditation, the effort is to suppress verbal thought; to relax while staying alert and maintaining one's attention on the meditation object (such as one's breath or the place between the eyebrows) each time it strays. This involves several nonverbal cognitive tasks at once. This process strongly implicates the right hippocampus, with its role in monitoring one's internal state. It's the primary source of the brain's theta activity, which commonly appears on EEG during meditation. Meditation is much more complicated than we're making it look here, but not everything about it is germane to understanding the states it creates.

The right hippocampus is not just intimately interconnected with the right amygdala; the two are actually joined. When one is very excited, the other tends to be quiet. We experience this directly when we're in a very emotional state and find it harder to think, and we can see it in the way some kinds of intellectuals are less emotional than some kinds of artists. When it's active enough to crowd out the amygdala, the right hippocampus can create a sense of detachment (or, *flattened affect* in psychiatric disorders). Detachment and equanimity, two of the fruits of successful meditation practice, actually rely on the same brain structures, and many kinds of meditation are pointed towards achieving them. In these states, our emotions either don't appear or they don't seem very important.

Prayer can be emotional, but there's not much emotion during some kinds of meditation. Meditation works with internal cognitions and a state of relaxation, but not many words. These silent states tend to calm the limbic emotional centers. Most meditation objects are nonverbal. Some examples are:

- watching the breath or counting breaths;
- visualizing objects, points or spheres of light, deities, or flows of imagined energy;
- Formal hand movements;[508]
- maintaining all your attention in one of your senses;[509]
- making sounds, such as "Aum", humming or chordal chanting;[510]
- imagining one's own death;
- staring at candles, lights, mirrors, the sun, or the moon;
- Imagining yourself in different forms.

All of these are nonverbal tasks. To do them correctly, you need to inhibit inner language or "mind chatter."

Even chanting involves suppressing words. "Hare Krishna, Hare Krishna, Krishna Krishna, Hare, Hare." "Holy Mary, Mother of God, pray for us sinners now and at the hour of our death." "If I have to live in this world, let it be on toasted eggs." Chanting keeps the brain's language centers busy with a single group of words and either suppresses other verbal thoughts or makes them appear much more slowly. Filling the mind with a mantra, as so many of its teachers have said, eventually means emptying it.

Meditation has prepared more people for enlightenment than any other way of working with the mind, and seems to do a better job of it, too. That's why it's used in so many spiritual traditions. Some spiritual traditions are less ambitious. They don't teach that meditation will make you enlightened. They tell you that meditation is calming and can make your life better. When hippocampus on the right is the focus of neural excitement, the right amygdala can be inhibited, along with its contributions to anxiety, fear, and sadness.

The same meditation that can keep the "silent thinking" and relaxation brain parts tuned and operating can also, in unusual circumstances, provoke anxiety and fear. Although it's rare, excess meditation has caused psychoses. Anything that excites the right hemisphere suddenly can disturb the fragile states meditation gradually creates.

When we become frightened of something, either from within the mind or from the world around us, the fear excites the right amygdala. Ordinarily, when a non-meditating mind experiences deep fear, it directs some of the activity into other areas, as we try to think our way out of the situation. In special cases, when the right hemisphere is already fully active, the person could be on the brink of terror, a sense of impending doom or the sense that they are dissolving. If the fear becomes strong enough, and the right hemisphere cannot accommodate any extra activity, the excitement can go past the right amygdala's capacity. The right hippocampus can also direct a load of activity into the right amygdala. If this happens when the whole right hemispheres is busy (a possibility for people who spend prolonged periods in meditation), there may not be anywhere for it to go but across the brain to the left amygdala. In other words, if the whole right side of the brain has become highly active through meditation, and the focus of excitement is in the right hippocampus, then the right amygdala may also be close to its full capacity without the person being in a state of fear, because. In this way, the right amygdala could be primed to dump activity into it's counterpart on the left, without even being the most excited structure.

If the person is an advanced meditator, the right hemisphere can already be more excited than usual, because of the many hours spent in meditation. Meditation will have tasked the right side of the brain, keeping it active and excited. When fear or dissociation is at its peak for such a person, the right amygdala can come to its maximum level of excitement very quickly. Any further input going into the right amygdala will need to escape somewhere. Where does it go? Out, by the most direct path in that moment, the path of least resistance, to the left amygdala. That's the moment of enlightenment. The same kind of interhemispheric intrusion is also behind visions of God, but without nearly so much right hippocampal involvement.

The Mechanism of Sudden Enlightenment

When the fearful right amygdala is working at its peak and the rest of the right limbic system is also highly active, the activity can burst over to the left side like an avalanche. In that moment, the left amygdala is suddenly and dramatically activated, and the entire situation turns around. A horrible moment becomes ecstatic. We've seen this pattern of brain activity in two other contexts. The first is in the God helmet experiments, and the second is in visions of God. In the next chapter, we will look at some examples of the same pattern of excitement in other situations. Here, we see it in enlightenment.

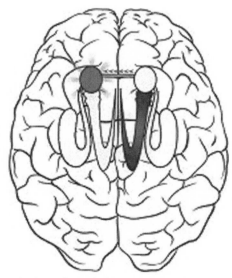

The basis for enlightenment seems to be a lasting excitement in the left amygdala and the right hippocampus[511], and a reduced or eliminated left-to-right communication along the anterior commissure.

It's as though this sudden activation of the left amygdala releases a kind of pressure from one on the right. However, the hippocampus on the right, with all its nonverbal functions and operations, can still outstrip its counterpart on the left, especially for people who've have exercised it through meditation. Just after enlightenment, both ecstasy and silent thinking are happening at or near their maximum. When an awful moment suddenly becomes delightful and harmonious, the person is also flooded with all kinds of insights, intimations, hints, and fragments of seemingly higher truth.

There have been many meditation studies, and they have added a wealth of information to the science of spirituality, but there is still no clear explanation for the personality changes meditation can create. There are several brain areas that become more active, and some that become quieter during meditation. In some cases, different have found the same areas becoming both more and less active. These studies contradict each other. One thing most agree on is that meditation stimulates the brain to produce more 'brain waves' in the lower frequencies, including delta waves, but especially theta waves. The right hippocampus is the main (possibly the only) source for theta waves[512].

Throughout this process, the left hippocampus remains quiet, outweighed by the cognitive activity in its counterpart on the right. The left caudate nucleus, which we believe contributes to arousal and excitement; can burst into activity[513], fed by the sudden activation of the left amygdala. Again, the caudate nucleus is directly connected to the amygdala, so the wave of bliss can include tremendous excitement. This has been called the "lion's roar" in Buddhism. Jesus said, "Shout it from the rooftops."[514] The feeling is so intense that it has to be acted out. Why a roar or a shout, but not a dance? Why vocal sounds? Remember: the left side of the brain, where the language centers are, is suddenly excited in the moment of enlightenment. We should expect something vocal – though dancing is not out of the question.

There's a small structure, *the anterior commissure*, which connects the two amygdalas. By connecting one set of emotions to the other, fear and joy can modulate and mute each other. For example, you're in a state of terror because your boss is about to fire you. His secretary then comes in and says, "He talked to me about the meeting. He's not going to fire you. He's just trying to scare you." You think, "Ahhh" and relax. The fear is starts to subside as soon as the reason for it is gone. The anterior commissure helps us feel the appropriate fear for each threat, and also helps us to stop feeling afraid when the danger has passed. Technically-inclined readers should recall that there are also connections between the two amygdalas that run through the frontal lobes.

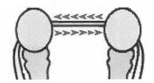

This is the anterior commissure connecting the left and right amygdala.

Communication between them flows equally in both directions. Here, both amygdalas are shown being quiet.

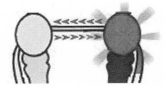

Here, the right amygdala is very excited, perhaps because something frightening has happened, or perhaps because the right hippocampus (below it) was over-excited, and dumped its load of activity into the right amygdala. In such cases, enlightenment might be an intra-limbic intrusion followed by another across the brain.

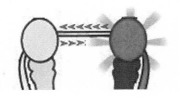

Here, we see more activity and excitement than the anterior commissure can handle. The electrical energy is pushing its way through, stripping away (inhibitory) synapses that would otherwise hold back activity moving from right to left.

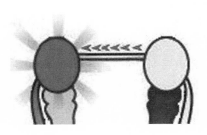

Here, we see the anterior commissure after one side has been pared away. Now, the right amygdala is quiet, and the one on the left is active and excited. The person is now enlightened, and activity flows from right to left much more easily than from left to right. The Caudate Nucleus is now active, and the person feels aroused and excited.

Not all enlightenment experiences would excite the left caudate. If the person was in a state of deep calm immediately before becoming enlightened, and the moment of fear (or other *dysphoria*) was brief enough, or involved few enough pathways, then the amount of excitement in the caudate might not change its levels of excitement in the process, leaving the person deeply relaxed and feeling a "peace which passeth understanding" instead of bliss.

From these illustrations, we see how activity was equally able to move in both directions across the anterior commisure before the moment of enlightenment. Afterwards, the activity can only run easily from right to left, from the fear structure to the bliss structure (so to speak). One would wonder why this changed. The answer is that all other conditions being equal, a sudden shock to the brain will remove more inhibitory synapses (which slow down activity) than excitatory synapses (that speed it up). Removing synapses that inhibit activity makes a brain part more excitable. A brain trauma eliminates more of the tiny pieces (synapses) that prevent things from happening (inhibitory) than the ones that help things happen (excitatory) [515]. If you prune away enough of the inhibitory right-to-left synapses along the anterior commissure, any significant excitement in the right amygdala will automatically shunt over to the left. Such a brain would be a lot less able to inhibit or prevent bliss.

Generally, a closed head injury, where the skull is cracked or severely shaken, will include a concussion. If it's severe enough, it will shake loose some inhibitory synapses. This can mean that all kinds of neural functions that are normally suppressed jump into action unexpectedly. Someone with a serious closed head injury could suddenly have severe bursts of anger or fear and wonder why their emotions are running amok. It's because some of the synapses that ordinarily inhibit them were lost. Most often, the phenomena they unleash in this way are unpleasant. In enlightenment, the limbic "injury" comes from only one direction, which limits its effects. Inhibitory synapses are pruned only from the right amygdala to the left, which ensures that enlightenment will feel good. If the synapses were shorn in the opposite direction, the result might be something like Post-Traumatic Stress Disorder; a lasting sensitivity to anything that feels bad, and an inability to hold onto good moods following fearful events, no matter how trivial.

These kinds of head injuries selectively break inhibitory synapses. Excitatory ones suffer far less damage. Enlightenment can be seen as a kind of injury that happens to the limbic system, but instead of coming from the outside, the "injury" of enlightenment comes from within. Instead of being painful, this one is blissful. We would expect that only the *anterior commissure* will be changed in this way for all enlightened people, though the connections between the two amygdala running through the frontal lobes could also be influenced.

For an enlightened one, whenever the fearful amygdala is turned on, most or all of its activity will automatically be directed to the blissful one, encouraging the perception that there are no problems and that there is never anything to fear. It will feel as if nothing is wrong, and nothing can ever hurt you. There are no threats; you are safe at all times and in all places.

Over time, a normal closed-head-injury patient will activate the brain's systems of reward and punishment, pleasure and aversion, without knowing they're doing it. The patient will do what he or she can to start building up new inhibitory synapses to suppress negative emotions and allow positive ("hedonic") ones. This process bypasses most of the pathways that help us feel good, because there's no need to inhibit positive feelings. Over time, the brain accommodates the new set of conditions. The brain's reward systems won't work to undo the changes that come with enlightenment, though it's worth noting that some enlightenment traditions maintain that the stress that can come from the pursuit of sensual pleasures can corrupt the experience, over time.

In the course of my work, I've encountered many people who've suffered various kinds of head injuries and then went into a turbulent period. A few of them said that when it was over, it turned out to be one of the best things that ever happened to them. Dr. Jill Bolte Taylor,[516] a neuroscientist, suffered a stroke, and doctors removed a blood clot the size of a golf ball from her brain. Afterwards, she had a phenomenal story to tell about becoming enlightened along the way. In spite of the many insights that she received, it was still a very turbulent enlightenment process. It remains to be seen whether her state will be permanent. Of course, she is a scientist, and not a meditator, so her right hippocampus may not be as easily excited as those of enlightened meditation masters, and the enlightenment that followed her stroke may well have a different flavor ("affective and cognitive dimensions"), so to speak.

The moment of enlightenment tends to be preceded by something extremely unpleasant. So far, we have only discussed the process of enlightenment in terms of bliss following an episode of fear, but other right hemispheric "negativity", like despair, dissociation or depression can also set the stage for it. In these cases, the right hippocampus is likely to have sent a jolt of energy into the right amygdala, bringing it to its tipping point, where it would then have sent another blast of excitement across the brain to the left amygdala. This would add a great deal of hippocampal information to the moment of enlightenment, making it, and its after-effects more cognitive (experienced through thought) than a vision of God, which relies on the same mechanism.

Why is enlightenment different in different people?

Let's look at the questions that I promised to answer at the beginning of this section. Why is it that some enlightened ones perform miracles, but others don't? Why do some Buddhas have lots to say and teach extensively, while others "go into silence"? The Buddha himself filled a five-foot shelf of books with his scriptural sayings, The Sutras. Why do some "liberated ones" look into your heart and see your innermost thoughts and show them to you in ways that transform you, while others don't?

Let's start by looking at why some enlightened ones talk more than others. In the moment of enlightenment, the left amygdala is suddenly filled with huge amounts of neural energy, coming from its counterpart on the right. It's unlikely the activity would just stay there when this happens. We would expect it to spill over into one or more of the other brain structures on the left. Let's look at how having this high level of activity, blasting into other areas connected to the left amygdala, might affect the brain and the mind.

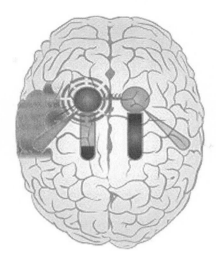

The activity might spill from the left amygdala into the left temporal lobe, where the language centers are. A loss of inhibitory pathways[517] along these routes could explain why some enlightened people can teach and put their insights into words easily, while others remain silent. An overload of activity from the left amygdala could create more connections to the language centers in and around the left temporal lobe than had existed before[518], and this would tend to increase their linguistic abilities. A blast of activity into the left hippocampus might do the same thing. If the same activity bypasses these areas, the newly enlightened person might be somewhat inarticulate.

If the activity overflowing from the left amygdala were to overflow into the left insula or the left caudate nucleus (not shown), the experience of enlightenment would be 'colored' by love and affection.

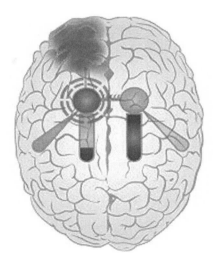

This activity could also overflow into the frontal lobes, with its many functions, not least of which is accessing our social skills, an *executive function*. The frontal lobes are deeply involved in relating to other people, with all the complicated social rules humans live by. If new pathways were created from the left amygdala to the frontal lobes, there'd be an extra load of social skills, which could include the ability to perceive other people's states of consciousness, traits, and habits. It might seem as if they can look into a person's soul.

Padre Pio, whose religious tradition recognizes sanctity, but not in terms of enlightenment, was able to tell people their sins before they began their confessions. Neem Karoli Baba, a contemporary Indian saint, often displayed his ability to know other people's thoughts, many of which were confirmed. Such "mind reading" could also be the result of a loss of the inhibitions that normally hold back one's intuition. It could also be a matter of greater sensitivity to information transmitted between brains, as we'll see in the next chapter. In such a case, the changes wrought by enlightenment could include a lasting alteration in a specific brain activity called "The Binding Factor", which we'll look at in another chapter.

An enlightened person can sometimes look at you and read your heart and mind (long-standing affective and cognitive traits) by seeing you make only a single gesture. As we saw in the chapter on brain parts, the amygdala is crucial in all these subtle perceptions. Whether it's forceful or gentle; abrupt or fluid, a single movement can reveal a great deal about you. A single tone of voice, the way you express yourself, and the nuances of your body language, can make you transparent to someone whose enlightenment expanded their social skills. Some can read your subtle cues and instantly understand their meaning. They can often tell you what they see, including things about yourself that even you aren't aware of. Such people can instantly know where you are in the many spectrums of human types. If they're trained in different meditation practices, they may be able to assign you to undertake a specific spiritual practice.

There are stories in the Hindu and Buddhist traditions in which people see "the master", who takes one look at them and says, "You go chant. Here's your mantra. Now go away and come back in three years. In the meantime, chant 30 minutes a day." A meditation master might assign you to sit and listen to your breathing. The practice might begin to have effects almost instantly. When coming out of meditation, the new disciple might think, "Wow, this really works for me. The master has amazing insight." They would have noticed an indefinable quality of the practice and matched it to an indefinable quality of the person. Such a master could no more tell you in words why a specific practice would work for you than a chef could say why oregano and not thyme belongs in a sauce.

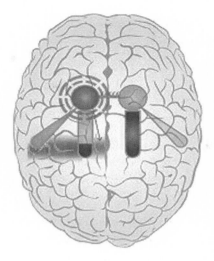

Activity spilling out of the left amygdala in the moment of enlightenment might also find its way into the parietal lobes. The parietal lobes are involved with our bodies. One section receives input from the body, and another section controls it. The enlightened person would then have an extra mastery over their body. Healing by 'laying on hands' is a widely known skill, but not all enlightened people have it or even claim to have it. Most spiritual traditions hold that some holy men or women can put their hands on a sick person, and make the illness vanish. Others can put their hands on someone's head, and impart some of their state of consciousness through their hands, briefly conveying their enlightenment experience. In India, the name for this is *Shaktipat*, meaning the direct transmission of spiritual energy.

I suggest that the different skills shown by enlightened people reflect the areas of the brain that were recruited when they became enlightened. Unusual states based in these parts of the brain become enduring 'special' traits, including the ones seen as signs of enlightenment. The more sensitive a brain area was before their enlightenment, the more likely it would be changed in the process. Enlightenment can turn spiritual traits the person had only sometimes into enduring spiritual states, which they can access at will.

Enlightenment Case Histories

The Buddha

Buddhist tradition tells us that the night before he became enlightened the Buddha was attacked by Mara, the Lord of Evil. His three daughters danced in front of the Buddha in skimpy clothes, tempting him with provocative poses. Their names were *desire, lust,* and *aversion.* Buddhist tradition holds that Mara put every possible distraction in front of the Buddha. However, the Buddha did not allow fear, desire, anger, or regret to take hold of him, and eventually, the temptations stopped. After that, Mara's armies attacked the Buddha.

The daughters of Mara dancing before the Buddha. Photo by Andreas Praefcke[519]

They fired spears and arrows at him. As they approached, they turned into flower blossoms that fell worshipfully to his feet. Many Buddhist teachers, and your author here, believe that this story is a symbolic telling of the tale of the Buddha's emotional turbulence as he struggled with his own negative thoughts and emotions. Perhaps he was tempted to return to his old princely life, with all its luxuries, but at the same time, horrified at how it would have meant his years as an ascetic were wasted.

It was probably a very stressful night, with fear and doubt in the forefront of the Buddha's mind; a struggle that ended with his enlightenment.

The story of the night before the Buddha's enlightenment may be more legend than history. It would be hard for many Buddhists to imagine that the founder of their religion could have been deeply tempted by lust, greediness, irritability and anger. Telling the story in symbolic form; turning it into a tale of struggle between the Bodhisattva and evil demons, would be easier to accept than hearing that this sacred being had such profane moments just before his liberation. The story of what happened the next morning is another matter. Once the dawn came, his mind returned to the calm he was known for. Buddhist tradition tells us that, as the sun rose the morning after his private battle, the Buddha gazed at the morning star, and became enlightened.

If we accept it as true, then we should look at the behavior of the planet Venus at sunrise. Venus is always close to the sun. Sometimes, when seen from the earth, it's on one side of the sun (the morning star), and on the opposite side (the evening star) at other times. As the evening star, it sets shortly after the sun does. In the morning, however, we don't see it set. Instead, it gradually fades from sight, disappearing when the sunlight becomes bright enough to wash out its light.

The Buddha cultivated deep concentration skills during his many years of spiritual practices. Perhaps the morning star became a spontaneous gazing (*tratak*[520]) meditation object. For him, just gazing at the morning star might have become so engrossing that when it disappeared as the sun rose, so did he.

The actual moment of his enlightenment is said to have occurred just as it disappeared from the sky that morning. The incredibly turbulent night he passed before this dawn must have given the process a powerful momentum. If the night was dominated by fear, then his right amygdala would have been in a very sensitive state. Any shock or surprise could have jolted it into extreme excitement. Seeing something vanish while you're totally engaged in looking at it can be a shock. The same is true for interrupting any meditation, whether it was based on gazing or watching the breath. If someone is completely caught up in meditation, a sudden disturbance can be jarring. If he was identified with his visual perception; that is to say, if he had *become the looking*, then *he* would stop when the thing he was looking at vanished. If the neural event that disrupted his right hemispheric sense of self (made more sensitive by regular disconnection from his thoughts, body sensations and emotions in meditation), were strong enough, it could have pared away many of the connections that would normally inhibit it. The *self* of someone who is so deep in meditation that they're completely identified with one of their senses will be unusually sensitive to an unexpected change in what that sense perceives. If you are listening to music through headphones, and suddenly everything goes silent, you'll be a bit shocked. If you're listening with powers of concentration built up through decades of meditation practice, you might even be disoriented.

When the morning star vanished from the Buddha's sight, it became possible for all the neural activity (whether inhibitory or excitatory) involved in the Buddha's spontaneous meditation (gazing at the morning star) to wash over into the other side of his brain. It would have been focused in the right limbic system. Increasing right hippocampal activity in such a sensitive mind may have triggered a jump in right amygdala activation; enough to push it past the low limit it would have after such a night of fear.

A similar story is told about the Zen nun *Chiyono*,[521] who was carrying a bucket of water and looking at the moon's reflection in it. The bottom of the bucket burst, the reflection of the moon vanished, and, as the story goes, she became enlightened. To this day, Zen Buddhism preserves many stories in which meditation masters shock their disciples into enlightenment.

The Fasting Buddha[522]

The Buddha's intense ascetic practices set the stage for his enlightenment. Tradition says that each day he ate no more food than one cupped hand could hold. Another tradition holds that he ate no more than three grains of rice per day. He became emaciated. He once rubbed his stomach and felt his backbone. He kept himself in a state of constant pain. Just three days before his enlightenment, he began to eat again, after realizing that this punishing practice could lead to his death before he achieved his liberation or enlightenment.

Three days before his enlightenment, a young maiden named Sujata, who came from a nearby village, brought the Buddha a bowl of rice cooked in milk with honey. He ate his first real meal in years. He knew how to deny himself, despite his body's demand for food. The relief when he finally ate that first meal, and allowed his body to take in sugar, carbohydrates, and protein all at once must have been enormous. The load of activation in his right amygdala would have been greatly reduced, but it would take weeks or months before his right limbic system, forced into a rare state of excitement by his intense spiritual practices, would quiet down again. He was just beginning to allow himself to feel good again.

He had almost starved to death, perhaps facing a strong death anxiety. Not only from an ordinary desire to avoid dying, but also of the social death that he would undergo having failed to meet the goal he worked to achieve for so many difficult years – attaining enlightenment. If he had given up meditation when he gave up starving himself, Buddhism might not exist today. He had chosen a new agenda for his inner work. He would stay in the middle. He wouldn't stop working on himself through meditation, but in all other things, he would be easy on himself and his body. In neural terms, he would no longer keep his right amygdala excited, but it wasn't going to quiet down abruptly. He would still have been prone to the occasional burst of excitement. His startle response could have been exaggerated for some time after. The mental torment of his visions of Mara, or the terrible moods they symbolized, were enough to overburden the right side of the brain, even after he stopped torturing himself. This brain activity could still come to a peak of right amygdala excitement, and then burst over to one on the left, precipitating his enlightenment.

Eckhart Tolle[523]

Another Enlightenment story belongs to Eckhart Tolle[524], author of *The Power of Now*. He wrote, "... until my 30th year, I lived in continuous anxiety, interspersed with periods of suicidal depression." The deep part of the brain most important for "anxiety, interspersed with suicidal depression" is the right amygdala.

"One night, not long after my 29th birthday, I woke up in the early morning hours with the feeling of absolute dread. I'd woken up with such a feeling many times before, but this time, it was more intense than it had ever been. The silence of the night, the vague outlines of the furniture in the room, the distant noise of a passing train. Everything felt so alien, so hostile, and so utterly meaningless that it created in me a deep loathing of the world. The most loathsome thing, however, was my own existence."

Focused on his sense of self, his deep unhappiness excited the right amygdala.

"I cannot live with myself any longer." This was a thought [that] I kept repeating to myself in my mind, and suddenly, I became aware of a peculiar thought; it was, "Am I one or two? If I can't live with myself then there must be two of me. The I and the self that I cannot live with. "Maybe," I thought, "only one of them is real."

Tolle understood that he had two senses of self. He was in a moment of self-loathing, which would put an unusual burden on both of them.

I was so stunned by this strange realization that my mind stopped. I was fully conscious, but there were no more thoughts. I felt drawn into what seemed a vortex of energy. It was a slow movement at first, and then it accelerated. I was gripped by an intense fear.

He was pulled in to a Tunnel experience.[525] His mind chatter had stopped, and he was in intense fear, meaning that his right amygdala, the next-door neighbor to the hippocampus, was very active. The right hippocampus itself, the silent brain part, was also busy. Next, he felt himself being sucked into a void, an experience that also appears in NDEs and from stimulation of the right hippocampus.

It felt as if The Void was inside myself rather than outside. Suddenly, there was no more fear; I let myself fall into that void. I had no recollection of what happened after that.

Falling into *The Void*, would mean his right hippocampus was the focus of his neural energy, confining it within the right hemisphere, and putting an end to his fear. These right hemispheric structures were at their peaks of activation. When the fear stopped, There was nowhere for the excitement to go except into the left amygdala, into enlightenment.

> I was awakened by the chirping of the birds outside the window. I had never heard such a sound before. My eyes were still closed, but I saw the image of a precious diamond. Yes, if a diamond could make a sound, this was what it would be like. I opened my eyes. The first light of dawn was filtering through the curtains. Without any thought, I felt [that] I knew that there was infinitely more to light than we realize. The soft luminosity filtering through the curtains was love itself. Tears came into my eyes.

As happens in near-death experiences (NDEs), Tolle went from an experience of *The Void* into an experience that involved light – from the right amygdala and hippocampus into the left amygdala. These phenomena can also happen during an NDE, though with a different manifestation. He was enlightened. I'm not saying that his book shows the best way to enlightenment, but his experience appears to be a typical enlightenment story. As in the Buddha's story, Tolle's dawn of enlightenment followed a hellish night.

The following is the story of Ramana Maharishi's enlightenment[526].

Ramana Maharshi[527]

"It was in 1896 that this great change in my life took place. I was sitting alone in a room on the first floor of my uncle's house. I seldom had any sickness, and on that day, there was nothing wrong with my health, but a sudden violent fear of death overtook me. There was nothing in my state of health to account for it, nor was there any urge in me to find out whether there was any account for the fear. I just felt (that) I was going to die and began thinking what to do about it."

It sounds as if he had a powerful anxiety attack, a wave of death anxiety, though it's not likely he would have called it that in 1896.

"It did not occur to me to consult a doctor or any elders or friends. I felt [that] I had to solve the problem myself then and there. The shock of the fear of death drove my mind inwards, and I said to myself mentally, without actually framing the words: "Now death has come; what does it mean? What is it that is dying? This body dies." And at once, I dramatized the occurrence of death. I lay with my limbs stretched out still, as though rigor mortis has set in, and imitated a corpse so as to give greater reality to the enquiry. . . . "Well, then," I said to myself, "this body is dead. It will be carried stiff to the burning ground and there burn and be reduced to ashes. But with the death of the body, am I dead? Is the body I? It is silent and inert, but I feel the full force of my personality and even the voice of I within me, apart from it. So I am the Spirit transcending the body. The body dies, but the spirit transcending it cannot be touched by death. That means [that] I am the deathless Spirit." All this was not dull thought; it flashed through me vividly as living truths [that] I perceived directly, almost without thought process."

In his state of death anxiety and despair, Ramana Maharshi allowed his thoughts to go in a very unusual direction. Instead of thinking of ways to avoid dying or escape from it, he *engaged* the experience. He even encouraged it. The internal pressure in the right amygdala accompanying his death anxiety made moving its activity over to its left hemispheric counterpart the path of least resistance. At the same time, his thoughts were pointed at something words can't describe. Death. He acquired the insight that he was not his body. It was a nonverbal (and hence, a right hippocampal) understanding, vividly flashing through him, and at that moment, the thought that he wasn't his body was enough to alter his sense of self. Indeed, many Hindu Traditions teach that contemplating the idea that you are not your body can be enough to change you.

Ramana Maharshi's enlightenment happened in a moment of deep death anxiety. For the rest of his life, he taught his students and disciples to look at what-they-are-not, like in the "neti, neti" method of Adi Shankaracharaya. This was Maharshi's most important way to attain 'truth', just as his own enlightenment followed the insight that he was not his body.

Just thinking about the fact that you are not your body won't have the same effect. A moment of mental turbulence can culminate in a spiritual experience, but the seemingly deep insight that can appear along with it will have no power at other moments. You have to be in a profound mood for the words to seem profound. You would probably be shaken up in the same circumstance, even if the words didn't appear. A deep insight can't do much if it's just a thought you have during an ordinary moment. The words are only a by-product. Spiritual teachers can talk about spiritual 'truths', but they won't transform the disciples unless real events naturally change the way their brains work. Because these events are usually going to be painful, no ethical Guru will ever try to *make* them happen. If you are ever drawn to a Guru or spiritual teacher who tries to set up their students to go through any kind of pain (sometimes called "showing you your ego"), get away from them as fast as you can. Being 'cruel to be kind' is more often an excuse for someone to act out their cruelty than it is a 'higher' form of kindness.

> I was something real, the only real thing about my present state, and all the conscious activity connected with the body was centered on that I. From that moment onwards, the "I" or Self focused attention on itself by a powerful fascination. Fear of death vanished once and for all. The ego was lost in the flood of Self-awareness. Absorption in the Self continued unbroken from that time. Other thoughts might come and go like the various notes of music, but the "I" continued like the fundamental shruti[528] (drone) note, which underlies and blends with all other notes."

The phenomena occurring in Ramana's enlightenment—(the insight into the nature of the Self) is reminiscent of the transcendent experience in NDEs. The phenomena of Ramana's *moksha* may have included a *Transcendent Experience* that happened outside the death process, with self as the object of inquiry instead of the nature of reality, as in so many NDE *transcendent experiences*. Such a substitution seems normal for Hinduism, with its strong belief that the world is a manifestation of the mind (either God's mind or one's own). Indeed, Ramana emphasized that we know the world is only through the mind, a teaching that seems to reflect his personal experience.

Osho Rajneesh, depicted in the locket he gave his disciples[529]

Bhagwan Shri Rajneesh, known in later life as Osho,[530] was called a spiritual criminal by several spiritual teachers, including J. Krishnamurti. Terrible things were done in his name by his underhanded secretary in the 1980s[531], and there were several scandals within his organization (though not with his centers and ashrams following his death). Rajneesh called himself "The Rich Man's Guru", and avidly collected Rolex watches and Rolls Royce cars.

His ashram conducted group therapy, with an "encounter group" so intense that arms and legs were broken in its worst moments. Entering a state of perfect bliss doesn't necessarily mean achieving a state of exemplary morality. Indeed, ethics and morality seem to have had no place in his teachings.

In this chapter, we have discussed "higher" states of consciousness without reference to morality. When the Emperor Napoleon asked the astronomer LaPlace about God's role in the universe, the scholar answered, saying "I had no need for that hypothesis." In explaining enlightenment, we have no need to refer to morality, perhaps because morality isn't one of its components. It's intrinsic to religion, but mystics often ignore the moral rules. One well-known example is the Sufi Al-Mansoor, whose realization led him to proclaim that he was God, a serious blasphemy in Islam. In fact, he was stoned to death for it.

Is morality an inherent part of enlightenment? Do the states of consciousness that motivate immoral, counter-adaptive, or bad behavior also inhibit progress towards enlightenment? There are no links with higher states of consciousness that guarantee that a higher morality will automatically appear with enlightenment. They may happen through the same processes (as taught in Theravada Buddhism), but they can also happen separately. Many enlightened ones have taught their disciples to cultivate compassion, but others haven't given it much importance. Some, like the Caucasian Gurdjieff, seem to be quite cruel. Enlightenment or sanctity doesn't seem to automatically bestow morality. Many 20th-century Christian evangelists or Holy Rollers (as they came to be known) have performed documented healings and made memorable impromptu sermons on Christian scriptures. Their skills in teaching religion didn't prevent them from sliding into alcoholism, committing sexual offenses and even embezzlement. In the 1990s, two Thai monks with large followings, Prah Nikom and Prah Ajhan Yantra, were found *in flagrante delicto*[532] with women followers. Both were expelled from the monkhood. Their scandals were front-page news in Thailand.

Rajneesh "worked on himself" for years, doing every kind of meditation practice imaginable. By the time his book of spiritual practices was published, there were over a hundred in the collection. His intensive spiritual practices whipped him into a state of extreme disassociation. He reached a point where he literally could not think.

One night, after a very intense yogic process that lasted a week, he found himself having an experience of light and bliss. He couldn't bear to be inside his little chamber. He had to get outside. A change in his spatial perception may have contributed to an overload. He felt a need to get outside, out of his small room. By increasing the amount of space around him, he tasked the hippocampus on the right and increased the workload of that spatial perception structure, even if only slightly.

He found himself drawn to a garden, and had to climb a wall to get inside it. All the trees were glowing, and one of them, a Maulshree tree, was glowing more brightly than the rest. He went and sat under it. His enlightenment happened as he sat there. All he could say about it was that it was a benediction beyond all words.

His enlightenment experience[533] was typical, except that instead of fear overloading the right side of the brain, he had gone into a state of deep dissociation. The burst of activity to the left side of his brain began in his right hippocampus, instead of his right amygdala. The shortest path from the right hippocampus to the left amygdala would have led through the amygdala on the right, and the enlightenment that would follow would have extra ineffable[534] cognitive nuances, reflecting the functions of the right hippocampus. Remembering that the right hippocampus functions in spatial reasoning and perception, it's not surprising that he felt the urge to 'change his space'. It's possible that if he hadn't been able to get outside, his enlightenment might not have happened when it did, or the way it did.

"On a dark night,
Kindled in love with yearnings —oh, happy chance!—
I went forth without being observed,
My house being now at rest …
… into a night more lovely than the dawn" (*St John of the Cross, "Dark night of the Soul"*)

Medication

A woman from California wrote to me after spending some time reading my website. She had been on antidepressants for years. Such medications should be tapered off slowly, but she stopped taking them abruptly, which any doctor would have told her not to do. All the controls to her depression had been removed suddenly. She went into a state of acute depression and anxiety. A group of antidepressants (primarily klonopin) had suppressed her fearful structure (again, dear reader, that's the right amygdala) for years. When these were abruptly withdrawn, her right amygdala burst into activity, this time without any chemical controls. That activity spilled into the left amygdala, and she became enlightened. Of course, she didn't need the pills after that. She continues as a spiritual teacher to this day, though teaching only women.

Another interesting case comes from a woman who was unable to achieve orgasm, and became desperate to breakthrough to the experience. She masturbated furiously every day, trying to have an orgasm, and had an enlightenment experience while resting after a session of prolonged masturbation.

> I am one of those lucky few who believe she has suffered a case of spontaneous enlightenment. I am not exactly sure how, but I do believe it has to do with the unfortunate fact that I do not climax... Tantric practices say that spiritual energy is the next energy after sexual energy, so all the built-up energy could have triggered it. I did not know what was happening to me, it was quite an experience. I felt on drugs for about two months. I was in euphoria, I was in a state of extreme happiness and surely felt quite disconnected with reality or should I say extremely connected, but to a reality that was still unknown to me.

> Her enlightenment "...was in fact precipitated by very intense sexual sessions (about four hours long) without climaxing. Then there was a good two months feeling euphoria, but there was also a more substantial change, the unlocking of something. I started to ... very strongly feel other's feelings, as if I connected with my empathy. But really, it's more that. I gained the knowledge that I was more than my body, that I felt

connected to everything. It's hard to explain because
I had never really been attracted to spirituality before,
but I felt a strong urge to jump in it.

What happened was a profound change; I really felt
I found myself. I look at pictures of myself from the last
five years and it feels as if I do not know this person
… But now, I feel I always have this joy in my heart."
(Author's collection)

What probably happened here is that the left Caudate Nucleus,
instrumental in sexual pleasure, became overloaded, and spilled its
activity into its next-door neighbor, the left amygdala. In another (or
additional) scenario, her sense of frustration may have excited her right
amygdala, which could well have transferred its excitement and activity
across to the left amygdala. Perhaps both happened at once.

One may wonder why some sudden and dramatic activations of the
left amygdala, appearing after episodes of deep suffering, elicit visions of
God while some culminate in enlightenment. The answer seems to be that
the periods just before enlightenment seem to have a hippocampal flavor
to them (so to speak). Introspection, disassociation, alienation, solitude
and a history of meditation and contemplation of the self can fill these
right-to-left neural avalanches with hippocampal information. In general,
it seems that such a dramatic interhemispheric intrusion will culminate in
enlightenment rather than a vision of God for those with a more excitable
right hippocampus. The more excitable the left amygdala is, the more
likely the experience will be a self-and-other phenomena, which might
be vision of God or something less dramatic, like a wave of love.

Gradual Enlightenment

Now, let's look at the gradual kind of enlightenment. How do
you attain enlightenment gradually? It's a bit like getting to Carnegie
Hall. A man carrying a trombone in Times Square meets a stranger
carrying a violin. "Excuse me. Can you tell me how to get to Carnegie
Hall?" The violinist says, "Practice, and keep practicing." How do

you get to gradual enlightenment? You do meditation, and practice, practice, and then practice some more. Never let up. Of course, other methods work, but meditation exercises the right hippocampus more than other techniques, and an excitable right hippocampus may make enlightenment more likely than an experience of God. If the most sensitive spot in *your* limbic system is in the caudate nucleus, you might do better with a body-based spiritual practice, like yoga, trance dancing or tai chi. If *your* most sensitive limbic spot is in the amygdala, you might have more success with chanting or prayer. However, more enlightened Buddhist teachers have taught meditation than any of its other methods.

When sitting in meditation, if your meditation object is your breath, don't pay attention to anything else. If your mind wanders into verbal thinking, stop and go back to your breath. If a wave of emotion comes over you, you disconnect from it as much as you can. If your body aches from the meditation posture or you have a little tickle, disconnect from it, and go back to your breath. If you're chanting a mantra, return to the mantra. No matter what the meditation object, keep returning to it, no matter what distractions appear. This exercises and trains your mind, as well as your brain, to avoid feelings and sensations that you don't want to experience. In meditation, that's *everything* - except the meditation object.

With rigorous, constant practice you can build up this ability, and use it when you're *not* meditating. You learn to withhold unwanted mental activity anytime you want to. You learn to disconnect from unpleasant events in your mind, just as you learn to avoid paying attention to them when you meditate. Instead of saying no to everything except the meditation object, you only say no to things that feel bad when you are not in meditation. You can allow the good stuff to run free. If you have a moment of fear, disconnect; don't 'put your energy there'; don't 'go there'. You have a moment of irritation. Disconnect; find another way of thinking about whatever's bothering you. When your body has pain, disconnect. Learn to keep still, as becoming stressed in the face of pain can often make it worse. Put your mind on something more pleasant, if you can[535]. Keep this up for years, months, decades, even a lifetime.

What you'll eventually find is an example of the brain's "use dependency" rule. "Use it or lose it." The best way to lose something is not to use it. You methodically atrophy your capacity for fear, anger, irritation, or depression. You slowly cut away at the synapses that support them until the strongest ones are those that direct your attention and states of consciousness onto joy, bliss, silent awareness or calm.

After this, you can be relaxed when you want to. If you want to, you can be aroused or excited, stand on the rooftop of the temple, and give that lion's roar. Gradual enlightenment seems to mean disconnecting slowly from the same structures that are abruptly disconnected in sudden enlightenment. In sudden enlightenment, you don't have a lot of choice about what comes after the crucial moment. With gradual enlightenment, you have a great deal of control. You also have a big job in front of you. Working hands-on with your consciousness to atrophy the bases for negativity is an unrelenting task. "Many are called, but few are chosen".

The neurology of gradual enlightenment is a large subject, and we're not really giving it the attention it deserves here. There are many studies on the effects of meditation on the brain and the mind, and they're not all in agreement. Building up a complete hypothesis for the mechanism of gradual enlightenment will mean reconciling a multitude of studies, each with different primary assumptions, methods, and results. No doubt a more complete picture of gradual enlightenment will eventually appear with further research. For us, for now, it appears to be a slow and deliberate atrophying of the right amygdala and the left hippocampus. When these two structures are quiet enough, they won't be as able to inhibit the left amygdala, so it can also burst into activity and, in rare moments, excite it in much the same pattern that appears during the moment of sudden enlightenment. This will make the person much more prone to mystic episodes, so that the one who reaches enlightenment gradually can be just as open to profound experiences as the one who attains it suddenly.

Now we can try to frame a definition for the word enlightenment. Enlightenment is the subjective experience of removing synaptic connections that inhibit positive affect. In simpler terms, it's the experience of pruning away connections that make it harder to feel good.

We are the product of Darwinian evolution, survival of the fittest, natural selection, and so forth. The sense of self, no matter how exalted it may seem, doesn't exist to attain enlightenment, but to avoid death and extinction. Individuals can choose enlightenment as a goal, but it may not ever be humanity's destiny unless and until our survival depends on it.

CHAPTER 13

Interhemispheric Intrusions

Suffering has an important place in the theologies of Christianity, Hinduism and Buddhism. In Christianity, the stress between sin and its forgiveness (or redemption) is what drives the human world. Suffering is thought to redeem sin but it can also be an offering to God. Many also believe that God uses suffering as a way to test people and to show them the limitations in their faith. The suffering of Christ on the cross, in the book of Job, and the martyrdoms of early Saints and Apostles provide the central examples of human suffering for Christians. Some believe that God forces people to suffer as punishment for their sins, though this view is less popular now than it was centuries ago.

Buddhism regards suffering as an intrinsic feature of human experience. It is present, in greater or lesser amounts, in every moment. In Buddhism, the solution to suffering is to build awareness through meditation, especially of how your own mind works, which makes it easier not to create suffering for yourself. Hinduism believes suffering is the result of bad karma, so that the suffering we experience now pays for our bad actions in the past, though there are many Hindus who think differently. More recently, there are "New Age" ideas encouraging one to find something sacred in suffering, be grateful for it and regard it as a teacher, or think of it as something we unconsciously want or choose to experience. The Aztecs thought blood was the offering the gods liked best, and that of course, implies pain.

Every religion has some teaching about why human beings experience suffering. In fact, no religion, would find many believers if it did not address the question of why people suffer. Buddhism is right. Being alive involves considerable unpleasantness. The connection between spirituality and suffering may reflect a pattern in mystic experiences. Following the path of the mystic is never easy, and at times it can involve some "wailing and gnashing of teeth". Pain and fear often drive people to embrace religion. No religion could survive without a belief showing the connection between suffering and destiny, God's will, or karma.

Buddhism teaches that suffering is caused by desire, and to overcome it, one should eliminate desire. This idea is far from ordinary experience. Common sense tells us that *fulfilling* our desires is the easiest response to suffering. Ignoring interpretations from religious beliefs, life has good moments without suffering and bad moments with it. *With* religious beliefs, there is nothing wrong with suffering or pain. Pain is the will of God. Accept it and be at peace. Pain is part of life. Offer your pain to Jesus; bear it for his sake, and store up riches in heaven. Disappointments happen only when we expect things. Drop your expectations, and you'll never be let down again. In Christianity, the glorification of pain and suffering allows those who suffer to feel they are drawing closer to God.

The New Age belief that one should be grateful for pain and suffering seems to rely on "higher wisdom". To me, it lacks common sense. New-agers tell us to be grateful for our pains and difficulties, because they give us opportunities to learn and grow. However, just because we are able to make the best of a bad situation does not mean it was good for us. We don't learn from pain. We learn more from our efforts to escape it. We learn far more while receiving treatment for our illness than we ever do from being sick. Nearly every religion and spiritual tradition has an interpretation of suffering that asks us to see its higher purpose and reject our natural responses to it. Our natural inclination to avoid and reject pain whenever we can is the most life-affirming attitude possible, given that our evolutionary programming is to preserve life. Unless you see it through the lens of religious ideas, suffering just feels bad. A common sense approach finds nothing good in it. We only want it to stop.

There is a real connection between suffering and mysticism, but it appears when suffering ends and not while we are going through it.

The *Interhemispheric Intrusion* principle (the *neural avalanche*) reveals how many traditional spiritual practices work. We have seen how these events can culminate on a vision of God or enlightenment. They begin when a person is in a state of pain, extreme mental turbulence, pushed to the limits of exhaustion, or feeling an intense yearning. All these can culminate in a spiritual experience. "Blessed are you who weep now, for you shall laugh."[536] "Weeping may endure for a night, but joy cometh in the morning."[537] The right amygdala, the primary neural foundation for fear, seems to be the most common place for these processes to begin.

When excitement in the right amygdala rises past a certain critical point, it may dump that activity into it's counterpart on the left (an *interhemispheric intrusion*). This breaking point will differ from person to person. This sudden dumping forces a dramatic change in a person's state of consciousness, including their emotional state. When it happens, the person's pain, fear, anguish, dissociation or despair can reverse themselves as an avalanche of finely tuned neural energy falls across the brain. Fear can become joy or bliss. A sense of purpose and fulfillment can replace hopelessness. When the circumstances match the individual brain, stress alone can be enough to trigger an interhemispheric intrusion.

It doesn't take a neural avalanche for a person to see God during the death-process. Remember, we work with the idea that the death-process is intrinsic to our species, so the pathways that support the experience of God in NDEs probably don't need higher levels of activity to excite them. We might say that death holds to key to the experience, while an interhemispheric intrusion is a bit more like breaking down the door.

Because the 'blast' of electrical activity across the brain literally overpowers the synapses that would usually inhibit them, the pathways can recruit or dis-inhibit the ones that function in the death-process. The experiences that follow can have the spiritual tone found in NDEs. This will not happen in every case. If the landing point for this activity is in the left hippocampus, then the result could be similar to a schizophrenic episode[538]. Our main point, throughout this book, is that (with a few exceptions) religious and mystic experiences are the result of activation of death-process pathways in other contexts, usually combining them with pathways that have no relation to dying, so that they often seem like very different experiences. Spaghetti and chocolate cake are both mostly made of wheat, but they taste different, have different textures, and the sauce that goes well with one will ruin the other. Of course, just as some people like ketchup on everything, some NDEers find that all spirituality hearkens back to their NDEs.

Not all interhemispheric intrusions will create mystic experiences. Some of them may culminate in sudden-onset psychiatric disorders, and some them might appear as moments of creative inspiration. These, of course, are outside the scope of this work. Interhemispheric intrusions are not part of the death-process. Nevertheless, these neural avalanches can engage its (rarely accessed) pathways while the person is still alive, and this can explain how many, if not most, mystic experiences happen.

Fear is not the only agent that can trigger an avalanche of activity across the brain. So can fatigue and boredom.

Charles Lindbergh, struggling against the monotony and sleeplessness of his one–man flight across the Atlantic, found that after 22 hours he:

> "... suddenly encountered a presence in the fuselage of *the Spirit of St. Louis.* Struggling to stay awake, and at times flying so low to avoid thunderheads that he could feel the spray from the surging Atlantic, Lindbergh became aware that he had company. In fact, he felt there was more than one being traveling with him. He recalled staring at the instrument panel, and then ...

> "The fuselage behind me becomes filled with ghostly presences - vaguely outlined forms, transparent, moving, riding weightless with me in the plane. I feel no surprise at their coming. There's no suddenness to their appearance. Without turning my head, I see them as clearly as though in my normal field of vision."

> Lindbergh felt the "phantoms" were speaking to him and he judged them to be friendly. He was in no way startled by these beings. He felt he knew them: they were familiar, and he felt that they were there to help "conversing and advising on my flight, discussing

problems of my navigation, reassuring me, giving me messages of importance unattainable in ordinary life."[539]

Stress or fatigue can also set the stage for an epiphany. When Admiral Byrd, the explorer, was assigned to stay alone at a forward Antarctic research station, his shelter, which was supposed to be completely buried in snow, actually protruded well above the surface of the pack ice, exposing it to the Antarctic winds. There was also a problem with his heater, which produced constant toxic fumes.

> "But now death was a stranger sitting in a darkened room, secure in the knowledge that he would be there when I was gone. Great waves of fear, fear I had never known before, swept through me and settled deep within. But it wasn't the fear of suffering or even death itself; it was a terrible anxiety over the consequences to those at home if I failed to return. ...

In the midst of his despair, Adm. Byrd had a kind of epiphany. He does not tell us what he experienced, but he does quote his diary, expressing a new-found understanding of life. He wrote:

> The universe is not dead. Therefore, there is an intelligence there, and it is all pervading. At least one purpose, possibly the major purpose, of that intelligence is the achievement of universal harmony. ... For untold ages man has felt an awareness of that intelligence. Belief in it is the one point where all religions agree. It has been called by many names. Many call it God."[540]

A similar account comes from a Korean woman who was in a department store that collapsed in July 1995. It killed More than 300 people, but Park Seung-Hyung survived.

> "She went without food and with little water for 16 days, surviving in a pocket beneath a crushed elevator

shaft, a space that was too small for her even to sit up in. All around her were the decomposing bodies of other victims. The young woman, who was suffering from severe dehydration when she was finally pulled from the debris, reported that a monk had appeared a number of times during her ordeal. "He gave me an apple, and this kept my hope alive," she said."[541]

Many classical spiritual techniques seem designed to facilitate interhemispheric intrusions. They can artificially create the stress, tension, pain and fatigue – even the frustration and desperation – that can set the stage for a spiritual breakthrough. Pilgrimages are one example.

Pilgrimage

Pilgrims undertake long journeys, usually to receive a blessing that they believe only happens at the place of pilgrimage, usually because of a sacred event that happened there. One example is Bodh Gaya, where the Buddha attained enlightenment. Others are places where people had visions of the Virgin Mary. So is the Garden of Gethsemane, where Jesus prayed the night before His crucifixion. The Kaaba, the first sacred space of Islam, is in Mecca, the home of the Prophet Mohammed (Blessings be upon him). It's the most important place of pilgrimage in Islam, and all Muslims are enjoined to make the pilgrimage there at least once in their lives.

Before railways and airplanes were invented, pilgrimages could be serious ordeals. Some took years to complete. Even today, many pilgrimages are done only on foot. In Tibetan Buddhism, there is a way of doing pilgrimages where the person lies down full-length, doing a full prostration with each step. Some Catholic pilgrimages include saying the rosary whenever one is actually moving. In others, like the one to the Shrine of Our Lady of Guadalupe in Mexico, some pilgrims climb the steps on their knees, reciting prayers as they go. These devotional practices make pilgrimages more demanding than simple journeys, and increase the stress involved. As the stress increases, so do the chances for an interhemispheric intrusion; a *peak experience,* at the journey's end.

As a person begins to travel, with whatever degree of difficulty, they do so with the anticipation of a peak moment; their arrival at the center of the holy place. It puts them in front of a sacred relic, a tabernacle, or a place where a saint or holy one had a profound experience. As the anticipation rises, so does the stress. Eventually the pilgrim arrives at Mecca, Lourdes, Bodh Gaya, Varanasi or some other sacred place. They arrive after the long effort to make the journey and a prolonged anticipation of a sacred experience. The sense of relief at reaching the goal can be enormous, and is usually followed by heartfelt prayers, or sitting down to meditate. The travail is over. The pilgrim's fear that they might not reach their goal excites the right amygdala as they travel towards their sacred goal. So does the exhaustion that can happen as they travel. Arriving at the holy place triggers the brain to release its stress. The activity in the right amygdala can then be shunted over to the one on the opposite side of the brain. The more stressful the journey, the more momentum the process will have. When they finally arrive at the sacred place, they're predisposed to have an epiphany. Their prayers on arriving at the sacred place, often the most joyous of their lives, makes it easy for them to feel the place is sacred, because that is where their prayers were the deepest.

> "Finally, after years of fantasy and impossible anticipation, pumped full of adrenaline from the strenuous ascent, I cast unobstructed eyes upon the throne of Shiva." ... "Reveling like a drunk in the sharp, angular light and rarefied air, I am filled with joy I could not have anticipated."[542]

One Pilgrim "went on foot to Loretto, the famous sanctuary of Mary. Again, he suffered many humiliations during this pilgrimage because of his poverty and ragged dress, as well as his humble bearing. He described himself once as ...

"… a very poor man, both physically and morally. My external appearance is so wretched that several times during my journey I have been taken for a criminal and almost was put in jail as such." At Loretto, he prayed almost uninterruptedly for seven days until he had the inner certainty that it was God's will that he should become a priest and found his missionary society."[543]

Ordination

The long road to ordination can also provide a long period of stress, tension and anticipation. The novice undergoes a strenuous effort to achieve their goal. Together with their studies in theology, they have to overcome all temptations to break their vows, and demonstrate their vocation to their superiors. Throughout the process, they are reminded of the very real possibility of failure. "Many are called, but few are chosen."[544] When the day of their ordination finally arrives, and they can finally let go of their worries and anxieties, the effect can be a dramatic experience; an epiphany. In our terms, it can be another example of an interhemispheric intrusion.

Father Francis Liebermann's ordination story has this to say:

"he entered the seminary at Strasbourg where his brother Samson gave them much valuable assistance, and finally reached the goal he desired so long and was ordained priest on September 18, 1841 the age of 39 … At his ordination, as at his baptism, he received Mystic graces. Immediately after the ceremony he writes to Samson: "I was ordained priest this morning. God knows what I have received on this great day. God alone knows it, for neither man nor angel can imagine it. And on the same day he tells another correspondent: "today immense and innumerable graces that descended on me and I am almost submerged by them: may God grant that I remain as it were drenched in his grace and his divine love."[545]

Another spiritual technique relying on anticipation and fulfillment is initiation, whether its initiation into adulthood, like the Catholic First Communion, the Jewish Bar Mitzvah or the manhood/womanhood ceremonies of American Indians and Africans. One of the more powerful initiations is the one into monkhood. It can also happen when a person who has converted to a new religion is finally accepted into its fellowship, congregation, or *Sangha*.

> In the story of Charles de Foucauld's (the French mystic) life we read, "Charles began to go to church, praying desperately: "my God, if you exist, make yourself known to me." Then he thought that it would be a good idea to discuss the doctrines of the church with an intelligent priest, ... And so one morning towards the end of October 1886, Charles entered his confessional, explaining that he had not come to make his confession but required some information about the Catholic faith. The Abbé, not usually given to dramatic gestures, told him to kneel down, make his confession, and go to Holy Communion straightaway. "At once", de Foucauld writes in a letter to a friend, "I believed that there was a God, I also understood that I could not do otherwise than to live for him: my religious vocation dates from the same hour as my faith."[546]
>
> Right after Pope Francis (the first of that name) was elected, he was "seized by a great anxiety". He later said that "to make it go away, I closed my eyes and made every thought disappear, even the thought of refusing to accept the position, as the liturgical process allows" "At a certain point I was filled with a great light. It lasted a moment, but to me it seemed very long. Then the light faded. I got up suddenly and walked into the room where the cardinals were waiting.[547]"

Thomas Merton, who later became the most influential Catholic theologian of the 20th century wasn't born "into the faith". He became interested in Catholicism, and soon acquired a desire to convert. "The more he learned, the more he began to "burn with desire for baptism." He felt that he was about to set foot on the shore, at the bottom of a ...

... seven-circled mountain of Purgatory; steeper and more arduous than I was able to imagine." He was anxious to begin the climb.

The date was set for 16 November. As the time got close, Tom began to get nervous. On the night of the 15th, he lay in bed awake, consumed with fear. All kinds of worries occurred to him. He might not remember what to do. Things might go wrong and humiliating. He couldn't sleep. What if he couldn't keep the eucharistic fast?"

After an anxious night, he arrived at the church to be baptized. The sacrament includes a ritual exorcism, in which the priest commands any impure spirits to leave the person. "What you want from the church, the priest demanded. Tom replied that he wanted to believe. Faith. He said it in Latin: *"Fidem!"* It was all in Latin.

The priest asked him faith in what, and Tom said: "life everlasting, *Vitam aeternam.*"

The priest now began the exorcism of Thomas Merton.

"Do you renounce Satan and all his works?"

Tom was thinking of his greedy ambitions, the lust for fame, the drive for self fulfillment. He said: "I do renounce Satan and his works. I do renounce them."

The priest breathed three times into Tom's face and said "Exi ab eo, spiritus immunde." Go out of him, unclean spirit, and make room for the Holy Spirit.

Tom felt a great wind of spiritual cleansing go through him. It frightened the Devils right out of him, "the Legion that had been living in me for twenty-three years ... I did not see them leaving, but there must have been more than seven of them. I had never been able to count them."

He was elated. "I have found the mountains of the spring where the Lord refreshes the morning. He has laid his hand on my shoulder."[548]

The Sweat Lodge & the Sauna

Sweating, participation in The American Indian sweat lodge ceremony (The *Inipi*) is another practice that can create an interhemispheric intrusion. The sweat lodge itself is small, extremely hot, and the ceremony can be grueling, especially the first time. It can last for several hours. The participants sing, chant and play drums. People often go limp in very hot weather, but in the Sweat Lodge, they must try to remain upright and alert.

My experience of a sweat lodge ceremony was that at the beginning, everyone was sitting up, shoulder to shoulder, but by the end, a few people were lying down. The medicine man said this happened often. The Sweat Lodge seems to become bigger as the Inipi progresses. Eventually, the heat, claustrophobic space and loud singing and drumming come to an end and everyone leaves the small lodge. The contrast between the heat and confinement and breathing cool air as well as having the freedom to move around again is so great to that some people are overcome with joy. They often experience enhanced visual acuity (when one's vision becomes clearer than usual). Some people even collapse as they leave the sweat lodge. It happened to me. The medicine man said it meant the spirits had entered me while I was in the lodge and when they left my body, it became my turn to fall down. "It was just your turn, that's all", the *wakanḳa* told me. I had an experience of Enhanced Visual Acuity, and the world looked amazingly beautiful.

Here is an account of an experience that followed a Sauna.

"Late one night, a group of men went to the sauna late. It was a mixed racial group. There were black men and white men and there was a Native American Indian chief. We were all sitting in the sauna, a bunch of maybe 30 to 40 men, and somebody suggested to the Native American: "Why don't you perform one of your ceremonies?" He agreed. He put his rug on the floor and took out his pipe and a few men made a circle around them. I was one of those who jumped at the opportunity to be sitting opposite him. He did the ceremony and we were all these naked men sitting there, smoking the pipe and calling the spirits to be present.

While the guy was doing the ceremony, something became important to me and I asked the question: "just show me the way. Show me what is it. What is the truth? I want to know. How do I find this out? I have tried all sorts of things and nothing seems to gel, nothing seems to be the answer. Is there an answer?"

After it was over, we hung around outside and cooled down it must've been about three or four in the morning." ... "So we were both walking back to the cabin, two naked men walking out on this grassy slope of the late, late night. Suddenly, I just stopped and he stopped and we just looked at each other and we just embraced. And all I can say is I disappeared. When I sort of came to, I said to him: "what happened?" He said: "I don't know. I just wasn't here." I said: "me too. There was nothing, was there?" And he said: "no, there wasn't." Suddenly, there was a dawning. "Actually, everything is me - everything I'm seeing here − the dew - the grass!"[549]

Perhaps the most powerful American Indian ceremony involving a sudden release from suffering is the Sundance. In the Sundance ceremony, men literally hang by their own flesh. Sticks are forced through their chests, and they dangle from leather straps tied around them. At one time, they forced the sticks through the pectoral muscles. Today, though, they normally put the sticks through cuts in the skin two or three inches apart. Usually the Sundancer blows a whistle made from the wing bone of an eagle as they hang. Those attending the ceremony sing as they dance in a circle around him. He stays there until he breaks away naturally. It can take a long time for a Sundancer to break free. It's an ordeal. Once the Sundancer is free, they lay him on a bed of sage and give him a chance to recover. When he gets up again, he is often in bliss. Once, I saw a Lakota Indian Sundancer, who spoke no English, after his dance was over. He was free; he walked around, with no shirt or bandages, allowing everyone to see his wounds. He was filled with such happiness that he couldn't speak, in any language. My knowledge of Lakota is scanty, but I said "Waśte; waśte yelo" (It is good). His answer was to look at me and grin even more widely. His mood was so joyful it was hard to look at him, because there was nothing I could do or say to match his feeling. A well-earned ecstasy had followed his long and tortuous ordeal.

Retreats

Retreats also create an opportunity for spiritual experiences. Remember, retreats are for laypeople. The rules and regulations for retreats are routine for monks and nuns, but they can be a hardship for ordinary people. Spending a number of days in prayer, meditation, contemplation and reflection exercises spiritual muscles, so to speak, and the strain can be severe. Unaccustomed to the efforts it requires, these "muscles" soon ache from the strain. In Zen retreats, one sits in meditation for hours, and endures pain in the back and legs. The need to stay still causes stress from which there is no escape unless someone breaks the rules. Even for experienced meditators, whose bodies have adjusted to the effort of maintaining the meditation postures, there is still the pressure to achieve a breakthrough. They feel the need to come away from the retreat with some new experience, insight or a restored sense of mindfulness.

Most spiritual retreats are intense. The leaders demand unflagging efforts. As the hours, days and sometimes weeks go by, the stress increases constantly. There can be a spiritual breakthrough or epiphany while it's happening. Activity builds up in the areas of the brain that get the most exercise. Of course, this will vary in different practices, and the practices differ from one religion to the next. During a successful retreat, it might spill over into other structures several times.

Here is Zen master Hakuin's story:

> "On one occasion the two of us monks engaged in a private session. We pledge to continue it for seven days and nights. No sleep. No lying down. We cut a three-foot section of bamboo and fashioned between makeshift *shippei* [A Zen stick for gently striking meditators who start falling asleep]. We sat facing each other with the shippei placed on the ground between us. We agreed that if one of us saw the others eyelids drop, even for a split second, he would grab the staff and crack him with it between the eyes.
>
> For seven days, we set ramrod–straight, teeth clenched tightly in total silence. Not so much as an eyelash quivered. Right through to the end of the seventh night neither one of us had occasion to reach for that cudgel.
>
> One night, a heavy snowfall blanketed the area. The dull, muffled thought of snow falling from the branches of the trees created a sense of extraordinary stillness and purity. I made an attempt at a poem to describe the joy I felt:

> If only you could hear
> the sound of the snow
> following late at night from the trees
> of the old Temple
> in Shinoda!"

"All at once, I found I had penetrated a verse that I have been working on, Master Ta-hui's "Lotus leaves, perfect discs, rounder than mirrors; water chestnuts needle spikes, sharper than gimlets." It was like suddenly seeing a bright sun blazing out in the dead of night. Overcome with joy, I tripped and stumbled and plunged headlong into the mud. My robe was soaked through, but my only reflection was, "what's a muddy road, compared to the extraordinary joy I now feel?"[550]

The stress, strain and effort end when the retreat finally is over. The extra excitement in the places that worked so hard during the retreat does not stop right away. Instead, it finds a new context, as the person is now free to relax and let go of the grueling efforts they have sustained. During the retreat, they were pushed to achieve an intense mindfulness or a more prayerful mood. Afterwards, they may carry less of it, but without any stress and effort. The spiritual mood continues, but mental strain is replaced by freedom to be calm and relaxed. Now they are free to "recite so much of the Quran as may be easy to them".[551] They often feel as though they are living in a completely new world. Of course, the world hasn't changed. They're in a new state of consciousness, and respond to the world around them with different thoughts and feelings. If this interhemispheric intrusion was powerful enough, it could cause the dropout of a few synapses that both inhibited spiritual states of consciousness, and also contributed to the sense of self. They might feel like a new person; "healed and made whole". They would have "returned to their center", or "remembered their true being." Even if the exact words they use to describe their feelings are ambiguous (like "my chakras are balanced"), the message is the same. Their sense of themselves will have changed. This is because the pathways involved in both prayerful and meditative spiritual practices also contribute to the human sense of self. When spiritual states happen more easily or more often, the sense of self changes, or feels like it has changed. You become a new being.

"… He went to the college to make his retreat. …" His spiritual guide "provided several books, the New Testament, of course, as well as a history of Christian Doctrine, showed in the garden and the refectory, and then left him severely alone. His complete solitude, the silence of the seminary, the absence of any occupation except reading and prayer, and above all, his terrible uncertainty of what he is going to do, produced at first the state of profound depression and anxiety. He prayed desperately that the God of his fathers should enlighten him; that he should make it clear to him whether the faith of the Christians was the true faith; that, if it were not, God should prevent him from embracing it.

After several weeks of uncertainty, his prayer was suddenly answered with overwhelming certainty: "I saw the truth; the faith penetrated my spirit and my heart." He read the history of Christian Doctrine and found that none of the teachings of the church presented any difficulty to him; he believed everything and had only the one desire to become a Christian."[552]

Austerities and self-torture.

One enduring spiritual practice, found especially in Hinduism and Christianity, is the practice of *austerities;* sometimes called *self-torture.* Both traditions share a belief in the merit of nonviolence, celibacy and silence. In the Catholicism, monks have beaten themselves with whips, gone without food, stayed awake for days on end, worn painful belts next to their skin, chains that cut into their flesh, crowns of thorns, and a range of other painful practices. In Hinduism, there are such practices as fasting, holding one arm above your head until it withers, being buried in the ground, meditation in difficult positions and on beds of nails. The ascetic life is a fertile ground for right amygdala excitement.

Catherine of Siena ...

> "... would only masticate a morsel of fruit or vegetable, swallowing the extracted juice and then spitting the rest out. Even this juice would often make her face swell, so that she had no ease until she had vomited, after one of her women friends had tickled her gullet with a feather. When she left the table for this purpose, she would say humorously "let us go and do justice to this miserable sinner." The vomiting itself was so painful that she frequently brought up blood. In the same way she virtually went without water or sleep, of which in her later years she permitted herself only half an hour every two nights. This, unlike her eating, was a voluntary penance, and something she found very hard. Her abstinence from food reached the point where she was unable to eat. How she existed is past understanding. ... From the sturdiness of her girlhood she gradually reached an extreme emaciation; she could have been sustained only miraculously. ... Almost every day she received heavenly visitors. Sometimes, too, she would meet them while walking the cool of the evening on the roof of the house. Then she would talk with them as with familiar friends. We hear of one occasion when she grew so absorbed in the conversation that not until rather late at night did she notice the hour. Then when she went to her room Christ and Mary Magdalene accompanied her, and she sat between them on her bed, their hostess, while the conversation continued."[553]

Butler's classic, *Lives of the Saints*, has many examples of Saints who both tortured themselves, and also experienced religious visions, miracles, and healings.

> One example is St. Elizabeth of Schönau, who "threw herself fervently into the religious activities of

the convent, and, though suffering from continual ill health, or a hairshirt, girded herself with an iron chain, and practiced other austerities. "The Lowliest of His Poor", she says of herself in one of her books, "I thank God That from the Moment I Entered the Order until This Hour, His Hand Is Pressed upon Me so Persistently that I have never ceased to feel his arrows in my body." From her twenty-third year onwards she was subject to extraordinary supernatural manifestations, celestial visions, and diabolic persecutions"[554]

"Many were the occasions when a disciple, searching for a revered ascetic, finally found the right cave in question, stepped up to the seated hermit, and touched his hand, only to witness the entire body collapse in a heap of dust. It was written, "behold, my son, for 95 years have I been in this cave ... I even ate dust ... From hunger, I drank water from the sea... Frequently they (demons) dragged me from here to the base of the mountain until there was no skin or flesh on my limbs ... Finally ... I saw the realms of the kingdom"[555]

Continually responding to pain and suffering maintains a constant pressure on the amygdala[556][557]. Ordinarily, when confronted with pain, a person does his/her best to remove its source. Nearly any pain will eventually cause damage if it's allowed to go unchecked (chronic pain syndromes are an exception, of course). Some can even kill. Not only does pain feel bad, but it also contains a warning that your body is under threat. There is always an element of fear in living with any pain, and the right amygdala is more implicated in processing pain than the one on the left. Pain not only inspires us to act in healthy ways, but it also encourages us to think about the long-term outcome of the problem. Maintaining a constant state of pain will include maintaining fear and anxiety, though a spiritual adept may be able to keep it in check. However, to be in this state constantly will mean that when something good happens, there is a ready reservoir of amygdala activity available to the one on the left, if the good feeling is strong enough to pass a certain threshold. Constant austerities can mean having one's life punctuated with moments of real joy. Of course, it probably wouldn't work if the person is depressed, but it seems unlikely that self-mortification, as a regular discipline, would have any appeal for people with depression. No doubt, many psychotics who "cut themselves" have hidden their psychoses behind the curtain of religious self-torture, but we shouldn't expect them to achieve any kind of mystic elation.

> St. Rose of Lima "practiced mortification since childhood. Where previously she had used only at discipline of knotted cords, she now used a chain with which to scourge herself. Her fasting became so drastic that she frequently went a whole week without food or drink. Now it was not a hairshirt that she wore but a belt of iron, which pierced her body with its sharp points. And she constructed a crown of iron which she wore under her tertiary veil, so that jagged spikes never ceased to remind her of the crown of thorns." "When she did attend Mass, everyone noticed that though she had to drag her body there – often when she did not go it was to avoid comments as to how ill and worn she looked – always after receiving holy Communion she went back to her place renewed, with a firm tread and a glowing face.[558] (Grammar corrected)

Continually tasking one's mind with pain can mean one is always poised for an interhemispheric intrusion. Bliss can appear at any moment. When appears without fear, it still excites the right amygdala[559]. Some monastics have gone through such practices for years, carrying a quiet joy from their faith that God will reward their suffering. In principle, a person who is actually happy with their self-denial and austerities will have lower chance for interhemispheric intrusions than those who think of it with dread and come close to despair. Like other spiritual practices found in so many traditions, self-mortification has a legitimate basis in the brain's operation. However, like any other spiritual practice, not everyone will have an equal chance of success. Some people could torture themselves for their entire lives and never have a moment of bliss. Others might have epiphanies through a single unpleasant episode. "Don't try this at home".

Prison

Prison can be hellish enough to precipitate mystic experiences. When Malcolm X was in prison, one of his Afro-American Muslim brothers spoke badly of the prophet Elijah Mohammed (accused of "improper relations" with his secretary).

> "It caught me totally unprepared. It threw me into a state of confusion." ... Feeling confused, Malcolm writes a letter to Elijah, in an attempt to defend his brother. That night, he experiences a vision of a man visiting his prison cell and believes it to be a "pre-vision" of Master W. D. Fard, "the Messiah, the one whom Elijah Mohammed said had appointed him."[560]

It looks as though his time in prison left him under constant stress, and the conflict between the prophet Elijah Mohammed and Malcolm X's brother in Islam was just enough to send him over the edge, and predispose him to a religious vision.

Baha'u'llah, the founder of the Baha'i religion, was imprisoned for his religious activities in a notorious prison known as the black pit (Síyáh-Chál). It was a huge underground pit that once served as a reservoir for public baths. It was absolutely dark. The air was foul, and it had only one entrance.

> "No pen can depict that place, nor any tongues describe its loathsome smell. Most of these men (about 150) had neither clothes nor bedding to lie on."[561] Baha'u'llah was forced to wear heavy chains, which cut through his skin and left him permanently scarred.

"Wrapped in gloom, breathing the foulest of air, his feet in stocks, and his neck weighed down by a mighty chain, Baha'u'llah received the first stirrings of God's revelation within His soul. Under these dreadful circumstances, the "Most Great Spirit" revealed itself to him, bidding him to arise and speak forth the Word of God.

At times, He would feel as if something flowed from the crown of His head over His breast, as a mighty torrent falls upon the earth from the summit of a high mountain. He saw the Maiden of Heaven suspended before Him, speaking to His inner and outer being, referring to Him as the Best–Beloved of the worlds, the Beauty of God, and the power of God's sovereignty. He was assured that He would be made victorious by Himself and by His Pen, and by the aid of those whom God would raise up.

Thus from behind the darkness of the black pit rose the Sun of Truth. ... The Baha'i revelation was born. Yet Baha'u'llah did not inform anyone of what had occurred. He would await the appointed hour, ordained by God, to make his mission known.[562]

His ordeal in prison culminated in an event very much like the death-process's Transcendent Experience. In his vision, as in Transcendent Experiences, he could see his purpose in life. Instead of fulfilling it in his next life, he did so in that one. NDE Transcendent Experiences, like Baha'u'llah's vision, can seem to reveal a person's true purpose. Both convey a sense of destiny and meaningfulness.

The second century Carthaginian Christian Martyr, St. Perpetua, wrote about her imprisonment:

"... During those few days, we were baptized, the spirit bidding me make no other petition after the rite than for bodily endurance. A few days after we were lodged in prison, and I was greatly frightened because I had never known such darkness. What a day of horror!

Terrible heat, owing to the crowds! Rough treatment by the soldiers! I was tormented with anxiety for my baby. Then Tertius and Pomponius, those blessed deacons who ministered to us, paid for us to be removed for a few hours for the better part of the prison and obtained some relief. Then all of them went out of the prison and I suckled my baby, who was faint for want of food. I spoke anxiously to my mother on his behalf and encouraged my brother and commended my son to their care. I was concerned because I saw their concern for me. Such anxieties I suffered for many days, but I obtained leave for my baby to remain in the prison with me, and being relieved of my trouble and anxiety for him, I at once recovered my health, and my prison suddenly became a Palace to me and I would rather have been there than anywhere else.

Then my brother said to me: 'lady sister you are now in great honor – so great that you may well pray for a vision in which you may be shown whether suffering or release be in store for you.' And I, knowing myself to have [the] speech of the Lord for whose sake I was suffering, confidently promised, 'tomorrow I will bring you word'. And I made petition and this was shown to me. I saw a golden ladder of wonderful length reaching up to heaven, but so narrow that only one at a time could go up ... And I went up and saw a large garden, and sitting in the midst a tall man with white hair in the dress of the shepherd, milking sheep; and round about were many thousands clad in white. And he raised his head and looked upon me and said, 'welcome child.' And he called me and gave me some curds of the milk he was milking, and I received my joined hands and ate; and all that were round me about said Amen.[563]

St. John of the Cross, the saint who wrote the canticle "Dark Night of the Soul", and helped to form the order of Discalced Carmelites ...

... "was taken prisoner in the night of 3 December, 1577, and carried off to Toledo, where he suffered for more than nine months close imprisonment in a narrow, stifling cell, together with such additional punishment as might have been called for in the case of one guilty of the most serious crimes. In the midst of his sufferings he was visited with heavenly consolations, and some of his exquisite poetry dates from that period."[564]

Torture

The most extreme moments of physical pain also offer a context for mystic experiences. One neuropsychiatrist tells the story about one of his patients who had been tortured by an agent of a South American drug cartel. This torture consisted of having a flap of skin slowly and carefully torn away from one of his buttocks.

"The victim "uttered a cry of absolute terror. He didn't know if he actually made a sound, but his mouth was wide open. Veins pulsated against the surface of his neck, the muscles straining. The side of his face pressed into the table. He stared at the green wood while his mind flashed on ancient images. Blistering sunburn when he was eight. The palms of his hands scraped raw when he fell off a bicycle at 14. And with every changing image, the pain grew. He tried to talk to the man behind him. The creature's silence only added to the horror of his predicament.

Another turn of the hemostat. Pain sparked through his body. He rode the pain along nerves he never knew existed. His cry turned into a scream that vibrated through his body and echoed in his brain. He found he could adjust the frequency of the scream so that it resonated with the pain. He became the pain. This allowed him to go ever deeper into his pain. Then, almost by accident, he hit just the right frequency at just the right moment, and a door opened.

He stepped through. There was no pain here. He turned around and caught a glimpse of his body wiggling in its torture like a frog on the dissecting tray. The body was still screaming. It had to. Otherwise, the sanctuary would cease to exist. But now he was in a place where no pain could touch him.

He was stretched out on the soft sand of the beach. A mist, warmed by the midday sun, sprayed over his body. He pressed himself into the beach digging with his hands until he reached wet sand. The grabbed a handful. This is reality, he told himself. Everything else seemed ethereal, like a fading memory. The ocean started to seep into the area he had dug, forming a pool around his hand. Reality is here, not there, he told himself. The air sparkled, fractured into tiny pieces of glass that rained down on him. He dug deeper into the wet sand. His fingers kept opening and closing on the reality of sand and ocean. He inhaled deeply and filled his lungs with the smell of salt water and a sweetish fragrance like gardenias. ...

Here was the mystery of the universe. And he was lying on top of it, his body pressed into it, fucking it, trying to possess its secrets. The essence of time and space, of life and death, all condensed into a single idea, almost within his grasp. He must try harder to reach it. He almost had it when the foam of the ocean came in. It swept over his feet, around his torso and up into his mouth. Then it receded, pulling him out, past the castle entrance and through the door.[565]

One Christian martyr (St. James Intercisus), pressured to recant his faith, refused and was tortured to death[566].

"This death which appears so dreadful is very little for the purchase of eternal life." Then turning to the executioners, he said "Why do you stand looking on? Begin your work." They therefore cut off his right thumb at which he prayed aloud "savior of Christians, receive a branch of the tree. It will putrefy but again will be clothed with glory. The vine dies in winter, but revives in spring. Shall not the body when cut down sprout up again?" When his first finger was cut off the cried out, "my heart hath rejoiced in the Lord, and my soul has exulted in his salvation! Receive another branch, O Lord." And at the lopping of every finger he exulted and thanked God afresh. When his fingers and toes have all been cut off, he said cheerfully to the executioner, "Now the boughs are gone, cut down the trunk". ... St. James still continued to pray and praise God, till a soldier by severing his head from his body, completed his martyrdom."

We also find a case where torture created a mystic experience in the scientific literature.[567]

"In 2009 a Black African man in his mid twenties attended for assessment to document alleged torture. He spoke fluent English and his only past medical history of note were symptoms of sleep paralysis. During the interview he described being detained and tortured eight years earlier in Africa to elicit information. He reported being repeatedly taken from a cell into a dedicated torture chamber where he was kicked, punched and beaten with batons and whips. His limbs were bound and he was suspended from the ceiling. During one interrogation a gun was pointed at him at close range. His aggressors were formidable torturers and the patient witnessed the death of another detainee. Scars on the patient's back, arms and legs were consistent with the injuries described. There was no electrocution reported during his torture. As a result of detention and torture, the patient was left with persistent symptoms consistent with Posttraumatic Stress Disorder (PTSD), including nightmares and flashbacks ..." During one of these interrogations" ... "he felt himself rising toward the ceiling of the torture chamber and looking down to observe his body being beaten below. There was a "pure white" light and a sound like "an open ocean". He felt as though he had "left suffering behind". At one point he heard familiar, "gentle voices". Images flashed before his eyes, for example of himself as a baby."

More stories of Interhemispheric intrusions.

When Bill W., The co-founder of Alcoholics Anonymous, was still a raging alcoholic, he went into *delirium tremens* one night, as his mental and physical health was collapsing. He was filled with fear and dread, as he lay in a hospital bed, both asleep and awake at the same time. He thought he was going out of his mind or perhaps even dying. Then, suddenly, the room was filled with light, and he was at peace. He experienced a comfort he had never known before. The next morning, the light was gone, but the peace remained. Like many who've had religious experiences, he soon found himself with a mission; a new purpose for his life: to help others recover from alcoholism.[568]

R. Buckminster Fuller, the engineer and philosopher, who pioneered several new engineering principles. These allowed him to develop the geodesic dome, a radical new car design, tensegrity masts, new ways of making maps of the Earth, and a host of other technical breakthroughs. Before he embarked on his career as an engineer, he found himself with no steady income, shortly after his daughter was born. He turned to drink, which provided him with some solace, but also gave him even more to be ashamed of. Several people were tearing down his reputation, because they had invested money in a company that failed while Fuller was the director.

"Although neither his nor (his wife's) families were excessively wealthy, he felt that if he removed the burden of his presence from everyone's lives, the two families would band together to support his wife and child. He also knew that his insurance policy would provide them with sufficient funds for several years. In weighing only that narrow range of personal issues, suicide appeared to be a viable alternative for Fuller that depressing day. 'Buckminster Fuller – life or death.' Bucky was suddenly seized by an experience, which would transform his life and his overall perception forever.

As he would later recall, he experienced what he thought was most significant of many seemingly mystical events which occurred throughout his life. During almost all of the lectures which followed that experience, he would recount that he had unexpectedly found himself suspended several feet above the ground enclosed in a "sparkling sphere of light." During the incident, time seemed to stop while he listened to a voice speaking directly to him. Although the experience was difficult for the pragmatic Fuller to accept as reality, he remembered not resisting and allowing himself to savor it fully. Because of that, he was able to remember the exact words he heard. The voice declared, "From now on you need never (add) any temporal attestation to your thoughts. You think the truth."

It continued," you do not have the right to eliminate yourself. You do not belong to you. You belong to universe. Your significance will remain forever obscured to you, but you may assume that you are fulfilling your role you apply yourself to convert your experiences to the highest advantage of others. [569]"

Michael Murphy, the founder of the Esalen Institute, tells a story about how he felt after a Rolfing (a kind of deep, forceful massage) session.

345

"Once, when Ida (Rolf) had done a session with me, spending most of the hour loosening and restructuring my sacrum, I walked onto a dock in the Gulf of Mexico. I experienced being a part of the sea breeze, the movement of the water and the fish, the light rays cast by the sun, the colors of the palms and the tropical flowers. I had no sense of past or future. It was not a particularly blissful experience. It was terrifying."[570]

This last story is especially interesting. The mechanism of interhemispheric intrusions, in which excited activity from the right amygdala is shunted over into the one on the left, can also happen in the opposite direction. Experiences that follow such a pattern would be unpleasant enough to look more like psychiatric symptoms than spiritual experiences. As we saw in the case of The Blessed Faustina Kowalska (in the chapter on God and the brain), feelings of joy or calm can be replaced by very negative emotions. Such cases are not common, but they do exist, and they make us realize that the same mechanisms that precipitate visions of God can also bring up visitations by "the devil and his minions".

Here is an example of anger culminating in a spiritual experience:

"... The next day I drove to Luxembourg, where I've been doing a lot of business. I was in the car on the road in Belgium, driving fast, and I suddenly started to cry and scream. I was so angry because all of my attempts my whole life to be a better person seem so trivial. ... I was really angry and shouting.

And then suddenly, the veil lifted. Suddenly, within all that turmoil it was as if a veil just fell on the floor or whatever. I lifted and I looked into this. God, I just still get ... I looked into this and there was no future, no past, nothing had ever happened. Oh God ... It's still amazing.

It's like ... It was incredible. At the same time, I was driving my car. I was seeing that there was no past,

346

that there never had been a past and also I had always known this. This had always been like this. There was no history. There was no attempt. There was nothing. There was absolutely nothing. It was amazing.[571]

Here, it looks like anger, building up in the left temporal and frontal lobes, crashed across the brain, and ended up in the right hippocampus. Of course, this is not going to be a common way for spiritual experiences to unfold, but they are possible for those whose right hippocampus is more sensitive than the right amygdala (an unusual set of thresholds).

During Stalin's terror, many people lived in constant fear of arrest and deportation to the gulags, and the constant anxiety this created could be enough to trigger an interhemispheric intrusion. The end of a lasting episode of anxiety can be all it takes to precipitate such an event. Here are two stories in which people had such experiences without actually coming to a point of extreme fear, but they also didn't have mystic experiences. Instead, they had simple episodes of joy.

"... This feeling was a thousand times stronger during epidemics of arrests when all around you they were hauling in people like yourself and still had not come for you; for some reason they were taking their time. After all, that kind of exhaustion, that kind of suffering, is worse than any kind of arrest, and not only for a person of limited courage. Vasily Vlasov, a fearless communist, ... Renounced the idea of escape proposed by his non-party assistants, and pined away because the entire leadership of the Kady district was arrested in 1937, and they kept delaying and delaying his own arrest. He could only endure the blow head on. He did endure it, and then he relaxed, and during the first days after his arrest he felt marvelous."

"In 1934, the priest Father Irakly went to Alma-Ata to visit some believers in exile there. During his absence they came three times to his Moscow apartment to arrest him. When he returned, members of his flock met him at the station and refused to let him go home, and for eight years hid him in one apartment after another. The priest suffered so painfully from this harried life that when he was finally arrested in 1942 he sang hymns of praise to God"[572].

The positive emotions that appear when a long period of intense anxiety is over can be so intense that even the horrors of prison, exile, and a diet of foul bread and water can seem like paradise.

War

The literature of war offers us a fertile ground, and shows that similar experiences can appear, even when the crises lack spiritual connotations.

Traumatic events activating the right amygdala can excite it enough that it dumps its activity into other structures on the same side of the brain. When this happens, the experiences can include sudden feelings of calm; out of body experiences; sudden psychic perception; moments of deep detachment; the experience of having time stop or slow down or even just falling asleep after a wave of intense fatigue. We can call these experiences 'intralimbic intrusions'; events where activity suddenly bursts out of a highly active structure into another one on the same side of the brain. Intrusions from the right amygdala to the right hippocampus are a likely source for battlefield epiphanies. If the battlefield conditions are stressful enough, and the person is sensitive enough, right-to-left 'intrusions' can also appear.

The level of fear appearing in battle is not always high enough to create interhemispheric intrusions that manifest as visions of angels, God, spirits and so forth. Trained soldiers, especially with battle experience know what to do in the worst moments, so they're less likely to go into complete helplessness or hopelessness, because. Their stress may not reach the crucial amygdala threshold where excess activity crosses over to the other side of the brain, but it can still be enough to slam activity into the amygdala's neighbors on the right. The right hippocampus, along with nearby surface cortical areas, is implicated in OBEs, inner imaging, time distortions[573] and non-verbal ways of thinking. A heavy load of fear during battle can make the two hemispheres work at such different levels that their normal connections are disturbed.

If the stress gets high enough, battles can create a wide range of altered states in traumatic moments. People who are very prone to altered-state experiences are usually more emotional, so they often don't make good front-line soldiers. Their extra measure of emotional sensitivity makes them less reliable when bullets start flying. However, stress, fear and terror, creating high levels of excitement in the right amygdala, can still reach the point where an interhemispheric intrusion can take place, even for a battle-hardened soldier. A person with a history of altered states will find their pathways of least resistance guiding the experience. Someone with no such history will have no such avenues. When a moment of deep terror creates more activity than their right amygdala can hold, the activity can spill out in many different directions. This means we should expect more variety in the weird moments that appear in war than we find in the epiphanies of people who do spiritual practices. For those who are good, mentally tough soldiers, the dam is higher, and when it overflows, it can flood out in many more directions. In the absence of worn-in pathways to direct the activity towards positive episodes, the brain can create demonic visitor experiences more easily than angelic ones. It's more likely to do so when the fearful event keeps on happening or when the person expects it to continue.

Let's look at some examples.

Mystic experiences on the battlefield [574]

One soldier, fighting in the battles following D-day in France, told the following story.

> "The fire was consistent, blasting our eardrums, spraying the lip of our hollow with sheets of mud. We couldn't get off more than one shot at a time. We were

trapped. We couldn't move forward or backwards. I figured that was the end. We'd had it."

He remembers a strange altered-state experience.

"I was looking down from above, and watching the episode unfold in slow motion. I remember feeling completely detached, but terribly sorry for the guys spread-eagled in that muddy little ditch".

The fear he experienced, based in the right amygdala, had abruptly spread into his right hippocampus, triggering an Out-of-Body Experience[575].

"We were within a few feet of the wounded man when the second round hit. It seemed right on top of us. It was like getting slugged with a baseball bat, and I went down. I had no idea how badly injured I was; it was in the thigh, but I had no sense of penetration. I remember the red cone of flame, and then, while falling, everything switched to slow motion".

Here's another incident from the same author[576]:

"The stench of cordite was heavy. I was hot and thirsty. I felt that premonition of danger, which is ludicrous to everyone, except those who experienced it and lived to tell of it. All my senses were exceptionally alert. A bristling, tingling feeling raced up my back. Each decision to move was made with great deliberation, then executed as rapidly as the Jesse Owens sprint. I had that sensation you have when you think someone is looking at you, and you turn around and you are right."

The experience of sensing a presence, fuelled by the fear of the being killed or wounded, can be expected to happen more often during a battle. Also, this last case invites the speculation that times of danger can elicit psychic skills. The response to danger is fear from the right amygdala, and the limbic basis for psychic skills appears to be in its next-door neighbor, the right hippocampus (as we'll see in our next chapter). Having the fearful amygdala able to trigger psychic perceptions or enhanced intuition could only tend to increase our chance of survival in such dangerous moments.

"Hallucinations are common in war. If you lie in a dark hole, listening to the sound of your own breathing, dead objects may rise and live, bald rocks may be transformed into men's pates, pinnacled stones may become witch's fingers. One of the commonest delusions is to see in the distance a buddy you know is dead, one you actually saw die, now very much alive. He's smiling at you. You run over and, of course, he isn't there."

The fear and dread soldiers live with in live warfare can build to the point where anything can trigger an "intrusion" experience, but their visions can be hellish. Activity building up in the right amygdala, and recruiting the right hippocampus, the source of dream imagery, can create horrific experiences while awake, the same way these two structures might combine to fill out a nightmare while we're dreaming.

Then there are the appearances of phantom nips.

I knew a major who dropped his pants in the bush on Guadalcanal and squatted to defecate. A shot rang out. Another Marine had spotted a Nip sniper in a coconut tree overhead. The dead sniper dropped 30 feet and plopped right in front of the major. Starting right then, he developed an extraordinary case of constipation. Every time he tried to empty his bowels, he saw Japs above him.... Similarly, a man in our 81mm mortar platoon awoke in his foxhole one night and saw himself ringed by Japs with fixed bayonets.

He grabbed his carbine and tried to turn off the safety. He hit the magazine release instead. The magazine fell out. He had a weapon, but no ammunition in it. He grabbed the barrel by the stacking level, turning the butt into a club and swatted away in all directions, crying for help. He was lucky the Marines around him didn't kill him. They wrestled him to the ground and convinced him that he was out of danger, but to the end of his life, three weeks later, he stubbornly insisted that those Japs had been real. And, of course, to him they were.

So it was with me that terrible night. Another flare revealed that my visitor was feminine. That was startling. What was a woman doing up here? My heart welling with pity, I thought she must be in nature, one of the innocent civilian bystanders, who were dying in the struggle for the island. Then the shock of recognition hit me. She wasn't harmless. She was evil. I was in the presence of the horror of death. ...

Her identity might have puzzled others. She lacked the grace and movements of a geisha; she wasn't even Oriental. Nor was she the stereotypical slut. She wore no black-net stockings, no flimsy negligee. She knew her mark too well for that. Corrupted innocence, not candid wickedness, was the right bait for an inhibited New Englander. She was, instead, dressed like the girls I remembered at Smith and Mount Holyoke: a cashmere twin-sweater set, a Peter Pan collar, a string of pearls, a plaid skirt, Bobby Sox, and loafers. Her dirty-blond hair fell in a shoulder-length pageboy coiffure, and when she turned her head abruptly to glance at her watch, she tossed her tresses like a young goddess. ... Her face was anything but appealing. It was deathly white, like a frog's belly, and covered with running sores. Twin lines of foul maggots appeared on her upper lip, entering her nostrils in endless, weaving columns. Gray fungus grew up her arms. Gaunt, tensile hands restlessly clutched at each other, like fingers stitching the shroud. When she grinned lewdly, as she presently did, she revealed vicious jagged teeth. Sharp enough to rip out your throat, as those of Java rats are said to lunge through your cheeks to reach the morsel of your tongue. She exhaled a foul stench. But it was her eyes, eyes as old as tombs, which were the most phenomenal. A direct stare is the boldest way to invade the sheath of privacy, which enveloped each of us, and she was using it devastatingly, diminishing the distance between us to the intimacy of a membrane. Our wide pupils were in turns fine, reptilian, shameless. She trembled suggestively. She was soliciting me, beckoning me towards cathexis[577].

None of this sounds inviting, let alone seductive. But the shell which had wiped out my squad had barely missed me. So close a call with death is often followed by eroticism. ... Just then a random shell ruffled over and landed a few yards away. In the flash she disappeared.[578]"

The same author described an episode of enhanced visual acuity during basic training.

"Physically I was delicate, even for a guy, but I had limitless reserves of energy, and I could feel myself toughening almost hourly. Everything I saw seemed exquisitely defined -- every leaf, every pebble looked as sharp as a drawing in a book."

Another story comes from one of the pilots in the Doolittle raid, the United States' first attack on Japan in World War II. The Japanese captured and imprisoned him until the end of the war.

On August 9, 1945, he awoke in his cell as the first ray of sunlight streaked through the morning haze, to a voice that told him in clear tones to 'start praying':

> "I asked, what shall I pray about?" "For Peace." I had prayed about peace, but very little, if at all, before that time, as it seemed useless. I thought God could stop the war anytime with the power which He had manifested." ... "About seven o'clock in the morning I began to pray. It seemed very easy to pray on the subject of peace. I prayed that God would put a great desire in the hearts of the Japanese leaders for peace. I thought about the days of peace that would follow. Japanese people would no doubt be discouraged, and I felt sympathetic towards them. I prayed that God would not allow them to fall into persecution by the victorious armies.
>
> At two o'clock in the afternoon the Holy Spirit told me, 'You don't need to pray any more – the victory is won'. I was amazed. I thought this was quicker and better than the regular method of receiving world news. ... It was then that (he) had a 'vision'. As he awoke on the morning of August 20, he was blinded by a bright light so radiant he could not see. A voice, the same one he had heard before, said, "Your travail will soon be over and you will be free. You will return to your loved ones and rejoice once more. But you are called to return to the Japanese people and teach them the way of the Lord." ... Later that day a prison guard opened his cell door wide and smiling, beckoned him to come out. "War over", he said. "You go home now."[579]

Haing Ngor, a survivor of the Cambodian holocaust, recounted this experience from one of his worst periods during that tragedy, after his wife had died.

"People saw me going out to the grave every evening with food, and they said I was crazy. I do not say that they are wrong, just that they hadn't been through what I had. No couple had been as close as Huoy and me. There was a night when I got back home from praying and lay down to sleep, and when I woke up someone was knocking on the door. Huoy's voice was calling to me. I opened the door and she was there, dressed in white, with a white veil.

"Please come often to visit me," she said.

She turned away from me and began to walk along the canal. It was still dark outside, but I could see her. I called after her to wait, wait, but although I followed her and she was walking very slowly, it was impossible to keep up with her. As she walked, the ends of her long veil floated in the air and bounced gracefully, like wings lifting her up and carrying her along. I ran after her, but she disappeared from sight."[580]

The stresses and tensions of war can also precipitate much quieter altered-state experiences. World War II veteran J. Glenn Gray, wrote,

"Then there was this strange feeling. I think every soldier must have felt at times that this or that happening fitted into nothing that had gone before; it was incomprehensible, either absurd, mysterious or both. If many events of this sort came to us, we began to feel foreign in our own skins, intruders in the world. More often than at home, we would wake up in the night and wonder where we were."[581]

This experience, very much like jamais vu (the opposite of Déjà vu), is not as dramatic or phenomenal as hearing a voice, seeing a ghost or going out of body. Nevertheless, such dissociative experiences can still have a powerful impact on the brains of those who have them.

Spiritual experiences can arise from some very unholy moments. The sudden shift in consciousness that can appear during a battle usually won't lead to a mystic experience. It's probably more common for an overloaded right amygdala to dump its load of activity, and shift the focus of excitement into the nearby right hippocampus, which will not produce a dramatic spiritual experience, but can create a moment of dispassion and detachment ("flattened affect") strong enough that the soldier can act without fear.

> "... In desperation I looked at our captain, lying among us behind a large rock. I watch as he returned the fire, shot after shot, with iron discipline. He handled the carbine of my dead comrade as if he were in a shooting gallery. Then, suddenly, a strange, rigid calm came over me that I had never known before. It became clear to me that I was also supposed to fire. Until then, I had not fired a single shot as I fearfully watched slowly advancing (East) Indians. I can still picture to this day a tall, broad Indian with a distinct black beard, jumping from a pile of rocks. For a moment I hesitated, the body next to me filling my whole mind, and I pulled myself together even though I was very much shaken. I fired and watched the Indian slump forward during his jump. He didn't move. I really can't say if I aimed correctly. He was my first kill! The spell was broken. Still unsure of myself, I began firing and firing, just as they had taught me in training."[582]

We cannot leave out one theme in the spirituality of war, "There are no atheists in foxholes". Here are two stories from the Russo-German war (WWII).

> "But though this was a generation (of Communists) that had seldom visited church, everyone observed the men who wore small silver crosses around their necks, hiding them under their shirts and explaining, if they

were challenged, that the trinkets were gifts from their grandmothers. Some made their own crosses by cutting shapes out of old tins. "They burned their party cards if they were going to die," a veteran remembered. "But they did not throw away the crosses." Very large numbers - perhaps a majority of rank and filers - cross themselves in the old Russian way before they faced the guns. The gestures and the words were totemic - echoes rather than formal evidence, of faith. "They said things like God save me' but what they believed I couldn't say,"a veteran explained. "I'm an atheist myself, but not very strongly. I came back to life. I suppose I live under a lucky star." "I had a Guardian Angel," (another) explained. "I could feel her beside me all the time." The angel, he told me, was in fact the spirit of his mother."[583]

"Before I (Ivan Schylaev) went off to fight, my mother gave me a written prayer, to act as a talisman. I kept it in my breast pocket. I never looked at it - I was, after all, a communist. But something was going on at Stalingrad, which I couldn't explain. I felt that, when we took the Mamaev Kurgan, a hill overlooking Stalingrad, the most strategic point in the city, and more strongly when we held out on 22 September.... I was an atheist. But being an atheist at Stalingrad was no longer enough. I could not explain how I was still alive, or how our Army was continuing to fight. The Germans should have destroyed us all that day. Reluctantly, I took out the prayer, opened it and gave thanks to God."[584]

On that day, September 22, 1942, the author's division was almost destroyed. They started the day with 3,000 men and ended it with just a few hundred.

There are (usually) no atheists in foxholes because the stress of battle creates and relieves high levels of excitement in the right amygdala — over and over. If it is 'dumped' into other structures, it might have other effects, like a lasting dissociation, or the first symptoms of PTSD. A lot

357

depends on where the activity in the right amygdala goes during and after the peak of excitement.

However, being prepared to fight was not the same as being prepared to survive, and his atheism became a casualty of war – on that day, at least. A wave of peace came over him after the fighting ended, as high levels of right amygdala excitement, sustained throughout that long day, finally subsided. Presumably, the areas in the left amygdala that support positive feelings were inhibited during the fighting, and started working again when it ended. At the same time, the right amygdala became quiet. The increase in left amygdala excitement and decrease in the one on the right triggered a wave of religious sentiment, but not a mystic experience. His gratitude went far beyond any he had ever felt before, and to put it into context, his brain manifested a cognitive hallucination (he felt the presence of a belief that wasn't in his mind at all). The hallucination was of *faith* – and a pure form of faith as well. He felt it without any beliefs to justify it or any intellectual basis. One moment, he felt that there was no God. In the next, he was saying prayers of thanksgiving.

In closing this chapter, we should note that some religious and mystic experiences are not preceded by negative emotions. If the sacred pathways are sensitive enough, or compromised by a head injury, or the person is just 'born that way', such experiences can happen in other circumstances. The interhemispheric intrusion mechanism is offered here as the most common door to mysticism, but not the only one. There are many published accounts of mystic experiences to be found in all sorts of different literature, but most of the time, only the epiphany itself is described. The events leading up to it are often left out. As this idea becomes more widespread, we hope to see future biographers of mystics looking into the events leading up to their spiritual breakthroughs more carefully.

CHAPTER 14

Psychic Skills

I want to begin this chapter by being clear about what type of psychic skills we'll be talking about. The first is telepathy. Here, telepathy, means 'the transfer of information between two brains'.

One of the most common kinds of stories about this kind of telepathic communication features a mother in Ney York (for example), who suddenly wakes up in the middle of the night, knowing that her daughter, thousands of miles away in California, is having some kind of trouble. She gets up, places a frantic call asking "What's wrong" and then finds the daughter at the other end of the phone saying "My boyfriend just went berserk", "I was in an accident" or some other crisis.

Information is somehow transferred across thousands of miles in this scenario. It seems to be most common between "intimates" - people who are closely connected - mothers and daughters[585], girlfriends and boyfriends, married couples, siblings, and so forth[586].

The second psychic skill we'll be talking about is remote viewing. Remote viewing is when someone in one location can focus their attention on another location and obtain valid, 'true' information about what's happening there.

There are some types of psychic skills that I won't be talking about very much. One of them is precognition. There may well some validity to precognition, and I'll be mentioning one of the studies that tended to validate it later on, but precognition involves getting information from the future to the present. This can be tricky because the idea of getting information from the future challenges physics' fundamental beliefs about the nature of time, and we want to do as little of that as possible. Some people may wonder what's wrong with telling physicists they're wrong, but physics is also the source of our understanding of time, and we can't reject the concepts we disagree with and keep the ones we like. The concepts of physics all fit together, and few metaphysically-minded people have the education to create replacements for the theories and hypotheses they don't agree with. I once had a friend who was sure (from their "higher wisdom") that time was a non-linear phenomenon. I asked; "if it's not linear, what kind of structure *does* it have?" As you might expect, they didn't have an answer. It was a trick question, because answering it requires very advanced math, and an understanding of some of the intricacies of Special Relativity.

We're not going to be talking about Tarot card readings, palmistry, tea readings, or crystal ball gazing - all these are in a different class of experiences. One of the things that distinguish telepathy and remote viewing from other kinds of psychic work is that all you need to do it is a human brain or a pair of brains. No tarot cards, no crystal balls, no tea, no séance room. The reason we're not covering these, and that discussion is possible at all, is because there is a fundamentally new kind of evidence from a recent technology, and so far, it's only been used in experiments with telepathy and remote viewing. Other psychic modalities haven't been studied using this new technology, so we'll be leaving them out of this discussion, to avoid going past our evidence, though we can speculate about a few of them, and put our principles of neurotheology through a few of its paces.

Technology for Psychic Skills

This device is known as *the Octopus* because it consists of eight film canisters, each with two magnetic coils, arranged around the head. These coils deliver magnetic fields with constantly changing strengths that, so these ordinary magnetic fields are also magnetic *signals,* modulated by both frequency and amplitude. Here is a picture[587] of the first prototype. The Octopus was developed by Dr. Michael Persinger and Stan Koren, who also developed the God Helmet. This 8-channel apparatus has been used to pioneer a new way of studying psychic perception.

Two signals have been used with this in laboratory experiments. One of them is a 'chirp' signal (one that gets lower in pitch as it goes along) and the other one is derived from the amygdala[588].

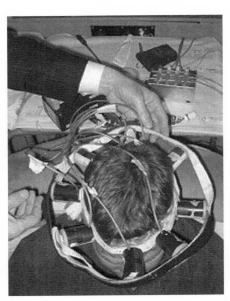

Each pair of coils puts out magnetic fields that rise and fall in very short periods of time, like 1 to 10 milliseconds. The magnetic fields they produce have a distinct pattern, and these are applied through each of the eight channels, one at a time.

Another such device is the *Shiva Neural Stimulation System,* developed by your present author, Todd Murphy. It replicates The Octopus, and was developed with the full cooperation and support of Stan Koren and Dr. M.A.

361

Persinger, who developed the original Octopus. It can be seen at www.shaktitechnology.com.

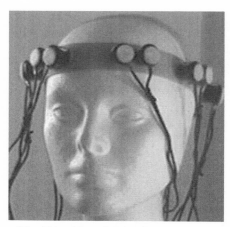

The Shiva Neural Stimulation System.

Remote Viewing

The Octopus was used in some experiments done with a well known remote viewer, Ingo Swann. Previously, he had been employed at an unspecified US government agency that sometimes used remote viewers. He did two experiments with Dr. Persinger, and these produced a great deal of information. In one of them[589], his job was to remote view a set of photographs. He would tell them when he was ready, and then someone in the next room would take out a picture from a manila envelope and place it on the table. He had no idea what the pictures would be. He sat in a completely silent room (an acoustic chamber) wearing the octopus headset. He had a light, but the door was closed. The room was equipped with an intercom that let him talk to the experimenters.

The original research paper even gave the length and the width of the table, as well as the length and the width of the manila envelopes they were stored in; very precise information.

The researchers gave him a fair amount of latitude. They even put the pictures exactly where Swann had told them to. They set up the experiment to show if his perceptions were wrong, but also to give him the best chance at doing well. In the other experiment (reported in the same research paper as the first), he was told to remote view specific researchers. He had met them in advance, so he knew who he was trying to 'track'. They went out into areas around the campus and the nearby town. Swann, an artist in his own right, was making sketches while he remote viewed both the photos and the researchers. Swann has a reputation as an artist, separate from his remote viewing activities.

44 Student 'raters' had the job of comparing the sketches Swann made in the lab with the actual pictures or people he was remote viewing. The times when Swann made his most accurate sketches (the ones the 'raters' thought showed the best match) were also times when his EEG showed a rare and distinctive pattern (7 Hz spiking – in the theta band) over his occipital lobes (back of the head; concerned with vision).

These experiments found that the accuracy of the drawings he made while remote viewing (either the researchers in various places away from the laboratory or the photos), was much higher when one of the two *Octopus* signals (a *chirp* signal) was revolving around his head, carried by its magnetic fields.

Validating his remote viewing this way, as well as stimulating and enhancing it, gave clear information about what's happening in a brain when a person is applying psychic skills.

They were also able to *block* his remote viewing[590]. They built a frame and put more of these magnetic coils around its edge, and ran a signal through all of these coils at once, using one of the signals also used in the experiment. However, the experiments where these signals (originating from the parallel port on a PC computer) were used to enhance remote viewing were run under the DOS computer operating system. When they ran this same DOS signal under Windows, he wasn't able to remote view through this magnetic screen, implying that the information he received through Remote Viewing was carried by magnetic fields.

The signals fed to the array of magnetic coils that screened his remote viewing were run under Windows, which added an extra component to the output (from the printer port – the Shiva System uses audio sources, which do *not* produce this distortion). This distorted the signal into a kind of fractal pattern, and the resulting chaos in the magnetic fields stopped Ingo Swann's remote viewing. Persinger didn't just confirm his remote viewing. He enhanced it, and also found a way to interfere with it. If you can create something in the laboratory, you're a lot closer to proving your understanding of it. If you can also stop it from happening, your proof is even stronger. One day, we may have a technology that will 'block' remote viewing, complimenting the *circumcerebral* (around the head) stimulation that can help create it.

That was the first of these experiments, involving just one 'exceptional' subject. Other experiments done with this technology used people who *weren't* trained psychics. None of them had any 'special' cognitive or emotional skills. This time, the researchers were dealing with ordinary people with ordinary minds, looking to see if more ordinary psychic perceptions would appear.

Brain to Brain communication (telepathy)

In one of these experiments[591] the subjects were pairs of 'intimates'; brothers and sisters, mothers and daughters, twins, and married couples. In these experiments, one from each pair received neural stimulation from the Octopus, while the other didn't. In one study, the one who didn't receive this *circumcerebral* (around the head) stimulation sat in a room and was shown pictures taken in the local area. One might be of a street; another might be a local monument. They had been asked what memories they might have had of being with the other person while they were in or near that location, such as "do ever remember being with your partner at the 'Big Nickel'"? (Sudbury, Ontario is home to the largest nickel in the world). The other one sat in a darkened and completely silent chamber, receiving the Octopus stimulation. They were equipped with a microphone and were told to free associate; share any thoughts, feelings, or any images that might come up while they were receiving this around-the-head magnetic stimulation.

The comments from the subjects receiving the Octopus stimulation (and free associating) were compared to the comments of the subject who was talking about memories of the other person provoked by the pictures.

Art by Me-Chan. Use by Permission.

As in the study with Ingo Swann, 44 students, each working independently, gave approximate ratings for how well the comments matched the pictures. They found that the matches came up 2.85 times more than they would by chance alone. That may not be impressive with a world class psychic like Ingo Swann, but it's enough to demonstrate that it's possible for two ordinary human brains to directly share and transfer information in certain circumstances.

As with Ingo Swann, Persinger found that accuracy improved when the subject doing the free association was being stimulated with a specific magnetic signal moving around their heads. The *congruence* (the amount of agreement the students saw) as they matched up the pictures with the free-associations yielded solid numbers that could then be analyzed. That's how we get a quantitative measure of psychic perceptions. This advance in statistical methods was one of the breakthroughs of this research. It allowed precise measurements of imprecise phenomena and that's also important because it satisfies the need to quantify lab results whenever possible.

One interesting thing about the signal is that it doesn't come from the brain. It's based on a fairly common signal (a kind of 'chirp' signal) that a piece of laboratory equipment called a function generator (sometimes called a tone generator) can produce. "Boxes" that can produce a perfect musician's "A" (440 hertz), can often produce this kind of signal, too. It doesn't have a frequency. It's an irregular signal with a range of frequencies.

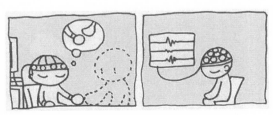

Drawing by Me-Chan. Use by permission.

In another experiment[592] with pairs of siblings, one of the pair sat in a room receiving the Octopus stimulation. The other one sat in another room, with their brain activity being monitored using EEG (electroencephalography). When the one getting the Octopus stimulation was asked to pretend they were touching their brother or sister, their sibling's EEG in the other room responded. If you are receiving circumcerebral magnetic stimulation and you pretend you're touching your brother or sister, their brain waves will show it. This experiment tends to support the idea that the people we know may be stimulating our brains when they think about us. However, we don't know how sensitive a person has to be to show the same response *without* the octopus stimulation. Perhaps we don't share psychic connections with the people we're close to, but one can be artificially created using this technology. Or perhaps we *do* have such connections people around us, and this experiment brought it out in the open. When we stop to consider how common 'psychic connections' with other people can be, it seems more likely that this experiment made them explicit that that it created them.

It's another example of transmission between two brains. This time they didn't need anyone to rate the 'congruence' of the effects for each subject. The times when the first person was imagining touching their partner matched the times when second person's EEG showed a response. That's a quantitative result – one that can't be attributed to chance. As far as I'm aware, no one has published anything criticizing either these experiments, or the ideas they're based on. That's significant when you stop to consider how surprising the results are for mainstream science. Sometimes, the scientific community amazes us by what it says. In this case, the surprising thing is what it hasn't said. Of course, there will eventually be skeptics, and we can expect that they won't have had any psychic experiences.

The next result is even more interesting[593], and offers a more decisive proof. It used pairs of subjects who didn't know each other before the experiment. This time, they *both* received the octopus stimulation.

One of them sat in a room looking at a flashing light. The other one, who was also wired up for EEG monitoring, sat in another room. They found that the EEG

Image by Me-Chan, Use by permission.

of the second subject responded in time with the flashing light that the first subject was seeing.

In the previous experiments with this technology, personal information was transmitted from one brain to another. This one was doing it with a flashing light, a very impersonal stimulus. A light has no personality, no personal 'vibration' or anything else a psychic might focus on. This was direct transmission from one brain to another, validated with brain imaging. It suggests that the transfer of information from one brain to another may be a capacity of all human brains. A house might be haunted with the spirit of a dead man, but who ever heard of a haunted light bulb? The experiment shows the brain is able to send and receive information even when it lacks thoughts or feelings.

It's been (mistakenly[594]) said that extraordinary claims require extraordinary proof. Here, the claim is that it's possible for information to pass from one brain to another without being expressed in any behavior or words. Its proof is indeed extraordinary.

There are also anecdotal reports from this technology. One user of the commercial version said:

> "The first six weeks (a series of six weekly sessions) finished the other week. While I'm not actively using the sessions to become psychic, my ability to feel what other people are feeling has become very good – sometimes to the point of overwhelming.[595]"

Another reported that her "horse whispering" became more effective. Others have reported enhancements in lucid dreaming and dream recall. One other person using the Shiva neural system, a spiritual healer, found that his healing abilities, which he felt are based on prayer, improved noticeably.

A Swiss research group, (under the direction of Dr. Rolf Bosch), has released a preliminary report[596] of an experiment with 100 subjects, all of whom actively did meditation, 'energy work' or other spiritual practices. Some of these subjects reported enlightenment experiences, as well as improvements in a range of psychic skills. Dr. Bosch also reported EEG confirmation of the subject's experiences, calling the system "Electronic Enlightenment". Clearly, it has more potential than the experiments to date have shown.

The stimulation

The devices we've been discussing use eight pairs of coils, arranged in a circle around the head. The signals move from one pair of coils to the next. The magnetic fields fluctuate, getting weaker and stronger with each passing millisecond.

The speed at which the fields move from one coil to the next changes each time they move. Suppose the field appears through the first coils for 50 seconds (for example – these are not the actual values). The next coils will have them for 40 seconds. The one after that will have them for 30 seconds, and so forth. The speed at which the fields move between the pairs of coils increases as it goes along. It keeps spinning faster. The rate at which it increases puts a theta range 'flicker' in the magnetic field for the whole head. Remember the association between theta activity in the brain, and trance, meditation, dreams, and the right hippocampus.

Like the God helmet, this technology uses electromagnets to produce ordinary magnetic fields. Magnetism is a field phenomenon (like gravitational fields). In the sciences, the word 'field' is defined by still other terms, including 'energy'. In the vocabulary of science, *Energy* is the capacity of a body, a mass, or a system that allows it to do *work*. *Work* is defined as anything that changes where a *force* is being applied. A *force* is anything that changes *inertia*. Magnetic fields are *forces*, not *energies*. Three things distinguish electromagnetic radiation from magnetic fields.

1) Electromagnetic (EM) radiation is a form of energy. Magnetism is a force, not a form of energy.

2) EM radiation has frequencies, and magnetic fields don't, unless they added by the source (like the fluctuating magnetic fields that appear around stereo headphones while music is playing through them).

3) Magnetic fields are not composed of quantum particles (like the photons that compose radiation).

The distinction between magnetic fields (whether coming from electromagnets or not) and EMF (electromagnetic frequencies) is important for this technology because the word *electromagnetic* can denote things like microwaves, and you don't want a microwave oven wrapped around your head. In contrast, magnetic fields are perfectly safe. The strengths of the magnetic fields coming out of the coils are close to the ones that come out of stereo headphones (which also have coils in them). As I'll be describing shortly, we're immersed in magnetic fields all the time, most importantly the earth's magnetic field. Some people express concern about the safety of magnetic brain stimulation, thinking that there could be a risk to brain tissues, but magnetic fields do no harm. Again, changing magnetic fields also appear from stereo headphones.

The magnetic fields from the God Helmet and the Octopus reach the brain because the scalp and skull don't have any insulation that could stop them. In fact, there is *no such thing* as a magnetic insulator. If anyone tells you that the fields aren't strong enough to influence the brain, you can be sure that they don't understand the physical laws that describe the behavior of electricity and magnetism.

Although two signals were used in the best known experiments, only one signal is used in some recent (unpublished) experiments[597], which have been more effective than its predecessors. The speed of the signal's movement, from one pair of coils to the next, goes up in each successive phase (there are seven of them) of the session. These two signals had each been studied in previous experiments, and found to have two very different ranges of effects. One of them is derived from the amygdala and referred to in literature as "burstx" because it duplicates the pattern that occurs with burst firing in the amygdala. It had gained a track record for producing spiritual experiences in the God Helmet experiments. The other one was based on a "chirp" pattern taken from a device called a function generator; both signals were also used in the God Helmet studies, and had been seen to induce powerful altered states. In the Octopus experiments, Burstx was applied first, and the 'chirp' signal was applied afterwards.

There are a few sensations that appear when using the session design that's proven most effective for enhancing spiritual practices (called the "Persinger Session"). Sometimes a mild altered state appears at the beginning of the session, which lasts about 40 minutes. Towards the end, a person can find they become very relaxed. Their inner monolog tends to slow down because the stimulation affects the brain more on the right, away from the language centers, than it does on the left. Right hemispheric events, experiences, phenomena, especially relaxation, tend to dominate the experiences during the session. The effects that appear after the session are another matter. To understand them, we need to look at a thing called the brain's *binding factor*.

The Binding Factor

The Octopus' arrangement of changing magnetic fields orbiting the head is designed to make them interact with a brain activity called the 'binding factor', which moves through the brain, from front to back, every 25 milliseconds. The binding factor reaches the surface of the brain from a deep structure called the thalamus. It sweeps from the bottom, beginning at the front of the brain and ending at the back, over and over again. Neuroscientists have called it the Forty Hertz component because it runs through the brain 25 times per second (1000 milliseconds ÷ 25 times per second = 40 Hertz). It's also called the *Binding Factor* because it's been said to bind consciousness to the sense of self.

The binding factor seems to be generated in the thalamus, which unites all of our sensory input; everything from our eyes, ears, nose, tongue, and skin. It also responds to our internal senses, like the one that lets you know you have to go to the bathroom, or the one that lets you know when you're hungry. More importantly, it responds to our thoughts and emotions ('affective and cognitive modalities'), including the ones we're not immediately aware of. These 'cognitive, affective, and sensory modalities' are all equal for the thalamus. The thalamus unites all of them into what we know as our present experience.

The binding factor isn't always present in the human brain. It's only there when we're awake; in normal consciousness, and it's there when we're dreaming[598] [599]. Dreams are a lot like normal consciousness. Doing something in a dream activates the same brain parts involved in doing that same thing while you're awake. The Binding Factor doesn't appear when we're in dreamless sleep. It's there when 'you' are there, but when *you* are absent, it's gone, too. We can only consolidate memories when the sense of self is present. We can remember things that happen when we're in our normal *states*. We can remember our dreams. We can't remember dreamless sleep. You can't create memories when your "self" isn't available.

In one moment of sleep, your sense of self is there, and in the next moment its not. The binding factor is also part of the mechanics of the sense of self. When you're in a dream, you're there, when you're in your normal states of consciousness, you exist, but where are you when you're in dreamless sleep? This is a slightly mind boggling concept. First, you're there, then you're not, then you're there, then you're not. The 40 Hz signal appears on an EEG, starting and stopping as someone goes in and out of dream (REM) sleep. Consciousness appears and disappears, over and over. It happens every night to everybody, but we feel 'we' exist all the time.

The binding factor has gotten the name the *binding factor for consciousness*. It keeps the sense of self bound to the things we are conscious of. My own belief is that is also binds us to our *repertoire of states of consciousness*. You have a range of states of consciousness, so does the remote viewer who can close his eyes and see what's going on with missile silos in Siberia. I can't do that. What's the difference? That state of consciousness is within his repertoire. It's not within mine. There are enlightened masters who are said to be able to put their hands on your head and make you see God. That skill, and the state they have to be in, is within their repertoire of states, but not mine. I've been able to use 'healing by laying on hands' to stop a couple of people's headaches and make a few aches and pains go away back when I was trying to learn spiritual healing, but I never even got close to what the real masters can do. Some people's repertoire of states of consciousness includes the *states* that support these and other 'special' skills. The range of *states* for most people doesn't. The binding factor, I believe, prevents us from leaving the range of states of consciousness we're accustomed to. We never lose hold of the states of consciousness that we rely on to relate to the people around us and to avoid threats to our survival, but we rarely access the less common states.

Let's look at how this technology works with binding factor. The magnetic signals are circulated around the head. The changing speed at which the signals move from one pair of coils to the next reflects the speed of the binding factor's movement. As you view the head from above, they go counterclockwise. The binding factor runs front to back. That means that when these signals are running over the left side of the head, they're running its current, and when they pass over the right side of the brain, they're colliding with the binding factor. The signals hold it back much more on the right side than the left.

The movement of the magnetic signals is *almost* at the same speed as the Binding Factor, but as they travel over the right hemisphere, it moves in the opposite direction; altering it – but only on the right side of the brain. Without the binding factor in place, the brain has an opportunity to access quite new states of consciousness, and makes it unusually sensitive to subtle phenomena, especially from the hippocampus. That means[600] that you are no longer bound to your habitual repertoire of states of consciousness while the session is happening, and for a time (up to five days) afterwards. This kind of stimulation changes what you can accomplish with your mind. The binding factor binds you to your normal range of states, and when you alter it; when you perturb it, when you make changes to it, you can temporarily have a broader range of cognitive skills. These can become permanent, but only If you exercise them. The range of your awareness can increase, as you become aware of phenomena that previously had been too subtle to perceive directly. As we saw with the Octopus experiments (where the subjects didn't know why their inner images came up), these cognitive skills may not be apparent to the person using them. Changing these skills so we can use them easily can mean *exercising* them. Spiritual practices, like meditation or visualization exercises, can have more and deeper effects after Octopus sessions, because such practices, being based on right hemispheric excitement, are affected when the binding factor in right hemisphere is 'deflected' in this way. Persinger has commented[601] that one Octopus session has its greatest effects when the sessions are done while the earth's magnetic field is unsettled. In short, psychic perceptions appear when the binding factor is muted, muffled, or held back. They should also appear more readily for people who've learned to change it at will. They may not know what's going on, but they know something is happening. "It's a thing that I do with the back of my head".

The binding factor is more flexible for a few days (3 to 5) after an Octopus (or Shiva Neural Stimulation System) "Persinger Session". Its habits are broken, so to speak. When meditation and psychic exercises push to include themselves into a person's repertoire of states of consciousness, the Binding Factor is unable to resist them, as it normally would. In the parlance of New Age psychology, there is an 'opening', and spiritual practices can go deeper. It's a bit like using steroids before a workout. The exercise does more than it usually would, but a lot less will happen if you take steroids *without* working out. To carry the metaphor a little further, the steroids are not the barbells, nor are they the workout itself.

If one does the *Persinger Session* repeatedly, but without any spiritual practices or psychic exercises, the result is usually a more subtle increase in psychic perceptions. In such a case, we would expect that they wouldn't go beyond the tasks that one's day-today life offers them. You might be better able to read your boss's moods, and know who's going to call soon, but the more exciting kinds of psychic perceptions will appear much more slowly. Your meditations and prayers offer a deeper context for the effects to emerge, and the result will be stronger psychic skills, more 'connected' (silent) prayers, and deeper meditations. How long it takes will depend on the individual. People looking for the "Persinger Session" to do the work for them will not be as successful as people who actively do spiritual practices.

The Role of the Earth's Magnetic Field

The earth's magnetic field plays a role. In the 'shared memories' experiment, they found that the subjects had a stronger response[602] when the earth's magnetic field was quietest. The stories those subjects told (the ones looking at pictures) matched the free associations of those receiving stimulation more closely when the earth's magnetic field was least turbulent. That's also the time when experiments with psychic phenomena or any kind of psychic or spiritual work is more effective, especially if it's introspective. The psychic perceptions that come in times of crisis, (like when a mother in one place knows when her daughter is in trouble, even though she's far away) are more likely when the earth's magnetic field is quiet.

The feeling of a 'sensed presence' is more likely when the geomagnetic measures are higher[603]. Out of body experiences are much more likely when the geomagnetic field is more active [604]. Psychic perceptions are quite different. They're more likely when the earth's magnetic field is quiet. The difference is because things like visions of God and sensing a presence affect both sides of the brain, while psychic perceptions seem to involve only right side. Psychic perception is easier when the earth's magnetic field is quiet, and spiritual experiences are more likely when it's busy. They're based on different brain processes[605].

An especially productive time for psychic perceptions is when the earth's magnetic field settles down to a very quiet level just after turbulence, like magnetic storms in the geomagnetic field. This quiet time offers a launch window for more effective psychic work. There are 'launch windows' when psychic perceptions are more available, suggesting that the brain makes small changes in its operations to accommodate changes in the earth's magnetic field. Our brains are overcompensating, not for geomagnetic noise, which you might think would interfere with the brain's functioning, but rather for geomagnetic *quiet*.

Persinger offered an 'exploratory' hypothesis[606] to explain these phenomena; that some portion of our consciousness is integrated with the earth's magnetic field. If this is so, and the geomagnetic field was shut off tomorrow, there wouldn't just be less magnetism around (and a change in electrical storms and other natural electric and magnetic phenomena). Each and every person on the planet might feel a shift in their state of consciousness, and possibly experience new *states*.

The shining blackness

Let's go back to the subject at hand – communication between brains. In the book *"Visuddhimagga"*, (The Path of Purification[607]), its author, Buddhagosha Acharya, said the way to acquire magic powers is to close your eyes and get into a state of consciousness where you're seeing an infinite space ("The Void") instead of the usual dull darkness that we see with our eyes closed. He discusses several meditation techniques intended to make that state of consciousness (the *realm of infinite space*) easier to achieve. Of course, it takes long practice with the right meditation technique to learn to do this. It's got to have that sense of spaciousness to it, or it's not the *realm of infinite space*. When some people are in that state of consciousness, they can visualize something, and get a clear mental image of it, appearing in the foreground – in front of the infinite space.

The limbic structure most implicated in both psychic phenomena and the experience of T*he Void* is the right hippocampus. The right hippocampus works with non-verbal information, and psychic information is usually non-verbal. It's also involved with producing the content of our dreams. Working together with other structures, it selects the images that appear in our dreams. It's characteristic output, theta waves, are also present when we're in twilight sleep. Twilight sleep is another time when images from the hippocampus can fill our minds, though they are usually somewhat disjointed and random compared with the images that fill our dreams.

This Buddhist tradition also says you can project an intention when you're in the void. The most common technique that I know of for this is a technique to put a thought in someone else's mind. You imagine the sound of their voice saying the thing that you want them to be thinking, while you're looking into the black space behind your eyelids. Unless there is some reason for them to resist it, those words will come to their consciousness. Several psychics have confirmed for me that it's a fairly normal technique and say that it will work even if the person is far away.

I used to do a simple parlor trick to illustrate this. I was having breakfast with a friend, and I said "I can make you say a word". He said, "Go ahead and try". I chose a word and imagined the sound of his voice saying that word. In that case, it was the word "Afghanistan". The word Afghanistan was still very much in the news, because the American war there had just broken out. So I wrote the word "Afghanistan" on a piece of paper, folded it up, stuck it in his pocket, reaching across the scrambled eggs to do so, and started imagining his voice saying the word "Afghanistan", while closing my eyes every few seconds to try to connect with *The Void*. At one point in the conversation he referred to a local shopkeeper, and he said, "The guy's Afghanistan. No, the guy is *from* Afghanistan" "He's *Afghani?*" I answered, and he replied, "That's it, he's Afghani". I told him to read the word on the paper in his pocket and when he took it out and read it, he was amazed. I had succeeded in putting the word in his consciousness. The reason why I chose that word was because, although it wasn't too common, it could still come up in a normal conversation. And it didn't have a religious, sexual, scientific or mathematical implication to it so that he would have no reason to over-react to it or resist it. If I used the word "polynomial" and he was one of those people who are convinced that he'll never learn math, I'd have failed.

Shared Psychic perceptions

There's a story I'd like to tell about another brain-to-brain event. As we saw from the discussion of the Octopus and it's 'around-the-head' stimulation, it's possible for information to be transmitted from one brain to another.

I had a girlfriend. The day came when she wanted to break up. Why, I can't possibly imagine, but she wanted to. She came over to my place and she said, "I don't want this relationship anymore. I'm getting another boyfriend". Actually, she used more words than that. I was upset about this, and went into a really bad state, not far from despair. She was upset, too. She wasn't completely sure she wanted to end the relationship. If I'd been nice enough to say "well, okay, its over. Bye. I need to go get a burrito now"; if I'd been that easy about it, it would've been easy for her. But it wasn't, and she got upset, too. Then something happened. It was as though we had both reached our limit for this bad mood at the same time and suddenly, I saw her head surrounded with a blue aura. I told her it was one of the most beautiful things I've ever seen. It was, too. She told me she was seeing the same thing around me, and said the she also found it beautiful. It wasn't a great relationship, but it was a magnificent moment. Something had happened, and our brains were sharing information. Our experience showed the pattern we've seen in other chapters. We both felt a very negative (dysphoric) emotion, followed by a positive experience. No doubt we were more prone to it because we were each actively doing spiritual practices at the time.

There was a case involving Shakti[608], a technology that's in the same family as the Octopus and God Helmet devices (both use complex magnetic fields), though much simpler. A woman had done a Shakti session[609] applying a signal derived from the amygdala over her temporal lobes. She had a six hour episode in which she saw auras around everybody. That day a group of people came to her home for a spiritual gathering. The others said they wanted to try it, so they did. They took turns, and one at a time, for 20 minutes each, everyone put on the headset using the same signal over the same area. They each went into the same state of consciousness, and had the same experience – strong aura vision.

Normally, this would be a very unlikely experience. With this class of technology, people usually have very individualized experiences - what you get is what *you* get. Another person gets what *they* get. You might see God, while someone else might get just a mood lift from the same stimulation. One would normally expect a wide range of responses. Yet here was a group of people who were all having the same experience one after the other. Most likely, they were each picking up the state that her brain was broadcasting (via its subtle magnetic fields), through something like sympathetic resonance[610]. Under its influence, they each went into the same experience. It was a spiritual group, and it's likely that they were more sensitive to altered states than most people. Other factors could have played a role. Of course, there haven't been any laboratory studies with groups of people, so no one really knows how common it could become.

Past Life Readings

Let's look at a couple of unlikely kinds of psychic readings. Past-life readings are a form of psychic reading that often inspires ridicule from skeptics and of course, those who don't believe in reincarnation. As with other kinds of psychic readings, just a few details about the person can be enough to intimate other times and places. An understanding of the person's emotional life and issues can suggest events encountered in their "past lives". These might be cases where the psychic actually accessed the person's past lives, but they could also be readings where the reader's sense of the person is accurate enough that they can unwittingly leave the subject with a story that's completely fabricated, yet still *feel* completely accurate. The reader may tell a person with anxiety issues that they lived through a very fearful situation in a past life. The character of their present fears might inspire a story that matches their present issues so accurately that the subject feels their fears are explained just by hearing it. The story could be a complete fabrication and yet can still be tremendously therapeutic.

The value of a past life story is not in its literal truth, but rather in how well it matches the circumstances of the person's present life. Being told that the cause of a dilemma in the present lies in a past life can help the person feel that they understand what's happening to them. Bruno Bettelheim, the folklorist, tells a story[611] about a child who had to go stay with his grandmother while his mother went to the hospital. Each night for about 10 days before she went to the hospital, the boy asked to hear the story of Rapunzel. The story, perhaps, worked with a theme that reflected the events in his life. It may have been the story's motif of the boy depending on the girl to make her hair, a "part of herself", available to the boy. It let him change his sense of the issue, and see his mother go into the hospital with a minimum of stress. The psychic, guided by their intuitive ability, might do exactly the same thing, with a past life story putting all the associations into a single context.

The hippocampus doesn't only put things into context; it also creates and retrieves memories. Its role in perceiving the past makes it easy for it to help create the feeling that the client's issues come from a past life. Because thinking of the past and the future activate different areas of the hippocampus[612] [613], it knows what the past *feels* like. It's involvement in a past life reading, whether veridical or not, can allow the psychic to choose to pay attention to perceptions that *feel* as though they come from the past. The same feeling could also help them avoid the ones that connote the present or anticipate the future.

Past-life readings may combine three of the hippocampus' functions. The first is where it accesses the guidelines for relating to others (our social, "executive" functions) through its extensive wiring to the frontal lobes. The second is where it obtains information from the past (through memory). The third is in its ability to find and create contexts for information of any kind. The first lets the reader see the person in front of them; inviting their intuition to dominate their thoughts. The second 'colors' their thoughts with a sense of the past. The third lets them 'find' a past-life, and an episode in it, that matches the issues their client is facing, like a knife matches the wound it makes. Like a dishonest detective, who can fabricate a knife to match any wound, the reading, real or not, will always match the issue.

Most past-life readers tell their clients that any issues that remain from past lives recur in the present, so that past-lives are never the only source of their problems. Resolving the issue, whatever it is, will involve "working it through" in the present. Such readings may be illusory, and have nothing to do with "actual" past lives, but they allow the clients to stop asking, "Why is this happening to me?", and helps move them towards finding ways to resolve their problems. The truth of the past-life story is separate from its value.

In our chapter on reincarnation, we arrived at the conclusion that past life information helps prepare us for social success by increasing our mating opportunities and the chances for our offspring grow to adulthood. Our karma divides our states of consciousness into two types; those to repeat, and those to avoid. The mechanism of reincarnation relies on preserving records of states of consciousness, not memories. This means we can't take it for granted that there are any such things as past life memories, but that doesn't mean they don't exist.

Medical Psychics

Medical psychics are very different from past-life readers. They work entirely in the present. Their unique skills allow them to look at someone, and 'feel' the nature of their illness. They can often have surprisingly accurate diagnoses to offer. At times, they have diagnosed illnesses which eluded mainstream doctors.

There is more than one kind of medical psychic. Some are essentially aura readers. They try to find problems in the person's body from the defects they see in the color or shape of the person's aura.

Some medical psychics are able to look at a person, and tell what's amiss intuitively, using a range of skills. One way this skill could happen through the right hippocampal ability to put large numbers of subtle observations into a single context. The way a person moves; the timbre of their voice; their posture; their body shape; the emotions they display; and a wide range of other factors all combine to allow a psychic to sense the nature of an illness. The clues medical psychics respond to may not be considered diagnostic markers by mainstream doctors, but this is only to be expected, as lab diagnostics are all quantifiable. Often, diagnostic signs from other paradigms are not (like Ayurvedic, Chinese, aboriginal, and Amish, to name only a few). In Chinese medicine, the pulses (there are five pulses in Chinese medicine) and an examination of the tongue are a guide to diagnosis. Some chiropractors use muscle testing to look into their client's problems, a technique which many ordinary doctors dismiss as quackery.

The holistic approach to medicine maintains that each illness affects the whole body, including its many systems. This paradigm includes the belief that there are a wide range of potential diagnostic signs that are unknown to mainstream medicine. Taking many such signs and putting them together into a single context is a job for the right hippocampus, the brain's contextualization engine for nonverbal information, and the limbic area most heavily implicated in psychic perceptions.

Aura Vision

The human aura may be a field of energy that surrounds the body which physics has yet to detect. However, it could also be something that exists only in the minds of those seeing it. In either case, only some people see auras, and that implies that it may be more a matter of who's doing the seeing, than of what's being seen. It doesn't matter whether auras are 'real'. It's more important that there is a real difference between the brains of those who see them, and those who don't, and that seeing auras is a useful skill. To claim that the human body is surrounded by an energy field or the body is emitting energies is to make a claim in physics. Remaining within the bounds of consensual science means that we should choose explanations that don't call for the laws of physics to be re-written.

Seeing auras is a skill (or function) that goes outside the limbic system. In the organization of the brain, it is below (or *prior* to) the amygdala, hippocampus, caudate nucleus and other limbic structures. Stimulation of the pulvinar nucleus of the thalamus has elicited aura vision in laboratory settings[614]. The thalamus gathers input from all our senses, and then organizes it all to form a coherent whole. The pulvinar, located at the back of the thalamus, lies on one of crucial visual pathways. Spiritual pathways extend out of the limbic system and include areas on the surface of the brain, above the limbic system. They can also include areas below it.

Aura vision could involve a distortion in our perception of the edges of objects around us. Our brains have specialized visual processes that perceive only the edges of objects, including other living things. Some people who see auras say that *everything* has one. Others say that they are unique to living things. Auras may exist around people, and only some perceive them, or they may exist only in the minds of those few who see them. In either case, an advanced aura reader can often read the state of a person's emotions, health, intelligence, and many other qualities. These are nonverbal perceptions, and this implicates the right hippocampus as its source in the limbic system.

Some skeptics reject the idea of aura vision outright, and speak as though such perceptions have no value. This view neglects the possibility that they are hallucinatory, but guided by valid perceptions.

It's not impossible that auras are hallucinations that summarize a person's mental and physical health. Like the sense of self, or perceptions of God's presence, it could be an *adaptive* hallucination. A few individuals with this trait could be of real value to their social group.

Developing Psychic skills

To finish this discussion of psychic skills, I'd like to offer a bit of practical instruction for those of you who want to develop them. We need to look at two brain structures the amygdala and the hippocampus - again. These two structures work very closely together. It's not just that they're connected by a bunch of nerve fibers, they're actually inter-grown. They have an intimate relationship with one another. Thoughts (hippocampus) can trigger emotions (amygdala), and emotions inspire thoughts. When one of them is extremely excited, the other tends to be quiet. They work in a kind of see-saw (*antagonistic*) relationship, each one continually inviting the other to take the top position. They don't always accept the invitation, but they're always capable of doing it. When some people do math, they can achieve cognitive *states* so focused that nothing appears in their minds but calculus. Others can attain emotional *states* so deep that everything is driven from their awareness except joy, fear or anger. One of the traditional teachings about how to acquire psychic skills is that emotions (usually, but not always) interfere with psychic perceptions. Emotions can crowd out psychic perceptions the way emotions tend to interfere with intellectual tasks in our normal daily lives.

Having used the Shiva device in its Octopus configuration, it's easy for me to know who's calling when the phone rings, like my mother, brother, or a friend. But when there's a call from someone with really bad news or a call with really good news, I usually won't know about it. If it's someone I really want to hear from and the phone rings, I'll usually guess it wrong. My desire to talk to them can be strong enough to prevent the calm that allow psychic perceptions to come through.

I'm sometimes asked how people can develop psychic perceptions. There are many answers for this question, and my opinions are just that – opinions. It seems to me that psychic perceptions are responses to events. When an event occurs, your mind; your brain, will produce a large number of responses to it, but you won't be aware of most of them. When something happens, one of the first responses could be a bit of information from inside your mind; an image or picture, a thought, a flash of music that reminds you of something, a phrase, or even a smell. It could be anything. Your very first, *instantaneous* response to the event, whatever it is, will constitute the psychic response to it. If it's a smell or a bit of music, you may have to interpret it, but if you want to develop psychic skills, it's worth paying attention to that perception, whatever it is,

What sets the psychic apart from others may only be that the psychic pays attention, knowing that their immediate, instant response *is* their psychic perception. The psychic doesn't move on to process their instant responses through the lens of their emotional habits or their default ways of thinking. The binding factor, which I take to mean a 'factor' that 'binds' us to our usual states of consciousnesses, either doesn't bind psychic perceptions to an habituated *state*, or it binds them to states the person developed while cultivating their psychic skills. There are a few people who have a more direct access to their psychic perceptions. For them, psychic states of consciousness (in which these immediate perceptions last longer, or perhaps remembered longer), *are* some of their normal states.

One might wonder how fast a psychic perception is. If someone isn't psychic already, and their psychic perceptions are subconscious, then the length of time the psychic perception is available for direct perception is probably about 25 milliseconds, or one fortieth of a second, because that's how long the binding factor takes to go through the brain. Developing psychic skills may well be nothing more than developing very close attention to fleeting information "from within", or learning to remember it as soon as it happens. That time might be longer if they're a psychic already.

I'd like to tell the story of how I actually learned what psychic perceptions were. There's a saying in the samurai arts that if you want to be a master swordsman, your sword must move as the flint flies from the steel. The flint hits the steel with a spark. There is no interval, no gap whatsoever, between striking the flint to the steel and the appearance of a spark. It's instantaneous – with no intervening stages of any kind. There is also no gap whatsoever between our perception of a thing, and the production of our psychic response to it (assuming that thing sparks a psychic perception).

I was visiting someone who had just moved into a new apartment; one they really liked. It was perfect for them. Actually, it was *almost* perfect. They said that there was only one thing they missed about their last home. As soon as they said the words: "there *is* one thing I miss here", I saw an image of fireworks in my mind, and I said "fireworks?" They said, "right, but how could you know that?" she told me that in her last home, there had been a small barbecue made of bricks set on the ground. She would sit in front of it, throw colored bath salts into a fire and the dye would ignite and give her different colored sparks. This was a kind of private devotional ritual for her. She was absolutely stunned, "how did you know that?" I said, "Well, when you said, you missed one thing here; I got an image of fireworks, so I said 'fireworks'".

That was the moment when I understood how to develop psychic skills. The responses from the hippocampus on the right won't be verbal, but they're still thoughts. The hippocampus on the right – away from the language centers on the left – responds to events with enormous speed. It doesn't need time to find the right words. The amygdala, with its emotional functions, responds even faster than the hippocampus, and can crowd out its responses, coloring events with emotion.

We experience an event. Is it a blessing or is it a curse? Is it a threat or can we benefit from it in some way? We immediately interpret events in terms of how they seem to affect us personally. What does this mean *to me*? The question that psychic perceptions answer is not *what does it mean to me* but rather *what is it*? As soon as you take it personally, you change it. Usually the amygdala, with it's slightly lower thresholds, will respond to things more readily than the hippocampus, and it may well be that psychic skills involve holding back responses from either amygdala long enough to allow us to be conscious of information from the right hippocampus. In other words, being psychic may mean staying detached from our immediate emotional responses long enough to see our cognitive ones.

Another question I hear regularly is: "can anyone be psychic?" The answer is yes, but not everyone will have the same challenges in developing such skills. If you're a heavily emotional person; if your emotions always respond first; if you feel you *are* your emotions, then you may have a harder time developing psychic perceptions, as emotional responses can quickly 'crowd out' the inner perceptions that inspire them. It may be a bit easier if you feel that you *are* your thoughts. If you're prone to feeling that your true identity lies with those thoughts that can't be expressed in words, then it gets easier still. If you feel deeply that *you* are something that cannot be expressed in words, then you'll have an even easier time. Of course, this is an over-simplification. Most people don't have just *one* feeling about who they are, and such feelings are often illusory "ego-trips".

We personalize our responses to things almost as soon as they appear, and this seems to interfere with psychic perceptions. We can agree with one of those traditional teachings from psychic teachers, and that's the role of the *ego*; the sense of self-importance. The feeling that a psychic perception is *important* because it came to *you* must be abandoned. What it *means* isn't important. It is, as some Buddhist teachers have called it, a matter of *tathata;* a matter of 'suchness'. *It is what it is.* Self-importance can interfere with psychic perceptions, because it provides a motivation to *demand* that psychic perceptions appear. It can also encourage psychics to want others to lend importance to their psychic perceptions, and make it easier for psychics to over-interpret them.

Developing psychic skills means learning to be dispassionate about our own perceptions. To be a successful psychic, you have to abandon the sense that your emotions are important. Anything that helps to develop equanimity, like meditation, can help.

Some psychics wish they could shut down their abilities a little. They would like to have a rheostat with settings for low, medium and high. They like it on high when doing psychic readings, but would like to turn it to medium most of the time, and turn it down to a low setting when they're with people they don't like. Unfortunately for them, there's no such switch, although I have heard that fatty foods can help. Once I even heard that McDonald's French fries was the best food for 'grounding'. I've heard of stranger things.

Developing psychic skills takes time, and paradoxically, the very desire to be psychic can itself be a sign that one may not have the aptitude.

CHAPTER 15

Prayer

"Lord, Hear my prayer." "On the back of Brother Eagle, I send a voice - that the people may live." "Homage to Him, the Blessed, the Exalted and the Fully Enlightened One." "Aum, I invoke the name of Shiva (Om Namah Shivaya)".

How prayer works

Prayer is the most widespread spiritual practice in the world. As we saw in earlier chapters, there is a neural basis for the experience of God, and for feeling the sense of a presence, whether it's God's presence or some kind of 'spirit being'. It happens when the senses of self in each side of the brain have too much or too little communication with each other, and the sense of self from the right hemisphere is directly perceived by the one on the left. When this happens, the right hemispheric self is felt as a spirit, being, entity or presence appearing outside the body.

Any technique that encourages the experience of a non-physical entity, most importantly, that of God's presence, will also tend to interrupt communication between the self on each side of the brain. The right hemispheric sense of self has access to the nonverbal right hippocampus, a structure that takes information from our memories and finds new contexts for them, as well as "scanning" them for things that remind it of anything happening in the present. Whether God exists only in our brains, or whether he exists outside of us, and communicates with us through our brains, the wisdom and insights that we can access through prayer reflect our life experience. In other words, no matter where God comes from, there are limits on our ability to perceive Him and "His will". At the same time, because right hemispheric information is far more subtle and complex than the information supported by the left hemisphere[615], the right brain's sense of self has access to huge amounts of information, and an ability to put it together in new ways, that the left hemisphere lacks. It's as though "we" (the left-brain 'self') are humbled by our own right hemispheric abilities, just as we might be when confronted with God, as we understand Him.

When we "pause" the left hemispheric sense of self's control over it's counterpart on the right, the right hemisphere is freed from the usual constraints language imposes on the way we think and feel. We are a linguistic species, and speech is a linear phenomena. When we're talking, we can only say one word at a time. When we're thinking of what we want to say, or gathering our thoughts while we're speaking, we gather one lump of information at a time[616]. Right hemispheric information can have a great deal more depth and subtlety than it does on the left. For example, harmony and counterpoint in music can be extremely complex, but such music will only sound right when everything is in place. You can immediately hear the difference when a harmonic structure is broken or when the counterpoint in a Bach fugue isn't played right. When we look at a picture, we can see details, one at a time, but we can also see the whole.

Prayer seems to be a process of trying to deliberately induce a visitor experience, where the left and right "self" work independently. The more excited the working pathways are, more powerful the experience. On the other hand (in principle), it should become *deeper* as communication between the two senses of self dwindles. Some people even become lost in prayer. Classical religious traditions might tell you that you are "getting out of your own way", as you feel God's presence more intimately, and also as your self on the right becomes more independent. Maybe, just maybe, it's possible to identify with the right hemispheric sense of self, and so achieve the Unio Mystica (mystic union) with God.

When the right hemispheric sense of self is free to operate on its own, it can learn new things from its database of memories and associations, combining them in new (non-linear) ways, and finding new contexts for them. Letting the self on the right side of the brain operate on its own taps a specific kind of creativity. It can happen naturally in dreams. If something is going on in your life, and you dream about it, you may wake up to find that you had different feelings about it. You might not have gotten any new ideas, but you may be more able to make a choice between the options you had before you went to bed. You "sleep on the problem", and it seems to change, even if only a little bit. It's hard to put a scientific name on "insight" of this kind, but I would be surprised if any but the most recalcitrant skeptical scientists didn't believe it existed.

I suggest that prayer accesses the same kind of creativity that chooses the content of our dreams. I'm *not* saying that prayer is a kind of dreaming; only that prayer and dreams have some cognitive skills in common. These may work differently in prayer than they do in dreams, but at the same time, dreams are often incomprehensible. The things we pray for, and the thoughts that come to us while we're praying, are usually quite clear, especially for people who've been praying for a long time. When we pray to God to help us with a problem, we're also focusing on our need to find a solution. Because the right side of the brain is more adept at problem solving, prayer can be a way for the left hemisphere to ask the right hemisphere for help. Because the right hemisphere knows more than the left, it's happy to oblige. If there is an actual God who comes to us through our right hemisphere, then this process provides him with a ready point of entry. "He" could commandeer the *sensed presence* experience and make it his own. People who believe in God might say that God's ability to contact us has no limits, but very few will say that we are all equally able to contact him. They might say we all have the potential for a rich prayer life, but developing it will be more challenging for some people.

Scientific studies on the effects of Praying for Others

Prayer has two kinds of effects. One is what it does for the people who pray, and the other is what it can do for the people we pray for. Over the last ten years, there have been many studies examining its clinical effects. These have been controversial, and they've shown very different results. In one case, people who knew others were praying for them even had "significantly *more* post operative complications than those not receiving prayer"[617].

Other studies concluded that prayer had no effect. One of these studies said that "prayer from a distance does not appear to improve selected clinical outcomes in HIV patients who are on a combination antiretroviral therapy[618]." Another study that looked at the effects of prayer on patients after heart surgery, found that intercessory prayer (prayers to intercede for someone) had "no significant effect[619]". There have been other studies with the same results. These have been skeptical studies, and many of them were designed to try to prove that prayer is useless.

Is Prayer *ineffective*? To find out, you can do a scientific experiment. Find people to pray, and find people for them to pray for. To make sure that the experiment is objective, and to make sure the people praying aren't prejudiced for or against the people they pray for, you put the patients they're praying for into random groups. Then, you assume that the people who are praying in your experiment are more willing to follow your protocols than their sense of what God wants them to do. Anyone with a well developed prayer life (and so, likely to be capable of 'more effective' prayer) will follow what they feel God wants from them, and not what a scientist tells them to do. If the people doing the praying speak to God as they usually do, they would not allow the protocol to influence their choice of words. Praying that God will help 'those people suffering from HIV infection at the Hospital' would not exclude the control group, and no one will pray that God ignore the control subjects. The prayer 'Lord, don't help the control subjects at all' would be unthinkable to anyone whose religion teaches compassion.

An intelligent and compassionate person would pray for the control group, too – and to hell with the protocols. Finally, you make sure that the people who are praying and the people they're praying for have no contact with each other. What kind of results will you get from this? Of course, you'll prove scientifically that prayer doesn't work. You'd be assuming that prayer can be studied as though it were just another drug, with randomized and placebo controlled protocols. This view has been criticized, even in the medical journals[620]. If effective prayer demands a good "set and setting", then randomized, 'blind', and controlled studies are doomed to fail. If you want to do a *really* rigorous scientific study, you can also slant your own results (so that other scientists won't laugh at you) to prove that prayer doesn't work by trying to control *how* people pray for others. You can do this by assigning a prayer, such as the Our Father, the Gayatri Mantra, or the Kaddish to the people who are praying, and then demand that they obey your experimental protocols. However, you might also be criticized if you do this. One scientific study has already found that a group of students who were praying for others "did not consider *reading* the prayer could constitute praying[621]" (emphasis ours). In other words, you'd have to give the people doing the praying the freedom to pray as they wish, and that's a terrible scientific protocol. On the other hand, trying to control the way people pray makes for terrible prayer.

It may be that no existing scientific method is really up to the job of studying intercessory prayer. New methods will have to be applied. The use of comparison groups, double–blind protocols, controlled laboratory conditions and placebos might hide the truth instead of revealing it.

Looking for results from prayer experiments designed to avoid contamination of the data is a bit like telling someone who says they're psychic "If you're psychic, then you should know who's going to win the next World Series." A skeptic will look for tests that are most likely to *fail*, or that are based on an atheist's naive idea of what they think prayer is supposed to be. If you study psychic perceptions, and believe that they have even a little validity, you'll choose methods to help make it clear how it works. In other words, by treating prayer as though it were a chemical drug, scientists miss the point, which may well include the brain-to-brain communication we looked at earlier.

When prayer studies aren't 'blind'

The results are very different when the people who're praying know the people they're praying for, even if only from a picture. In one such study, the people receiving the prayers had anxiety and depression. The people "sending" the prayers had pictures of the people they were praying for. They also knew their names. In that study, the patients showed "significant improvements" shown by eleven measures of mental well-being[622]. The people who were praying also showed improvement in their mental health, as shown in ten of the measures.

In another study with depression and anxiety[623], the people weren't just prayed for; they had direct contact with the people who were praying for them. In fact, they had weekly hour-long prayer sessions. The patients who received the prayers showed "significant improvements in depression and anxiety, as well as increases of daily spiritual experiences and optimism, compared to the controls". One could claim that prayer is an effective type of psychotherapy, but this would agree with the belief that prayer "has power". It's possible that brain-to-brain communication is already a feature of prayer and psychotherapy sessions are also a context for it.

One might think that prayer was only effective for psychiatric disorders, but not physical problems. In a study of the effects of prayer on patients with bloodstream infections, where the ones who were praying only knew the first names of the people they were praying for, both the length of the patient's stay in the hospital, and the duration of their fevers were significantly shorter then the ones in the control group[624]. By making sure that the people who prayed for the patients knew who they were praying for, the chances that they would pray for the control group was reduced. Even then, they could only pray for the control group as a whole, because they didn't know the names of the people in the control groups.

One very interesting result in prayer studies[625] found that injured Bush babies (a kind of lemur), recovered from their wounds much more quickly, and showed more healthy social behavior (grooming) when people were praying for them. The research report suggested that intercessory prayer experiments with humans might have confounds; factors that confuse the results. One obvious suggestion is that there is brain-to-brain communication happening between the people who were praying and the ones they're praying for, which we looked at in the chapter on psychic skills. One might suppose that other social species, like other primates, have more of these non-verbal communication skills than we do. It's possible that language skills supplanted some of our psychic skills when we acquired the ability to speak. Of course, this is speculation, but it does help to explain why prayer seems to be more effective for Bush babies than it is for people. It's a very intriguing result. If other scientists follow up on it, they might also make discoveries about prayer, brain–to–brain communication, and perhaps shed new light on the origins of Homo Sapiens.

One study[626] commented that "when bacteria are prayed for, they tend to grow faster; when seeds are prayed for, they tend to germinate quicker; when wounded mice are prayed for, they tend to heal faster." … "Mice, seeds, and microbes presumably do not think positively." It may be, however, that thinking positively is less important than not thinking negatively. The "power of positive thinking" has commanded so much attention that the "power" of avoiding negative thinking has been neglected, at least by scientists who try to investigate spirituality.

It looks like prayer has effects on illness, both mental and physical, when the prayers are for individuals, and not anonymous groups of randomized subjects. Praying for people at random doesn't seem to work very well. One study actually assigned people to pray for patients they knew only as a case number[627] ("Lord, please help case number 108"), and found no effect. But then, that's not how people pray for others naturally. Usually, it's for people they know personally. Parents pray for their children. Family members pray for the one who is ill, or in trouble. When Japan is hit by an earthquake, we might pray for its people, but if you *know* someone there, you will pray for *them*. You might even have faith that your prayers will help the rest of the country, too. Our most heartfelt prayers are for people who mean something to us.

Prayer and Coping

A great deal of media attention has been given to the studies of prayer in which one group of people prayed for another group of people. In point of fact, there are more studies on the effects of prayer when people pray for themselves. In short, these studies have found that prayer is an effective means of coping with health troubles. One study[628] found that prayer was significantly related with pain tolerance (remember that the right amygdala is involved in pain). The same study also found a moderate relationship between prayer and the severity of pain. In other words, people who prayed were less bothered by their pain, and their pain was a little less severe than that of those who didn't pray about it.

One interesting study[629] found that patients with severe head injuries who received prayer stayed in the hospital longer, but those patients who were in the habit of praying for themselves actually recovered better. Very few studies of the effects of prayer took note of whether or not the people who received prayer had a prayer life of their own.

Another study[630] looked at how often patients with advanced cancer thought of committing suicide. The study found that these patients fit the criteria for posttraumatic stress disorder, and that the ones who reported suicidal thoughts were more likely to lack a religious affiliation. Presumably, this means they did not pray very much, although there could be exceptions.

Still another study[631] found that heart surgery patients who prayed had fewer symptoms related to postoperative stress. Another research report[632] found that the most effective ways of coping with having a critically ill person in their family included talking the problem over with friends, and praying. Still another study[633] found that prayer, as understood by American Indians, was a powerful way to cope with the stress of hemodialysis.

Yet another study of this type looked at several factors that could affect people with PTSD after Hurricane Katrina in New Orleans, most importantly, how much time they spend watching television to see the latest news, and prayer. Prayer was associated with a decrease in PTSD symptoms[634] keeping up with the news (presumably including news about relief efforts) didn't help at all.

A further study[635] compared the relationship between children's prayer habits and their levels of stress and health behaviors. Prayer was found to be associated with social connectedness and a sense of humor. The same study found children who prayed often had more positive health habits, like eating balanced meals and brushing their teeth, and exercising. However, the same study also found kids who prayed suffered the same stress as those who did not.

Yet another study tried to analyze the psychological processes through which prayer contributes to better health. After surveying over almost 800 Catholic Mexican-Americans, the researchers found that a *belief* in prayer led to doing it more frequently. This was associated with a stronger belief that God mediates one's state of health. This, in turn, led to more optimism, and that led to a better perception of their own health[636].

You Gotta Believe! – or– leave your skepticism at the door

One study[637] looked at Christians who attended prayer meetings led by charismatic Christian ministers. It found that one area of the brain, the *ventral medial prefrontal cortex*, was much more likely to be deactivated in the subjects who believed the speakers had healing powers. Another study[638] found that this same area is activated when people hear statements they believe, whether the statements are religious or not. In other words, it looks like there may be a difference between religious belief, and religious faith; the *sense* that one is hearing the truth, and not intellectual agreement. It may be that faith involves both disconnecting from one's beliefs as well as suspending *disbelief*. Belief (as we use the word here) is intellectual, while faith is not. To use a metaphor, it's like the difference between *feeling* that we should take care of the people we love, and *thinking* that we should show some responsibility towards their needs. The *feeling* of love that inspires us to take care of them is more akin to faith. Extending the metaphor a little further, let's say that wondering "is this really love?" makes it harder to feel it. Skepticism toward your own romantic feelings tends to corrupt them.

In other words, religious faith is not a matter of *thinking* something, but rather has to do with the *feeling* that it's true. In order to have either religious or romantic faith, you have to avoid critical thinking about it; you need to avoid finding fault with it. You have to stop choosing between "true" and "false". Trying to measure the validity of someone's faith by looking at the truth (or lack of it) of their beliefs is like trying to persuade a patient who seems healthy that they are not in any pain. If a patient says they experience pain, then they almost certainly are.

Science may seem to be a source of truth, but today's theories are tomorrow's history. Some theories, like the theory of evolution, look like they will stand for a long time, but even they become so embellished with additions and re-statements of their fundamental principles that, over time, they become almost unrecognizable to the people who learned them while they were still new. There is no final truth in science. Facts may be true, but the theories and hypotheses that interpret these facts are eventually replaced. Nevertheless, there are skeptics for whom scientific truth becomes almost a religion. Such people will argue in favor of their beliefs, ignoring the fact that they are temporary, and disdain ideas they disagree with, with the same passion as a devout religious believer.

Belief and disbelief

Interestingly, there are also areas of the brain that are known to be associated with disbelief.

> "The areas especially engaged in disbelief included the limbic systems cingulate gyrus and the anterior insula, a brain region known to report visceral sensations such as pain and disgust and to be involved largely negative appraisals of sensations like taste and smell[639]."

Active skepticism and hatred of religion both act out an emotional response to conflicting beliefs. The religious believer who is offended when presented with ideas they find blasphemous has the same motivation as a skeptic who is offended when they think something is untrue. I once asked an active skeptic why the idea of life after death made him so angry. He answered me saying "because it's bullshit". I asked him why "bullshit" made him angry and they said he didn't like to see people led away from the truth. I asked him why seeing people departing from the truth made him angry, but he had no other answer than the one he had already given. It's an emotional response. Hatred or disgust toward (what *you* think is) nonsense has nothing to do with the "love of truth". The skeptical atheist who is offended by religious belief is no different than the committed Christian who is offended by other religions. Someone who simply doesn't believe won't be angry when they're presented with ideas they disagree with, and that reminds me of a joke:

"What's an agnostic?"

"I don't know – what's an agnostic?"

"An agnostic is someone who doesn't know if there is a God, – and doesn't think that you know, either."

Skepticism is important in science. Without it, scientists working to support specific theories would be less careful, and errors would creep in more easily. But scientists are often a bit naive about religion, and often miss the distinction between the ideas religions are based on, and the moods it creates. These moods are important for maintaining effective ways to cope with the stress everyone encounters as they go through life. Prayer, religion, and faith make life easier. Its been said that skeptics are only good at tearing down ideas they don't like, and are often not much good at building up ideas of their own. Skepticism does not offer a fertile field for creativity. On the other hand, faith concerns a person's own place in the world, their sense of their destiny, as well as the meaning of their life. It requires creativity. Not surprisingly, Persinger found that several kinds of creativity are more likely to appear in people with religious, paranormal, and spiritual beliefs.

If you meet a skeptic, and find yourself getting into a conversation about spirituality with them, pay close attention to their emotional state. If ideas they disagree with seem to make them angry, then don't bother trying to persuade them that yours are valid. You will never succeed, anymore than you will persuade a fundamentalist Christian that other religions aren't "tools of Satan". Fundamentalism is found in both religion and in science, and it's equally destructive in both places.

The Experience of Praying

In many forms of prayer, such as contemplative prayer, feeling the presence of the deity is considered a deeper, better, or "higher", way. If the right–sided self is completely separated from its partner on the left, we might feel ourselves in the presence of God. Many people really feel God is with them when they pray. If so, then they are in the presence of a very wise being. They are, too; their own right hemispheric self. God isn't always nice company. Many have felt that God was angry or disappointed with them. The experience can be very unpleasant. Even when someone is told that their sins are forgiven, their own personal sense of guilt can still color their prayers. However, although I have heard stories of people who felt that God did not love them in the moment they were praying, I have never heard anyone say that they didn't feel that God was either infinitely wise, or much, much wiser than they were. God is believed to be all-knowing, and the (right hippocampal) experience of deeper prayer seems to buttress this belief.

Because the right hemispheric sense of self has its own type of intelligence and insight, inducing God's presence through prayer opens a reservoir of wisdom: those based on right hemispheric cognitive skills.

It can happen that people intending to pray for one thing as they plan their prayers, find themselves praying for something slightly different. Sometimes they just can't remember what they had planned to pray for. Nonverbal thoughts, with their extra ability to see the connections between things, and their implications for each other, may find a prayer to be unreasonable, or at least very difficult to resolve. Some people pray that they will win the lottery. If you believe in the power of prayer so strongly that you pray for improbable things to happen, you may find that your prayers lack depth. Our own right hemispheric knowledge does us the most good when we pray for the things that are within our experience. Winning the lottery isn't something many people know first-hand.

Are Prayers Answered?

Another question is whether praying for something makes it more likely to happen. People who believe in God insist that their prayers are answered very often.

As we saw above, prayers for medical cures seem to be more effective when the people know the ones they're praying for. When we pray for other people, or pray about our relationships with them, or about problems we have with them, we usually have some sense of their presence, even if it's a faint one. We know "who they are"; apart from their appearance, the sound of their voice, or the way they carry themselves.

As we saw in the chapter on psychic skills, brain-to-brain communications may be a normal feature of our species. Our prayers for others (or about them) may have a chance to influence their behavior and increase the possibility that they will act in concert with our prayers. If we consistently pray that a friend who is in trouble receives some money, we could actually influence their brain, their dreams, and their behavior so that they have a greater chance of leading themselves towards it.

When we pray for ourselves, we may really increase our own chances for finding solutions to the problems we pray about. When we pray about others, there is a chance we actually influence their behavior.

As we've seen, there are benefits to prayer whether or not there is a God to pray to. It helps us cope with times of trouble, it may help with health and life issues, and it may help us to act in ways that benefit us. Prayer may be effective by eliciting subtle changes in the way we behave. It may help others by taking advantage of the human capacity for brain-to-brain communication. In other words, we can see benefits to prayer that have nothing to do with God's existence or nonexistence. The problem is that if you don't believe in God, you may short-circuit the mechanisms of prayer. Not by failing to think positively about it, but rather by thinking about it negatively. Prayer is a skill, and just as the belief in one's own weakness makes it impossible to become an athlete, or believing that you can't dance can make you clumsy, believing that prayer is pointless will put you in a mood that will prevent the mechanism behind the *sensed presence* from working, as well as cutting off the right hemisphere's cognitive and psychic skills.

How to Pray – a guide for atheists

I believe that the capacity for prayer is part of our evolutionary heritage. It forms a "backup" cognitive style that allows us to find solutions to problems that don't lend themselves to our ordinary ways of thinking, and this is why we find it in every culture without exception.

Feeling God's presence may depend on a specific brain process, but that process only works when we feel that God exists outside ourselves. If you try to pray believing that God exists in your own brain, you're praying to yourself, and that doesn't seem to work very well. In fact, I've never met a single person who did it ("I pray to myself" is absurd in all religious traditions). God may appear in or through the right hemisphere, and just as the sense of self on the right side of the brain can be experienced as a being or presence outside of ourselves, we can access our capacity for insight through prayer, but only if we feel that God exists outside of ourselves. Intellectual belief in God is quite another matter.

There are good reasons to pray, as we saw above, but prayer is usually predicated on a belief in a God who exists outside ourselves. So if you can see the benefit of prayer, but don't believe in God, then you are left with *pretending* that there is a God, and indulging that pretension until it becomes a *sense* of God's existence. Not a belief. If you don't believe in God, but you want to experiment with prayer, start by recognizing that the sense of God's existence is separate from belief. Belief is not the same as faith.

The idea that the universe was created by a single entity, who now watches over you, along with each and every other person on this earth, is hard to accept. On the other hand, the idea that there aren't any spirit beings who hear our prayers contradicts ordinary human experience, which leaves us feeling moved by the presence of others, even if the only exist in our imagination.

I believe atheism runs outside of our evolutionary programming, which is not designed to help us know the truth, but rather behave in adaptive ways. I've read atheists saying that pretending to believe in God is intellectually dishonest, and that you shouldn't do it in order to avoid "cognitive dissonance" (a favorite atheist phrase) when reality doesn't match the points of your faith. Suppose there were a God, after all. The difference between his choices and ours, as well as his nature and our ability to understand it, does indeed cause cognitive dissonance. But, the same cognitive dissonance will be waiting for you even if you don't believe in God, when you look at the difference between the life you have, and the one you'd like to have.

We can't escape the often uncomfortable differences between our desires and the world, but I suggest that the cognitive tools our evolutionary history has provided most people include prayer, making life easier and less stressful, though to be sure, not everyone is equally prone to the desire to pray. Some people see faces (and the occasional rabbit) in the clouds, and others don't.

The way to pray for atheists begins with accepting that one's feelings aren't always supposed to match one's beliefs. Someone asked Candice Pert, the discoverer of opiate receptors in the brain, if she believed in God. Her answer[640] was "Yes, I believe in God. I'm a member of a species that believes in God". As a scientist, she probably was an atheist, or at least unwilling to try to persuade the scientific community to believe in God along with her. However, her belief in God, while not scientific in itself, was based on sound scientific reasoning.

"…when you give alms, let not your left hand know what your right hand does.[641]" This saying of Jesus cuts to the heart of this idea. When you're being generous, do what you must do, but don't tell yourself what a charitable person you are. Allow a gap between your understanding and your experience of yourself. If you're an atheist, and you want to pray, even to see what it's like, cultivate a sense of a presence, ignoring whether or not it's not real. Let this book be "Mister Book".

"Men turned to stone when they ceased to believe
in the beauty of the impossible" - *Arabian Nights.*

The realism of skeptical atheists is based on the notion that knowing the truth is more important than finding adaptive responses to our life circumstances. I am not among them. I believe that it's best to refer to objective truth when you're doing science, law, or mathematics. In many other circumstances, an unfettered sense of subjective truth can be far better. Imagination is a desirable quality, and it's more available when we forget literal truth. Prayer is as much a mood as a "cognitive strategy".

I don't suggest that anyone who doesn't believe in God change their ideas. I suggest that people who don't believe in God *pretend* that there is a being in the room with them, and that being *is only described* as a manifestation of the God that actually exists within the right hemispheric sense of self, in certain circumstances. One should pretend the *feeling*, not the belief. If you're an atheist, and you choose to undertake such an experiment, and someone asks you why you have a statue of the Virgin Mary or the God Shiva, you can answer that you use it as a focus for your imagination.

When you pray, you need to use your own words. The classical prayer recitations are only useful as prayers when one is mindful of the meaning of the words. If the prayer a short, and repeated enough, it becomes a mantra. Chanting is a good spiritual practice, but it's not the same as prayer. On the other hand, faced with a being that your guts, if not your mind, tells you is God, "Which maketh Arcturus, Orion, and Pleiades, and the chambers of the south[642]" can be a little intimidating. So, many religious traditions combine one's own words with chants. In Hinduism and popular Buddhism, there is the practice of chanting briefly before making ritual offerings of things like candles, incense, flowers, and devotional songs. In Catholicism, there is the practice of saying novenas. These are formal prayers in which there is a specific section where one states there intentions or prayer requests. For an example, let's look at the novena for St. Philomena. She is a Catholic saint known only by the discovery of her remains in the early 19th century. Her tomb was marked by a lily, arrows, an anchor and a lance, iconography that suggests that she died as a martyr and a virgin. Later on, a few mystics claimed to have had revelations about her, filling out the cult that surrounded her with a biography. Her novena is printed as follows:

Statue of St. Philomena, Germany[643]

Prayer to St. Philomena

"Illustrious virgin and martyr, St. Philomena, behold me kneeling in spirit before the throne on which it has pleased the most holy Trinity to place thee. Full of confidence in thy protection, I beseech thee to intercede for me with God. From the height of thy heavenly country, deign to cast a look upon thy humble servant. Spouse of Jesus Christ, console me in my troubles, strengthen me in temptations, protect me in the dangers which surround me on every side; obtain all the graces necessary for me, especially [*here mention your particular intention*], and above all, assist me at my death. Amen."

In this prayer, traditionally said once a day for nine days, there is a mix of formal words and those of one's own choosing. The formal words, when spoken mindfully, help to establish a prayerful mood. It doesn't need to be a very long prayer to help someone shift their mood. A few sentences are enough. Some traditional American Indian prayers begin with the ritual words: "On the back of brother Eagle, I send a voice; that people may live." A small amount of ritual can help get one get started praying. The Lord's Prayer, the Hail Mary, reciting a mantra a few times, or any other sacred words can demarcate the beginning and the end of prayer. In between the first words, and the final "Amen", there is a short time which is supposed to be held sacred.

Another way of helping prayer along is to follow a specific structure. For example, in several religious traditions, prayers follow the ritual sequence of first praying your thanks for all the good things that have happened to you. After that, you pray for other people, and ask that the creator of the universe, or the Great Spirit, or one's chosen deity help them. After that, you pray for yourself and your own needs. Praying with a structure like this means that you always know what you're about to pray for, and you don't have to think about it very much before you begin. It also means that you try to deliberately think of things that inspire gratitude and compassion for others before you pray for yourself.

You should slowly be able to cultivate a sense of the presence of the deity you're praying to as the practice develops. It may be something like deliberately creating an "invisible friend". Usually, children are better at that than adults are, but I think it may be because adults resist the process more than children do, at least in our present modern and scientific age.

In closing this chapter, I would like to restate my position. I am an atheist who prays. By extension, I'm an atheist with faith in God (or the Gods). Intellectually, I understand that the God of my prayers is an expression of my own right hemispheric sense of self. As a point of faith, I understand that this, my own personal God, is a presence I *sense*. Thus, logically, I do believe in God – except that I don't. Sometimes it's vague, and sometimes it's clear. My prayer life is fraught with contradictions, but I believe I am explicit enough here not to be considered a hypocrite. My beliefs and feelings contradict each other, and I think that's the way it's supposed to be, because humans did not evolve for truth, but rather for survival, and letting go of stress feels good. It helps people survive. I believe that's why our evolutionary strategy has made prayer a part of what makes us human. Not everyone is the same, and some people will never be drawn to pray whether they think there's a God or not. At the other end of the same spectrum, there will be people who feel they simply cannot live without prayer.

God may be within, but faith and prayer does more for us when we project it onto something that feels like it exists outside ourselves. The "truth" has nothing to do with it.

CHAPTER 16

The Earth Beneath our Feet

States of Consciousness and the Geomagnetic Field.

There was a violent earthquake, for an angel of the lord came down from heaven ... His appearance was like lightening and his clothes were as white as snow. *Gospel according to Matthew 28:2-3*

It's a basic fact of physics that electricity and magnetism are intimately related. Electrical currents create magnetic fields, and moving magnetic fields create electrical currents. There's a formula that expresses the exact relationship, called *Maxwell's Equation*. It tells you just how much electrical current will create how much magnetism.

Minute magnetic bursts accompany the electrical pulses running between neurons in the brain. In the background, the earth's magnetic field, with its constant changes, makes it own contributions. It has storms and quiet times. The strength of the earth's magnetic field also changes. Its value goes up and down by as much as 20 percent. This range is called the *variable portion* of the earth's magnetic field. Whenever there are changes in the earth's magnetic field, there also are changes in the way our brains work. Most of these are too subtle for us to notice, and many of us never even feel the strongest of them, though very few people keep track of the geomagnetic 'weather'.

Dr. Michael Persinger has published scores of studies about the effects of the earth's magnetic field in a series of publications called "Geophysical variables and human behavior" in the journal "Perceptual and Motor Skills". Other researchers have also published findings on the subject. Sleep paralysis, in which a person can wake up and find they are unable to move, is more likely three days after the geomagnetic field was especially active[644]. It's possible that this observation can't be explained by changes in the magnetic field strengths alone. It could also be that people who are prone to sleep paralysis in the first place are responding to a signal that appears in the earth's magnetic field during geomagnetic storms.

Sleep paralysis, or anything else that the Earth's magnetic field contributes to, isn't *caused* by geomagnetic storms. It's caused by factors at work inside the human brain. The geomagnetic storm makes it more likely that these factors will start operating, but if a person isn't prone to sleep paralysis, the aftermath of a geomagnetic storm won't make it happen. Changes in the earth's magnetic field make many experiences more likely, but that's not the same thing as *causing* them.

Geomagnetism, Paranormal Perceptions, and Psychic Skills

Let's take a quick look at a few studies. Many of these follow paranormal themes, and there are always people who respond to any mention of the paranormal with ridicule. To them, I say that they should understand that these studies don't focus on paranormal experiences. Instead, the emphasis is on *reports* of paranormal experiences. Even if one is unable to believe that telepathy is a human skill, one can still accept that *reporting* telepathic perceptions is a human behavior, and is as worthy of study as any other. Its one thing to say that you don't believe in clairvoyance and another thing to say that you don't believe there are any such things as *reports* about it. There are skeptics who'll deride it as a waste of time and scientific efforts, but there's no denying that the propensity to make reports of paranormal experiences can be subjected to scientific scrutiny and statistical analysis. As it happens, reports of paranormal experiences correlate with geomagnetic changes.

Other people have had paranormal and psychic experiences themselves, and are satisfied that events have proven them right. They won't think like academic skeptics. They'll be more interested in what these studies reveal than the scientific method they used. Here are a few sample studies from this richly-researched phenomenon.

In one study[645], intense paranormal experiences focusing on the death or illness of friends or family (such as when the deceased 'visits' grieving loved ones) occurred on days when the geomagnetic activity was lower than the average for the month in which they happened.

In another study[646], reports of telepathic experiences were analyzed and it was discovered that the ones that communicated a death or a crisis (when a person in one place has a vision or striking intuition that someone they know has died) happened on days when geomagnetic activity was far lower than on the three days before or after.

Another study[647], involving reported telepathy during dreams, found that the dreams were more accurate when they occurred on days when the geomagnetic activity was weaker than it was on the days just before and after.

In one case study[648], a 20-year-old woman with a history of several different kinds of psychic experiences had 23 sessions in which she tried to guess which symbol was on the back of some standard ESP cards. The scores for her accuracy were highest on days when geomagnetic activity was at its lowest.

Poltergeist activity was examined in one study[649], which found that geomagnetic activity on the day (or the days) after these episodes began was far higher than on the days before or after.

Another study[650] found that the "sensation of being detached from one's body" or out of body experiences were more likely during times of elevated geomagnetic activity.

Another researcher[651], investigating extrasensory perception using featureless white visual fields, called Ganzfelds, found that ESP scores related to high geomagnetic activity the day before the experiments but not to the days of the experiments themselves. This only partly agrees with other studies in the same field, but we can wait for more evidence to appear.

Another interesting one[652] involved fifty-seven cases of telepathic experiences involving the death or illness of a friend, lover, or family member where one person – at a distance – had some sort of psychic warning about the other person. The telepathic experiences occurred on days when geomagnetic activity was lower than on the days immediately before or after.

Here's one that can make skeptics reach for some flimsy arguments. This study[653] is especially interesting, because it didn't examine individual reports of ESP, but instead analyzed the results of 185 ESP (Extra-Sensory Perception) experiments. It compared ESP studies and found that the years in which researchers published the *most* robust ESP effects were also the years with the *quietest* geomagnetic activity. It was a *meta-analysis*, a study that looked at the results of many similar studies.

It's not all about spiritual or psychic experiences and geomagnetism. Female but not male suicide is more likely during geomagnetic storms[654]. One study[655] found that the number of first-time admissions to psychiatric facilities went up when geomagnetic activity went down.

Another study[656], looking at mining accidents (minor enough to be handled with first-aid) found that they were higher on days of elevated geomagnetic activity. The difference is high enough that geomagnetic variations accounted for 23 percent of all variations in the amount of first-aid used in the mine they studied.

One very interesting result comes from a study[657] where claimed precognitive perceptions of future events showed that geomagnetic activity for the day of the perception correlated with geomagnetic activity for the day of the event (in cases where the prediction and the event were separated by at least four days). This study's certainty may be reduced by using self-reported validations of precognition, but that still leaves us wondering why these reports show correlations with geomagnetic levels.

Of course, this is significant. If even *some* precognitive experiences are accepted as valid, then some people can access information from the future. One can speculate that time itself is being influenced by the earth's magnetic field, or that magnetic fields can convey information from the future, but it's also possible that it's our *perception* of time that's at work. In either case, it implies that there is some feature of time, fields (like those of magnets or gravity or subatomic forces) and consciousness that physics doesn't yet understand.

There is a scenario in which a mother in one region wakes up from a nightmare about her child at the same time as her (grown-up) child is having an accident in a different region. That's most likely to happen on a day of high geomagnetic activity happening between days of low geomagnetic activity. Precognition; remembering things before they happen, doesn't manifest the same effect. Is information as able to travel backwards in time as easily as it's transmitted through space? Are there features of time which most of us can't perceive and the few that can only do so in relatively uncommon geomagnetic circumstances?

I cannot help but wonder if precognitive experiences occur as some brain functions are disinhibited – ones that ordinarily act to screen out (mostly irrelevant) information from the future, borne on magnetic fields, which are not subject to Special Relativity (which apply to matter and energy, but not fields). The earth's magnetic field seems to be the medium in which information is transmitted through space, from one brain to another, but it's much more speculative to think that information from the future is also carried by the geomagnetic field. No matter how tentative or hesitant we are with speculations to explain the physical basis for precognitive perceptions, we'd have to create hypotheses about the physics of time. Those can become very complicated, very quickly.

The physics of time relates to the physics of space, and the physics of space relates to the physics of matter. If we change one of them in order to include explanations for precognition, we'll end of making changes to all of them. We would be re-creating the world as seen in physics to suit just one set of observations. While it might be a good idea for modern physics to undergo another revolution, it's probably not going to happen because someone has had a new and clever thought about precognitive experience. Revolutions in modern physics must come from crises within that field. The need for a new paradigm in physics that accounts for precognition may seem obvious to some people, but need alone is not enough to precipitate a new way of seeing the world. It only changes when there are both enough new facts that the old theory can't explain, and a new hypothesis that *does* explain them.

There is huge interest in paranormal experiences, both among researchers and the general public. More people are interested in telepathic experiences than are interested in nail biting, to name only one example. Do people bite their nails more or less during a geomagnetic storm? Is it possible that you get a good night's sleep during geomagnetic quiet, and you tend to toss and turn more during geomagnetic storms? Most studies of human behavior take no account of the effects of the geomagnetic field, so we really don't know how many things are affected by its changes. Probably, there are many awaiting discovery. The fact that there are so many studies correlating geomagnetic conditions with psychic skills and spontaneous spiritual experiences partly reflects the fact that there's so much interest in these things. When it facilitates an experience we have all the time, we won't see anything unusual about it. Let's suppose for example, that the experience of having a melody run through your head is more likely on days of geomagnetic storm. Actually, we don't know this. It hasn't been studied. But let's suppose.

Music running through your head is a common experience. If it happened one day, you wouldn't think there was anything strange about it. On the other hand, if you had a string of paranormal experiences, all on the same day, like knowing who was calling on the phone before you picked it up, or thinking of people and then meeting them by accident, you might think something strange was going on. One seems to call for an explanation, and the other doesn't. How many television programs have you noticed about the paranormal, and how many have you seen about music playing in the mind?

The information embedded in the earth's magnetic field changes constantly and at random, reflecting unpredictable movement deep in the earth, solar winds, and other influences. Much of it will be meaningless static. There are no patterns to geomagnetic storms. Geomagnetic input into our brains is never regular. They come when they come and don't follow any regular schedule. Any specific field strength that makes psychic perceptions more likely is going to appear sooner or later. It may be sheer coincidence that some experiences respond to certain patterns in geomagnetic activity, but I think it's more likely that the evolution of our brains included making use of environmental factors that affect it. We evolved into our present form in the geomagnetic environment, so it wouldn't be surprising if we (and other species) had found some way to take advantage of its resources. Indeed, birds are known to use the geomagnetic field for navigation.

Humans are a very diverse species. Some of us are irritable. Some of us are very demure. Some of us are very intelligent. Some of us are very sexual. Some of us are very anxious. We keep a high level of diversity within our population at all times. Traits that appear in one person can be absent in others. No single individual needs to have all the skills it takes to keep all humans alive. It may also be possible that our species could derive some benefit by having traits that appear intermittently for just a few days at a time. Imagine our early ancestors. Suppose a few people in their group had the ability to garner information from the future only on those days of when the geomagnetic conditions are just right. That would mean that some individuals, probably the shamans or spiritual leaders, would occasionally have a chance to find information that would benefit their group. If a shaman had the ability at all times, they might find that they were seeing deaths (for example) more often than they liked and their motivation to go on with their ordinary activities might be lost. If they were constantly getting information from the future, they might find that they were seeing too many unpleasant events. Most psychics will tell you that directing their attention onto something specific helps a lot in getting psychic information about it. They have to 'focus' on the thing they want to know about. If they don't learn this focus, they won't have any psychic perceptions, no matter how psychic they might be. Having this 'focus' as a prerequisite skill would mean that they aren't usually overwhelmed by psychic perceptions, because they don't have to pay attention when they don't want to.

Most psychics will tell you that they have days when they're "on" and days when they're not. A few psychics will tell you that they are always on, and they can do their work at any time. There are no numbers to support this, because no such studies have been done. But let's imagine that an early human's social group, like a tribe, consisted of about 50 people. The number seems pretty reasonable; it's close to the numbers you can find in groups of nomadic people today. Now, let's imagine that only one out of a hundred people are very powerful psychics, able to use their skills at any time. That would mean that for groups of humans living a nomadic life, such a psychic would appear only once in two generations. Clearly, we will do better to understand the common, ordinary psychic perceptions of common, ordinary psychics, and even ordinary people who usually aren't psychic at all. Understanding the processes at work with the most powerful psychics will not contribute as much to our understanding of psychic perceptions in the human species. It would be like trying to figure out how fast we could get away from predators by studying Olympic sprinters.

The relative scarcity of powerful psychics in our early evolutionary history means that any advantage derived from having psychic skills would likely appear in ordinary people, not the 'special' psychics we hear of today (unfortunately today's marketing techniques are as available to fakes as they are to authentic psychics).

All of the preceding discussion has been about reports of telepathic, psychic, extrasensory, and precognitive experiences. Except for precognition, there is a tendency for them to be more likely on days of geomagnetic quiet. In the previous examples, we've been discussing *global* geomagnetic activity; fluctuations in the magnetic field of the entire earth. However, it appears that smaller areas, even places just a few miles across, can have their own effects.

Sacred Lands

What makes one place different from another in this regard is *tectonic strain* - the stress that builds up in the earth and is later discharged in earthquakes. A few studies have demonstrated that many, if not all, luminous displays can be explained as manifestations of tectonic strain. Most often, it builds up in areas near fault lines. Luminous displays are lights in the sky that are often interpreted as UFOs, but they can take other forms, including ball lightening and earth lights. The earth's magnetic field is expressed differently in these areas. It picks up information, as the rocks under pressure beneath the surface generate small amounts of piezoelectricity[658] with signals being imposed by the size and structure of the crystals in the rock. The result can be lights that appear in and around earthquake-prone areas, but only until an earthquake releases the strain.

Put simply, the explanation is that UFOs (and other lights in the sky) are explained as electrical products of the stress and strain on the earth's crust that culminates in earthquakes. Most rocks have a crystalline structure, and most crystals generate an electric charge when they're under pressure or being bent. This electric charge is called *piezoelectricity*. Places with lots of seismic activity will have a charge, and the more electricity, the more magnetism. Under extreme conditions, this creates an environment where charged particles can actually light up the sky around the places under strain. These seismic regions can be large or small. They can appear far away from the epicenter of the earthquakes that eventually discharge it.

Like the magnetic field for the whole Earth, the geomagnetic field in areas with high seismic activity can have an impact on human states of consciousness. In general, the people with the most sensitive temporal lobes are the most likely to enter an altered state, whether the trigger is a geomagnetic event or not. The person watching a glowing light in the sky can enter an altered state, and impose a hallucinatory shape on it. It's a bit like seeing shapes in the clouds. If you look at clouds long enough, you might begin to see some that look like faces. Once you've seen one that way, it can be very hard to look at it without seeing the face.

The altered states that appear from tectonic strain (or from information that only appears when the field is stronger) might also facilitate the transfer of information directly from one brain to another, as we discussed in another chapter. This would make it possible for a group of people in such an environment to see the same thing. Geomagnetic quiet facilitates brain-to-brain communication. Geological strain doesn't mean geomagnetic storm.

The researchers who investigated the connection between geomagnetic changes and psychic experiences found that their research tools were equally suited to investigating the down-to-earth basis for UFOs.

The *distance* between the earthquake and the lights in the sky that preceding it can be short or long. The *time* between lights in the sky and the earthquakes that follow can also long or short. In one case, in southwestern Missouri[659], both happened in the same region and the most phenomenal displays happened the day before the earthquake. In another example (from Utah), large numbers of reports of UFOs correlated with seismic activity 150 to 250 km away[660]. One study found a connection between lights in the sky and earthquake activity 1000 km away[661]! In another case[662], in Mississippi Valley, the lag between the luminous displays and the seismic activity (compounded by the extra tectonic strain imposed by the weight of the Mississippi River in flood) was about six months. Another study found correlations between numbers of UFO reports and earthquake activity in Sweden[663], also emerging when the data was looked at over periods of six months.

Another study examined the numbers of UFO reports in the amount of seismic activity over thirty years, in the area surrounding the Rio Grande rift system. Over time, UFO reports clustered closer and closer to the center of the area under study. As it turned out, that was also the epicenter of a group of earth tremors[664].

UFO reports are more likely with earthquakes of five or less on the Richter scale, and less likely with earthquakes of six or more[665]. In other words, minor earthquakes and tremors are more likely to create luminous displays than major ones.

There are several problems involved in studying reports of lights in the sky. Often there won't be anyone to see the luminous display – they usually don't last long. Another is that people who see them may not want to report them. Telling people that you've seen a UFO is an easy way to get yourself ridiculed. Beyond that, even if someone does see a luminous display, they may have no idea who to report it to. Moreover, the experience of seeing a light in the sky can be so compelling that some people won't report it because picking up the phone and dialing a phone number for UFO reports can ruin their mood.

Once, while I was walking across a parking lot at night in Southeastern Michigan, a woman approached me and asked "did you see those lights?" I hadn't. She told me that the sky had been covered with blue lights, and she wanted to follow them. She found them enchanting, and walked on, enraptured, trying to chase them. She was oblivious to everything else. I don't think she would have called a UFO report hotline. For her, it was a very personal experience. The next day, the front page of the newspaper had a story about the "UFO sightings", though the woman I'd spoken with didn't say anything about UFOs. She had seen lights and that's what she called them.

The experience of seeing lights in the sky can be very personal. A person can project their own images on the luminous display, a bit like the way we see faces in clouds. It's something less than hallucination, but more than imagination. As we saw another chapter, it's actually possible for people to share information coming as images. If we want to make sense of the next geomagnetic phenomena, we need to suppose that it's possible for a single image to be shared between many brains, a phenomenon often dismissed as "mass hysteria".

Marian Apparitions

In the years 1968 and 1969, large groups of people had repeated sightings of the Virgin Mary above a Coptic Orthodox church in Zeitoun, Egypt. Huge crowds formed to see them. Sometimes, her whole body appeared, and sometimes just her head and shoulders. In all cases, observers, including a delegation from an Orthodox Patriarch, saw a bright halo around her head. Some people took photos and made drawings of the apparition, and it seems they were all seeing about the same thing. There were also smaller lights. They didn't last long, and they moved around quickly. These were nicknamed "doves". There were also lights like stars, and a sideways cross was sometimes seen over the church. Of course, from the right direction, it would have been upright. At times, a smell like incense would hang in the air. There were even reports of miraculous cures.

When John Derr and Michael Persinger looked into the event[666], they found that the Zeitoun apparitions of the Virgin Mary began one year before earthquake activity in the region (in the southern tip of the Sinai Peninsula, about 350 miles away) showed a dramatic increase. In fact, it had gone up by 10 times. In 1974, there was another cluster of earthquakes about 35 miles north of Zeitoun. When the earthquakes ended, so did the apparitions.

So what had happened? The correlation between the beginning and the end of these swarms of earthquakes with the apparitions was very strong, and it's consistent with the results from the other studies we've already mentioned. There are details that can't be worked out by comparing the times of the earthquakes and the times of the apparitions alone, but if you don't mind a little speculation, here's what may have happened.

Deep in the earth's crust, pressure was building up under the southern tip of the Sinai Peninsula. The earth's crust under the surrounding area, extending hundreds of miles away, had to bear an unusual amount of strain. Usually, there are three or four earthquakes in that small area per year. In this case, it took almost 40 quakes to release the strain. The land itself was unaccustomed to this higher-than-usual burden. Meanwhile, to the north, a second area was building up the same kind of geological stress. The church at Zeitoun lay between these two geological hotspots.

The earth's magnetic field was passing through Zeitoun, just as it always had. However, the extra strain and stress imposed on the land – from two directions – was literally crushing astronomical numbers of very tiny crystals in the ground. As any geologist can tell you, most crystalline materials will put out a kind of static electricity when it's under strain (piezoelectricity). While crystals in the bedrock had probably been vibrated, twisted, and kept under pressure over the long geological history of the place, the swarms of earthquakes that occurred indicated unusually high strain on the bedrock. This seems a reasonable inference, given that there was 10 times more seismic activity than usual during the years of the apparitions. The bedrock itself began pouring electricity out; electricity that would be accompanied by magnetic fields.

The people in Zeitoun were standing between two geological pressure points, one far to the south, and one much more nearby in the north. Each new strain from either of these points would reverberate all throughout the region, the way guitar string resonates after being plucked.

This strain is enough to produce luminous displays all by itself. Earth lights. Ball lightening. Lights in the sky. Things like that. So how does a luminous display become the Virgin Mary?

The electrical activity in their brain is going to be affected as people walk through an area where the earth beneath their feet is emitting

416

large amounts of static electricity. The temporal lobes of the brain, the area that's most sensitive to this kind of stimulation, will be pushed into excitement. Some people are more sensitive than others, so not everyone is equally affected. The ones who *are* affected may begin to find that they have odd sensations as their temporal lobes become more active. They might feel tingling sensations. They might feel a little bit dizzy as they look at the top of the church. They might experience déjà vu. But what comes next drives all of this from their minds, and if they remember these subtler sensations at all, they'll interpret them in terms of what comes next (as "signs from God").

Their brains would have reached the point where the temporal lobes are no longer producing transient, minor experiences, and are now closer to full-fledged hallucination. One part of their brains is responding more than the rest: the amygdala on the left side. In laboratory settings, stimulation of the amygdala on the left side using the God helmet has elicited apparitions, uplifting sensations and visions of light. So, if we ask which part of the brain participates most in these apparitions, we have to say the amygdala on the left. If the right amygdala responded more than the one on the left, the result would be a negative experience. Its possible that people's expectations could 'weight' the experience in favor of a positive one, and that the information broadcast from other people's brains could also tend to make the experience a positive one. There is also the possibility that the local geomagnetic field could have borne information that triggered left amygdala excitement more readily than excitement from the one on the right. If anyone were to have a right amygdala-based (fearful) experience, they might interpret it as God's wrath or displeasure, or a vision from Satan. They might tend to focus on their own failings and sins, and be less likely to talk about the experience, out of shame or the sense that their experiences either can't or shouldn't be talked about. They might think the place was haunted

This strange and unusual stimulation, coming from all around them, finally triggers a vision. The intense magnetic fields and the glowing flow of ions from under the earth might be faintly visible, and is transformed (or confabulated) into a vision of a being that one would expect to see in the sky. The Virgin Mary; the Holy Mother. Why would it appear as a woman? Most Catholics and Orthodox Christians already knew stories about visions of the Virgin Mary. Moreover, our earliest and most emotionally evocative relationship with another person is almost always with our mothers. We have a ready-made template for seeing the "divine in the feminine" (mapping spiritual qualities onto females) that we don't have for seeing the divine in the masculine. Too bad for men, eh? Another speculative possibility is that the magnetic fields surrounding the apparition's luminous display received information from the brains of the people looking at it through the direct transmission of information between brains. One person seeing the lights as the Blessed Mother makes it more likely that another person will see them the same way.

People predisposed to see Christian symbolism would have become very excited when a cross appeared in the sky. Naturally, this would have been remembered and photographed far more often than random displays. One photo of a cross above the church in Zeitoun showed a somewhat irregular Christian cross in the sky - but only if you saw it from one direction. If the display looked like a rocking chair, no one would have noticed.

As the amygdala on the left becomes more excited, its activity can spread into other structures, like the hippocampus, where the apparition's size and location in space acquire greater definition. The olfactory bulb is directly connected to the amygdala, and as activity in the amygdala spreads there, it perceives smells as though they had been stimulated from outside, even though the excitement came from within, and the air will seem to be filled with a fragrance. By now, the religious theme has taken over completely, and the only smell to be easily hallucinated (or confabulated) into the context is the smell of incense. And so, the air itself seems to become sanctified around the church.

More Speculation:

Someone, probably very early in the period of the apparitions, experienced the Virgin Mary as having a specific, particular, appearance. That person's brain, emitting its own signals, imposed an interpretation for the state of consciousness that easiest to enter when they were close to that church (there could have been many states of consciousness appearing for different people), and was able to impose a specific, concrete vision onto the brains of those for whom it was still just an 'unformed' altered state. It may have taken on the shape of the Virgin Mary because the onlooker's brains were imposing information on a system that was otherwise quite random. Photographs of the luminous display above this region under tectonic strain showed the Virgin Mary. It seems that the image was projected onto the displays by the brains of the people congregated there, especially in view of the lack of allegations of photographic fakery (remember, this happened before photoshop existed), though we should remember that religious fakery is commonplace.

A single nonrandom element can organize an otherwise random system in what are called stochastic processes. The total energy input into the local electromagnetic environment from a crowd of human brains would be insignificant compared to the forces unleashed by the stress and strain on the earth's crust. However, the *information content* from those brains could easily organize the whole local geomagnetic system, if that system had no significant information content of its own. Thereafter, the luminous display, created out of tectonic strain, stopped being a blob of light, and became The Holy Mother.

As we'll be seeing in the second volume of this work, left hemispheric activation, including activation of the left amygdala, is a common theme in tales of miraculous healings. For now, we can say that if our other speculations are right, then inexplicable healings are to be expected.

A Catholic believer might say that this is how God chose to allow the Immaculate Virgin to place herself before the world, and pass on her messages. In the end, Christian believers are turned back to their primary beliefs. They are left with the choice to have faith, or not to.

This explanation for the details of the Zeitoun apparitions is quite speculative. You could even call it guesswork. It addresses the details in a way that allows us to see how the earth itself participates in many of the religious visions the world remembers. There have been other famous apparitions of the Virgin Mary. Our Lady of Guadalupe was seen in a vision in Mexico, a region prone to earthquakes. The same is true for our Lady of Fatima, who comes from Portugal, another geologically active area. Our Lady of Lourdes comes from Southwest France, not far from the fault lines that are also the source of Portugal's many earthquakes. The Holy Mother of Akita, (who appeared between 1973 and 1982), and whose veneration is now approved by the Catholic Church, appeared in Japan, a very seismically active region.

There have been many apparitions of the Virgin Mary, going back as far as 250 A.D., when one appeared in Neo-Caesaria, in Asia Minor. It's not possible to analyze all of them, because some of them may have never happened, the distances from the apparitions to the nearest fault is not always known, and because the amount of tectonic strain needed to elicit such events may vary with the distance from the displays and the thickness of the earth's crust. Some of the seismic activity that came towards the end of episodes of luminous displays happened as much as a thousand kilometers away, though as we will see in the next section, lights in the sky can be seen within a mile or two of a fault line. You can look at almost any example of an apparition, and find a fault line somewhere. Explaining specific apparitions with better certainty is a matter of careful statistical analysis. Earthquakes that are five or less on the Richter scale are more likely to be associated with luminous displays than earthquakes of six or more. If you look at seismic activity and lights in the sky, and compare the times when they happen in terms of days, you don't get very much. If you make the same comparison in terms of periods of three to six months, the correlations begin to emerge. It seems that there's a certain minimum amount of time that the earth's crust has to be under stress before it will start contributing to luminous displays.

There's a lot of room for variation. This explanation discusses luminous displays, UFOs, and visions of the Virgin Mary, in terms of electromagnetic phenomena. There could be other electromagnetic circumstances that can create the same phenomena, so that geological and geographic processes may not be enough to explain them all. But it's certainly enough to explain most of them.

Lake County, California – Earthquakes Every Day

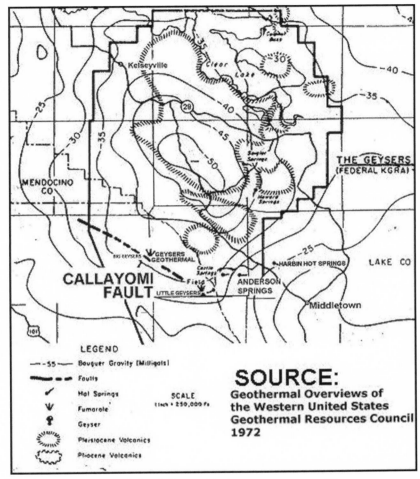

The area around the Callayomi fault gets an average of 5 tremors of 1.5 or more on the Richter scale every day[667].

I once spent a year living in Middletown, California, about six miles from the Callayomi fault. It's an interesting fault line. It's only eight miles long, but it produces large numbers of low magnitude earthquakes. In the area just north of Middletown, which had a huge number of earthquakes, you could hear the earthquakes rolling over the land with a low rumbling noise that grew louder as they approached you. You would feel the ground shake a little bit, and the earthquake would go on past you. These were usually not very intense.

I once obtained a large map of the area, attached it to some cardboard, took it out to the local grocery store, where I stood for couple of hours asking people if they had ever seen any kind of lights in the sky in the area. 80 percent had. That's a very high rate of local reporting. There appeared to be three types of lights (when seen at a distance). The first were small lights that moved in unusual ways. The second were said to look something like arc welding lights either floating in the sky or hovering closer to the ground, and this type comes in several colors. The last kind had been described to me as looking like comets that streak across the sky and lights up the area for a second or two after it passes by, as though it had an impossibly long tail. This last type I have heard of only twice and both reports were from an area about seven miles northeast of Middletown. There seem to be areas where they are most common. They are: Northeast, northwest of Middletown, and due north of it; in that order.

Photo of a Luminous Display[668] taken in Lake County, CA

These lights could come in any color, but most often they were white or blue. I asked people to point out where they had seen lights on the map. None of them were more than six miles from the fault line, and several people said that the lights were moving, and pushed on the map to show the direction, usually parallel with the fault line.

Some of them were right over the fault line, and all the movement was parallel to it. I remember speaking to one woman who told me that while she was driving home from work out of Middletown to the Northeast, she saw faint lights in the sky almost every day. If I left

Middletown going northwest on a moonless night, I would see a faint blue halo just above the tree tops, as though the earth itself had an aura.

It's tempting to think that the reason the Callayomi lights were so close to the earthquakes, while the Zeitoun apparitions were hundreds of miles away is because the Callayomi fault is so very short, only eight miles from one end to the other. That might be the reason, but the Callayomi fault has another difference. Most earthquakes happen when there is stress on a tectonic plate. The earthquakes around the Callayomi fault are caused by movements of the earth's magma, pushing up against the bedrock. The earth's crust is very thin in the area. There is even a geothermal power plant.

As we saw in the chapter on the visitor experience, visitors can be positive or negative. I spoke with one person there who had seen an angel, but only once, and another who kept seeing a "spiky guy" in her backyard. She had a clear feeling that he was evil.

I talked to several people who heard voices in their head when they were living in Middletown or the area north of it, but never anywhere else, and I also talked to people who heard voices regularly, but *not* while in Middletown.

There are other oddities in the area, less phenomenal than UFOs by far, but still worth looking at.

Lake County has the highest death rate of any county in California, even when you take its high population of seniors into account[669]. It has the highest AIDS rate for any small county in the state[670]. It's a low-income county, but there are other areas in California about as poor.

Per 100,000 people Lake County has a:

- Suicide rate of 25.3, while the average for the rest of the state is 10.7.
- Fatal Lung Cancer rate of 58.1, while the rest of the state has a rate of 31.8.
- Fatal Heart Disease rate of 117.9, while the rest of the state has a rate of 100.6.
- Fatal Stroke rate of 35.5, compared to 26.3 through the rest of the state.

- Drug-related death rate of 15.4, compared to 8 elsewhere in the state.

I know an epileptologist who lives in the area. She had written a book on how to self-manage epileptic seizures. She told me that she sells more of her books (by mail order) in Clearlake (northeast of Middletown) than any where else in California, excepting major cities. We should find that this area has a higher rate of epilepsy than other counties in the state, as local electromagnetic changes give unstable parts of the brain more to adjust to. Interestingly, I had reports from people who said their Temporal Lobe Signs (déjà vu, etc.; common in epilepsy) stopped after coming to Lake County. If this were concrete enough to allow conclusions (and really, it isn't) to be drawn, I'd say that the local geomagnetic environment adds a factor that dampens some aspects of epilepsy, and enhances others.

I have heard of an area about 14 miles northwest of Middletown where, my informant claimed, everybody who goes there gets a strange Déjà Vu-like feeling. Another person I spoke to who lived in that area said she had déjà vu almost constantly. I don't think that it's possible for there to be a place where everybody has Déjà Vu, but I can see how a place could bring it out in anyone who was prone to it.

People seem to have more trouble sleeping in Lake County. Especially in the area about 7 miles northwest of the fault line. It seems to be a special kind of insomnia, too. What I kept hearing about was that when insomnia hits people around there, they often find that their thoughts run in odd directions. They would think of things they otherwise never enter their minds, and seem to be unable to 'get a grip on themselves.' One resident said that he would wake up in the middle of the night and feel completely isolated; as though there wasn't another person for hundreds of miles around. Another said that he would wake up and find himself imaging suicides. Not his own, but other people's. This didn't happen to him in other places; only while staying north of Middletown. It didn't happen in the northwest (where he had lived for a few months) or in San Francisco; only at a place about three miles due north of Middletown.

Another person, who had moved to the area a year before I spoke to him, said that his cats stopped running to him when he moved there.

Southern Lake County has a lot of spiritual centers. The Adi Daist (Adi Da is the name of their spiritual teacher) 'Mountain of Attention Sanctuary,' and the 'Age of Enlightenment' Transcendental Meditation™ center. A town about four miles northeast of Middletown is the home of a Tibetan Buddhist center (it's not open to the public, so I can't give you the name), and a Zen Buddhist center. There is a hypnotherapy office in Middletown, a town that can't support even one Xerox copy shop. Middletown also has a massage store and an acupuncturist, but no bookstores. It boasts exactly one accredited school of Shiatsu and Massage. And exactly one liquor store. Last, but not least, is Harbin Hot Springs, a clothing-optional spiritual retreat center where the food is vegetarian, and there is a different meditation or yoga taught just about every night. South of Middletown, there used to be an organization called the 'Star Cross.' They were, I believe, waiting for alien spacecraft to land and carry off their true believers.

The extra helping of spiritual centers is not only for minority religious believers. It also seems to apply to more mainstream, Christian groups. For a town of its size (population 1,323 in 2010), Middletown sure has a lot of churches. Catholic, Methodist, Seventh-Day Adventist, Fundamentalist, and others. All this in a town so small that it wouldn't support half its number of churches anywhere else. Of course, its parishioners came from nearby towns, as well.

In Middletown, I heard 11 to 15 year olds who swear that there are spots where they always felt scared at night, riding by on their bicycles. One of them said, as if unable to imagine that anyone might think it strange, that there was a gnome who lived outside her home. The Zeitoun events left people feeling good. This place has spots where people feel bad. It's possible that somehow, the Zeitoun events activated the amygdala on the left, while the 'scary spots' of Middletown activate the one on the right. Or, they're both emotionally neutral, and people felt what they expected to feel, directing the activity to one amygdala or the other through their expectations.

They seem to reflect an interaction between the earth's electrical and magnetic environment with the one in the brain. Taken together, these somewhat strange stories, all from one location, might just prove the local nickname for the place: Flake County.

Few places in the world have a greater reputation for being sacred than the Himalayas. For centuries, Hindu believers who want to follow the path of mysticism have stayed there as a spiritual retreat. One accepted way for a man to end his life is simply to walk into the Himalayas, not looking back, and keep going until he can go no further, and then lie down and die[671]. It's the home of Tibetan Buddhism, with its heavy emphasis on "inner work". Hindu culture preserves many stories of yogis going into the Himalayas to practice austerities; rigorous spiritual practice that are said to confer magical powers on its longtime practitioners. There is a Hindu legend that the God Shiva lives on the top of Mount Kailash. The Himalayas were formed as the Indian subcontinent, once a vast island, pushed into the land mass of Asia. The Himalayan region remains seismically active, and the tectonic strain, as the two continental plates push into each other, is enormous. Perhaps the reason the Himalayas have this reputation is because of these huge forces, pushing them even higher, and influencing the brains of those who live there. The conditions that precipitated the apparitions of the Virgin Mother in Zeitoun might have something in common to those in the Himalayas.

Most of what I've written about Middletown and Southern Lake County is based on anecdotes and stories. This isn't the most exact way to work, but it does give us a broad overview of many phenomena that can appear in places with high seismic activity. I hope to return there and gather more careful data one day.

Afterward

To sum up the main hypotheses in this book, we can say that:

1) Reincarnation pre-adapts us to live in a human culture, where it increases our chances for social success, which in turn means raising our chances to see our children grow to have kids of their own.

2) The death-process in a crucial part of the mechanism of reincarnation, because it indicates which states of consciousness are most likely to inspire adaptive behavior. The states may not be re-affirmed when cultures change, and instead are re-labeled, so to speak, to suit the new context, when old behaviors can now have new consequences.

3) A person will have a religious or mystic experience when the neural pathways that support any part of the death-process are excited during life.

4) These pathways can be excited while we're still alive are through a 'neural avalanche' (interhemispheric intrusion). Spiritual practices, brain stimulation, or hallucinogenic drugs can make these death-process, 'sacred' pathways more sensitive than before.

The core idea can still stand even if one rejects the idea of reincarnation. In that case, we need only accept that the death-process is part of our evolutionary strategy, without knowing exactly what it's for. The "sacred pathways" that function for it can still be the basis for mystic experiences. Nevertheless, invoking reincarnation allows us to understand why we have a death-process in the first place, and that's a crucial question.

Even the evidence from the God Helmet experiments isn't essential. One could still arrive at the same hypotheses (concerning the left amygdala and interhemispheric intrusion); reasoning from completely different kinds of evidence, now that neuroscience understands that the left amygdala is specialized for positive emotions. We must also understand that our arguments would be the stronger if we made fewer speculations, but they also wouldn't explain as much. We've enjoyed our freedom to speculate, but without crossing the edge of objectivity.

The ideas presented in this book constitute an integration of science and human spirituality. Now that it exists, science will never be without an explanation for spiritual experiences, and disagreement from other scientists cannot change that. The history of science shows that once a scientific paradigm appears in a field, it can only be displaced by a better one. The inevitable skeptics who will denigrate the paradigm presented here will not affect it unless they can offer better explanations. Dismissing or ridiculing the phenomena, or the people who experience them, will not be enough.

Inevitably, the ideas in this book will be replaced. Their replacements may be better versions of the same concepts, or they may be totally new ideas that do a better job of explaining the same things. When Einstein's theory replaced those of Sir Isaac Newton, the arguments first put forward against Newton were irretrievably put on the rubbish heap of history. So it will also be with arguments against this paradigm that ignore the self-evident phenomena that mystics know first-hand.

Nothing lasts forever, and the ideas you've been reading here are no exception.

Some religious thinkers will denounce this book. However, the advance of science into our cultures is a trend that can't be reversed. Science is now a part of basic education, no matter how rudimentary, in every country on earth; even the poorest of them. An understanding of spirituality that agrees with science will inevitably supplant religion whose only basis is in traditional scriptures. The beauty of traditional religion will always inspire, and its teachings will remain good for people. However, in the present era, only science can offer explanations that will endure, even though those explanations can and will change.

I hope to contribute to human spirituality. Although science is not attacking religion, it cannot help encroaching on it, and only more science will preserve it.

As religion and spirituality respond to the challenges science has given it, the only way 'out' is 'through'. In the end, a scientific understanding of spirituality can only help us live spiritual lives. We need not fear the demise of older religious beliefs. Their end will be a rite of passage for humanity in which we will surrender the intolerance, bigotry and abuses of religion, and embrace our own lives as the most sacred pathway of all.

Author, 2007

Photo by my neighbor (Thanks, Elizabeth!).

Todd Murphy
www.spiritualbrain.com

Author Todd Murphy is a long-time member of Laurentian university Behavior Neurosciences research group, which operates under the direction of Dr. Michael A Persinger. He has published in the Journal for Near-Death Studies, Psychology Reports, *Activitas Nervosa Superior,* and the journal, *Neuroquantology*. His 9-hour lecture series can be seen on www.youtube.com. He is also the developer of the Shakti and Shiva Neural stimulation systems, which made Dr. Persinger's pioneering neural stimulation work available to the general public. His studies in the field of neurotheology began in 1985, becoming increasingly formal until his work found publication in academic journals, beginning in 1998. This is the first volume of his projected two (or three) volume series "Sacred Pathways: The Brain's role in Religious and Mystic Experiences."

See us online at:
www.sacred-pathways.org

Endnotes

References for Chapter 2 – Darwinian Reincarnation

1. Murphy, Todd, "The Structure and Function of Near-Death Experiences: An Algorithmic Reincarnation Hypothesis, *Journal of Near-Death Studies*, Vol. 20, Number 2 - December, 2001

2. Note that throughout this book, the term 'evolution' refers to evolution through natural selection; Darwinian adaptation, and not spiritual or personal evolution.

3. In traditional logic, a postulate is a "proposition not proved or demonstrated but considered to be either self-evident or subject to necessary decision". Therefore, its truth is taken for granted, and serves as a starting point for deducing and inferring other (theory dependent) truths. The crucial phrase is 'Subject to necessary decision'. The reader needs to decide whether or not to accept it as a working assumption. If they cannot accept it, then they will also find themselves rejecting everything based on it.

4. An anomaly is something whose relevance to a field of science is evident, but which that field cannot explain.

5. Illustration from A Thai comic book, under Fair Use Act.

6. Lundahl, Craig R., "Angels in Near-Death Experiences" Journal of Near-Death Studies, 11 (1) Fall 1980

7. http://www.shaktitechnology.com/bkknde.htm

8. There has been research implicating the visual cortex as the basis for the Tunnel experience. However, this seems to apply only to seeing the Tunnel, and not the NDE experience of traveling through it. The visual cortex is not involved with the *sensation* of movement that occurs in the Tunnel experience. The Tunnel is more than a reflection of the structure of the visual

cortex. It's an episode in NDEs with a tactile, vestibular and often auditory component, which together implicates many areas in the brain. Blackmore, S. J., and T. Troscianko. 1988. "The Physiology of The Tunnel." *Journal of Near-Death Studies* 8: 15–28.

9   Illustration from Van Scott, Miriam *"The Encyclopedia of Hell."* . St. Martin's Press. ©1998, under Fair Use Act

10   Illustration from Wiki Commons. Public Domain. http://commons. wikimedia.org/wiki/File:19th_century_black_heaven.jpg

11   Greyson, Bruce, M.D. "A Typology of Near-Death Experiences." American Journal of Psychology, 1985 142 : 8 967-969

12   Eleven Thai Near-Death Experiences http://www.shaktitechnology.com/bkknde.htm

13   Eleven Thai Near-Death Experiences http://www.shaktitechnology.com/bkknde.htm

14   Eleven Thai Near-Death Experiences http://www.shaktitechnology.com/bkknde.htm

15   `Near-death` Experiences Vastly Different For Japanese' Chicago Tribune, January 20, 1992

16   Reproduced under Fair Use Act.

17   Illustration by Mi-Chan, Use by Permission.

18   Sandars, N.K. "Poems of Heaven and Hell from Ancient Mesopotamia", Penguin Books, 1971

19   "If any one bring an accusation of any crime before the elders, and does not prove what he has charged, he shall, if it be a capital offence charged, be put to death".

20   Many NDEers have reported that their thoughts and feelings occurred with amazing speed.

21   Akashic comes from the Sanskrit word "Akasha", meaning space.

22   Illustration from a Thai Religious postcard. Reproduced under the Fair Use Act.

23   His explanation for World War II was that it happened in order to show the world its own capacity for brutality and mass murder before the spread of nuclear weapons had taken place. If nuclear weapons had been invented and World War II had not happened, the reality of mass death would not have been understood by the global mind until after it was already too late.

24 Traditionally, Yama is represented either with horns, or wearing a crown adorned with horns. His skin is dark, sometimes red, and his servants carry tridents or spears. The iconographic resemblance to Satan is obvious. Of course, Yama punishes sins and rewards virtue, making him an ally of the gods, and not God's enemy, like Satan in the Judeo-Christian traditions.

25 "Reality" is a difficult word to define in this context. The concept of two realities or of multiple realities is actually self-contradictory unless you already believe in more than one. We might say "Ontological Environments" instead of 'different realities', but the conundrum still remains, so we'll work on the assumption that the 'reality' we experience while we're alive is 'objective', and the ones that come after death are 'subjective'. Of course, our position is that alternate realities are manifestations of non–ordinary states of consciousness.

26 There is a popular, but much misunderstood theory in neuroscience called the *Triune Brain Theory*, which says we share the deeper levels of our brains with other species. This theory has been misunderstood to mean that our brains are composed of a human layer on top of a mammalian layer, on top of a reptilian layer. In fact, the deeper structures in our brains, considered to be "mammalian" are also uniquely human. The amygdala, a structure placed in the mammalian brain, has only 7 nuclei in cats, 12 nuclei in chimpanzees, and 21 nuclei in humans. The mammalian brain, in humans, is more complicated than in other species. In humans, the mammalian brain (including the limbic system) has been adapted to meet human needs.

27 Uomini NT, Meyer GF (2013) "Shared Brain Lateralization Patterns in Language and Acheulean Stone Tool Production: A Functional Transcranial Doppler Ultrasound Study". PLoS ONE 8(8): e72693. doi:10.1371/journal.pone.0072693

28 There is disagreement among anthropologists about whether language and complex culture appeared suddenly, following simultaneous changes in our brains, or appeared gradually, being elaborated as we evolved from more ancient primates species. The reincarnation hypothesis here agrees with hypothesis that language appeared suddenly. (See: Noble, William, & Davidson, Iain "The Evolutionary Emergence of Modern Human Behaviour: Language and its Archaeology" *Man* Vol. 26, No. 2, Jun., 1991)

29 We could also say that reincarnation gives us the capacity to learn the rules of culture, which would make it an example of a Baldwinian adaptation

in which selected offspring would tend to have an increased capacity for learning new skills rather than being confined to genetically coded, relatively fixed abilities.

30   An example of this is found in the Book of Deuteronomy, where God told the Hebrews "...in the cities of the nations the LORD your God is giving you as an inheritance, *do not leave alive anything that breathes.* Completely destroy them—the Hittites, Amorites, Canaanites, Perizzites, Hivites and Jebusites—as the LORD your God has commanded you." (Deuteronomy (20: 16-17, New International Version – Italics ours)

31   Small, Meredith, "What's Love Got to Do with It?" Anchor Books, 1996

32   "If a damsel who is a virgin be betrothed unto a husband, and a man find her in the city and lie with her, then ye shall bring them both out unto the gate of that city, and ye shall stone them with stones, that they die — the damsel, because she cried not, being in the city, and the man, because he hath humbled his neighbor's wife; so thou shalt put away evil from among you. (Deuteronomy 22:23-24)

33   Exodus, 20:14 & 17

34   Kellehear, Allan, Ph.D. "Culture, Biology, And The Near-Death Experience: A reappraisal" The Journal of nervous and Mental Disease", 181 (3), 1993

35   Persinger, MA. "Out-of-body-like experiences are more probable in people with elevated complex partial epileptic-like signs during periods of enhanced geomagnetic activity: a nonlinear effect." Perceptual and Motor Skills. 1995 Apr;80(2):563-9.

36   From http://etacar.put.poznan.pl/piotr.pieranski/Physics Around Us/Physics around us.html Reproduced under the Fair Use Act.

37   Kosevich et al. "Magnetic Soliton Motion in a Nonuniform Magnetic Field Journal of Experimental and Theoretical Physics" Volume 87, Number 2 / August, 1998. The physics of magnetic solitons is quite advanced, but some information can be gleaned from online sources.

38   There is an entire theory of memory developed by Karl Pribram, based on the idea that our memories are preserved holographically, known as the holographic theory of memory. It is an extremely influential theory not only of memory, but also of mind.

39   Photo taken on the Oregon Coast, reproduced under the fair use act. by Terry Toedtemeier http://www.portlandart.net/archives/2008/12/memorial_for_te.html

40   Sympathetic resonance (or sympathetic vibration) is a harmonic phenomenon wherein a passive vibratory body responds to external vibrations to which it has a harmonic likeness.

41   Holy Bible, John 3:16 (paraphrased)

42   Van Buitenen, J.A. B. (translator and editor) "The Bhagavadgita in the Mahabharata" University of Chicago Press, 1981

43   However, the finest grained structure of a magnetic field could mean a structure at the quantum level, and as there are no quanta associated with magnetic fields at present, finding such evidence could take time and a theoretical breakthrough in physics. Without such a breakthrough, we would not know what we were looking for, or how small the 'finest grained' structure of a magnetic field might be.

44   The Straw Man is a logical fallacy committed when a person ignores a person's actual position, substituting a misrepresented version of that position, and then argues against their own interpretation of it.

45   Speculation means to reason based on inconclusive or incomplete evidence. Speculative science calls for evidence, without assuming that that none is possible.

References for Chapter 3 – Some Brain parts:

[46] Miller, Lisa A; Collins, Robert L; Kent, Thomas A (2008). "Language and the modulation of impulsive aggression." *The Journal of neuropsychiatry and clinical neurosciences* **20** (3): 261–73.

[47] Kuhn, T.S. "The Structure of Scientific Revolutions" University Of Chicago Press, 1996

[48] Gupta R, Koscik TR, Bechara A, Tranel D. "The amygdala and decision-making." *Neuropsychologia.* 2011 Mar;49(4):760-6.

[49] Gupta R, Koscik TR, Bechara A, Tranel D. "The amygdala and decision-making." *Neuropsychologia.* 2011 Mar;49(4):760-6.

[50] Burkhard Ludescher, MD. Petros Martirosian, PhD. Uwe Klose, PhD Thomas Nägele, MD. PhD Fritz Schick, MD, PhD and Ulrike Ernemann, MD Determination of the rCBF in the Amygdala and Rhinal Cortex Using a FAIR-TrueFISP Sequence *Korean Journal of Radiology.* 2011 Sep-Oct; 12(5): 554–558.

[51] Gloor, P., "The Role of the Amygdala in Temporal Lobe Epilepsy". Appeared in *"The Amygdala: Neurobiological Aspects of Emotion, Memory, and Mental Dysfunction"* Wiley-Liss, 1992

[52] Kawashima R, Sugiura M, Kato T, Nakamura A, Hatano K, Ito K, Fukuda H, Kojima S, Nakamura K. "The human amygdala plays an important role in gaze monitoring." A PET study. *Brain.* 1999 Apr;122 (Pt 4):779-83.

[53] Hadjikhani N, de Gelder B. "Seeing fearful body expressions activates the fusiform cortex and amygdala." *Current Biology.* 2003 Dec 16;13(24):2201-5.

[54] Grèzes J, Pichon S, de Gelder B. "Perceiving fear in dynamic body expressions." *Neuroimage.* 2007 Apr 1;35(2):959-67.

[55] Goleman, Daniel "Social intelligence: the new science of human relationships" Bantam Books, 2007

[56] Han T, Alders GL, Greening SG, Neufeld RW, Mitchell DG. "Do fearful eyes activate empathy-related brain regions in individuals with callous traits?" *Social Cognitive and Affective Neuroscience* 2011 Oct 22.

[57] Sobhani M, Bechara A. "A somatic marker perspective of immoral and corrupt behavior." *Social Neuroscience.* 2011 Oct;6(5-6):640-52.

[58] Dunbar RI. "The social brain meets neuroimaging." *Trends in Cognitive Science.* 2011 Dec 15.

59   Kanai R, Bahrami B, Roylance R, Rees G. "Online social network size is reflected in human brain structure." Proceedings. *Biological Sciences / The Royal Society* 2011 Oct 19. [Epub ahead of print]

60   Gordon I, Voos AC, Bennett RH, Bolling DZ, Pelphrey KA, Kaiser MD. "Brain mechanisms for processing affective touch." *Human Brain Mapping.* 2011 Nov 29.

61   Juruena MF, Giampietro VP, Smith SD, Surguladze SA, Dalton JA, Benson PJ, Cleare AJ, Fu CH. "Amygdala activation to masked happy facial expressions." *Journal of the International Neuropsychological Society.* 2010 Mar;16(2):383-7.

62   Ji G, Neugebauer V. "Hemispheric lateralization of pain processing by amygdala neurons." J *Neurophysiology.* 2009 Oct;102(4):2253-64.

63   Sander K, Scheich H. "Left auditory cortex and amygdala, but right insula dominance for human laughing and crying." *Journal of Cognitive Neuroscience.* 2005 Oct;17(10):1519-31.

64   Adamic, Robert E., Morgan, Hywel D. "The effect of kindling of different nuclei in the left and right amygdala on anxiety in the rat" *Physiology and Behavior* 1994, Jan, v55 (n1): 1-12

65   Baeken C, De Raedt R, Ramsey N, Van Schuerbeek P, Hermes D, Bossuyt A, Leyman L, Vanderhasselt MA, De Mey J, Luypaert R. "Amygdala responses to positively and negatively valenced baby faces in healthy female volunteers: influences of individual differences in harm avoidance." *Brain Research.* 2009 Nov 3;1296:94-103.

66   Morri, J.S., Frith, C.D., Perrit, D.I., Rowland, D. et al., "A Differential Response in the Human Amygdala to Fearful and Happy facial expressions." *Nature* v383, n6603 (Oct. 31, 1996

67   Morri, J.S., Frith, C.D., Perrit, D.I., Rowland, D. et al., "A Differential Response in the Human Amygdala to Fearful and Happy facial expressions." *Nature* v383, n6603 (Oct. 31, 1996)

68   Persinger MA, "The neuropsychiatry of paranormal experiences." *Journal of Neuropsychiatry and Clinical Neuroscience.* 2001 Fall;13(4):515-24.

69   Murray, Elizabeth A., et. al. "Amygdala function in positive reinforcement". Appeared in "The Human Amygdala" Whalen, Paul J. & Phelps, Elizabeth A., editors. Guilford Press, 2009

70   Brennan PA, Kendrick KM. "Mammalian social odours: attraction and individual recognition." Philosophical Transactions of the Royal Society of London, Series B, *Biological Sciences.* 2006 Dec 29;361(1476):2061-78.

71 Mormann F, Dubois J, Kornblith S, Milosavljevic M, Cerf M, Ison M, Tsuchiya N, Kraskov A, Quiroga RQ, Adolphs R, Fried I, Koch C. "A category-specific response to animals in the right human amygdala." *Nature Neuroscience*. 2011 Aug 28;14(10):1247-9.

72 Lanteaume L, Khalfa S, Régis J, Marquis P, Chauvel P, Bartolomei F. "Emotion induction after direct intracerebral stimulations of human amygdala." *Cerebral Cortex* 2007 Jun;17(6):1307-13.

73 The frontal cortex, the insula, and the left caudate nucleus to name only three.

74 Persinger MA, Makarec K. "The feeling of a presence and verbal meaningfulness in context of temporal lobe function: factor analytic verification of the muses?" *Brain and Cognition*. 1992 Nov: 20(2):217-26.

75 Bower GH, Sivers H., "Cognitive impact of traumatic events." *Developmental Psychopathology*. 1998 Fall: 10(4):625-53

76 Compton WC. "Meaningfulness as a mediator of subjective well-being." *Psychological Reports*. 2000 Aug: 87(1):156-60.

77 Barbalet JM. "Boredom and social meaning". *British Journal of Sociology*. 1999 Dec: 50(4):631-46.

78 Carlson JM, Greenberg T, Mujica-Parodi LR. "Blind rage? Heightened anger is associated with altered amygdala responses to masked and unmasked fearful faces." *Psychiatry Research*. 2010 Jun 30;182(3):281-3. Epub 2010 May 21.

79 Harmon-Jones E. "Contributions from research on anger and cognitive dissonance to understanding the motivational functions of asymmetrical frontal brain activity." *Biological Psychology*. 2004 Oct;67(1-2):51-76.

80 Hayano F, Nakamura M, Asami T, Uehara K, Yoshida T, Roppongi T, Otsuka T, Inoue T, Hirayasu Y. "Smaller amygdala is associated with anxiety in patients with panic disorder." *Psychiatry and Clinical Neuroscience*. 2009 Jun;63(3):266-76.

81 Beaton EA, Schmidt LA, Schulkin J, Antony MM, Swinson RP, Hall GB. "Different fusiform activity to stranger and personally familiar faces in shy and social adults." *Social Neuroscience*. 2009;4(4):308-16.

82 Cannon R, Lubar J, Baldwin D. "Self-perception and experiential schemata in the addicted brain." *Applied Psychophysiology and Biofeedback*. 2008 Dec;33(4):223-38.

83 McEwen BS. "Protective and damaging effects of stress mediators: central role of the brain." *Dialogues in Clinical Neuroscience*. 2006;8(4):367-81.

84   Woon FL, Hedges DW. "Amygdala volume in adults with posttraumatic stress disorder: a meta-analysis." *Journal of Neuropsychiatry and Clinical Neuroscience.* 2009 Winter;21(1):5-12.

85   Smith SD, Abou-Khalil B, Zald DH. "Posttraumatic stress disorder in a patient with no left amygdala." *Journal of Abnormal Psychology.* 2008 May;117(2):479-84.

86   By internal language, I mean information encoded in EEG traces derived from the amygdala and to which the amygdala principally responds, when magnetic copies of the signal are applied to the brain.

87   Wallentin M, Nielsen AH, Vuust P, Dohn A, Roepstorff A, Lund TE. "Amygdala and heart rate variability responses from listening to emotionally intense parts of a story." *Neuroimage.* 2011 Oct 1;58(3):963-73.

88   Gloor, P., "The Role of the Amygdala in Temporal Lobe Epilepsy". Appeared in *"The Amygdala: Neurobiological Aspects of Emotion, Memory, and Mental Dysfunction"* Wiley-Liss, 1992

89   Derntl B, Habel U, Windischberger C, Robinson S, Kryspin-Exner I, Gur RC, Moser E. "General and specific responsiveness of the amygdala during explicit emotion recognition in females and males." *BMC Neuroscience.* 2009 Aug 4;10:91.

90   Goleman, Daniel "Social intelligence: the new science of human relationships" Bantam Books, 2007

91   Watson DR, Bai F, Barrett SL, Turkington A, Rushe TM, Mulholland CC, Cooper SJ. "Structural changes in the hippocampus and amygdala at first episode of psychosis". Brain Imaging and Behavior. 2011 Nov 3.

92   Hajek T, Kopecek M, Kozeny J, Gunde E, Alda M, Höschl C "Amygdala volumes in mood disorders--meta-analysis of magnetic resonance volumetry studies." Journal of Affectinv Disorders. 2009 Jun;115(3):395-410.

93   It's not clear if these changes are due to the disorder, its medication, or a combination of both.

94   Gainotti G. "Unconscious processing of emotions and the right hemisphere." Neuropsychologia. 2012 Jan;50(2):205-18.

95   Kiernan JA. "Anatomy of the temporal lobe." *Epilepsy Research and Treatment.* Epub 2012 Mar 29.

96   Irwin W, Anderle MJ, Abercrombie HC, Schaefer SM, Kalin NH, Davidson RJ. "Amygdalar interhemispheric functional connectivity differs between

the non-depressed and depressed human brain." Neuroimage. 2004 Feb;21(2):674-86.

[97] Howard LR, Kumaran D, Ólafsdóttir HF, Spiers HJ. "Double dissociation between hippocampal and parahippocampal responses to object-background context and scene novelty." *Journal of Neuroscience*. 2011 Apr 6;31(14):5253-61.

[98] Amat JA, Bansal R, Whiteman R, Haggerty R, Royal J, Peterson BS. "Correlates of intellectual ability with morphology of the hippocampus and amygdala in healthy adults." *Brain and Cognition*. 2008 Mar;66(2):105-14.

[99] The area of the brain's surface near the hippocampus is the 'hippocampal complex'. It includes the parahippocampal gyrus, the entorhinal cortex (from whence the hippocampus get's much of it's input from the cortex), the dentate gyrus, and the perirhinal cortex. In many places, we will refer to all these areas simply as the hippocampus, even though some neuroscience teachers might roll their eyes.

[100] Via the cingulate gyrus.

[101] Burgess N, Maguire EA, O'Keefe J. "The human hippocampus and spatial and episodic memory." Neuron. 2002 Aug 15;35(4):625-41.

[102] Shinohara Y, Hirase H, Watanabe M, Itakura M, Takahashi M, Shigemoto R. "Left-right asymmetry of the hippocampal synapses with differential subunit allocation of glutamate receptors." Proceedings of the National Academy of Sciiences of the United States of America 2008 Dec 9;105(49):19498-503.

[103] Shinohara Y. "Left-right asymmetry of the hippocampal synapses." Seikagaku. 2009 Sep;81(9):806-11.

[104] Harrison PJ. "The hippocampus in schizophrenia: a review of the neuropathological evidence and its pathophysiological implications." *Psychopharmacology (Berlin)*. 2004 Jun;174(1):151-62.

[105] Woon FL, Sood S, Hedges DW. "Hippocampal volume deficits associated with exposure to psychological trauma and posttraumatic stress disorder in adults: a meta-analysis." *Progress in Neuropsychopharmacology and Biological Psychiatry*. 2010 Oct 1;34(7):1181-8.

[106] Anger relies on several brain areas which, including the hippocampus and the primary areas supporting it, are all on the left. Surprisingly, the study of the anatomy of anger is still in its infancy, although its chemical basis is well understood. One researcher commented: "Very little is known about the neural circuitry guiding anger, angry rumination and aggressive personality." Denson TF, Pedersen WC, Ronquillo J, Nandy AS. "The angry brain: neural

442

correlates of anger, angry rumination, and aggressive personality." Journal of Cognitive Neuroscience. 2009 Apr;21(4):734-44.

107 Herrero N, Gadea M, Rodríguez-Alarcón G, Espert R, Salvador A. "What happens when we get angry? Hormonal, cardiovascular and asymmetrical brain responses." *Hormones and Behavior.* 2010 Mar: 57(3):276-83.

108 Stewart JL, Levin-Silton R, Sass SM, Heller W, Miller GA, "Anger style, psychopathology, and regional brain activity." *Emotion.* 2008 Oct: 8(5):701-13.

109 Denson TF, Pedersen WC, Ronquillo J, Nandy AS., "The angry brain: neural correlates of anger, angry rumination, and aggressive personality." *Journal of Cognitive Neuroscience.* 2009 Apr: 21(4):734-44.

110 De Smedt B, Holloway ID, Ansari D. "Effects of problem size and arithmetic operation on brain activation during calculation in children with varying levels of arithmetical fluency." *Neuroimage.* 2011 Aug 1;57(3):771-81.

111 Poppenk J, Walia G, McIntosh AR, Joanisse MF, Klein D, Köhler S. "Why is the meaning of a sentence better remembered than its form? An fMRI study on the role of novelty-encoding processes." *Hippocampus.* 2008;18(9):909-18.

112 Cipolotti L, Bird CM. "Amnesia and the hippocampus." *Current Opinions in Neurology.* 2006 Dec;19(6):593-8.

113 Stickgold, R. (2005, October 27). "Sleep-dependent memory consolidation." *Nature, 437*(7063): 1272–1278.

114 Bramão I, Faísca L, Forkstam C, Reis A, Petersson KM. "Cortical brain regions associated with color processing: an FMRI study." *The Open Neuroimaging Journal.* 2010 Nov 5;4:164-73.

115 Gaffan D, Parker A. "Interaction of perirhinal cortex with the fornix-fimbria: memory for objects and "object-in-place" memory." *Journal of Neuroscience.* 1996 Sep 15;16(18):5864-9.

116 Schwenzer M, Mathiak K. "Numeric aspects in pitch identification: an fMRI study." *BMC Neuroscience.* 2011 Mar 9;12:26.

117 Fujioka T, Zendel BR, Ross B. "Endogenous neuromagnetic activity for mental hierarchy of timing." *Journal of Neuroscience.* 2010 Mar 3;30(9):3458-66.

118 Trost W, Ethofer T, Zentner M, Vuilleumier P. "Mapping Aesthetic Musical Emotions in the Brain." Cerebral Cortex. 2011 Dec 15. [Epub ahead of print]

119 Koelsch S. "Investigating emotion with music: neuroscientific approaches." *Annals of the New York Acadamy of Science.* 2005 Dec;1060:412-8.

120 Gosselin N, Samson S, Adolphs R, Noulhiane M, Roy M, Hasboun D, Baulac M, Peretz I. "Emotional responses to unpleasant music correlates

with damage to the parahippocampal cortex." *Brain*. 2006 Oct;129(Pt 10):2585-92.

[121] Watanabe T, Yagishita S, Kikyo H. "Memory of music: roles of right hippocampus and left inferior frontal gyrus." *Neuroimage*. 2008 Jan 1;39(1):483-91.

[122] Hirshhorn M, Grady C, Rosenbaum RS, Winocur G, Moscovitch M. "The hippocampus is involved in mental navigation for a recently learned, but not a highly familiar environment: A longitudinal fMRI study." *Hippocampus*. 2011 May 16. doi: 10.1002/hipo.20944.

[123] Aradillas E, Libon DJ, Schwartzman RJ. "Acute loss of spatial navigational skills in a case of a right posterior hippocampus stroke." *Journal of Neurological Science*. 2011 Sep 15;308(1-2):144-6.

[124] Pereira AG, Portuguez MW, da Costa DI, Azambuja LS, Marroni SP, da Costa JC, Pereira-Filho AA. "Route learning performance: is it a hippocampus function?" *Cognitive and Behavioral Neurology*. 2011 Mar;24(1):4-10.

[125] O'Keefe J, Burgess N, Donnett JG, Jeffery KJ, Maguire EA. "Place cells, navigational accuracy, and the human hippocampus." *Philosophical Transactions of the Royal Society of London, Series B Biological Sciences*. 1998 Aug 29;353(1373):1333-40.

[126] Postma A, Kessels RP, van Asselen M. "How the brain remembers and forgets where things are: the neurocognition of object-location memory." *Neuroscience and Biobehavioral Reviews*. 2008 Oct;32(8):1339-45.

[127] Maguire EA, Woollett K, Spiers HJ. "London taxi drivers and bus drivers: a structural MRI and neuropsychological analysis." *Hippocampus*. 2006;16(12):1091-101.

[128] Rodriguez PF. "Human navigation that requires calculating heading vectors recruits parietal cortex in a virtual and visually sparse water maze task in fMRI." *Behavioral Neuroscience*. 2010 Aug;124(4):532-40.

[129] This refers to the *Vestibular system*.

[130] Hüfner K, Strupp M, Smith P, Brandt T, Jahn K. "Spatial separation of visual and vestibular processing in the human hippocampal formation." *Annals of the New York Acadamy of Science*. 2011 Sep;1233:177-86.

[131] Lopez C, Blanke O. "The thalamocortical vestibular system in animals and humans." *Brain Research Reviews*. 2011 Jun 24;67(1-2):119-46.

[132] Engström M, Pihlsgård J, Lundberg P, Söderfeldt B. "Functional magnetic resonance imaging of hippocampal activation during silent

mantra meditation." *Journal of Alternative and Complementary Medicine.* 2010 Dec;16(12):1253-8.

133 Lazar SW, Bush G, Gollub RL, Fricchione GL, Khalsa G, Benson H. "Functional brain mapping of the relaxation response and meditation." *Neuroreport.* 2000 May 15;11(7):1581-5.

134 Lou HC, Nowak M, Kjaer TW. "The mental self." *Progress in Brain Research.* 2005;150:197-204.

135 Luders E, Toga AW, Lepore N, Gaser C. "The underlying anatomical correlates of long-term meditation: larger hippocampal and frontal volumes of gray matter." *Neuroimage.* 2009 Apr 15;45(3):672-8.

136 Chiesa A. "Vipassana meditation: systematic review of current evidence." *Journal of Alternative and Complementary Medicine.* 2010 Jan;16(1):37-46.

137 Hölzel BK, Ott U, Gard T, Hempel H, Weygandt M, Morgen K, Vaitl D. "Investigation of mindfulness meditation practitioners with voxel-based morphometry." *Social Cognitive and Affective Neuroscience.* 2008 Mar;3(1):55-61.

138 There is more grey matter in the hippocampus of long-term meditators.

139 Ekstrom AD, Caplan JB, Ho E, Shattuck K, Fried I, Kahana MJ. "Human hippocampal theta activity during virtual navigation." *Hippocampus.* 2005;15(7):881-9.

140 Chen CY, Yang CC, Lin YY, Kuo TB. "Locomotion-induced hippocampal theta is independent of visual information in rats during movement through a pipe." *Behavioral Brain Research.* 2011 Jan 20;216(2):699-704

141 Gruzelier J. "A theory of alpha/theta neurofeedback, creative performance enhancement, long distance functional connectivity and psychological integration." *Cognitive Processing.* 2009 Feb;10 Suppl 1:S101-9.

142 Lee AC, Rudebeck SR. "Investigating the interaction between spatial perception and working memory in the human medial temporal lobe." *Journal of Cognitive Neuroscience.* 2010 Dec;22(12):2823-35.

143 Smith PF, Brandt T, Strupp M, Darlington CL, Zheng Y. "Balance before reason in rats and humans." *Annals of the New York Academy of Science.* 2009 May;1164:127-33.

144 Kesner RP, Hopkins RO. "Short-term memory for duration and distance in humans: role of the hippocampus." *Neuropsychology.* 2001 Jan: 15(1):58-68.

145 Postma A, Kessels RP, van Asselen M. "How the brain remembers and forgets where things are: the neurocognition of object-location memory." *Neuroscience and Biobehavioral Reviews.* 2008 Oct;32(8):1339-45.

146 The Book of Daniel, 5:27

147 Smith PF, Brandt T, Strupp M, Darlington CL, Zheng Y. "Balance before reason in rats and humans." Annals of the New York Acadeny of Science. 2009 May;1164:127-33.

148 Lavallee, Christina F., Hunter, Mathew D., Persinger, Michael A. "Intracerebral source generators characterizing concentrative meditation." *Cognitive Processes* (2011) 12:141–150

149 Kronmüller KT, Schröder J, Köhler S, Götz B, Victor D, Unger J, Giesel F, Magnotta V, Mundt C, Essig M, Pantel J. "Psychiatry Res. 2009 Oct 30;174(1):62-6. Epub 2009 Oct 1. "Hippocampal volume in first episode and recurrent depression." *Psychiatry Research.* 2009 Oct 30: 174(1):62-6. Epub 2009 Oct 1

150 Weiler JA, Suchan B, Daum I. "When the future becomes the past: Differences in brain activation patterns for episodic memory and episodic future thinking." *Behavioral Brain Research.* 2010 Oct 15;212(2):196-203.

151 Howard RJ, ffytche DH, Barnes J, McKeefry D, Ha Y, Woodruff PW, Bullmore ET, Simmons A, Williams SC, David AS, Brammer M. "The functional anatomy of imagining and perceiving colour." *Neuroreports.* 1998 Apr 20;9(6):1019-23.

152 Dotta, Blake Tiberius, & Persinger, Michael A. "Dreams, Time Distortion and the experience of future events" A Relativistic, Neuroquantal Perspective" *Sleep and Hypnosis* 2009;11(2):29-39

153 Johnson JD. "The conversational brain: fronto-hippocampal interaction and disconnection." *Medical Hypotheses.* 2006;67(4):759-64.

154 Piolino P, Giffard-Quillon G, Desgranges B, Chételat G, Baron JC, Eustache F. "Re-experiencing old memories via hippocampus: a PET study of autobiographical memory." *Neuroimage.* 2004 Jul;22(3):1371-83.

155 Plailly J, Delon-Martin C, Royet JP "Experience induces functional reorganization in brain regions involved in odor imagery in perfumers." *Human Brain Mapping.* 2012 Jan;33(1):224-34.

156 Roll WG, Persinger MA, Webster DL, Tiller SG, Cook CM. "Neurobehavioral and neurometabolic (SPECT) correlates of paranormal information: involvement of the right hemisphere and its sensitivity to weak complex magnetic fields." *International Journal of Neuroscience.* 2002 Feb;112(2):197-224.

157 Putative means 'believed to be'.

158 Venkatasubramanian G, Jayakumar PN, Nagendra HR, Nagaraja D, Deeptha R, Gangadhar BN. "Investigating paranormal phenomena: Functional brain imaging of telepathy." *International Journal of Yoga.* 2008 Jul;1(2):66-71.

[159] Frank MJ, O'Reilly RC, Curran T. "When memory fails, intuition reigns: midazolam enhances implicit inference in humans." *Psychological Science*. 2006 Aug;17(8):700-7.

[160] Though I don't remember who called it that.

[161] Miller, Robert "Cortico-hippocampal interplay and the representation of contexts in the brain" Springer-Verlag, 1991

[162] Rodriguez PF. "Human navigation that requires calculating heading vectors recruits parietal cortex in a virtual and visually sparse water maze task in fMRI." *Behavioral Neuroscience*. 2010 Aug;124(4):532-40.

[163] *Somatic* means having to do with the body.

[164] Gerdes AB, Wieser MJ, Mühlberger A, Weyers P, Alpers GW, Plichta MM, Breuer F, Pauli P. "Brain Activations to Emotional Pictures are Differentially Associated with Valence and Arousal Ratings." *Frontiers in Human Neuroscience*. 2010 Oct 28;4:175.

[165] Arnow BA, Desmond JE, Banner LL, Glover GH, Solomon A, Polan ML, Lue TF, Atlas SW. "Brain activation and sexual arousal in healthy, heterosexual males." *Brain*. 2002 May;125(Pt 5):1014-23.

[166] Fisher H, Aron A, Brown LL. "Romantic love: an fMRI study of a neural mechanism for mate choice." *Journal of Comparative Neurology*. 2005 Dec 5;493(1):58-62.

[167] Starkman MN, Giordani B, Gebarski SS, Schteingart DE. "Improvement in mood and ideation associated with increase in right caudate volume." *Journal of Affective Disorders*. 2007 Aug: 101(1-3):139-47. Epub 2006 Dec 15.

[168] Hayashi A, Abe N, Ueno A, Shigemune Y, Mori E, Tashiro M, Fujii T. "Neural correlates of forgiveness for moral transgressions involving deception." *Brain Research*. 2010 Mar 19.

[169] Noriuchi M, Kikuchi Y, Senoo A. "The functional neuroanatomy of maternal love: mother's response to infant's attachment behaviors." *Biological psychiatry*. 2008 Feb 15;63(4):415-23.

[170] Stevens, Charles F. "The Neuron" Appeared in : *The Brain* W.H. Freeman and Co., 1979

[171] Kalat, James W. "Biological Psychology (2nd Ed.)" Pg. 46, Wadsworth Publishing Co. 1981

[172] Kirschvink, Joseph L., Kobayashi-Kirshvink, Atsuko & Woodford, Barbera J. "Magnetite Biomineralization in the Human Brain", *Proceedings of the National Academy of Science* 1992, 89 7683-7687

447

References for Chapter 4 – Principles From Neuroscience

173 Newberg A, Alavi A, Baime M, Pourdehnad M, Santanna J, d'Aquili E. "The measurement of regional cerebral blood flow during the complex cognitive task of meditation: a preliminary SPECT study." *Psychiatry Research*. 2001 Apr 10;106(2):113-22.

174 A vector is a quantity, determined by two values, like time and height. If a water level goes up and down over time, the *average* water level is a vector.

175 Prosody, (from Greek *prosoidia*) means the rhythm, stress, and intonation of speech.

176 Persinger MA, "The Neuropsychiatry of Paranormal Experiences." *Journal of Neuropsychiatry and Clinical Neuroscience*. 2001 Fall;13(4):515-24.

177 Sander K, Scheich H. "Left Auditory Cortex and Amygdala, but Right Insula Dominance for Human Laughing and Crying." *Journal of Cognitive Neuroscience*. 2005 Oct;17(10):1519-31.

178 Sander K, Scheich H. "Left Auditory Cortex and Amygdala, but Right Insula Dominance for Human Laughing and Crying." *Journal of Cognitive Neuroscience*. 2005 Oct;17(10):1519-31.

179 Meyer M, Baumann S, Wildgruber D, Alter K. "How the brain laughs. Comparative Evidence from Behavioral, Electrophysiological and Neuroimaging Studies in Human and Monkey." *Behavioral Brain Research*. 2007 Sep 4;182(2):245-60.

180 Let the reader take note that this is the author's idea, and published for the first time in this book. This means, of course, that there has been no exposure to the scientific community, and so it has not yet found any agreement there. Of course, this also means that there has been no disagreement either.

181 Kronmüller KT, Schröder J, Köhler S, Götz B, Victor D, Unger J, Giesel F, Magnotta V, Mundt C, Essig M, Pantel J. "Hippocampal Volume in First Episode and Recurrent Depression." *Psychiatry Research*. 2009 Oct 30;174(1):62-6.

182 Von Gunten A, Ron MA. "Hippocampal Volume and Subjective Memory Impairment in Depressed Patients." *European Psychiatry*. 2004 Nov;19(7):438-40.

183 Horowtiz, M.J. & Adams, J.E. "Hallucinations on Brain Stimulation; Evidence for Revision of The Penfield Hypothesis" Appeared in: Origin and mechanism of Hallucinations, Plenum Press, 1970

[184]   Baker-Price L, Persinger MA. "Intermittent burst-firing weak (1 microTesla) magnetic fields reduce psychometric depression in patients who sustained closed head injuries: a replication and electroencephalographic validation." Perceptual and Motor Skills. 2003 Jun;96(3 Pt 1):965-74.

[185]   Richards PM, Koren SA, Persinger MA. "Experimental stimulation by burst-firing weak magnetic fields over the right temporal lobe may facilitate apprehension in women." Perceptual and Motor Skills. 1992 Oct;75(2):667-70.

[186]   Healey F, Persinger MA, Koren SA. "Enhanced hypnotic suggestibility following application of burst-firing magnetic fields over the right temporoparietal lobes: a replication." International Journal of Neuroscience. 1996 Nov;87(3-4):201-7.

References for chapter 5 – The God Helmet

187   Schobel SA, Kelly MA, Corcoran CM, Van Heertum K, Seckinger R, Goetz R, Harkavy-Friedman J, Malaspina D. "Anterior hippocampal and orbitofrontal cortical structural brain abnormalities in association with cognitive deficits in schizophrenia." Schizophrenia Research. 2009 Oct;114(1-3):110-8.

188   For more information, go to www.pubmed.com and search for the name 'Persinger'.

189   Persinger MA. "Religious and mystical experiences as artifacts of temporal lobe function: a general hypothesis." Perceptual and Motor Skills 1983 Dec;57(3 Pt 2):1255-62.

190   Or when the frontal lobes aren't able to dampen left temporal lobe activity.

191   Public domain image from Wikimedia commons.

192   Public Domain Image from Wiki Commons

193   Roberts DL, Tatini U, Zimmerman RS, Bortz JJ, Sirven JI. "Musical hallucinations associated with seizures originating from an intracranial aneurysm." Mayo Clinic Proceedings. 2001 Apr;76(4):423-6.

194   Persinger MA. "The neuropsychiatry of paranormal experiences." *Journal of Neuropsychiatry and Clinical Neuroscience.* 2001 Fall;13(4):515-24.

195   See the chapter on principles from neuroscience.

196   Miller, Lisa A; Collins, Robert L; Kent, Thomas A (2008). "Language and the modulation of impulsive aggression.". *The Journal of neuropsychiatry and clinical neurosciences* **20** (3): 261–73.

197   I have often thought that self-esteem is nothing more than how we feel about what we think other people think of us. Our sensitivity to the things other people say to us shows how deeply our 'social selves' are integrated with our linguistic selves, and the sense of self. A child who grows up constantly hearing themselves denigrated will usually either abuse others in similar ways, and/ or sink into a lifetime of low self-esteem.

198   Public Domain Image from Wiki Media Commons. Provided by Dr. MA Persinger.

199   Persinger MA. "The neuropsychiatry of paranormal experiences." *Journal of Neuropsychiatry and Clinical Neuroscience.* 2001 Fall;13(4):515-24.

200   A Swedish research group, attempting to replicate Persinger's results, ran their equipment in a DOS shell while running Windows 95 (known to distort

the signals), and got no results. The Swedish group assumed that it would be the same. It wasn't.

[201] Persinger MA. "The neuropsychiatry of paranormal experiences." *Journal of Neuropsychiatry and Clinical Neuroscience.* 2001 Fall;13(4):515-24.

[202] In Newberg's studies, a part of the parietal lobes was quieter in the 'absorption states', that appear in Buddhist meditation. It may be that pathways from the parietal lobes to the temporal lobes are also quieted, freeing up matrices of neurons that function during the death-process. The neurophenomenological principle (which tells us that the most active portion of the brain dominates the content of consciousness), and Crick's 'Astonishing Hypothesis' tell us that the functions of the most active area of the brain, moment-to-moment, are reflected in the content of our minds, moment-to-moment. Mental forms follow neural function.

[203] Newberg A, Pourdehnad M, Alavi A, d'Aquili EG. "Cerebral blood flow during meditative prayer: preliminary findings and methodological issues." Perceptual and Motor Skills. 2003 Oct;97(2):625-30.

[204] Photo by Author. See www.spiritualbrain.com

[205] Frank, Lone, "The Neurotourist", Oneworld Publications, 2011

[206] http://caloriecount.about.com/god-helmet-ft123438-1

[207] Wired Magazine, Novenber, 1999, "This is your Brain on God."

[208] BBC Report: "God on the Brain" *Horizon*, 17 April, 2005, http://www.bbc.co.uk/science/horizon/2003/godonbrain.shtml (retrieved 02-2012)

[209] The commercial "God Helmet" device, "Shiva", works with ordinary computer sound devices, and is designed to run under Windows.

[210] St-Pierre LS, Persinger MA. "Experimental facilitation of the sensed presence is predicted by the specific patterns of the applied magnetic fields, not by suggestibility: re-analyses of 19 experiments." International Journal of Neuroscience. 2006 Sep;116(9):1079-96.

[211] Many people have made the mistake of thinking that this involves EM emissions. By definition, EMF emissions must be composed of photons (radiation), or ions (charged particles), which this technology does not use.

[212] Some commentators in online forums have speculated that these low-intensity magnetic fields are not strong enough to penetrate the brain. In fact, there is no such thing as a magnetic insulator. There is no way to stop magnetic fields. Nature must find a way to return the magnetic field lines back to an opposite pole. This is covered by one of Maxwell's equations (del dot B = 0).

213 A 'burst-firing' pattern.

214 This can occur with epilepsy, but is very rare in our normal lives.

215 Persinger MA, Tiller SG, Koren SA. "Experimental simulation of a haunt experience and elicitation of paroxysmal electroencephalographic activity by transcerebral complex magnetic fields: induction of a synthetic "ghost"?" Perceptual and Motor Skills. 2000 Apr;90(2):659-74.

216 In the sciences, there is an adage "You can't prove a negative". It implies that it's impossible to prove there is no God; and that no such proof will ever be possible. Although this is good scientific structuralism, it doesn't recognize that standards for proof are not the same in the sciences as in religion and spirituality. The religious faithful have always held that they are right to hold onto their faith, until such time as there is incontrovertible proof that God doesn't exist. Skeptics have always held that they are right in denying God's existence until there is iron-clad proof of it. There is one standard for truth in the Sciences, another in Law, another in Religion, and yet another to be found in the minds of ordinary non-specialists. None of these, in this author's opinion, have any right to demand that others apply any criteria but their own.

217 There actually is some evidence, although controversial, that one *can* change one's world through prayer.

218 The amygdala is a mesio/basal temporal lobe structure, meaning that it's in the middle and deeper areas of the temporal lobes.

219 St-Pierre LS, Persinger MA. "Experimental facilitation of the sensed presence is predicted by the specific patterns of the applied magnetic fields, not by suggestibility: re-analyses of 19 experiments." International Journal of Neuroscience. 2006 Sep;116(9):1079-96.

References for Chapter 6 – Stages of Near-Death Experiences

220 In fact, most people who clinically die do not have NDEs, and the difference may lie in how sensitive the temporal lobes of their brains are. The hypothesis of this book encourages us to presume that everyone who is dead, even temporarily, has a death-process, but the two thirds of the population with less sensitive temporal lobes are less likely to remember their experiences. Even the one-third of those who die clinically and remember such experiences is a large number; too large to be explained as random processes.

221 We'll use the phrases "death process" and "near-death experiences" almost interchangeably through much of this book.

222 See the chapter on Principles of Neuroscience.

223 Salisbury, Harrison, E. "The 900 days: The Seige of Leningrad" Harper & Row, 1969.

224 Eadie, Betty J. & Taylor, Curtis, "Embraced by the light", Gold Leaf Press, 1992

225 Heim, A., "Notizen ueber den Ton durch Absturz" Jahrb Schweiz Alpenklub 27, (1882): 327.

226 Noyes, Russell, & Slymen, Donald, "The Subjective Response to Life-Threatening Danger" Omega, Vol.9, 1978-1979, 313-321

227 Osis, Karlis, Ph.D. & Haraldsson, Ernendur, Ph.D. "At the Hour of Our Death", Avon books 1977

228 Morse M.D., Dr. Melvin, & Perry, Paul "Closer to the Light: Learning from the Near-Death Experiences of Children". Ivy Books, 1990

229 Moody, Raymond, "Life after Life and Reflections on Life after Life." Guidepost Books, 1975

230 Morse, Melvin, MD, et. al. "Childhood Near-Death Experiences" American Journal of Diseases of Children, Vol. 140, Nov 1986, 1110-1114

231 Randle, Kevin D., "To Touch The light", Pinnacle Books, 1994

232 Ring, Kenneth, Ph.d. & Lawrence, Madeline, R.N., Ph.D. "Further Evidence for Veridical Perception during Near-Death Experiences", Journal of Near-Death Studies, 1993 11 (4) 223-229

233 Tibiri, Emelio, "Extrasomatic Emotions", Journal of Near-Death Studies, 11(3), Spring, 1993

234 An hallucination is where you see something that doesn't exist. An illusion is a distorted perception of something that does exist.

235 Eliade, Mircea "Shamanism" Princeton University Press, 2004

236 Varga, Josie Visits from Heaven, A.R.E. Press, 2009

237 Steiger, Brad, "One with The Light", Signet Books, 1994

238 Morse, Melvin, M.D & Perry Paul, "Transformed by The Light", Ivy Books, 1992

239 Persinger, Michael; Saroka, Kevin; Mulligan, Bryce; Murphy, Todd "Experimental Elicitation of an Out of Body Experience and Concomitant Cross-Hemispheric Electroencephalographic Coherence" NeuroQuantology, Vol 8, No 4 (2010)

240 Vissudhikoon, Phra Bhavana "Vipassana meets Consciousness", Pg. 145-154 "Tie Laeow Fuhn" (no publisher or date information, accessed 1995), Bangkok.

241 Steiger, Brad, "One with The Light", Signet Books, 1994

242 Author's collection (edited for spelling and grammar)

243 Image copyright by author.

244 Randle, Kevin D., "To Touch The light", Pinnacle Books, 1994.

245 Moody, Raymond, "Life after Life and Reflections on Life after Life." Guidepost Books, 1975

246 Ring, Kenneth, "Life at Death, A Scientific Investigation Of the Near-Death Experience", Coward, McCann & Geoghegan, 1980

247 McNay, Roxy Ian, "Close Encounters: A Journey of Spiritual Discovery and Adventure". Roximillion Publications, 1991

248 Moody, Raymond A. "Life After Life" Bantam Books, 1975

249 Morse, Melvin, M.D & Perry Paul, "Transformed by The Light", Ivy Books, 1992

250 Nanamoli, Bhikku (trans.) "Visuddhimagga: "The Path of Purification of Bhandantacariya Buddhaghosa" (IV, 95-98) Buddhist Publication Society, Kandy, Sri Lanka, 1975

251 Nanamoli, Bhikku (trans.) "Visuddhimagga: "The Path of Purification of Bhandantacariya Buddhaghosa" (IV, 95-98) Buddhist Publication Society, Kandy, Sri Lanka, 1975

252 Morse, Melvin, M.D & Perry Paul, "Transformed by The Light", Ivy Books, 1992

253 Steiger, Brad, "One with The Light", Signet Books, 1994

254 Morse, Melvin, M.D. & Perry, Paul, "Parting Visions: Uses and Meanings of Pre-Death, Psychic, and Spiritual Experiences" Harper Paperbacks, 1994

255 Morse, Melvin, M.D & Perry Paul, "Transformed by The Light", Ivy Books, 1992

256 Suwannatat, Thong Thaew "Experiences Through Consciousness", Vol 2. Bangkok, 1992

257 Moody, Raymond Jr. MD. "Reflections on Life After Life" Bantam Books, 1977.

258 Reproduced under the Fair Use Act.

259 Pronounced yah-ma-TOOT.

260 From Greek, meaning "From within".

261 Bascom, Lionel C. & Loecher, Barbera, "By the Light" Avon Books, 1995

262 Morse, Melvin, M.D & Perry Paul, "Transformed by The Light", Ivy Books, 1992

263 Bascom, Lionel C. & Loecher, Barbera, "By the Light" Avon Books, 1995

264 Moody, Raymond, "The Light Beyond", Bantam Books, 1988

265 Randle, Kevin D., "To Touch The light", Pinnacle Books, 1994.

266 Lee, Carolyn, "The Promised God-Man is Here" Dawn-Horse Press, Middletown, California, (1998)

267 Da, Adi, "The Knee of Listening", TDL Trust, 1995

268 Within the definition of enlightenment we will use in the chapter on enlightenment.

269 There are also NDEs in the West where people have hellish experiences, though researchers don't agree on how many. Usually, these have negative emotions, not visions of hell, though such visions have been reported. Negative NDEs in the West are usually not unpleasant throughout. More often, they have a fearful message or episode. A hellish NDE can also have some very joyous moments.

270 "in thy presence is fullness of joy; at thy right hand there are pleasures for evermore." Psalms 16:11

271 Victa, Lori & Chiero, Kathy "Don Piper: At Heaven's Gate" *The 700 Club* http://www.cbn.com/700club/features/amazing/donpiper_heaven051104. aspx Accessed 01/17/2012

272 Serdahely, W. J. (1995). Variations from the prototypic near-death experience: The individually tailored hypothesis. *Journal of Near-Death Studies*, 13, 185-196.

273 Morse, Melvin, M.D & Perry Paul, "Transformed by The Light", Ivy Books, 1992

274 Morse, Melvin, M.D & Perry Paul, "Transformed by The Light", Ivy Books, 1992

275 The Gainsville Times "From the Brink of Death, a Mission is Born" October 28, 2006. Edited for subject anonymity.

276 Vincent, Ken "Visions of God from the Near-Death Experience" Larson Publications, 1994

277 Morse, Melvin, M.D & Perry Paul, "Transformed by The Light", Ivy Books, 1992

278 Morse, Melvin, M.D & Perry Paul, "Transformed by The Light", Ivy Books, 1992

279 Vincent, Ken "Visions of God from the Near-Death Experience" Larson Publications, 1994

280 Castaneda, Carlos, "The Fire from Within" Simon & Schuster, 1984

281 "Otherworldly Journeys", (Carol Zalesky)

282 In some Thai NDEs, Yama is found sitting at a desk instead of on a throne.

283 Many will argue that the Buddha is not a deity, but rather the embodiment of enlightenment. However, in the popular religion of Thailand, he is the principle object of religious worship - a status imposed by centuries of devotional practice.

284 "Experience through consciousness" (Prasobkhan Tahng vinnanna) by Thong Thaew Suwanathat Vol. 2 Pg. 126-136.

285 There is a biblical belief that an angel will read the 'Book of Life" to see if the name of the person being judged appears, but this has not been reported in any NDEs of which I am aware.

286 Detail from Thai religious poster. Under Fair Use Act

287 In one Thai NDE, they were actually called by this word – 'accountant'.

288 Subrahmanyam, S.V. (Trans.), *The Garuda Purana*, Forgotten Books, 2008

289 Elementary school rooms in Thailand still display two banners, provided by the Department of Education. One says "We love our mothers and fathers, and we love The King". The other says "Your mother and father gave you life. You owe them a debt you can never pay".

290 Moody, Raymond Jr. MD. "Reflections on Life After Life" Bantam Books, 1977.

291 Brinkley, Dannion, "Saved by The Light" Villard Books, 1994

292   Brinkley, Dannion, "Saved by The Light" Villard Books, 1994

293   Bascom, Lionel C. & Loecher, Barbera, "By the Light" Avon Books, 1995

294   Vissudhikoon, Phra Bhavana "Vipassana meets Consciousness", "Tie Laeow Fuhn" (no publisher or date information, accessed 1995), Bangkok.

295   Atwater, PMH, "Beyond The Light" Avon, 1994

296   Kellehear, Allan, Ph.D. "Culture, Biology, And The Near-Death Experience: A reappraisal" The Journal of nervous and Mental Disease", 181 (3), 1993

297   Illustration by Gustav Doré. Public Domain.

298   From an uncopyrighted Thai postcard collection. Reproduced under the fair use act.

299   Indra is the King of heaven and God of thunder. *Loka* means 'world'.

300   The Akashic Records, remembered in theosophical beliefs, are a repository of all possible knowledge; including the knowledge that the gods hold.

301   Randle, Kevin D., "To Touch The light", Pinnacle Books, 1994

302   Sutherland, Cherie, Ph.D. "Within the Light", Bantam Books, 1993

303   In at least two NDEs, this council had 12 members. This is same number of sub-personalities shown by some people with Multiple Personality Disorder.

304   Harris, Barbara, and Bascom, Lionel C. "Full Circle - The Near Death Experience and Beyond", Pocket Books, 1990

305   Moody, Raymond, "Life after Life and Reflections on Life after Life." Guidepost Books, 1975

306   Suwannatat, Thong Thaew "Experiences Through Consciousness", Vol 2. Bangkok, 1992

307   Randle, Kevin D., "To Touch The light", Pinnacle Books, 1994.

308   Augustine, Keith, "Hallucinatory Near-Deah Experiences", secularweb, 2003 (updated 2008).

309   Suwannathat, Experience through Consciousness (*Prasobkhan Thang Vinanna*) Vol. 2, Pg. 220-239 (No date or publisher)

310   Greyson B. "A typology of near-death experiences." American Journal of Psychiatry. 1985 Aug;142(8):967-9.

311   Jim Chapman, "Come back to life", Bettger Books, 2006

312   These are drawn from the *Garuda Purana*.

References for Chapter 7 – The Neural Bases for the Stages of Near-Death Experiences

313 Dolgoff-Kaspar R, Ettinger AB, Golub SA, Perrine K, Harden C, Croll SD. "Numinous-like auras and spirituality in persons with partial seizures." *Epilepsia.* 2011 Mar;52(3):640-4

314 Britton WB, Bootzin RR. "Near-death experiences and the temporal lobe." *Psychological Science.* 2004 Apr;15(4):254-8.

315 Saver JL, Rabin J. "The neural substrates of religious experience." *Journal of Neuropsychiatry and Clinical Neuroscience.* 1997 Summer;9(3):498-510.

316 TL seizures can create lots of other phenomena, too. In fact, only a small percent of TL seizures include altered states. The most common TL seizure phenomena is lip-smacking, a thing that's very far from the spiritual experiences for which TLE has become so well known.

317 Morse, Melvin & Perry, Paul, "Parting Visions: Uses and Meanings of Pre-Death, Psychic, and Spiritual Experiences" Harper Collins, 1996

318 Kubler-Ross 'On Death and Dying'. New York, Macmillan Publishing Co, 1969.

319 Ball T, Derix J, Wentlandt J, Wieckhorst B, Speck O, Schulze-Bonhage A, Mutschler I. "Anatomical specificity of functional amygdala imaging of responses to stimuli with positive and negative emotional valence." Journal of Neuroscience Methods. 2009 May 30;180(1):57-70.

320 This is based on the fact that the right hippocampus is the primary source of Theta brain waves, which are associated with trance, mediation, hypnosis, and other states that depend on relaxation.

321 I use the phrase "in and through unusual pathways" within certain brain parts to convey that, although each phenomenon is dominated by a brain structure, there will always be more than one structure involved. When only one brain part is supporting the phenomenon of the moment, it will be very intense. In the overwhelming majority of our experiences, groups of structures are working together, with one in the lead. It can be more active, or its parts may work in closer unison, but there will always be one structure which is the most excited at any given time and which will dominate the experience. Dr. Persinger uses the phrase 'matrices of neurons', instead of the more common term 'pathways'. This helps to imagine neural circuits, running through several brain parts, spread out over a wide area.

322 Kavanau JL. "Memory, sleep, and dynamic stabilization of neural circuitry: evolutionary perspectives" *Neuroscience and Biobehavioral Reviews* 1996 Summer;20(2):289-311.

323 "Shared" psychic experiences are another question, and we'll be looking at them later on.

324 See the chapter on "neural phases of NDEs".

325 A skull of a deformed child, dated at 530,000 years ago, was found in Spain. The skull belonged to a 10-year-old child, who had a birth defect in which the plates of the skull fuse together. This debilitating disease increases pressure on the brain. This would have made it impossible for the child to take care of itself. The wounded, the sick, and the elderly were also taken care of, if their nation is at all like the hunter/gatherer societies we see today. *Discover magazine January / February, 2010.*

326 Yamdhood is a Sanskrit word meaning "messenger from Yama".

327 Morse, Melvin, M.D. & Perry, Paul, "Parting Visions: Uses and Meanings of Pre-Death, Psychic, and Spiritual Experiences" Harper Paperbacks, 1994

328 Persinger MA. "Neuropsychological principia brevita: an application to traumatic (acquired) brain injury." *Psychological Reports.* 1995 Dec;77(3 Pt 1):707-24.

329 Hoffmann, Yoel "Japanese Death Poems: Written by Zen Monks and Haiku Poets on the Verge of Death," Charles E. Tuttle Company, 1986, p. 27.

330 Speer, Albert, "Inside the Third Reich", Bonanza Books, 1970

331 Eadie, Betty J. & Taylor, Curtis, "Embraced by the light", Gold Leaf Press, 1992

332 Macropsia and Micropsia are known to happen with seizures that begin in the amygdala and hippocampus, though it can also happen from other causes as well. Macropsia seems to associate with the left hippocampus and the area around the left angular gyrus, but it's not clear if it's exciting or inhibiting activity there. It's a spatial illusion, which implicates the right side, so the associated activity in the left side of the brain may be suppressing excitement on the right, and the functions of the stimulated areas on the left might be picked up by the same areas on the right. In the Penfield case, it doesn't say which side of the brain is involved, though the diagrams show the left side.

333 Barrack, Samuel "Hippocampal and parahippocampal seizures" *Journal of Neurology*, November 10, 2009

334 Wilder Penfield, the famous Canadian Brain surgeon, used the same electrical stimulation to map the areas of the brain that connect to specific areas of the body.

335 Penfield, Wilder, & Jasper, Herbert, "Epilepsy and the functional Anatomy of The Human Brain" Little, Brown, & Co., 1954

336 The hippocampus, the areas on the surface of the brain close to it, and the occipito-temporo-parietal region, which contains the angular gyrus.

337 Schacter, Steven C, MD, "Brainstorms: Epilepsy in our words" Raven Press, 1993

338 LaPlante,Eve, "Siezed: The story of Temporal Lobe Epilepsy", Harper Collins Books, 1993

339 Eadie, Betty J. & Taylor, Curtis, "Embraced by the light", Gold Leaf Press, 1992

340 Penfield, Wilder, O.M., C.M.G., M.D., *BSc.*, F.R.C.S., *F.R.C.S.* "The Role Of The Temporal Cortex in Certain Psychic Phenomena", *Journal of Mental Science*, July 1955 388, (101) 451-465

341 Penfield, Wilder, & Jasper, Herbert, "Epilepsy and the functional Anatomy of The Human Brain" Little, Brown, & Co., 1954.

342 Baldwin, Maitland & Baily, Pearce, "Temporal Lobe Epilepsy", Charles C. Thomas Pub. 1958

343 Persinger, M.A. "Out Of Body Experiences Are More Probable In People With Elevated Complex Partial Epileptic-Like Signs During Periods of Enhanced Geomagnetic Activity: A Nonlinear Effect." *Perceptual and Motor Skills*, 1995 80, 563-569

344 This refers to the "Shakti" neural stimulation systems, available through www.spiritualbrain.com.

345 Author's collection. Stimulation was over the right temporal lobe and angular gyrus.

346 Blanke, O., Ortigue, S., Landis, T., Seeck, M. "Stimulating Own-Body Perceptions". *Nature*, 419, 269 – 270, (2002).

347 The occipital-temporal-parietal area, which includes the Angular Gyrus.

348 Schacter, Steven C, MD, "Brainstorms: Epilepsy in our words" Raven Press, 1993

349 Persinger, Michael, Saroka, Kevin, Mulligan, Bryce P Murphy, Todd R "Experimental Elicitation of an Out of Body Experience and Concomitant

Cross-Hemispheric Electroencephalographic Coherence" *NeuroQuantology*, Vol 8, No 4 (2010)

350 Russell NA, Horii A, Smith PF, Darlington CL, Bilkey DK "Lesions of the Vestibular System Disrupt Hippocampal Theta Rhythm in the Rat." *Journal of Neurophysiology.* 2006 Jul;96(1):4-14

351 Smith PF, Horii A, Russell N, Bilkey DK, Zheng Y, Liu P, Kerr DS, Darlington CL "The Effects of Vestibular Lesions on Hippocampal Function in Rats". *Progress in Neurobiology.* 2005 Apr;75(6):391-405

352 Note that these are rat studies. Deliberately damaging the brain to learn what it does is limited to animals, for obvious ethical reasons.

353 See the chapter on "Some brain parts".

354 Persinger, M.A. "Out Of Body Experiences Are More Probable In People With Elevated Complex Partial Epileptic-Like Signs During Periods of Enhanced Geomagnetic Activity: A Nonlinear Effect." *Perceptual and Motor Skills,* 1995 80, 563-569

355 Kirschvink, Joseph L., Kobayashi-Kirshvink, Atsuko & Woodford, Barbera J. "Magnetite Biomineralization in the Human Brain", *Proceedings of the National Academy of Science* 1992, 89 7683-7687

356 Hagerty, Barbara Bradley "Are Spiritual Encounters All In Your Head?" NPR (National Public Radio) January 16, 2012 Online at http://www.npr.org/templates/story/story.php?storyId=104291534

357 Penfield, Wilder, & Jasper, Herbert, "Epilepsy and the functional Anatomy of The Human Brain" Little, Brown, & Co., 1954.

358 Schacter, Steven C, MD, "Brainstorms: Epilepsy in our words" Raven Press, 1993

359 The smell of bananas here is an example of an epileptic *aura*. In epilepsy, an aura is a sensation or perception (usually hallucinatory or illusory) that tells the patient that a seizure is about to begin. The word *aura* comes from the Greek word meaning 'breeze' or 'breath'.

360 Health24.com "The aura: an early warning sign" Last updated: Friday, October 08, 2004. Retrieved 01/17/2012 http://www.health24.com/medical/Condition_centres/777-792-809-1676,17434.asp

361 Talaei SA, Sheibani V, Salami M. "Light deprivation improves melatonin related suppression of hippocampal plasticity." *Hippocampus.* 2010 Mar;20(3):447-55.

362 Gorfine T, Zisapel N. "Melatonin and the human hippocampus, a time dependent interplay." *Journal of Pineal Research.* 2007 Aug;43(1):80-6.

363 Chaudhury D, Wang LM, Colwell CS. "Circadian regulation of hippocampal long-term potentiation." *Journal of Biological Rhythms.* 2005 Jun;20(3):225-36.

364 Author's Collection.

365 Schacter, Steven C, MD, "Brainstorms: Epilepsy in our words" Raven Press, 1993

366 Blackmore, Susan: Dying to Live: Near-Death Experiences (1993). London, Grafton.

367 Author's collection (edited for spelling and grammar).

368 Author's Collection.

369 Author's Collection.

370 Author's collection

371 Author's Collection.

372 KLTV News Report, 11/06/06 "Back From the Dead: Woman Says She Visited Heaven's Doorstep. http://www.kltv.com/Global/story. asp?S=5641928 Accessed 01-17-2012.

373 Siegel, Ronald "Fire in the Brain: Clinical tales of "hallucination" Dutton books, 1993

374 http://www.shaktitechnology.com/bkknde.htm

375 Personal communication.

376 The Shakti neural stimulation system. See www.spiritualbrain.com

377 Author's Collection.

378 Aron A, Fisher H, Mashek DJ, Strong G, Li H, Brown LL. "Reward, motivation, and emotion systems associated with early-stage intense romantic love." *Journal of Neurophysiology.* 2005 Jul;94(1):327-37.

379 Bartels A, Zeki S. "The neural basis of romantic love." *NeuroReport* 2000; 11(17): 3829-3834.

380 Noriuchi M, Kikuchi Y, Senoo A. "The functional neuroanatomy of maternal love: mother's response to infant's attachment behaviors." *Biological Psychiatry.* 2008 Feb 15;63(4):415-23.

381 Augustine, James R. "Circuitry and functional aspects of the insular lobe in primates including humans" *Brain Research Reviews* 22 (1996) 229-244

382 Riem MM, Bakermans-Kranenburg MJ, Pieper S, Tops M, Boksem MA, Vermeiren RR, van Ijzendoorn MH, Rombouts SA. "Oxytocin modulates

amygdala, insula, and inferior frontal gyrus responses to infant crying: a randomized controlled trial." *Biological Psychiatry.* 2011 Aug 1;70(3):291-7.

383 Liu X, Hairston J, Schrier M, Fan J. "Common and distinct networks underlying reward valence and processing stages: a meta-analysis of functional neuroimaging studies." *Neuroscience and Biobehavioral Review.* 2011 Apr;35(5):1219-36.

384 Persinger MA. "Geophysical variables and behavior: LV. Predicting the details of visitor experiences and the personality of experients: the temporal lobe factor." Perceptual and Motor Skills. 1989 Feb;68(1):55-65.

385 Schmidt, Richard Penrose, M.D. & Wilder, B. Joe, M.D. "Epilepsy" (Contemporary Neurology Series), F.A. Davis Company, 1966

386 Penfield, Wilder and Phanor Perot, "The Brain's Record of Auditory and Visual Experience" *Brain*, Vol 86, Pt.4, December 1963

387 Arzy S, Seeck M, Ortigue S, Spinelli L, Blanke O. "Induction of an illusory shadow person." *Nature.* 2006 Sep 21;443(7109):287.

388 Persinger MA., "The Neuropsychiatry of Paranormal Experiences". *Journal of Neuropsychiatry and Clinical Neuroscience.* 2001 Fall;13(4):515-24.

389 Kellehear, Allan, Ph.D. "Culture, Biology, And The Near-Death Experience: A reappraisal" *The Journal of nervous and Mental Disease*", 181 (3), 1993

390 A flashback, or *involuntary recurrent memory*, is a psychological phenomenon in which an individual has a sudden, powerful, re-experience of a past experience or elements of a past experience.

391 Penfield, Wilder & Rasmussen, Theodore, "The Cerebral Cortex of Man", Macmillan, 1955b Penfield, Wilder and Phanor Perot, "The Brain's Record of Auditory and Visual Experience" *Brain*, Vol 86, Pt.4, December 1963

392 Penfield, Wilder, O.M., C.M.G., M.D., *BSc.*, F.R.C.S., *F.R.C.S.* "The Role Of The Temporal Cortex in Certain Psychic Phenomena", *Journal of Mental Science*, July 1955 388, (101) 451-465

393 The Shakti Neural System - see www.spiritualbrain.com

394 Author's collection.

395 Persinger, M.A. "Elicitation of Childhood Memories in Hypnosis-like Settings is Associated With Complex Partial Epileptic-like Signs For Women But Not Men: Implications for The False Memory Syndrome". Perceptual and Motor Skills, 1994, 78, 643-651

396 396 Mendez MF, Fras IA. "The false memory syndrome: experimental studies and comparison to confabulations." Medical Hypotheses. 2011 Apr;76(4):492-6.

397 Mendez MF, Fras IA. "The false memory syndrome: experimental studies and comparison to confabulations." Medical Hypotheses. 2011 Apr;76 (4):492-6

398 Strehler BL. "New theory of hippocampal function: associated rehearsal of multiplexed coded symbols." *Synapse.* 1989;3(3):182-92.

399 Beebe-hill, Ruth "Hanta Yo" (introduction), Doubleday, 1979

400 Suwannathat, "Experiences through Consciousness" (no publisher listed), Bangkok Vol. 2, Pg. 220-239

401 During long-term potentiation.

402 Author's collection.

403 Augustine, Keith, "Hallucinatory Near-Death Experiences" Secular web, 2008 http://www.infidels.org/library/modern/keith_augustine/HNDEs.html

404 Persinger MA, Makarec K. "The feeling of a presence and verbal meaningfulness in context of temporal lobe function: factor analytic verification of the muses?" *Brain and Cognition.* 1992 Nov;20(2):217-26.

405 Steriade M, Deschenes M. "The thalamus as a neuronal oscillator." *Brain Research.* 1984 Nov;320(1):1-63.

406 Tiberi, E. (1993). Extrasomatic emotions. *Journal of Near-Death Studies, 11*(3), 149-170.

407 Persinger, Michael A, Ph. D. "Near-Death Experiences: Determining the Neuroanatomical Pathways by Experiential Patterns and Simulation In Experimental Settings", Appeared in: "Healing: Beyond Suffering and Death", Bessette, Luc, MD (Ed), MNH Publications, 1994

408 A transforming insight is a new cognition, often about one's self, that compels one to make changes in one's life and behavior.

409 There is one other kind of mystic experience, which we will examine in a later chapter. These include experiences of "oneness", or of "being beyond the world of form", or of "transcending or going beyond duality".

410 Source unknown.

411 The Akashic records, a teaching preserved in Theosophical and Wiccan traditions (to name only two), can take many forms. A library, filled with books, is one of them. Another is a magic pan, filled with water, where images appear, and the images show the answer to any question. Naturally,

belief in the Akashic record is also popular among active psychics, some of whom believe that their cognitive skills work by accessing it.

[412] These implicate the right hippocampus, and the right occipito-temporo-parietal region, the area where deer have their antlers.

[413] Persinger MA. "Geophysical variables and behavior: LV. Predicting the details of visitor experiences and the personality of experients: the temporal lobe factor." Perceptual and Motor Skills. 1989 Feb;68(1):55-65.

[414] Persinger MA, Makarec K. "The feeling of a presence and verbal meaningfulness in context of temporal lobe function: factor analytic verification of the muses?" Brain and Cognition 1992 Nov;20(2):217-26.

References for Chapter 8 – The Sensed Presence.

[415] Technically, an illusion is a distortion of a real perception, and a hallucination is a perception of something that isn't there at all.

[416] Murphy, Todd "Recreating Near-Death Experiences: A Cognitive Approach" *Journal of Near-Death Studies*, 1998, Volume 17, Number 4, Pages 261-265

[417] Persinger, MA, Personal communication.

[418] These experiences are known as signs of complex partial epileptic (temporal lobe) seizures, but they also happen to non-epileptics. Instead of having epileptic temporal lobes, many just have very sensitive temporal lobes, so that they have these same sensations and perceptions, but without either accompanying epileptic brain activity or seizures.

[419] It's emotional "valence".

References for Chapter 9 – Out-of-Body Experiences.

[420] Image from Wiki commons. Generated by *Database Center for Life Science*

[421] Blanke O, Ortigue S, Landis T, Seeck M. "Stimulating illusory own-body perceptions." Nature. 2002 Sep 19;419(6904):269-70.

[422] Tong F., "Out-of-body experiences: from Penfield to present." *Trends in Cognitive Science* 2003 Mar; 7(3):104-106.

[423] Penfield, Wilder, O.M., C.M.G., M.D., B.Sc., F.R.C.S., F.R.S. "The Role Of The Temporal cortex in certain Psychic Phenomena", Journal of Mental Science, July 1955 388, (101) 451-465

[424] Image Source: Penfield, Wilder, O.M., C.M.G., M.D., B.Sc., F.R.C.S., F.R.S. "The Role Of The Temporal cortex in certain Psychic Phenomena", *Journal of Mental Science*, July 1955 388, (101) 451-465

[425] Penfield, Wilder, O.M., C.M.G., M.D., B.Sc., F.R.C.S., F.R.S. "The Role Of The Temporal cortex in certain Psychic Phenomena", Journal of Mental Science, July 1955 388, (101) 451-465

[426] Baldwin, Maitland & Baily, Pearce, "Temporal Lobe Epilepsy" Charles C. Thomas Pub. 1958

[427] Saroka, Kevin, Mulligan, Bryce P., Murphy, Todd R. and Persinger, Michael A. "Experimental Elicitation of an Out of Body Experience and Concomitant Cross-Hemispheric elctroencephalographic Coherence" NeuroQuantology |December 2010 |Vol. 8 |Issue 4 |Page 466-477

[428] Author's Collection.

References for Chapter 10 – God and the Brain

429 Penfield, Wilder, & Jasper, Herbert, "Epilepsy and the functional Anatomy of The Human Brain" Little, Brown, & Co., 1954

430 Penfield Wilder, & Perot Phanor "The brain's record of auditory and visual experience. A final summary and discussion." *Brain* 1963: 86; 595–696.

431 Anecdotal: Based on personal observation, case study reports, or random investigations rather than systematic scientific evaluation.

432 Persinger, Michael A. "Religious and mystical Experiences As Artifacts Of Temporal Lobe Function: A General Hypothesis" Perceptual And Motor Skills, 1983, 57 1255-1262

433 In interior locutions, a person receives a set of ideas, thoughts, or inner voices and experiences them as coming from an outside spiritual source. Usually, these are auditory – 'hearing voices', instead of 'seeing things'.

434 Persinger MA, "Death anxiety as a semantic conditioned suppression paradigm." Perceptual and Motor Skills. 1985 Jun;60(3):827-30.

435 In Piaget's stages of cognitive development.

436 A *conditioned suppression paradigm*.

437 One exception to this is the Buddhist teaching of "no–self". In this teaching, the diffuse experience of having a self is regarded as an illusion, and can't be reduced to any of its components. In this teaching, one way to perceive that the sense of self is an illusory perception is to inquire into the nature of self through meditation and other spiritual practices (such as asking yourself "who am I?" constantly, for several days). However, among the common faithful, one's own existence is taken for granted, and the doctrine of "no–self" is either forgotten or only rendered lip service. It's a teaching "more honored in the breach".

438 The word Darshan means 'vision'. Seeing ones Guru is referred to as 'taking darshan'.

439 Such as 'fake' gurus who fabricate stories to make themselves seem more holy than they really are, as well as people who claim "divine revelations" they have never received to justify their actions within their own spiritual communities. In Theravada Buddhism, a monk committing such an act can be immediately defrocked.

440 This, and all other similar illustrations, copyright by author.

441 There are other positive emotions that are not 'housed' in the left amygdala, like calm and peace, but these are not 'affective states' in neuroscience, though they certainly are so in common language.

442 Persinger MA, Richards PM, Koren SA. "Differential ratings of pleasantness following right and left hemispheric application of low energy magnetic fields that stimulate long-term potentiation". *International Journal of Neuroscience.* 1994 Dec;79(3-4):191-7.

443 Richards MA, Koren SA, Persinger MA. "Circumcerebral application of weak complex magnetic fields with derivatives and changes in electroencephalographic power spectra within the theta range: implications for states of consciousness." Perceptual and Motor Skills. 2002 Oct;95(2):671-86.

444 Nielsen TA, Stenstrom P, "What are the memory sources of dreaming?" Nature. 2005 Oct 27;437(7063):1286-9.

445 Dotta, Blake Tiberius and Persinger, Michael A. "Dreams, Time Distortion and the Experience of Future Events: A Relativistic, Neuroquantal Perspective." Sleep and Hypnosis 2009;11(2):29-39

446 Persinger MA, Koren SA, Tsang EW. "Enhanced power within a specific band of theta activity in one person while another receives circumcerebral pulsed magnetic fields: a mechanism for cognitive influence at a distance?" Perceptual and Motor Skills. 2003 Dec;97(3 Pt 1):877-94.

447 Acevedo BP, Aron A, Fisher HE, Brown LL. "Neural correlates of long-term intense romantic love." Social Cognitive and Affective Neuroscience. 2011 Jan 5.

448 Noriuchi M, Kikuchi Y, Senoo A. "The functional neuroanatomy of maternal love: mother's response to infant's attachment behaviors." Biological Psychiatry. 2008 Feb 15;63(4):415-23. Epub 2007 Aug 7.

449 Beauregard M, Courtemanche J, Paquette V, St-Pierre EL. "The neural basis of unconditional love." Psychiatry Research. 2009 May 15;172(2):93-8.

450 The evidence for this comes from people who have used a neural stimulation device ("Shakti", not unlike the God Helmet) that applies a typical EEG signal for the caudate nucleus using a magnetic field as a carrier. These people experienced arousal and excitement, sometimes as "edginess", following stimulation over the left, and relaxation following the same stimulation over the right. The supposition is based on a small number of reports. It cannot be considered conclusive, and awaits confirmation or falsification from laboratory studies. Its contribution to our bodies' state of relaxation and arousal may

follow the amygdala's activity. For now, it's a "working hypothesis" in that we will work with the idea as though it were true, knowing that it could be sent "back to the drawing board" later on. The caudate nucleus may not have left/right specializations of its own. Its contribution to our bodies' state of relaxation and arousal may be directed by the amygdala's activity.

[451] "What is whispered in your ear, shout from the rooftops". (Matthew, 10:26)

[452] Horga G, Parellada E, Lomeña F, Fernández-Egea E, Mané A, Font M, Falcón C, Konova AB, Pavia J, Ros D, Bernardo M. "Differential brain glucose metabolic patterns in antipsychotic-naïve first-episode schizophrenia with and without auditory verbal hallucinations". Journal of Psychiatry & Neuroscience. 2011 Sep;36(5):312-21.

[453] Richards MA, Koren SA, Persinger MA. "Circumcerebral application of weak complex magnetic fields with derivatives and changes in electroencephalographic power spectra within the theta range: implications for states of consciousness." Perceptual and Motor Skills. 2002 Oct;95(2):671-86.

[454] Lagopoulos J, Xu J, Rasmussen I, Vik A, Malhi GS, Eliassen CF, Arntsen IE, Saether JG, Hollup S, Holen A, Davanger S, Ellingsen Ø. "Increased theta and alpha EEG activity during nondirective meditation." Journal of Alternative and Complementary Medicine. 2009 Nov;15(11):1187-92.

[455] Vøllestad J, Sivertsen B, Nielsen GH. "Mindfulness-based stress reduction for patients with anxiety disorders: evaluation in a randomized controlled trial." Behavior Research and Therapy. 2011 Apr;49(4):281-8. Epub 2011 Jan 27.

[456] This is a direct consequence of the Vectoral Hemisphericity hypothesis.

[457] We need to distinguish between the vision of God and other experiences that can be called by the same name. The vision of God is one where a person feels themselves in the immediate presence of God. This is different from insights into the nature of God, deeper experiences during prayer or peak moments in the development of faith. There are many Christians who insist they are always seeing God in their hearts. This is a different experience from the one under discussion here. We will discuss the vision of God in the classical sense of meeting 'Him' - face to face.

[458] This refers to a system that fluctuates, but is in balance overall.

[459] While traveling on the road to Damascus, Saul was struck by a vision of Jesus, who asked him: "why are you persecuting me?" He is said to have seen a vision of the risen Christ (1st Corinthians, 15:3-8). History does not record what Paul was thinking or feeling prior to his vision, although many

Christians might say he could have been overcome by guilt over his actions, which included stoning St. Stephen to death.

460 Allen & Gorski, "Sexual Orientation and the size of the Anterior Commisure in the Human Brain" Proceedings of the National Academy of Sciences, Vol. 89, 7199-7202, August 1992"

461 Positive emotions rely on many other areas of the brain, including some on the right side. We referred to positive emotions as based in the left amygdala to keep the text simple. This footnote is to keep it from being too simple.

462 Irwin W, Anderle MJ, Abercrombie HC, Schaefer SM, Kalin NH, Davidson RJ. "Amygdalar interhemispheric functional connectivity differs between the non-depressed and depressed human brain." Neuroimage. 2004 Feb;21(2):674-86.

463 Many people think they would enjoy better mental health if their brains were 'balanced', meaning that both sides of their brain were equally active. This is not really true. If your brain were perfectly balanced in this sense, you would be equally prone to fear as you would be to happiness – not a desirable way to live. Being happy will mean more activity in certain structures on the left, and less on the right. Distinctly 'out of balance'.

464 Persinger MA, Makarec K. "The feeling of a presence and verbal meaningfulness in context of temporal lobe function: factor analytic verification of the muses?" Brain and Cognition 1992 Nov;20(2):217-26.

465 Straube T, Sauer A, Miltner WH. "Brain activation during direct and indirect processing of positive and negative words". Behavioral Brain Research 2011 Sep 12;222(1):66-72.

466 See the chapter on enlightenment.

467 The amygdala is crucial for our emotions, and responds to the emotions of others. This is a vital function in social contexts. In earliest human history, as today, almost all emotions, except the fear of personal injury or death, were inspired by social events and situations.

468 In conjunction with other structures

469 Persinger, Michael A. "Religious and mystical Experiences as Artifacts of Temporal Lobe Function: A General Hypothesis" Perceptual And Motor Skills, 1983, 57 1255-1262

470 In some scientific literature, the phrase "matrices of neurons" is used instead of "groups of pathways".

471 This image is in the public domain due to its age. From Wiki Commons.

472   *Moroni* (pronounced more-OH-nigh)

473   This image is in the public domain due to its age. From Wiki Commons.

474   Ullman, Robert; Reichenberg-Ullman, Judyth, "Mystics, Masters, Saints and Sages", Conari Press, 2001

475   *His Istadevata.* The aspect of god chosen for worship, devotion and contemplation.

476   Menendez, Sister Josepha, "The Way of Divine Love" Tan Books and Publishers, 1972

477   Walsch, Neale Donald "Conversations With God", Putnam Publishers, 1996

478   Painting by Alonso del Arco (1635-1704)

479   A 'purge' is when the stomach is filled with water, and the patient is forced to vomit.

480   Image declared to be in the public domain by copyright administrator at Marians of the Immaculate Conception.

481   *Beatify:* to honor a dead person by stating officially, he or she is especially holy. Once beatified, Blessed is always placed before the name or title of that person.

482   Another possibility is that she had a 'reversed' or 'left-handed' amygdala. Activity from one left-hemispheric structure could more easily find its way into the fearful amygdala, which in her case, was possibly, found on the left, the opposite of normal hemispheric specialization. Of course, this is speculation.

483   Public Domain Image.

484   Matthew 4:3 Scriptures taken from the Holy Bible, King James Version, unless otherwise noted.

485   Deuteronomy 8:3

486   Psalms 91:11-12

487   Matthew 4:10

488   Matthew 4:11

489   Murphy, Todd R. "The Role of Religious and Mystic Experiences In Human Evolution: A Corollary Hypothesis for NeuroTheology", *NeuroQuantology*, Vol 8, No 4 (2010)

490   The reader may wonder about the word "excite". It refers to activity that makes things happen instead of preventing things from happening. Most brain activity is inhibitory; stopping things from happening or slowing them

down. "Activation" simply means that an area is busy, either exciting it or inhibiting it.

[491] Persinger MA, Makarec K. "Greater right hemisphericity is associated with lower self-esteem in adults." Perceptual and Motor Skills. 1991 Dec;73(3 Pt 2):1244-6.

[492] Horgan, John, "Rational Mysticism", Mariner Books, 2003

References for Chapter 12 – Enlightenment

493   One example of this in recent history is Neem Karoli Baba, described in Ram Das' *Miracle of Love*.

494   This is reminiscent of the line in *Alice in Wonderland*, which actually reflects Lewis Carol's experiences with temporal lobe epilepsy. Alice says: "I seem to be going out like a candle." It appears to be an instance in which the brain's involvement in maintaining the sense of self is interrupted; you can actually stop existing for a few moments.

495   Illustration copyright by author.

496   One of the sillier conventions of neuroscience, one that has led to a great deal of confusion, is that despite the fact that there are two amygdalas, one on each side of the brain, together they are referred to as "the amygdala." This convention often creates a lot of confusion, as it glosses over the very different emotional tone that each amygdala can add to our moment-to-moment experiences. In deference to the of neuroscience conventions, we will use the word amygdala as both singular and plural.

497   In those studies, the amygdala was being assaulted by electrical stimulation whose strength and patterns were quite different from its natural ones. When all other conditions are equal, the amygdala is more likely to mistake something beneficial as a threat, rather than the other way round. If you're afraid of things that you don't understand, then you'll treat them with caution. This means they're less likely to hurt you. After learning a little about it, you may recognize that it offers more benefit than potential for harm. You won't get bitten by snakes as much if you avoid pieces of rope, but if you assume that anything that looks like a piece of rope is just that, then sooner or later you'll pick up a snake by mistake. Ouch.

498   The left frontal lobe, for example plays an important role in producing anger.

499   These differences include the hippocampal layer named CA1 and the dentate gyrus. (Duvernoy, et al. *The Human Hippocampus: Functional Anatomy, Vascularization and Serial Sections with MRI.* 3rd ed. Springer; 2005)

500   Via the cingulate gyrus.

501   This observation is based on reports from people using a hippocampal-derived complex magnetic signal (based on long-term potentiation) applied by the *Shakti* "mind machine."

502 Butters MA, Aizenstein HJ, Hayashi KM, Meltzer CC, Seaman J, Reynolds CF, Toga AW, Thompson PM, Becker JT; "Three-dimensional surface mapping of the caudate nucleus in late-life depression. "American Journal of Geriatric Psychiatry. 2009 Jan;17(1):4-12.

503 McGillchrist, Iain, "The Master and His Emissary" Yale University press, 2009

504 Persinger, Michael A.; Saroka, Kevin; Koren, Stanley A.; St-Pierre, Linda S. "The Electromagnetic Induction of Mystical and Altered States within the Laboratory" Journal of Consciousness Exploration & Research Vol 1, No 7 (2010)

505 Cook CM, Persinger MA. "Experimental induction of the "sensed presence" in normal subjects and an exceptional subject." Perceptual and Motor Skills. 1997 Oct;85(2):683-93.

506 The phrase "all perceptions" treats thoughts, feelings, and somatic (bodily) processes as all being equal. Collectively, they can be called "sensory and cognitive modalities."

507 Image from Wikipedia commons. Licensed by Ministry of Education, Culture, Sports, and Technology (MEXT) Integrated Database Project, Japan

508 As found in Gurdjieff's dances, SUMA Ching Hai's Method of Instant Enlightenment, the Latihan of Subud, and others.

509 As in the Hindu scripture *Vigyana Bhairava Tantra*.

510 For example, as practiced by the Gyuto monks (among others) in Tibetan Buddhism, where the person sings two or more notes at once.

511 Image copyright by author.

512 See the chapter "Some Brain Parts".

513 Not all tales of enlightenment include the feeling of excitement. Some speak of a tremendous calm.

514 "There is nothing concealed that will not be disclosed, or hidden that will not be made known. What I tell you in the dark, speak in the daylight; what is whispered in your ear, proclaim from the roofs" (Matthew 10:26–28, NIV).

515 Persinger MA. "Neuropsychological principia brevita: an application to traumatic (acquired) brain injury." Psycholgical Reports. 1995 Dec;77(3 Pt 1):707-24.

516 Dr. Jill Bolte Taylor's story can be found on YouTube.com and in her book *A Stroke of Luck: Beyond the Blue.*

517 The technically-minded reader should note that this can happen either through 'synaptic dropout' (where synapses are pruned away) or through 'kindling', in which pathways become more sensitive the more often they are used, as happens with epileptic seizures.

518 The load of activity would strip away more inhibitory synapses than excitatory ones, so areas affected by this process would become more excitable, as it would now have fewer controls. Often, more activity means more inhibition, but in a process like this, more activity would mean greater neural excitement.

519 Public domain photo by Andreas Praefcke, released to wiki commons.

520 Tratak (fixed gazing) is a method of meditation that involves concentrating on a single point such as a small object, black dot, a mirror, or candle flame. Crystal ball gazing is an example of this technique.

521 There is another story about Chiyono (1223–1298), in which she, after being refused admission to a monastery because her outstanding beauty would distract the monks, built a fire. She put her face into it and destroyed her beauty. After that, moved by her determination, the abbot granted her admission.

522 From Wiki Commons. Licensed under Creative Commons Attribution-Share Alike 3.0 Unported.

523 Image from Wiki Commons, **by** Kyle Hoobin, under Creative Commons Attribution-Share Alike 3.0 Unported license.

524 Tolle, Eckart, "The Power of Now" New World Library, 2004

525 *The Void* in near-death experiences (NDEs) is not just an empty space. It's energetic and full of meaning. Both The Void and the Tunnel usually have a center point. For The Void, this center point is a point of light in the middle of the visual field, and for the Tunnel, it's the light at the end of it. Both experiences have many other forms. The variations seem endless, but the center point here is more common than most, and it seems to be a more direct reflection of hippocampal spatial cognition. A vortex also has a center point, whether in a whirlpool or a tornado. An *experience* of an inner energy vortex may be a variation on the spatial theme and the underlying neural substrates seen in The Void and the tunnel experiences.

526 Ullman, Robert, & Reichenberg-Ullman, Judyth "Mystics, Masters, Saints, and Sages: Stories of Enlightenment" RedWheel / Weiser, 2001

527 Image from Wiki Commons. Public Domain.

528 *Shruti* means "that which is heard." In this sense, *shruti* refers to the tonic *do* note (as in do, re, mi) to which a Tamboura, the drone instrument in Indian Classical music, is tuned. As the tonic note for the drone must match the tonic note for the other instruments, the tonic for the drone imposes the musical key on Indian music, whether it's a raga or a trashy Bollywood song.

529 Photo by author.

530 The name Osho is an onomatopoeic way of calling him "the Oceanic One," as well as being a name that Zen Masters sometimes used when addressing each other.

531 These included immigration fraud, attempted murder (by poisoning), aiding and abetting potentially lethal violence in his therapy groups, and election tampering.

532 Having sexual intercourse.

533 Rajneesh, Bhagwan Shree, "The Discipline of Transcendence" Vol. 2, Chap. 11, Rajneesh Foundation (1978)

534 Ineffable means *incapable of being expressed in words.*

535 Of course, this is not so easy to do. "Never was there a philosopher who bore the toothache patiently". Shakespeare, *Much Ado about Nothing.*

References for Chapter 13 – Interhemispheric intrusions

[536] Luke, 6:21

[537] Psalms 30:5

[538] The hippocampus on the left is smaller in those studied after their first episode of schizophrenia. The lower volume could be interpreted as the atrophy of some tissue in that structure. It might also be due to problems during the brain's development. See: Adriano F, Caltagirone C, Spalletta G. "Hippocampal volume reduction in first-episode and chronic schizophrenia: a review and meta-analysis." *Neuroscientist.* 2012 Apr;18(2):180-200

[539] Geiger, John, "The Third Man Factor", Canongate Publishers, 2009

[540] Byrd, Richard E. "Alone", G.P. Putnam's Sons, New York, 1938

[541] Geiger, John, "The Third Man Factor", Canongate Publishers, 2009

[542] O'Reilly, Sean and O'Reilly, James, "Pilgrimage: Adventures of the spirit". Traveller's Tales Publishers, San Francisco, 2000

[543] Greaf, Hilda, "Mystics of our Times", Hanover House Publishers, 1962

[544] Matthew 22:14

[545] Greaf, Hilda, "Mystics of our Times", Hanover House Publishers, 1962.

[546] Greaf, Hilda, "Mystics of our Times", Hanover House Publishers, 1962.

[547] Associated Press report, Oct 1st, 2013

[548] Süssman, Irving & Cornelia, "Thomas Merton: The Daring Young Man on the Flying Belltower." MacMillan publishing Co., Inc., New York 1976

[549] Bongers, Sally. "Everyday Enlightenment: Seven Stories of Awakening." Non-Duality Press, 2008

[550] Ullman, Robert "Mystics, Masters, Saints and Sages: Stories of Enlightenment" Conari Press, 2001

[551] See The Holy Koran, Sura 73.

[552] Greaf, Hilda, "Mystics of our Times", Hanover House Publishers, 1962.

[553] Maynard, Theodore, "Saints for our times". Image books, 1955.

[554] Thurston, Herbert J and Attwater, Donald, (editors). "Butler's Lives of the Saints", Christian Classics, 1996, Volume 2, page 579.

[555] Thurston, Herbert J and Attwater, Donald, (editors). "Butler's Lives of the Saints", Christian Classics, 1996,.

[556] Ji G, Neugebauer V. "Hemispheric lateralization of pain processing by amygdala neurons." Journal of Neurophysiology. 2009 Oct;102(4):2253-64.

557 Moont R, Crispel Y, Lev R, Pud D, Yarnitsky D. "Temporal changes in cortical activation during conditioned pain modulation (CPM), a LORETA study." *Pain*. 2011 Jul;152(7):1469-77.

558 Greaf, Hilda, "Mystics of our Times", Hanover House Publishers, 1962.

559 Ji G, Neugebauer V. "Hemispheric lateralization of pain processing by amygdala neurons." Journal of Neurophysiology. 009 Oct;102(4):2253-64.

560 Bloom, Harold, "Bloom's Guides: the Autobiography of Malcolm X", 2008

561 Baha'u'llah, "Epistle to the Son of the Wolf", CreateSpace Publishers, 2011.

562 Baha'u'llah, Ruhi, Book 4, 101-102. Philosophical Library, 1970

563 Thurston, Herbert J and Attwater, Donald, (editors). "Butler's Lives of the Saints", Christian Classics, 1996, Volume 1, page 494.

564 CATHOLIC ENCYCLOPEDIA: St. John of the Cross: http://www. newadvent.org/cathen/08480a.htm

565 Siegal, Ronald K. "Fire in the Brain: Clinical Tales of Hallucination", Dutton Books, 1992

566 Butler, Alban "The Lives of the Saints", Volume XI, 1866

567 Cooper MJ. "Near-death experience and out of body phenomenon during torture-a case report." *Torture*. 2011;21(3):178-81.

568 As shown in the 1989 film "My name is Bill W." Out of respect for the conventions of Alcoholics Anonymous, Bill W's full name is not used here, and no "AA" texts are quoted.

569 Sieden, Lloyd Steven, "Buckminster Fuller's Universe". Basic Books, 1989

570 Murphy, Michael, "The Future of the Body", Tarcher Perigee Publishers., 1993, Pg.395

571 Bongers, Sally. "Everyday Enlightenment: Seven Stories of Awakening." Non-Duality Press, 2008

572 Solzhenitsyn, Alexander "The Gulag Archipelago", Harper & Row, 1973.

573 Persinger's Experiments with time distortion used the "Octopus", an apparatus that stimulates the right hemisphere much more than the left, and in a way that elicits theta output. The right hippocampus is well-known to be the primary, perhaps the only, source of theta waves (4 to 8 Hz.) in the brain.

574 Our thanks to an anonymous colleague for providing us with some of these case histories. "Thanks, Hamlet."

575 Leinbaugh, Harold P. & Campbell, John D. "The Men of Company K: The Autobiography of a World War II Rifle Company", William Morrow & Co., Inc. 1985

[576] Manchester, William "Goodbye, Darkness: A Memoir of the Pacific War", Little, Brown & Co. 1980

[577] *Cathexis* refers to the process that attaches psychic energy, essentially libido, to an object.

[578] Manchester, William "Goodbye, Darkness: A Memoir of the Pacific War", Little, Brown & Co., 1980

[579] Glines, Carroll, "Four Came Home: The Gripping Story of the Last Survivors of Doolittle's Tokyo Raid", Van Nostrand Reinhold Co., 1981

[580] Ngor, Haing S. "Surviving the Killing Fields: The Cambodian Odyssey of Haing S. Ngor", Pan Books, Ltd, 1988

[581] Gray, Glenn, J. "The Warriors: Reflections on Men in Battle" Harper and Row Publishers, 1970.

[582] Hoss, Rudolf, "Death Dealer: The memoirs of the SS Kommandant at Auschwitz, Da Kapo Press, 1996

[583] Merridale, Catherine, "Ivan's War: Life and death in the Red Army, 1939-1945" Picador Books, 2006

[584] Jones, Michael K. "Stalingrad", Casemate Publishers, 2007

References for Chapter 14 – Psychic Skills

585   Sanchez R. "Empathy, diversity, and telepathy in mother–daughter dyads: an empirical investigation utilizing Rogers' conceptual framework." *Scholarly Inquiry for Nursing Practice.* 1989 Spring;3(1):29-44.

586   Thomas G, Fletcher GJ "Mind-reading accuracy in intimate relationships: assessing the roles of the relationship, the target, and the judge." *Journal of Personality and Social Psychology.* 2003 Dec;85(6):1079-94.

587   Images from the Laurentian university neuroscience research group website. Use by permission.

588   This refers to the amygdala "burst-firing" pattern.

589   Persinger MA, Roll WG, Tiller SG, Koren SA, Cook CM. "Remote viewing with the artist Ingo Swann: neuropsychological profile, electroencephalographic correlates, magnetic resonance imaging (MRI), and possible mechanisms." *Perceptual and Motor Skills.* 2002 Jun;94(3 Pt 1):927-49.

590   Koren SA, Persinger MA. "Possible disruption of remote viewing by complex weak magnetic fields around the stimulus site and the possibility of accessing real phase space: a pilot study." *Perceptual and Motor Skills.* 2002 Dec;95(3 Pt 1):989-98.

591   Persinger MA, Cook CM, Tiller SC. "Enhancement of images of possible memories of others during exposure to circumcerebral magnetic fields: correlations with ambient geomagnetic activity." *Perceptual and Motor Skills.* 2002 Oct;95(2):531-43.

592   Persinger MA, Koren SA, Tsang EW. "Enhanced power within a specific band of theta activity in one person while another receives circumcerebral pulsed magnetic fields: a mechanism for cognitive influence at a distance?" *Perceptual and Motor Skills.* 2003 Dec;97(3 Pt 1):877-94.

593   Persinger MA, Saroka KS, Lavallee CF, Booth JN, Hunter MD, Mulligan BP, Koren SA, Wu HP, Gang N. "Correlated cerebral events between physically and sensory isolated pairs of subjects exposed to yoked circumcerebral magnetic fields." *Neuroscience Letters.* 2010 Dec 17;486(3):231-4.

594   The adage that extraordinary claims require extraordinary proof means, in effect, that scientific method is not enough for claims that a skeptic ***thinks*** are 'extraordinary'. It gives permission for anyone to 'raise the bar' for results they consider surprising, and to dismiss results that don't have an (unspecified) degree of extra proof. When the subject relates to spirituality or spiritual

skills, it implies that one religious orientation (atheism, for example) can dismiss ideas that conflict with it. The adage often amounts to nothing more than religious intolerance at play in the fields of science, and the abandonment of established scientific methods. When skeptics demand extra proof, they, being disbelievers, are often unfamiliar with the phenomena they reject, and so aren't qualified to design experiments that study it. Instead of examining the phenomena, they examine the claim.

595 Author's collection.

596 http://www.deepfocus.eu/New_Folder/Elektronische%20Erleuchtung.pdf (original German) or http://www.shaktitechnology.com/shiva/deepfocus_report.htm (English)

597 This includes the earlier-mentioned Swiss study that did 400 sessions for 100 subjects and elicited enhancements in psychic perception as well as some enlightenment experiences.

598 Llinás R, Ribary U. "Coherent 40-Hz oscillation characterizes dream state in humans." *Proceedings of the National Academy of Science* U S A. 1993 Mar 1;90(5):2078-81.

599 Llinás RR, Paré D. "Of dreaming and wakefulness." Neuroscience. 1991;44(3):521-35.

600 This assumes that I'm correct in my interpretation of the binding factor as 'binding' not only consciousness, but also binding us to our usual repertoire of states of consciousness.

601 Personal communication.

602 More of the 44 student 'raters' found matches between what the pairs of subjects said at the same time.

603 Booth JN, Koren SA, Persinger MA. Increased feelings of the sensed presence and increased geomagnetic activity at the time of the experience during exposures to transcerebral weak complex magnetic fields. *International Journal of Neuroscience*. 2005 Jul;115(7):1053-79

604 Persinger MA, "Out-of-body-like experiences are more probable in people with elevated complex partial epileptic-like signs during periods of enhanced geomagnetic activity: a nonlinear effect." *Perceptual & Motor Skills*. 1995 Apr;80(2):563-9.

605 Persinger MA. "Paranormal and religious beliefs may be mediated differentially by subcortical and cortical phenomenological processes of the temporal (limbic) lobes." *Perceptual and Motor Skills*. 1993 Feb;76(1):247-51.

606 Persinger, M.A. "Out Of Body Experiences Are More Probable In People With Elevated Complex Partial Epileptic-Like Signs During Periods of Enhanced Geommagnetc Activity: A Nonlinear Effect." Perceptual and Motor Skills, 1995 80, 563-569

607 Visuddhi means "Purity" and Magga means "path" or "trail".

608 Author's Collection.

609 www.shaktitechnology.com

610 Sympathetic resonance is the phenomenon where one vibrating object, such as a string or a bell, can induce the same vibration in another, with the only physical contact coming from the vibrations in the air.

611 Bettleheim, Bruno "The Uses Of Enchantment", Vintage Books, 1977

612 Addis DR, Schacter DL. "Constructive episodic simulation: temporal distance and detail of past and future events modulate hippocampal engagement." *Hippocampus.* 2008;18(2):227-37.

613 Addis DR, Pan L, Vu MA, Laiser N, Schacter DL. "Constructive episodic simulation of the future and the past: distinct subsystems of a core brain network mediate imagining and remembering." *Neuropsychologia.* 2009 Sep;47(11):2222-38.

614 Persinger, Dr. MA, Personal communication, 1998.

References for Chapter 15 – Prayer

[615] McGillchrist, Iain, "The Master and His Emissary" Yale University press, 2009

[616] There is a great deal of disagreement among linguists, neuroscientists and cognitive scientists as to how this process works. Rather than take sides in this long-standing discussion, I will simply refer to "lumps" of linguistic information, and assume that, at least some of the time, there are discrete units of linguistic thinking. I will let other people decide whether these lumps are syntactic, grammatical, or perhaps reflect some kind of intrinsic brain logic.

[617] Roberts L, Ahmed I, Hall S. "Intercessory prayer for the alleviation of ill health." *Cochrane Database of Systematic Reviews.* 2007 Jan 24;(1):CD000368.

[618] Astin JA, Stone J, Abrams DI, Moore DH, Couey P, Buscemi R, Targ E. "The efficacy of distant healing for human immunodeficiency virus--results of a randomized trial." *Alternative Therapies in Health and Medicine.* 2006 Nov-Dec;12(6):36-41.

[619] Aviles JM, Whelan SE, Hernke DA, Williams BA, Kenny KE, O'Fallon WM, Kopecky SL. "Intercessory prayer and cardiovascular disease progression in a coronary care unit population: a randomized controlled trial." *Mayo Clinic Proceedings.* 2001 Dec;76(12):1192-8.

[620] Turner DD. "Just another drug? A philosophical assessment of randomised controlled studies on intercessory prayer." *Journal of Medical Ethics.* 2006 Aug;32(8):487-90.

[621] Belding JN, Howard MG, McGuire AM, Schwartz AC, Wilson JH. "Social buffering by God: prayer and measures of stress." *Journal of Religion and Health.* 2010 Jun;49(2):179-87.

[622] O'Laoire S. "An experimental study of the effects of distant, intercessory prayer on self-esteem, anxiety, and depression." *Alternative Therapies in Health and Medicine* 1997 Nov;3(6):38-53.

[623] Boelens PA, Reeves RR, Replogle WH, Koenig HG. "A randomized trial of the effect of prayer on depression and anxiety." *International Journal of Psychiatry in Medicine.* 2009;39(4):377-92.

[624] Leibovici L. "Effects of remote, retroactive intercessory prayer on outcomes in patients with bloodstream infection: randomised controlled trial." *BMJ (Clincal Research Edition).* 2001 Dec 22-29;323(7327):1450-1.

625 Lesniak KT. "The effect of intercessory prayer on wound healing in nonhuman primates." *Alternative Therapies in Health and Medicine.* 2006 Nov-Dec;12(6):42-8.

626 Mathai J, Bourne A. "Pilot study investigating the effect of intercessory prayer in the treatment of child psychiatric disorders." *Australasian Psychiatry.* 2004 Dec;12(4):386-9.

627 Leibovici L. "Effects of remote, retroactive intercessory prayer on outcomes in patients with bloodstream infection: randomised controlled trial." *BMJ (Clincal Research Edition).* 2001 Dec 22-29;323(7327):1450-1.

628 Dezutter J, Wachholtz A, Corveleyn J. "Prayer and pain: the mediating role of positive re-appraisal." *Journal of Behavioral Medicine 2011* Dec;34(6):542-9.

629 Vannemreddy P, Bryan K, Nanda A. "Influence of prayer and prayer habits on outcome in patients with severe head injury." *American Journal of Hospice and Palliative Care.* 2009 Aug-Sep;26(4):264-9.

630 Spencer RJ, Ray A, Pirl WF, Prigerson HG. "Clinical correlates of suicidal thoughts in patients with advanced cancer." *American Journal of Geriatric Psychiatry.* 2012 Apr;20(4):327-36.

631 Ai AL, Peterson C, Tice TN, Huang B, Rodgers W, Bolling SF. "The influence of prayer coping on mental health among cardiac surgery patients: the role of optimism and acute distress." *Journal of Health Psychology.* 2007 Jul;12(4):580-96.

632 Hunsucker S, Flannery J, Frank D. "Coping strategies of rural families of critically ill patients." *Journal of the American Academy of Nurse Practitioners.* 2000 Apr;12(4):123-7.

633 Walton J. "Prayer warriors: a grounded theory study of American Indians receiving hemodialysis." *Nephrology Nursing Journal.* 2007 Jul-Aug;34(4):377-86

634 McLeish AC, Del Ben KS. "Symptoms of depression and posttraumatic stress disorder in an outpatient population before and after Hurricane Katrina." *Depression and Anxiety.* 2008;25(5):416-21.

635 Rew L, Wong YJ, Sternglanz RW. "The relationship between prayer, health behaviors, and protective resources in school-age children." *Issues in Comprehensive Pediatric Nursing.* 2004 Oct-Dec;27(4):245-55.

636 Krause N, Bastida E. "Prayer to the Saints or the Virgin And Health Among Older Mexican Americans." *Hispanic Journal of Behavioral Science.* 2011 Feb 1;33(1):71-87.

637 Schjoedt U, Stødkilde-Jørgensen H, Geertz AW, Lund TE, Roepstorff A. "The power of charisma--perceived charisma inhibits the frontal executive network of believers in intercessory prayer." *Social Cognitive and Affective Neuroscience*. 2011 Jan;6(1):119-27.

638 Harris S, Kaplan JT, Curiel A, Bookheimer SY, Iacoboni M, Cohen MS. "The neural correlates of religious and nonreligious belief." *PLoS One*. 2009 Oct 1;4(10):e0007272.

639 Wheeler, Mark "Different areas of brain respond to belief, disbelief, uncertainty" UCLA newsroom, December 11, 2007 - http://newsroom. ucla.edu/portal/ucla/ucla-study-shows-different-areas-40881.aspx

640 Hooper, Judith & Teresi, Dick, "The Three Pound Universe", Dell Publishers, 1987

641 Matthew 6:3, King James Bible.

642 Job 9:9

643 Image under GNU license, from Wiki Commons. Bamberg Germany, Church of our blessed Mother, 2008 Photo by Andreas Praefcke

References for Chapter 16 – The earth Beneath your Feet

[644] Conesa J. "Isolated sleep paralysis, vivid dreams and geomagnetic influences: II. *Perceptual and Motor Skills.* 1997 Oct;85(2):579-84.

[645] Persinger, Michael A. "Geophysical variables and behavior: XXX. Intense paranormal experiences during days of quiet, global geomagnetic activity" *Perceptual and Motor Skills* 1985 Aug v61 (n1): 320-322

[646] Arango, Manuel A. ; Persinger, Michael A. "Geophysical Variables and Human Behavior: LII Decreased Geomagnetic Activity and spontaneous Telepathic Experiences from the Sedgwick collection. *Perceptual and Motor Skills,* 1988 Dec v67 (n3):907-909

[647] Persinger, Michael ; Krippner, Stanley. "Dream ESP and Geomagnetic Activity" *Journal of the American Society for Psychical Research,* 1989 Apr v83 (n2):101-116.

[648] Makarec, K.; Persinger, Michael A. Geophysical variables and behavior XLIII "Negative correlation between Geophysical Variables between accuracy of card-guessing and geomagnetic activity: A Case Study" *Perceptual and Motor Skills,* 1987 Aug, v65 (n1) 105-106

[649] Gearhart, Livingston; Persinger, M.A. Geophysical variables and behavior XXXIII. Onsets of historical and contemporary poltergeist episodes occured with sudden increases in geomagnetic activity. *Perceptual and Motor Skills,* 1986 Apr v62 (n2) 463-466

[650] Persinger MA. "Out-of-body-like experiences are more probable in people with elevated complex partial epileptic-like signs during periods of enhanced geomagnetic activity: a nonlinear effect." *Perceptual and Motor Skills.* 1995 Apr; v80 (2):563-9.

[651] Haraldsson, Erlendur; Gissurarson, Loftur R. "Does geomagnetic activity effect extrasensory perception? *Personality and individual differences,* 1987, v8 (n5):745-747

[652] Schaut, George B. Persinger, Michael A. "Subjective telepathic experiences, geomagnetic activity, and the elf hypothesis: I Data Analysis" *PSI Research,* 1958 Mar, v4 (n1):4-20

[653] Berger R.E.; Persinger, M.A. "Geophysical variables and behavior: LXVII. Quieter annual geomagnetic Activity and effect Size for Experiemntal psi (ESP) studies over six decades". *Perceptual and Motor Skills,* 1991 Dec, v73 (n3, Pt2 Spec issue):1219-1223

[654] Berk M, Dodd S, Henry M. "Do ambient electromagnetic fields affect behaviour? A demonstration of the relationship between geomagnetic storm activity and suicide" *Bioelectromagnetics.* 2005 Nov 22;27(2):151-155

[655] Raps A, Stoupel E, Shimshoni M. "Geophysical variables and behavior: LXIX. Solar activity and admission of psychiatric patients. Perceptual and Motor Skills. 1992 Apr;74(2):449-50.

[656] Persinger, Michael A.; Nolan, Michael "Geophysical variables and behavior XX. "Weekly numbers of mining accidents and the weather matrix: The importance of geomagnetic variation and barometric pressure. *Perceptual and Motor Skills,* 1984 Dec, v59 (n3):719-722

[657] Lewicki, Dougals R.; Schaut, George H; Persinger, Michael A. "Geophysical variables and behavior XLIV. Days of subjective precognitive experiences and the days before the actual events display correlated geomagnetic activity" *Perceptual and Motor Skills,* 1987, aug, v65 (n1):173-174

[658] The *piezoelectric* effect describes the relation between a mechanical stress and an electrical voltage in solids. Mechanical stress elicits electrical current from many materials, including a large number of minerals.

[659] Persinger, Michael A. "Geophysical variables and behavior: L Indications of a tectonic strain factor in the Rutlidge (UFO) observations during 1973 in southwest Missouri" *Perceptual and Motor Skills,* 1988 Oct, v67 (n2): 571-575

[660] Persinger, M.A.; Derr, J.S. "Geophysical variables and behavior: XXII. Relations between UFO reports within the Uinta Basin and local seismicity" *Perceptual and Motor Skills* 1985, Feb; 60 (1) :143-152

[661] Persinger, M.A.; Derr, J.S. "Geophysical variables and behavior: XXXII. Evaluations of UFO reports in an area of infrequent seismicity: The Carmen, Manitoba episode." *Perceptual and Motor Skills,* 1985 Dec, v61 (n3, Pt1): 807-813

[662] Derr, J.S.; Persinger, M.A. "Geophysical variables and behavior: LXXVI. Seasonal hydrological load and regional luminous phenomena (UFO reports) within river systems, the Mississippi Valley test" *Perceptual and Motor Skills,* 1993 Dec, v77 (n3, Pt62), 1163-1170

[663] Matteson, Dan; Persinger, M.A. "Geophysical variables and behavior: XXXV. Positive correlations between numbers of UFO reports and earthquake activity in Sweden." *Perceptual and Motor Skills,* 1986 Oct, v63 (n2, Pt2) 921-922

[664] Persinger, M.A.; Derr, J.S. "Geophysical variables and behavior: LXII. Temporal coupling of UFO reports and seismic energy release within the Rio Grande rift system: discrimative validity of the tectonic strain theory." *Perceptual and Motor Skills*, 1990 Oct, v71 (n2): 567-57

[665] Persinger, M.A.; Derr, J.S. "Geophysical variables and behavior: XIX Strong temporal relationships between inclusinve seismic measures and UFO reports within Washington state. *Perceptual and Motor Skills*, 1984, 59, 551–566

[666] John S. Derr & Michal A. Persinger 'Geophysical Variables and Behavior: LIV. Zeitoun (Egypt) Apparations of the Virgin Mary as Tectonic Strain-induced Luminosities. *Perceptual and Motor Skills* 1989, 68, 123-128

[667] Reproduced under the Fair Use Act.

[668] Author's collection.

[669] Middletown Times Star (4/16/98)

[670] Middletown Times Star (4/16/98)

[671] The *Laws of Manu*